THE WORD BECAME FLESH

Australian College of Theology Monograph Series

SERIES EDITOR GRAEME R. CHATFIELD

The ACT Monograph Series, generously supported by the Board of Directors of the Australian College of Theology, provides a forum for publishing quality research theses and studies by its graduates and affiliated college staff in the broad fields of Biblical Studies, Christian Thought and History, and Practical Theology with Wipf and Stock Publishers of Eugene, Oregon. The ACT selects the best of its doctoral and research masters theses as well as monographs that offer the academic community, scholars, church leaders and the wider community uniquely Australian and New Zealand perspectives on significant research topics and topics of current debate. The ACT also provides opportunity for contributors beyond its graduates and affiliated college staff to publish monographs which support the mission and values of the ACT.

Rev Dr Graeme Chatfield
Series Editor and Associate Dean

The Word Became Flesh

A Rapprochement of Christian Natural Law
and Radical Christological Ethics

DAVID GRIFFIN

Foreword by Gordon Preece

WIPF & STOCK · Eugene, Oregon

THE WORD BECAME FLESH
A Rapprochement of Christian Natural Law and Radical Christological Ethics

Australian College of Theology Monograph Series

Copyright © 2016 David Griffin. All rights reserved. Except for brief quotations in critical publications or reviews, no part of this book may be reproduced in any manner without prior written permission from the publisher. Write: Permissions, Wipf and Stock Publishers, 199 W. 8th Ave., Suite 3, Eugene, OR 97401.

Wipf & Stock
An Imprint of Wipf and Stock Publishers
199 W. 8th Ave., Suite 3
Eugene, OR 97401

www.wipfandstock.com

PAPERBACK ISBN 13: 978-1-4982-3925-7
HARDCOVER ISBN 13: 978-1-4982-3927-1

Manufactured in the U.S.A.   05/05/2016

To Jenny and Jonathan, whose lives of Christ-like kindness are worthy of my imitation.

Contents

Tables and Diagrams | viii
Foreword by Gordon Preece | ix
Acknowledgments | xi
Abbreviations | xii

Introduction | 1

Part One: Natural Law Christian Ethics
1 Philosophical, Theological and Biblical Considerations | 7
2 Protological and Teleological Natural Law Theories | 35

Part Two: The Radical Tradition of Christian Ethics | 65
3 Theological, Textual and Philosophical Considerations | 69
4 Historical, Confessional and Ethical Considerations | 91

Part Three: The Word Became Flesh—Chalcedonian Christology and Moral Reasoning
5 Chalcedonian *Logos* Ethics | 127
6 *Logos* Cosmology and Christological Ethical Reasoning | 155
7 The Christological Redetermination of Natural Law Ethics Through Barth's *Church Dogmatics* | 208

Conclusion | 261

Bibliography | 267

Tables and Diagrams

Tables

Table 1: Aristotelian Bifurcated Rationality | 17

Table 2: Aristotle's Duplex Scheme of Law | 47

Table 3: Maximus's Threefold Taxonomy of Law | 169

Table 4: The Murphy/Ellis Classification of Disciplines with Christological Natural Law Implications | 198

Table 5: The Structure of Barth's Ethics in *Church Dogmatics*. The Perichoretic Act of the One God in His one Command in Jesus Christ in Three Spheres | 210

Diagram

Diagram 1: The Theological and Ethical Structure of 1 Peter 2:21–25 | 102

Foreword

In a recent meeting with David Griffin in Australia's capital Canberra, he was reminiscing about his youth in the Sydney seaside suburb of Cronulla. It was there we first met, and fellowshipped and ministered together. And it was there that he spent whatever time he could surfing, he still does. Truth be known, half of his school was at the beach in school hours. David was a much better board-rider than I, but behind that passion, lay a larger passion for God as Creator, the one who can stir up a mighty swell, and the aesthetic but dangerous arc of a beautiful break. It seemed to me that surfing for David, like Norman Maclean's 1976 book, now Robert Redford film, *A River Runs Through It*, through fly-fishing, encountered a form of liquid Logos. And the face of that creative God is expressed utterly and finally in flesh, in Jesus Christ.

I mention this biographical detail because the reader of this thesis turned to book, *The Word Became Flesh*, will find not only a powerfully coherent argument marshalling major streams of the Great Tradition, East and West, Reformed, Lutheran, Catholic, Orthodox and Anabaptist, but a book that profoundly links the Logos and created life. For the streams that David draws together, in ways perhaps unlikely to some, have been separated to the detriment of each, in a series of theological schisms. They have sometimes torn the Alpha and Omega of Christ, the Creator and new Creator, apart, so that the purpose and point of the whole alphabet of life is somehow left out.

I mentioned our national capital Canberra, where David pastors at North Canberra Baptist Church, because I believe that while much of this book is high-level dogmatic theology, it also has a powerful impetus towards an incarnational ethics and public theology. David is a fine example of what Kevin Vanhoozer and Owen Strachen have called *The Pastor as Public Theologian* (Baker 2015). For several decades David has kept alive and sharpened his linguistic and exegetical skills, his wide and deep theological and ethical reading in a seasoned way that will be of great benefit, not only to academic theologians, but theologically literate pastors and laity.

David is nothing if not ambitious in this book. He surfs the great wave of the Great Tradition, but in a way that joins the two waves of the Classical tradition of the Logos with the radical Christocentric Anabaptist tradition. His is a story of theological peace-making between sometimes seeming enemies. He does this through sympathetic listening to the historical nuances of both traditions but with robust argument in a richly synthetic re-reading of what many claim to be opposed. Put aside your scepticism for a while to see what coherence he uncovers through this rapprochement and what radical theological and ethical fruitfulness potentially follows. I commend *The Word Became Flesh* to your diligent reading. It will take time to digest, but will provide rich sustenance, even if you find you cannot swallow it whole.

Rev'd Dr Gordon Preece,
Director of Ethos: Evangelical Alliance Centre for Christianity and Society,
Melbourne, Australia.

Acknowledgments

THE FOLLOWING ARE ACKNOWLEDGED for their support during the writing of this project:

Reverend Dr Gordon Preece, supervisor and friend.

Reverend Dr Doru Costache, St Andrew's Greek Orthodox Theological College, Sydney, for initial guidance in Orthodox Patristics.

Mr Christopher Harvey, Librarian, St Andrew's Greek Orthodox Theological College, Sydney, for resource assistance in Orthodox Patristics.

My wife Jennifer, for her unstinting support.

Jervis Bay Baptist Church, for granting a year of study leave from ministry.

Abbreviations

ANF	Ante Nicene Fathers
CD	Church Dogmatics
CHSS	C. Henry Smith Series
CNTC	Calvin's New Testament Commentaries
CRR	Classics of the Radical Reformation
ICR	Institutes of the Christian Religion
JSNT	Journal for the Study of the New Testament
LCC	Library of Christian Classics
MQR	Mennonite Quarterly Review
NIB	New Interpreter's Bible
NICNT	New International Commentary on the New Testament
NPNF	Nicene and Post Nicene Fathers
SAMH	Studies in Anabaptist and Mennonite History
TDNT	The Theological Dictionary of the New Testament
TNIGTC	The New International Greek Testament Commentary
WBC	Word Biblical Commentary

Introduction

"WE ARE NOT ANIMALS!! Clean up after you!" If this staffroom notice indicates anything, it is that natural law never seems to go away. Its most recent "eternal return"[1] in relation to positive law dates from the Nuremberg Trials.[2] More recently, the new natural law theory has sought its rehabilitation in personal ethics.[3]

"Jesus. Prophet of Islam." This billboard likewise indicates the enduring public interest in Jesus, despite attempts by more secular cultures to place an interdiction upon his public presence. Within the church this christological focus has increased as some confessions that have inherited classical trinitarian forms desert them for a more contemporary Jesus style.

However, the relationship between natural law and radical christological ethics is more often a fraught conversation than a respectful co-rationalism. This thesis offers a modest christological rapprochement of this relationship.[4]

A brief overview will help delineate the argument.

Natural law is here divided into two broad types, the protological and teleological. The protological emphasizes human origins, the teleological human ends and purposes. Both understand human nature as the primary object of moral enquiry. Their concern to establish a ubiquitous, real and perduring base for human ethics is well justified, especially in the light of dehumanizing political and social practices. However, their claim to transparent moral self-evidence is a burdened venture in the light of vigorous

---

1 Murray, *We Hold These Truths*, 295–336.

2. Thielicke, *Theological Ethics*, 384.

3. See Finnis, *Fundamentals of Ethics*, *Moral Absolutes*, and *Natural Law and Natural Rights*; Grisez, *Fulfillment in Christ*; Black, *Christian Moral Realism*; Biggar and Black, *Revival of Natural Law*.

4. Hauerwas et al, "Natural Law, Tragedy and Theological Ethics," in *Truthfulness and Tragedy*, 57–70.

moral disagreements, which indicate incommensurable rational traditions and *a priori* presuppositions about reality.[5] Yet even within this debate, natural law theories tend to be silent about Jesus.

This project suggests that any ethical theory that takes human nature, and that which is proper to it, as its base criterion, cannot avoid the consubstantial humanity of the incarnate eternal *Logos*, Jesus Christ, if it is to be properly Christian. The principle of adjectival congruence applies: as Aristotle is proper to Aristotelian ethics, Christ is proper to Christian ethics.

Because classical Christology affirms the perfect nature of Christ's humanity, practical moral reasoning about the goodness that is proper to human nature and action is unsound if this nature is avoided. Understanding health precedes remedial prescription. In this regard, the radical Anabaptist tradition is rightly centered on christological moral reasoning.

Yet this focus on Jesus tends towards sectarianism due to its perceived historicism, and the voluntarism of its "discipleship ethics."[6] When Jesus is put in his particular cultural and religious place, his universal and substantive claims are minimized. The modern understanding of the individual as essentially self-determining exacerbates this.[7] Explicit christological ethical claims are thus considered intrusions of personal opinions into public moral space. A reticent moral posture may result, particularly in secular and pluralistic contexts.[8]

Furthermore, embracing Jesus as morally normative is possible without holding a classical two-nature Christology. Such a "religious-ethical" Christology is noted for both the "modesty of its soteriological interest," and also for "rejecting . . . all metaphysical elements in the doctrine of God."[9] Whereas natural law typically overlooks the human Jesus, christological ethics may easily become theologically minimalist because of a hesitancy regarding Jesus' divinity. While natural law tends to avoid the Gospels altogether, radical ethics tends to avoid John, the primary source of "Alexandrian" and Chalcedonian *Logos* Christology.

---

5. See MacIntyre: *Whose Justice?*, *After Virtue*, and *Three Rival Versions*.

6. For instance, Spohn, *Go and Do Likewise*, 10: "Disciples become apprentices of someone who knows what they need to learn."

7. O'Donovan, *Resurrection*, 16—18.

8. This holds even though all claims to truth have universal intent; see Newbigin, *Truth to Tell*.

9. Pannenberg, *Jesus–God and Man*, 45, and *Basic Questions in Theology*, 99, on Schleiermacher and Ritschl. Metaphysics here means basic principles of reality as a whole, including God. Ontology is a subset of metaphysics concerning sentient and intelligent being.

Part One discusses and upholds the enduring appeal of natural law, yet argues that its "christological lack" renders it inadequate as a Christian ethic. Part Two appraises and affirms the christological focus of radical Anabaptist ethics, yet argues that its tendency towards a "metaphysical lack" destabilizes its universal appeal. Both of these parts are mainly analytical and evaluative.

Part Three proposes a rapprochement between these two ethics through Chalcedon's *logos* and double *homoousios* Christology. It discusses the relationship between being and act, the concept of the *logos* in John's Gospel, and *logos* cosmology and reasoning. Barth's *Church Dogmatics* is discussed as it may bear upon the subject.[10]

Because the project is christological, there is little attention given to the Spirit and Father. This does not indicate a lack of awareness of how these may be worthwhile areas for more research. In particular, a Spirit anthropology would provide further significant ways of reframing the ethics of human nature in a Christian fashion.

---

10. This project is not an exhaustive account of Barth's ethics.

Part One

Natural Law Christian Ethics

I

Philosophical, Theological and Biblical Considerations

1. Introduction

NATURAL LAW AFFIRMS THAT both nature generally, and human nature specifically, are intrinsically and inherently ethical. Human value consists in and is simultaneous to its factuality, constituting it an ontological and ethical realist theory. Thus three alternatives are discounted: the Humean rejection of value-laden facts, the Cartesian separation of objective fact and subjective value, and existentialism's voluntarist manufacture of post-existence essence. Natural law affirms moral existence and moral essence as simultaneously co-inherent.

Historicism rejects natural law's metaphysical realism along with its static anthropology: historical consciousness opposes both *mythos* (primordial creation dramas legitimizing static social order and nature, including the human), and the realist philosophies of antiquity (the eternal and timeless *one* against the changing *many*, as seen in Parmenides and Plato).[1] "The mythic focus on primordial time gave human beings security against the uncertain historical future," while philosophy "identified the essential with the abiding," with both sharing "a reserve towards history."[2] Accordingly,

---

1. Pannenberg, *Anthropology*, 495–502. For a sustained debate with and trinitarian critique of the Parmenidean *one* and Heracladean *many*, see Gunton, *The One, The Three and the Many*.

2. Pannenberg, *Anthropology*, 497.

natural law as a form of substantive ethics is one center of an elliptical debate, with historicism and its dynamic developmentalism the other center.

The contemporary renaissance of natural law's realism contests four expressions of historicism: first, unjust state positivism; second, various forms of moral subjectivism and non-cognitivism; third, the perceived failure of the enlightenment ethical project; and fourth, ethnology's culture-specific diversity undergirding relativism. The critique of positivism is based on the thesis that human rights, grounded in human nature, are pre-legal.[3] This echoes Cicero, discussed below. In all four cases, human ontology, understood as invariant, singular and real, acts to correct perceived unstable societal practices, historicism and unjust legal positivism.

Non-theistic contemporary natural law theory is predicated "on the supposition that reality is completely rational and can be known by human reason." This realist rationalism provides non-theological legitimacy for the "continuation of the natural law in the circumstances created by the modern consciousness of freedom,"[4] sustaining commensurable cross-ideological rational moral discourse in a non-theistic setting.[5] Thus "the term 'natural law' in the context of moral theology also denotes a 'cognitive' ethics, or one 'guided by reason,' which claims to be able to distinguish between good and evil, and correct and false, in such a way that it establishes substantial norms."[6] By contesting non-cognitivism it implies that reason is itself moral and not dependent upon external moral foundations or canons.

This thesis functions with a *duplex* taxonomy of natural law: protological and teleological. They are not mutually opposed and may be combined. Both theories tend to ontological and instrumental optimism.[7] However, three factors render protological natural law currently problematic: first, the contested views of human origins and therefore essence and existence; second, the modern situation of free historical consciousness, which opposes natural law's static character that is grounded in the two presuppositions of non-developmental fixed realist human ontology, and a realist metaphysic

---

3. On Nazi Germany's strong positivist legal culture eclipsing natural law: "It is tragically significant that the country where formal jurisprudence was developed to its utmost perfection was also the country where legality offered least resistance to the challenge of new and disruptive forces." A. P. d'Entreves, *Natural Law: An Introduction to Legal Philosophy*, 105, in Montgomery, *Jurisprudence*, no pagination. Recourse to natural law indicates a crisis in history according to Thielicke, *Ethics*. 149–150.

4. Schockenhoff, *Natural Law*, 2—3.

5. This is a function of natural law in Hauerwas, *After Christendom?*, 58. Also Grabill, *Rediscovering the Natural Law*, 7.

6. Schockenhoff, *Natural Law*, 2.

7. Calvin however has a mixed view, below.

of divine immutable ontology; and third (as a more specific form of the second), the postmodern malleable and decentered self. Thus contemporary natural law theories tend to be non-eschatologically teleological (ends), rather than metaphysical (origins), as universal human goods and ends are more perspicuous, historically adventurous and less controversial than protological claims. Primary consideration will be given to Cicero and Calvin as protological theorists, and Aristotle,[8] Augustine and Aquinas as teleological theorists, as well as the new natural law theory of the Finnis school.

Two recent attempts to soften natural law's realism with virtue ethics are Boyd's and Black's. Boyd argues that virtue ethics needs a proper understanding of human nature, and natural law needs the warmth of structured human relationships in the virtues. Human relations and deontological rules exist reciprocally, but the relational element is primary (e.g., "Sabbath made for man").[9] Black argues that Hauerwas and Grisez are "capable of functioning as mutually enriching . . . forms of ethics."[10] As virtue ethics are often teleological —"What type of person do I want to become?"—this is unsurprising.

Because natural law is primarily a realist ethic, the philosophical matters of critical realism and naturalism will be first examined, followed by theological and biblical concerns.

2. Philosophical Considerations

a. Critical Moral Realism

The emergence of critical realism in the twentieth century has enabled the confident determination of theology from its own material content.[11] This project utilizes McGrath's tri-dimensional critical realism in developing christological ethics: it is metaphysical, "there exists a reality or realities . . .

---

8. "Aristotle and the Stoics formulated a comprehensive way of thinking about human life that has had enormous influence on European thought," Engberg-Pedersen, *Paul and the Stoics*, 45. That Paul's anthropology and ethics only becomes coherent when seen as expressing the basic structure of Stoicism, 33, 46, may overstate the case. This structure is threefold: the "I" as unconverted, converted, and new, 33–44.

9. Boyd, *Shared Morality*, 255. When quoted, "man" retained throughout to avoid anachronism.

10. Black, *Christian Moral Realism*, 316.

11. Barth being the pioneer. McKenzie and Myers, "Dialectical Critical Realism," 49–66, discuss theological and scientific realism. Also La Montagne, *Barth and Rationality*, 118: "For Barth, the reality of God in revelation actively criticizes all our knowledge."

independent of and external to the enquiring human mind"; epistemological, "this reality can be known"; and semantic, "this reality may be depicted . . . at least as approximations to the truth."[12] Neo-Kantian object-skepticism is thus rejected. Porter's term is "speculative realism," which she contrasts with what she sees as the naïve realism of McGrath.[13] Rasmussen's theory is bi-dimensional, consisting of ontological realism (the existence of beings, rather than reality more broadly conceived) that grounds epistemological realism (the knowledge of the existence and nature of these beings).[14] La Montagne's typology has two constitutive elements in four basic propositions. As realism, it asserts a) the reality of the other-in-itself, and b) that the knowing subject can have real knowledge of the world. As critical, it a) asserts that all such knowledge is mediated, and b) requires a critical theory about the nature and limits of all knowledge.[15]

Critical realism affirms that "genuine knowledge in any field involves knowledge of that field in accordance with the realities with which we have to do in it, and knowledge of those realities in terms of their internal relations or intrinsic structures."[16] In this situation, the object or objective field determines the subject's epistemology and semantics: epistemology (the knowing subject's apprehension) and semantics (the subject's description) are parasitic upon, determined by and congruent with metaphysics/ontology (the knowable object), yet are open to cross-discourse description. Rationality is thus not a justifying criterion that exists external to that which is being investigated, but lies within the object and its attendant fields. Thus entities and their relations impose upon the observer their own reality and configuration, thereby shaping the mind's theoretical structure and object-specific description of that object.[17] Accordingly, "a disclosure model in natural science is a conceptual construct forced upon us by the intrinsic intelligibility of some field as we inquire into it, and it is developed as a theory through which we seek to let the structures of that field disclose themselves to us."[18] This is depicted biblically in Psalm 19:1–6 where the heavens and skies (the subject, v. 1) declare (v. 2–4) the glory of God and the work of his

12. McGrath, *Scientific Theology*, vol. 1, 75–76.

13. Porter, *Nature as Reason*, 57–68.

14. Douglas B. Rasmussen, "The Importance of Metaphysical Realism for Ethical Knowledge," in Paul et al., *Objectivism*, 56, n. 4.

15. La Montagne, *Barth and Rationality*, 14–16.

16. Torrance, *Ground and Grammar*, 146.

17. The significance of relations is explored by Polkinghorne, *Trinity and Entangled World*, 1–14.

18. Torrance, *Ground and Grammar*, 125.

hands (the object, v. 1). Hence the ontological reality (God's glory) and the physical reality (his work) coordinate and co-inhere. This disclosure model is not limited to natural science, but extends to all forms of human knowing. Calvin expresses this regarding Scripture: "The same Spirit, therefore, who has spoken through the mouths of the prophets must penetrate into our hearts to persuade us that they faithfully proclaimed what had been divinely commanded."[19] Calvin here approximates Irenaeus's coordination of the Father's two hands, for both the Word (Gen 1:3; Ps 33:6a) and the Spirit (Gen 1:2, 2:7; Ps 33:6b, 104:30) create and sustain creation. Not only does this mean that creation is intelligible and open to rational description, but that this coherent intelligibility extends to the moral dimension of creation because *Logos* and *Pneuma*, the agents of creation, are not Stoic or Hegelian abstractions respectively, but the moral persons of the Son and Holy Spirit. Because the Spirit is coordinate with the Word (Ps 33:6), there is neither a subjective departure from reason, nor a rationalistic abandonment of subjectivity.

Thus if viewed spatially, critical moral realism elliptically unites objectivism and subjectivism. Objectivism affirms there "is or must be some permanent, ahistorical matrix or framework to which we can ultimately appeal in determining the nature of rationality, knowledge, truth, reality, goodness and rightness," while subjectivism avers that "when we turn to the examination of those concepts . . . —whether it is the concept of rationality, knowledge, truth, reality, the good, or norms—we are forced to recognize that in the final analysis all such concepts must be understood as relative to a specific conceptual scheme, theoretical framework, paradigm, form of life, society, or culture."[20] Similar is Polanyi's theory of personal knowledge where the "personal and objective are fused . . . in the act of establishing contact with reality."[21] By disabling the view that rationality is an external reality to which all disciplines must be subjected, critical realism established that the knowing and describing of any object or relation is internal to that object or relation, and also rehabilitated fallibilism as epistemologically acceptable.[22] Such critical realism means that the Incarnation renders obsolete any sense that the objective and subjective are *exclusive* polarities, as their contested claims become the one claim of the enfleshed Word, the objective as the subjective, the divine object of the Word as the divinely knowing

---

19. Calvin, *ICR*, I.vii.4.
20. Bernstein, *Beyond Objectivism*, 8.
21. Thomas F. Torrance, "Notes on Terms and Concepts," in *Belief in Science*, 141.
22. McCormack in La Montagne, *Barth and Rationality*, viii.

subject of the flesh, of the ahistorical eternal Word as the historical incarnate Word. Jesus knows the eternal *Logos* because he is internal to it.

Moreover, the structured order and thus intelligibility of the creation is implied in biblical monotheism, in contrast with the "anarchia" and "polyarchia" of pagan religious philosophy, which produced a world without order and a world of fractious order, respectively, and thus dissolution. "Only a divine 'monarchia,' therefore, could salvage order in the world."[23] The Cappadocians "posited a fundamental philosophical connection between the correct doctrine about God's being and the quest for the world order," although not without classical antecedent.[24] Furthermore, and akin to Torrance, "as the 'Maker of heaven and earth,' God was 'the Creator even of the essence of beings,' not merely 'an inventor of figures' but the Creator of 'the *ousia* with the form [eideis].'"[25] Thus the co-inherence of form and being in God is the philosophical basis for a similar co-inherence in creation as a whole. Such a creative process possesses three aspects: 1) the divine idea of any *ousia* included both its form and matter; 2) the divine creation of matter in its form; and 3) the systematic coherence of form and matter in each *ousia*, and also between all created realities. Thus "one *ousia*" underlies all humanity.[26] Hence in the *Logos ensarkos*, the divine order and coherence of creation's (especially humanity's) form and matter became focused in an unprecedented fashion such that natural law as that which is proper to human nature is necessarily christological. In contrast, voluntarism, positivism and constructivism tend to tease apart the co-inherence of form and matter, subject and object. They do this by imposing *a priori* presuppositions and semantics that are alien to and non-congruent with the object. This subjective determination separates moral matter from moral form: being formally human corresponds to no material human morality, enabling the decentered self to freely determine its own moral nature that may be alien to its real humanity.

Critical moral realism differs from both naïve metaphysical realism and constructivism. First, simple or naïve metaphysical realism acknowledges the real existence of things but denies real knowledge or description of them due to the theory-laden character of all knowledge and language,

---

23. Pelikan, *Christianity and Classical Culture*, 77; citing Gregory Nazianzus, Orations, 29.2 (SC 250:178). Eastern trinitarianism locates God's unity in the Father's monarchy, rather than in a single *ousia* as in Western, particularly contemporary, theology. This reflects the Bible's emphasis on persons rather then substance.

24. Ibid., 91, 94.

25. Ibid., 97; citing Gr. Nyss. Hom.opif.29 (PG 44:233), Bas. Hex.2.3 (SC 26:148).

26. Ibid., 97.

rendering realism not false but unintelligible.[27] This reflects the modernist precedence of the human subject over objective entities. However, Rasmussen unnecessarily assumes that all such theory-laden knowledge is non-congruent with objects, being inevitably constructed in such a fashion that it imposes consciously or unconsciously upon, rather than reflecting, the object. Thus, while appearing epistemologically modest it betrays a form of anthropocentric hegemony over objects, for it fails to acknowledge that the human mind may be acted upon and truthfully shaped, not wholly passively, but in an object-determined and congruent fashion. The relationship between the mind and objects is dialectical, the primary status being accorded to the object, and the subject functioning with a listening attitude towards the object or reality, being obediently receptive to disclosed forms, structures and laws. Thus, in moral terms, receptive object-determined epistemology is an intellectual virtue possessing the moral character of humility, while a constructivist, imposed, object-nondetermination (or subject-determination) epistemology is the moral vice of pride.

Similarly, yet more radically, critical moral realism contrasts with perspectival constructivism, which functions from acknowledged *a priori* presuppositions and non-congruent thought-forms imposed upon the object. Such imposition has nominalist overtones by denying that entities belong to *a priori* kinds, and allows arbitrary predication and description of entities and their relations. Here the object-determined yet dialectical mode is replaced by a subject-determined positivism where objects are forced to fit pre-existing beliefs. This epistemology leads to an impasse in understanding, unresolvable anomalies, a false interpretation, or the final collapse of the theory and its replacement by a better explanation that accords with the object itself. An example would be the reduction of persons to economic utility, which finally collapses due to the universal valuing of financially dependent persons such as the chronically unemployable.

In contrast to both naive metaphysical realism and constructivism, critical moral realism maintains an object-subject dialectic, "where the human being and nature interact, affect, and influence each other . . . [here] the emphasis is . . . on the relation, the interaction that brings the different entities together into community and communion."[28]

Critical realism is thus not naïve realism (Porter's mis-description of McGrath), which is more appropriately attributable to forms of natural

27. Douglas B. Rasmussen, "The Importance of Metaphysical Realism," in Paul et al., *Objectivism*, 61; describing Hilary Putman's position, which is akin to Kantian skepticism, and historicism.

28. Argyris Nicolaidis, "Relational Nature," in Polkinghorne, *Trinity and Entangled World*, 95.

law possessing an optimistic anthropology and a high epistemology of self-evidence. The tendency in these forms is to conflate natural law with convention, as Augustine does with slavery, noted below. Reformed thought is ambiguous here: its negative hamartiology preferences divine commands over natural law (e.g., Barth), yet its strong theology of general revelation, common grace and providence may support natural law.[29] In contrast, McGrath and Torrance have produced Reformed critical realist approaches, McGrath from the natural sciences and Torrance from theoretical science, the key distinction from naïve realism being the predicate "critical."

Torrance's fundamental principle is that "we know things in accordance with their natures, or what they are in themselves; and so we let the nature of what we know determine for us the content and form of our knowledge."[30] Thus "nature must be courted, not imposed upon."[31] This is theologically derived: God is known as God (being) in his self-disclosure (act) to those who attend to him in the epistemic mode congruent to his essential nature found in his self-revelation (faith). This process applies to all aspects of his good creation as reflecting his character. Thus human nature is revealed and understood as one entity within and one aspect of the matrix of divine created reality, bearing the *imago Dei*. This being so, Christian metaphysical realism implies ontological realism: or to put it another way, divine ontological realism implies human ontological realism. Hence Torrance: "Laws of nature are thus the dogmas that are imposed on the scientific mind by the immanent rationality of the universe."[32] Such rationality is inherent in the universe by the act of its creation by the intelligent and intelligible rational Creator, not by hypostasizing the universe, as in Cicero. Thus the knowledge of the moral world is *formally* identical to the knowledge of God in that both epistemologies are determined by canons of rationality that lie, not external to God or humanity, but internal to them as necessary elements of their reality.

Similarly regarding jurisprudence, Torrance attacks legal positivism on the basis of Einsteinian science's "unity of being and form, or substance and structure . . . in every sphere of human enquiry" which involves the "integration of ontology and epistemology in rigorous fidelity to the fact that empirical and theoretical factors are found already inhering in one another

---

29. As in Grabill's *Rediscovering the Natural Law*.

30. Torrance, *Ground and Grammar*, 8. Barth's argument with Harnack concerned theology's proper object and its knowledge: Busch, *Karl Barth*, 147, 165–166.

31. Torrance, *Ground and Grammar*, 9.

32. Ibid., 51.

in objective reality."[33] Rejecting the Greek bifurcation of reasoning (theoretical and practical reasoning) which legitimizes the detachment of formal law from its content and objective ground[34] (contrary to Athanasian *logos* theology[35]), he suggests that jurisprudence should "seek to ground judicial law in the objective intelligibilities of that created reality."[36] This echoes Ciceronian natural law (noted below) but with a modern scientific justification. Torrencian scientific realism thus suggests that contingent positive law ought to possess science's internal structure if is to escape the pitfalls of arbitrariness, a key concern of natural lawyers and justice advocates. Extended to natural law, this suggests moral structures are inherent in reality as the result of God's free and morally good act of creation as expressing his essential being. Consequently humanity, as one aspect of this created reality, possesses moral freedom (as a form) as an element of its substantial nature (its being) as the *imago Dei* so that human moral freedom is freedom to be, realize and reflect its nature.[37]

Consequently, moral realism is congruent with Christian theology as one aspect of creation's intelligibility. To affirm scientific realism while denying moral realism repeats the errors of both Greek rational bifurcation (theoretical verses practical reasoning)[38] and the Cartesian split of fact and value. As science reveals the intrinsic coherent intelligibility of the universe's physical essence and form, ethics reveals the coherent inherent intelligibility of its moral essence and form. In traditional theology, this has been described as the general revelation of moral goods, laws and rules.

There lies a problem with natural law's rationalism, however, and it concerns the human will. Two volition-based problems exist: will-to-power (hubris), and will-enfeeblement (sloth).[39] Nietzschian will-to-power can be seen in forms of purposive theory-laden constructivism in hard sciences

---

33. Torrance, *Juridical Law*, 24–25. Torrance proposes physical/scientific realism as a model for a realist corrective of Lockean and Benthamite legal positivism, and hence ethics.

34. Ibid., 30.

35. Torrance, *Ground and Grammar*, 151.

36. Torrance, *Juridical Law*, 33.

37. So John Paul II, *Veritatis Splendour*.

38. For a discussion of the relation between the two, see Germaine Paulo Walsh, "The Problematic Relation between Practical and Theoretical Virtue in Aristotle's Nicomachean Ethics," in Grasso and Hunt, *Moral Enterprise*, 59–81. Walsh is an inclusivist: human eudemonia in Aristotle is a composite of both practical and theoretical virtue, because human nature is composite.

39. Aristotle, *Nicomachean Ethics* VII, 1–10, sees sloth (his "incontinence") as incompatible with practical reasoning.

(fudging the data to support the hypothesis), and politically skewed statistics, as well as ethical voluntarist positivism. Will-enfeeblement is seen in the Pauline self-woe oracle of Romans 7.[40] In contrast, both naïve ethical epistemic realism and simple rationalistic ethics deny will-enfeeblement, holding that moral knowledge leads inexorably to moral acts, despite empirical observations indicating otherwise.[41] This problem of the will in most natural law theories constitutes one of its basic omissions, whereas christological ethics that include pneumatology take both will-to-power and will-enfeeblement seriously through the doctrines of repentance and regeneration.

In this respect, 2 Peter 2:12 describes some human behavior as expressing the irrational behavior of animals.[42] Such an association of irrationality, ignorance and nature suggests human nature can be degraded by unnatural practices or orientations contrary to proper reason, necessitating critical modification of naïve or absolute realism regarding nature.[43] However, this modification is not nominalistic or hard-constructivist grounded upon conscious *a priori* imposed presuppositions, but responds to entities and reality within constraints: the moral task is constructivist in an object-determined fashion. This is a form of epistemic fallibilism but not skepticism, for it asserts the truth of its propositions and the possibility of true knowledge, whereas skepticism denies both. It also differs from absolute or naïve realism in its openness to modification by new object-related information or more adequate description, as well as from revelation: it holds its truth more modestly. Thus, *aloga* softens excessive realist claims.

40. The identity of the self is immaterial here.

41. As seen in humanism's social panacea, education, and certain catechetics where Bible knowledge *sans* other means of grace guarantees sanctification.

42. That instincts are negatively attributed to irrational animals suggests they are not equivalent to proper natural human inclinations.

43. "Knowledge is constructed by fallible humans in particular social contexts, and ... our knowledge is at the best approximate" (McKenzie and Myers, "Dialectical Critical Realism," 49). The moral aspects of irrationalism and ignorance are highlighted in 2 Peter 2:12–22. Reason "supplies . . . moral alibis and *ex post facto* rationalizations which serve its purpose," like a harlot serving desire (Thielicke, *Ethics,* 142). Smith attempts to rehabilitate the Augustinian model of persons as "embodied agents of desire or love" over reason: "we are fundamentally non-cognitive affective creatures" (Smith, *Desiring the Kingdom,* 47, 53). Henriksen locates desire in God (his wish for human fellowship) and in the synoptic love command, which is fulfilled eschatologically (Henriksen, *Desire, Gift and Recognition,* 27–38, 125–32). The insatiability of normative desire makes it possible for us "to enjoy the creation more fully and enduringly" (Jan-Olav Henriksen, "Desire: Gift and Giving," in Shults and Henriksen, *Saving Desire,* 6).

Consequently natural law can be understood as the critically real knowledge and description of the divine and human moral natures. Yet because objects determine such knowledge and description, natural law miscarries as a Christian ethic to the extent that it excludes Christ's two natures as the proper object of such inquiry. Because critical realism implies that natural law's rationality is internal to these two natures, Jesus Christ is the focal instance of natural law. Critical realism also contests Humean ethical skepticism, which is now assessed.

b. The Naturalistic Axiom

Moral realism's naturalistic axiom ("ought" being derivable from "is") has been problematic since its Humean fallacious critique. As the object(s) of theoretical reasoning are prior realities, and the object(s) of practical reasoning are yet-to-be realities originating in human action, the two forms of reasoning are considered logically incommensurable: see Table 1.

Factor	Is	Ought
Type of reasoning	*Theoretical*	*Practical*
Object of reasoning	*Pre-existent*	*Consequent*
Goal of reasoning	*Truth*	*Good*
Purpose	*Knowledge*	*Action*
Linguistic form	*Descriptive*	*Evaluative*
Grammatical mood	*Indicative*	*Imperative*
Anthropology	*Mind*	*Body*

Table 1: Aristotelian Bifurcated Rationality

One novelty of the Finnis-Grisez school is their affirmation of both moral realism and the naturalistic fallacy, the latter based on Aristotelian bifurcated rationality.[44] As any conclusion must be implicit in its premises, it is asserted that practical reasoning cannot be grounded in theoretical reasoning, as the latter contains no practical element.

Where practical conclusions appear derivable from theoretical premises, Black asserts that the premise contains a hidden practical (i.e., ethical) component, which makes the ethical conclusion appear logically derivable

---

44. On natural lawyers having shown that ethical norms are derivable from facts, Black states: "They have not, nor do they need to, nor did the classical exponents of the theory dream of attempting any such derivation," *Moral Realism*, 33. Despite this, Finnis rejects the Humean subjectivist interpretation of ethics, *Fundamentals*, 27, 57–8.

from the theoretical premise.[45] This presupposes that truly descriptive statements are necessarily ethically empty, and that ethically true statements are descriptively vacuous. Yet this disjunction is problematic because such abstraction "imposes on thought a dualism between form and matter or structure and being which gives rise to a formalistic and artificial picture of things."[46] It is preferable to see reason as simply an abstract noun which describes a single human activity in variegated forms: bifurcated modalities of reasoning are philosophically interesting, but are non-descriptive of actual reasoning, for people reason dialectically both indicatively and imperatively.[47] The following statement is illustrative:

God is,

I ought to love God.[48]

The Humean tradition asserts this statement as logically fallacious, yet it expresses Jesus' love command. Black's contention that the premise contains an implicit ethical dimension is grammatically untrue, and the naturalistic fallacy is an analytic/linguistic argument. Even if the premise is predicated as in the synoptic Gospels ("Lord," "your God," and "one"), it is still a descriptive statement: "Lord" is a name, "your God" describes a pre-existing covenant relation, and "one" is numerical or metaphysical, thus non-evaluative.

The command's antecedent (Deut 6:4) inverts the order: the imperative "Hear, O Israel" precedes the indicative "The Lord your God, the Lord is one." Here the practical reasoning demands assent to an object of theoretical reasoning. However, if logical deduction from reality to practice is fallacious, logical induction from practice to reality is equally fallacious, so that urging (the ethical imperative) acceptance of any reality (the realist indicative) is fallacious. Thus, "You must accept (ought, imperative mood, ethical, practical reasoning) you have cancer (is, indicative mood, realistic, theoretical reasoning)," is fallacious and illogical. This is contra self-evident.

The premise "God is" is linguistically indicative and an instance of theoretical reasoning, yet the lexical item "God" is moral by definition.[49] Thus Black is right in suggesting that the above premise has an ethical com-

---

45. Black, *Moral Realism*, 27–33.

46. Torrance, "Notes," *Belief in Science*, 133.

47. Combining the "theological *cum* 'cosmological'" and ethical, Engberg-Pedersen, *Paul*, 6.

48. "God is our Father, we ought to hallow his name," is Phillips's is/ought example. His argument proceeds from the institution of human fatherhood and the moral obligation of children: "God and Ought," in Ramsay *Christian Ethics*, 133–139. Black rejects Phillips; see Black, *Moral Realism*, 26–33.

49. Barth's reworking of "God is" as "God loves" is discussed in Part Three.

ponent, although it is arguable whether that component is hidden. Whilst the language is indicative/theoretical, the content is not, demonstrating the inadequacy of the Humean tradition, which is based on grammar. Therefore while ethical content expressed in ethical/imperative language maintains matter/form congruity (as mathematics expressed in mathematical formula), the necessity of such linguistic congruence is non-absolute. That is, invariant material can be commensurable between multiple linguistic forms and moods: cross-discourse translation is possible. Therefore, while matter/form congruity is a base requirement for any matter to be discourse-coherent (as in Torrance, above), matter/form non-congruity is not excluded so long as it remains secondary to and parasitic upon the congruent forms, thus avoiding voluntarist constructionism. To prioritize descriptive-language premises over prescriptive-language conclusions in ethics constitutes illegitimate descriptive-language hegemony, and begs the question of alternative linguistic hegemonies. To invalidate an argument due to it possessing more than one verbal mood renders language almost useless.

Rather than prioritizing one language form over another, or asserting their separation, maintaining all forms as connected and mutually dependent in a coherent matrix maintains the realist unitive view of the co-inherence of form and substance. It is also a grammatical expression of relational reality. Whilst the separation of the two language forms leads either to existentialism or linguistic philosophy,[50] their co-inherence maintains the unitary/relational view of moral life and human existence that is lived everyday, enabling commonsense ethics to reason from the way things are to the way people ought to act.

Furthermore, considered analytically, "God" is lexically vacuous. Although nouns have meaning on their own, such meaning implies the noun's internal self-predication. Self-evidence means a predicate is contained in the subject itself. For instance, the ontological argument predicates greatness to "God" for the purpose of the argument. When confronted by a lexically unpredicated subject that appears non self-evident, the reader supplies a predicate to create meaning. Thus the noun "God " begs the question, "What or who is 'God'"? And as non-contradiction is the only rule governing predication, ethical predication cannot be excluded. Therefore the term "God" in the above premise "God is" can be legitimately understood morally, as in Barth's "God loves." As Thomas states, "Any proposition is said to be self-evident in itself, if its predicate is contained in the notion of the subject." For Thomas a human is self-evidently a "rational Being."[51] Simi-

---

50. Torrance, *Ground and Grammar*, 32–5.
51. Aquinas, *ST*, Ia2æ, q. 94. 2.

larly, "God" is self-evidently understood as morally "good." Thus Thomas's attribution to Boethius: "Certain axioms or propositions are universally self-evident to all";[52] and Aristotle: "Since 'good' has as many senses as 'being' (for it is predicated both in the category of substance, as of God and of reason)."[53] Substantive good, when attributed to God, takes on a moral sense, necessarily. In Barthian terms, the term "God" is non-substantive, anti-realist, arbitrary and fictional unless predicated as Father, Son and Holy Spirit, known as moral through his self-revelation. Thus "God is" contains moral meaning even though its grammatical form is otherwise. Therefore deducting imperative conclusions (an "ought") from linguistically descriptive premises (an "is") is non-fallacious and ethically legitimate when God is the premise.

We cite five further arguments against the Humean tradition. First, the assertion that ethical actions cannot be logically based upon prior real beliefs contests natural mental inclinations and reasoning. "I must move the baby," is a natural ethical response to "There's a baby on the road." To assert that it contains an implicit ethical premise ("babies are precious") illustrates the point above: that descriptive language often contains ethical content. To declare, "You moved the baby off the road due to illogical reasoning," would be met with universal offence, for if the reasoning upon which a morally good act is based is illogical, the moral agent is illogically motivated. Thus morally good acts are patronizingly accused of fallaciousness, which is pejorative and unethical.

Second, the fallacy renders theological propositions ethically inert, contrary to the biblical use of therefore (οὖν, *oun*) which links the theologically indicative to the paraenetic imperative moods.[54] The acts of *heilsgeschichte* provide the indicative justification for the imperatives of the Decalogue (Exod 20:1–2), the psalmist's call to worship (Ps 81:1–5), and prophetic oracles (Isa 1:2–3). Jesus' initial preaching (Mark 1:15) consists of a foundational double perfect followed by a consequent double imperative. The imperative, "Be perfect," is predicated upon (οὖν) the fact that God in heaven "is perfect" (Matt 6:48). The merciful activity of God (Rom 9—11) is the antecedent basis (οὖν) of Paul's exhortation (Rom 12:1–21). Finally "the end of all things is at hand, therefore (οὖν) keep sane and sober in your prayers" (1 Pet 4:7, RSV) contains a descriptive eschatological premise

---

52. Ibid.

53. Aristotle, *Nicomachean*, I. 6. 1096a15.

54. Hauerwas is noted as an exponent, Black, *Moral Reasoning*, 7. Pauline paraenesis (imperative) urges the actualization of the new self (indicative), Engberg-Pedersen, *Paul*, 8.

(the "end") in the indicative mood and an imperative ethical conclusion ("keep sane and sober"). Verb mood cannot be the criterion of logical moral discourse.

Third, the naturalistic fallacy excludes ethical texts as sources for practical moral reasoning, because such texts preexist the act of moral reasoning and therefore cannot act as bases for the moral action that they themselves actually encourage. The *Nicomachean Ethics* is rendered illogical, as it purports to be a true description (theoretical reasoning) about the good (practical reasoning). Likewise, Scripture becomes morally incoherent when it states that "these things happened to them to serve as an example and they were written down to instruct us on whom the ends of the ages have come," (1 Cor 10:11). The fallacy renders textual moral argument and exhortation ethically inert.

Fourth, the naturalistic fallacy excludes past good actions (which exist prior to the act of reasoning) as sources for practical moral reasoning, as no ought is derivable from past events. Yet such actions constitute an "is" and are capable of plural descriptions in multiple discourses. A youth assisting an elderly person can be described psychologically (operant conditioning), politically (community welfare), and religiously (honoring elders). However, the naturalistic fallacy denies that such behavior is explicable by the youth as copying his father—"Dad did it (an 'is'), so I should too" (an 'ought')—without it being labeled logically fallacious. It follows that to draw any psychological, political or religious consequences is also necessarily fallacious, unless there are equivalent psychological, political or religious hidden premises. Therefore all conclusions cognate to their premises (e.g., political conclusions of a political premise) are logically fallacious if such conclusions contain an imperative. The fallacy renders all descriptions (premises) as non-objective, non-descriptive and thus materially inconsistent (i.e., hidden imperative) with their form (grammatically descriptive). This is counterintuitive: for instance, government surveys consist of description (the "is" of quantitative research) followed by recommendations ("oughts") to maximize human goods.

Fifth, if hortatory language is logically not derivable from description, exhortation is non-substantive and circularly self-referential. Yet exhortation begs the question, "*Why* should I do that?" To answer that doing so is a self-evident good is unhelpful for three reasons. First, "*Why?*" a central question in moral discussion, implies non-self-evidence: self-evidence renders "*Why?*" redundant, necessarily. Second, "*Why?*" expects a realistic and substantive answer, the questioner being insulted if a purely hortatory answer is repeated. Third, citing self-evident goods constitutes a substantive answer, which it is argued cannot function as a premise for imperatives, which renders such argument illogical.

Consequently, the naturalistic axiom is sustainable and arguments based on bifurcated reasoning are problematic, theoretically inconsistent, and unwarranted by biblical literary forms and practical living. Critical moral realism rejects bifurcated reasoning which separates essence/substance/being from form/structure/act, and the indicative from the imperative, asserting that critical real knowledge of real being(s), entities and their relations, and reality, exists; and necessarily discloses real forms, structures, and acts, including those that are moral; and that these can be properly, although not perfectly, described. It is fallibilistic but not skeptical, and thus open to reassessment. However, it dismisses the view that such real knowledge and description necessarily leads to moral acts due to the problem of the will and *aloga*. Following these philosophical matters, biblical and theological concerns are now assessed.

3. Theological and Biblical Considerations of Nature

a. Nature and Natural

Reason constitutes the essence of human nature in traditional natural law. Such anthropology fails to be sufficiently cognizant of broader non-rational[55] human dimensions, and as such constitutes a truncated ontology.[56] MacIntyre convincingly demonstrates that reason is inseparable "from the intellectual and social traditions in which it is embodied,"[57] which leads to "rival conceptions of rationality, both theoretical and practical."[58] Similarly, there are contested theological, biblical and material conceptions of nature, although they all function to legitimize an action as proper.

Natural law differs from natural theology by its object. Natural law asserts truthful rational moral knowledge of good conduct, whilst natural theology asserts truthful rational theological knowledge of the true God. While both God and the good are inextricably linked, they possess different

---

55. As distinct from irrational.

56. "Rational action ought therefore to be subject to the control of contemplation, which is exercised through faith," Augustine, "Reply to Faustus," 27, 283. Aristotle also qualifies practical rationality by virtue, "virtue in the strict sense . . . involves practical wisdom," *Nicomachean*, VI. 13. 1144b5. Also Smith, "We are primarily desiring animals," Smith, *Desiring the Kingdom*, 26.

57. MacIntyre, *Whose Justice?*, 8.

58. MacIntyre, *Three Rival Versions of Moral Enquiry*, 13.

focal concerns.⁵⁹ Both are philosophically realist, drawing conclusions from what are considered observable self-evident facts, and both possess an optimistic rationality and concept of conscience, whilst minimizing the epistemological effect of sin.⁶⁰

In theological usage, a transition from the medieval "nature as sacrament" in the neo-Platonic Augustinian synthesis of grace and nature to "nature as object of God's specific creative acts" in the Reformation is noted by Torrance. "In the former outlook the world was interpreted in its attraction to God, in the latter it was interpreted in God's action upon the world."⁶¹ This action means that "man and nature belong to the same order of rationality so that when we bring to scientific formalization human relations with nature we lay bare the natural order and structure of created existence."⁶² Thus the inherent moral structure of human existence is rationally apprehensible as one element of the wider created order, including the opportunity to "ground juridical law in the objective intelligibilities of created reality."⁶³ Consequently, nature is synonymous with truth and reality, not simply with a surface reading of phenomena.⁶⁴

McGrath proposes a threefold scientific meaning of nature: 1) the realist and scientifically measurable "structures, processes and causal powers" of the physical world; 2) the metaphysical, which "allows humanity to posit its distinctive nature and identity in relation to the non-human"; and 3) a surface concept referring to the ordinary observable phenomena of the world, especially "in modern ecological discourse."⁶⁵ As in Aristotle, *phusis* is distinct from *techné*.⁶⁶

Furthermore, McGrath establishes that "nature" is a socially constructed polysemous term expressed in historically determined metaphors, proposing the term "creation" as the proper Christian term.⁶⁷ Such polysemony produces conflicting theories of natural law in respect of matter,

59. Because of this difference, Hauerwas's *With the Grain*, while not without importance, is not a primary text for this thesis.

60. Later Reformed orthodoxy's more pessimistic doctrines of the noetic effects of sin and the enslaved will are an exception: see the discussion of Calvin later. For a contrary thesis see Grabill, *Rediscovering the Natural Law*.

61. Torrance, *Theological Science*, 67. Thomas's concept of humanity's attraction to God-given goods is noted below.

62. Ibid., 298.

63. Torrance, *Juridical Law*, 33.

64. Torrance, *Divine Meaning*, 211, on Athanasius.

65. McGrath, *Scientific Theology*, vol. 1, 82.

66. Ibid., 93–4.

67. Ibid., 102–33. Space prohibits discussion of the biblical term *ktisis*.

means and ends. For instance, Aquinas's human nature (a rational soul), Calvin's prayerfulness (as a necessary means) and The Westminster Confession's chief end (to know God) are not self-evident diachronically, diaconfessionally or diaculturally, although not necessarily opposed either. Nature contested is natural law contested.

Boyd offers three meanings of nature: first, "the object of various scientific inquiries that focuses upon explanations of how natural objects and living beings act and are acted upon"; second, "a principle of corruption resulting from a primeval fall of humanity wherein the active power of nature is contrasted with the restorative powers of grace"; and third, "the fulfilment of the natural *telos* embedded in humans in creation; it includes but is not reducible to" nature in his first sense.[68]

O'Donovan offers two proper theological meanings of nature: first, the ontological in contrast with the Hegelian historical; and second, the epistemological in contrast to the revelatory. An improper third meaning refers to fallen humanity.[69] Both the proper meanings refer to "everything that is not the self-giving of God in Jesus Christ . . . which does not depend directly upon Jesus,"[70] constituting a sharp distinction between nature (creation), and grace (revelation).

The theological tradition describes human nature in four broad ways, three of which are found in the natural law tradition. First, nature describes *pre-lapsum* humanity (and creation and its goods) and is found in protological natural law theories.[71] Original human *phusis*[72] is a morally good divine creation, and open to truthful rational cognition. Humanity's common *ousia* gives natural law universal significance. Being grounded in creation, it

68. Boyd, *Shared Morality*, 39.
69. O'Donovan, "The Natural Ethic," in Wright, *Essays*, 32–3.
70. Ibid., 33.
71. Rom. 1:26, discussed below.
72. If we augment *phusis* with *ousia*, we strengthen the metaphysical basis of the natural law ethic, as every hypostasis possesses its concomitant *ousia* and vice versa. Thus the link between human phenomenology (the focus of ethics in "the modern consciousness of freedom," Schockenhoff, *Natural Law*, 2–3) and human essence is strengthened. This locates any particular hypostasis in a given *phusis* or *ousia*, ontologically grounding it. As there is no *physis anhypostasis*, it is not possible to propose a personal ethic agent (hypostasis) separated from its concomitant *ousia* or *phusis*, or vice versa. McIntyre cites Aristotle's Categoriae c. 5. as the basis for such logic when applied to two-nature Christology: Aristotle's in rebus thesis means that forms or universals are neither antecedent to (ante res, as in Plato), or posterior to (post res, as in nominalism) particulars, but are "only . . . realized in particular subjects." See McIntyre, *Shape of Christology*, 88; see 86–103. Thus universal human *ousia* and *phusis* only exists in particular human hypostases.

is prior to and independent of revelation that subsequently attests to it. Thus "the fundamental ethical command imposed on the Christian is precisely to be what he or she is. 'Be human.' That is what God asks of us, no more and no less . . . Christian ethics is human ethics, no more and no less."[73]

Second, nature refers to *post-lapsum* humanity, the empirical datum of moral reasoning.[74] This use is uncommon and concedes natural law's inefficacy due to sin, as with revealed law. In both, the law itself is good, but the human response is noetically or volitionally inadequate, rendering its efficacy ambiguous. An acute sense of this inadequacy was one reason for the breakdown of classical forms of moral reasoning in the Reformation.[75]

Third, nature possesses the eschatological teleological sense of humanity's final good as the end of the perfective process.[76] This sense is found in means/ends/goods theories, where humanity's *telos* determines the natural practices and dispositions that are congruent with—and function instrumentally to attain—such goods and ends. It is common in the New Testament where eschatology frequently functions morally (e.g., 1 Thess 4:17–18), although Christian and classical approaches differ as to the content of the final end. Whereas Aristotle's *telos* is peaceful social existence, Augustine's *telos* is the peaceful eschatological vision of God, humanity's infinite, final and proper good.

The fourth sense, renewed pre-eschatological nature, is insignificant in natural law due to its specific Christology, soteriology and pneumatology which are viewed as sectarian and thus problematic due to compromised ubiquity.[77] However, the "grace perfecting nature" thesis alleviates this problem, maintaining the priority of nature over grace, of creation over salvation.

The moral standing given to human nature and its capacities determines the status and viability of natural law ethics. *Pre-lapsum* and eschatological emphases contribute to a positive assessment of natural law's validity and efficacy, as it is reasonable and defensible to build a moral theory upon positively evaluated human data. Anthropologies that stress humanity's *post-lapsum* situation tend to minimize natural law as a possible source of moral guidance because it is considered incoherent to determine ethical

---

73. T. O'Connell, *Principles for a Catholic Morality*, 39–40, as cited in Katongole, *Beyond Universal Reason*, 15.

74. Ephesians 2:3, discussed below.

75. So David Solomon's reading of MacIntyre: see "MacIntyre and Contemporary Moral Philosophy," in Mark C. Murphy, ed. *Alasdair MacIntyre*, 135.

76. See 2 Peter 1:4, discussed below, regarding human participation in the divine nature.

77. For example, 2 Corinthians 5:17; Colossians 3:10–11, although *phusis* is not used.

ideals or moral values from that which is not good. In all approaches, Christology is minimal.

In common usage, "natural" possesses three general meanings. First, quantitatively, it describes statistical frequency of an act or disposition, meaning common, and implies the normativeness of the act or disposition. "Pre-marital sex is natural" means it is common, conventional. "Natural" is thus quantitatively determined, akin to McGrath's third sense, with the added sense of moral approval. It is a variety of the naturalistic axiom, whereby the "is" of statistical frequency of acts and/or dispositions implies the "ought" of moral acceptance.

Second: natural means primal, endocrinological, pre-rational, and vital. Such atavism opposes *phusis* to perceived distorting analytical and rationalistic *techné*, and is the opposite to the traditional sense of nature as reason and its governance of negative desire.[78] Such use is found in hedonic, erotic, and ecstatic theories of the good (e.g., Romanticism), heroic societies of aggression and power, and in Nietzsche.[79]

Third, natural is synonymous with individual subjectivity when qualified by a personal pronoun. For instance, practices previously considered unnatural (in the first and second senses) become natural if psychological dispositions and physical acts are congruent. Congruence implies normativeness: what is natural *for me* is taken as naturalness *per se*, in that particular instance, implying moral approval.[80]

Theological, biblical and common uses of "nature" demonstrate that although it is materially variant, it functions invariantly as a morally legitimizing term, describing a perceived good, thus bearing out Aristotle's thesis that practical reasoning about human nature is directed to a good. A basic question for Christian natural law is the correct determination of human nature within various biblical contexts, the two locations being the Garden

---

78. Although "no scholastic would interpret reason in such a way as to drive a wedge between the pre-rational aspects of our nature and rationality," "these [pre-rational] tendencies may be expressed in ways that are destructive and repugnant," Porter, *Natural and Divine Law*, 93, 143–146.

79. Berkowitz, *Nietzsche*, 49: Christianity's moral themes include "an ardent hostility to the instincts, passions."

80. The unity of desire and reason may indicate reason's capture by passion. The eighteenth-century transformation of Platonic order (*kata phusis* = *kata logon*) to deist design (*kata phusin* = *kata* sentiments) via subjective inclinations is argued by Taylor, *Sources of the Self*, 278–284. Compare Lady Gaga's apology *Made That Way*: an inclination/disposition becomes morally self-justifying.

or Golgotha.[81] The development of a Chalcedonian determination of human nature, which unites these two locations, occupies Part Three.

b. Φυσις *in the New Testament*

I. PAUL

Φυσις (*phusis*) is primarily a Pauline term (Rom 1:26, 27; 2:14, 27; 11:21, 24; 1 Cor 11:14; Gal 2:15, 4:8; and Eph 2:3[82]). Of particular interest is the κατα φυσιν/παρα φυσιν (*kata phusin/para phusin:* according to nature/ against nature) couplet, the latter taking on "the exclusive sense of 'instead of.'"[83] The *kata/para* usage suggests *phusis* functions as a moral canon that assesses actions as either according to, or against, a basic rule. Like the classical tradition, *phusis* stands in opposition to both dishonorable passions (Rom 1:26) and unnatural desire (v. 27). Christian natural law theories draw primarily upon Romans 2:14–16 and secondarily upon Romans 1:26–27, and are contested.[84] The theologically rich lexical contexts determine *phusis* as possessing no hypostatic self-existence: for Paul "there is no nature either detached from God or identifiable with God."[85] In Romans 2:14–16, Gentile obedience to divine law originates in *phusis* due to the law's requirements being written in their hearts (v. 15), constituting *phusis* and *kardia* as functional equivalents. The echoes of Jeremiah 31:31 lead Wright to interpret verse 15 as referring to Gentile Christians, meaning *phusis* in verse 14 refers to regenerate Gentile human nature, demonstrating *phusis'* polysemous character.[86] But what is written on the heart is not the law but the law's requirements (v. 14, 15) yet it "has the same goal as the idea of νόμος ἄγραφος, namely, that of setting mankind under an unconditional obligation."[87] The validity of this law's moral judgment is provisionally coordinate with the

---

81. Schockenhoff, *Natural Law,* 21.

82. Read as Pauline.

83. Käsemann, *Romans,* 48, commenting on Romans 1:26. This parallelism is found in Romans 1:26–27, and 11:21, 24.

84. "Concerning . . . φυσει . . . in Paul, theologians and philosophers are engaged in hot debate," Käsemann, *Romans,* 63 (full discussion, 62–8). "If Paul makes use of Stoic ideas . . . he does so without surrendering his thought to them," Dunn, *Romans 1–8,* 99. Romans 2:14–15 is "Paul's treatment of the *stoa,*" Bayer, *Freedom in Response,* 61. Aquinas's only reference to these texts when discussing natural law is a dismissal of an invalid exegesis of Romans 2:14 in *ST,* Ia2æ, q. 94. 6.

85. Käsemann, *Romans,* 48.

86. Wright, *Romans,* 441–442.

87. Käsemann, *Romans,* 64.

witness of conscience and the juridical accusation of one's inner thoughts (v. 15b), yet finally determined eschatologically according to Paul's gospel (v. 16), denoting a christological determination of *phusis,* conscience, and inner thoughts. Thus Paul coordinates four morally determining objects: the law's standards written on the heart, conscience, inner accusing thoughts, and the gospel. The first three are subjective, hidden (v. 16b), and determine current moral existence (although inner thoughts also performs an eschatological role, v. 15b–16a), while the gospel is the objective, eschatological, and final arbiter of previous moral judgments. Paul's use of *phusis* is conditioned by christological considerations at all points.

Significantly for the natural law tradition, there is a marked absence of explicit noetic moral psychology in Romans 2:14–16. *Nous* is absent, and although *kardia* does possess an intellectual component, it is not pre-eminent.[88] Paul's use of *kardia* rather than *nous* suggests that this principal natural law text miscarries if it is understood to refer primarily to human reason.

In Romans 1:26–27 *phusis* and *para phusis* refer to both cognition and affection. Human acts that are *para phusis* manifest dishonorable passions, affirming the traditional opposition between *phusis* and *pathé*. Verse 26 uses *phusis* in an instrumental fashion: the judgment is upon sexual acts that are not in accord with nature. Verse 27 is similarly affective, although desire (*orexis*) replaces dishonorable passions (*epithymia*). The cognitive aspect is found in both positive and negative senses: in verse 25, truth as opposed to falsehood, and in verse 28 a debased mind *(nous)*.

Phusis is thus not self-evident or self-explanatory. Actions described as *para phusin* are understood within the context of revelation (Rom 1:18), while the description of God's invisible qualities as plain and clearly understood (v. 19–20) suggests that revelation is coordinate with, not simply supplementary to, natural knowledge, and that the category of self-evidence is more nuanced than proposed. Epistemologically, God's invisible qualities are understood from what is seen, while historically they are known since the creation of the world (v. 20). In contrast to rationalistic theories where self-evidence is central both substantively and cognitively, wisdom is displaced by folly (v. 22), epexegetically glossed as futile thinking (v. 21) and a debased mind (v. 28). The denial of revelation is the causal link (v. 26a) to acts that are *para phusin*. The four divinely determined consequences of such denial are mutual bodily degradation (v. 24), degrading passions (v.

---

88. *Kardia* "is the concept that pre-eminently denotes the human ego in its thinking, affections, aspirations, decisions, both in man's relation to God and to the world surrounding him," Ridderbos, *Paul*, 119.

26), debased minds, and improper actions (v. 28). Thus the following terms are coordinate: *para phusin*, folly, futile thinking, and a debased mind. All are contra revelation and truth (v. 18), making *para phusis* determined by salvation history.[89]

Romans 11:21 and 24 presents the second use of the *kata phusin/ para phusin* form. *Phusis* is determined by divine election and will: Jews are the cultivated olive branches *kata phusin* (v. 21) while Gentiles are the wild olive branches *kata phusin* (v. 24a). The divine ingrafting of these wild olive branches into the cultivated stock is *para phusin*. Both grafting and re-grafting are due to God's power (v. 23). The agricultural metaphor illustrates Paul's elastic use of *phusis*, here possessing neither ethical nor ontological meaning, but referring to salvation history. The same also occurs in Romans 2:27, where Gentiles are uncircumcised by nature.[90] Nature is determined by its surrounding theological modifiers.

Galatians 2:15 presents *phusis* as birth status determined by salvation history. Ethnic (birth) Jews are "natural Jews," whereas the Gentiles may be "faith Jews," that is, offspring of the person of faith (Gal 3:29). Thus *phusis* contains a distinctly biological and ethnic flavor, although determined by election.

In Galatians 4:8 *phusis* has a realist metaphysical sense: by nature idols are not gods. Despite their external form, such objects possess no divine *phusis*, which suggests that non-congruence between structure (form) and substance (matter) constitutes deception, illustrating the Torrencian realism described earlier. Positivist predications of internal essence to an entity (in this case, divine *phusis* to an act of human *techné*) thus potentially break the inhering unity and self-referentially authenticating and self-evident character of such entities, necessitating their assessment by criteria located in revelation. Such differentiation between *phusis* and its attributions constitute acts of falsehood.

---

89. Romans 12:1-2 christologically reverses the process of 1:18-32: see Thompson, *Clothed With Christ*. Romans 1:18-32 is the assessment of Gentile morality by the apostle to the Gentiles, whose defense of Gentile inclusion led to the Jerusalem Decree (Acts 15). Bockmuehl, *Jewish Law*, argues that a natural law ethic grounded in the Noachide commands (Genesis 9) lies behind this decree, which appropriated Jewish Halakah for Gentile converts. This suggests that "natural" is still dependent upon revelation and not reason. That an ethic is universal is not identical with it being a natural law ethic.

90. Whether *phusis* means "nature," "convention" or "physically" does not alter the priority of election.

Ephesians 2:3 ("we were by nature, children of wrath") is universal in scope.[91] Here *phusis* takes a double sense. First, it describes human *post-lapsum* nature (sin and death, v. 1). Second, it has the sense of judicial dessert: what is fitting and appropriate, or consequentially right and just due to this sinfulness and its actions (v. 1–3). The appropriate natural consequence in this case is wrath. This is a morally and juridically consequential/deductive use of *phusis*, as in, "This is a cow, so naturally it gives milk," and could be rendered "thus."

A use of *phusis* which is "unique in the Pauline corpus"[92] is found in 1 Corinthians 11:14. The constituents of this paraenesis are creation (v. 7–9, 11–12), angels (v. 10), self-critical awareness (v. 13), apostolic recognition, and catholic practice (v. 16). *Phusis* possesses a morally educative power causing both male shame (v. 14) and female glory (v. 15) in respect to the cultural practice considered. *Phusis* stands with other considerations in determining what is proper (v. 13). Here Paul's appeal to *phusis* as a basis for Christian practice functions within the broader context of salvation history, and theological, pastoral and ecclesial categories.

As the natural law tradition understands revealed divine law as a *post-lapsum* instantiation of natural law, Paul's discussion of God's law in Romans 7:22–23 is apposite, despite the absence of *phusis*. There is a distinction between the inmost self and the external somatic elements (v. 24). It is this "somatic law" which overpowers God's law, causing captivity to sin. This moral psychology places the mind *(nous)* in the destructive power of members of the body of death, which renders obedience to God's law problematic or impossible (v. 23–24) unless the whole person (v. 24) is delivered, enabling the mind to serve the law of God (v. 25). In broad Pauline terms, sin morally degrades *phusis* and *nous* into *sarx*,[93] which renders natural law's moral psychology problematic due to reason's captivity. Despite inwardly delighting in God's law (Rom 7:22), practical moral inability is experienced (Rom 7:24).

In summary, Paul's use of *phusis* is non-reducible to the rationalism of the standard natural law tradition. Although he uses it primarily ethically, it can also refer to matters such as election and salvation. As a moral canon it stands within and is interpreted by fundamental theological categories,

---

91. The change from "you" (v. 1) to "we all" (v. 3).

92. Fee, *Corinthians*, 526–527.

93. The interplay of *sarx* and *soma* in nuanced here, because Christ is *somatic* yet *asarkic* (v.4). *Soma*'s "range of meaning is close to that of σάρξ," Dunn, *Romans 1–8*, 397.

including Christology. By itself it is an inadequate basis for a Christian moral theory.

II. Peter

In 2 Peter 1:4 *phusis* describes eschatological humanity as sharing the divine nature. *Phusis* has a clear ontological meaning, constituting a form of theandric *ousia*. The Palamite tradition interprets this participation to be in the energies, not the essence, of God, coordinating divine nature (v. 4) with divine power (v. 3), thus avoiding pan(en)theism. This participation approximates the "in Christ" formula of John and Paul. Participation in future glory (1 Pet 5:1; see also 2 Pet 1:3b), and being made like Christ (1 John 3:2) both share the eschatologically and ontologically transformative sense of 2 Peter 1:4.

This transformation is moral as well as ontological, for participating in God's nature involves escaping worldly corruptions caused by lust (v. 4). This moral dimension of *phusis* is evident in the virtue paraenesis immediately following (v. 5–10), and in a rare New Testament use of virtue, *arête* (v. 3). The teleological/eschatological sense means that human transformation will reach beyond current renewal, and is promissory (v. 4, 11). This constitutes a virtue-teleological natural law ethic, or an acts/end theory, as the end (*theosis*, v. 4) not only comes about through the moral practices and dispositions listed (v. 5–10), but also determines those acts and dispositions. The ascended Christ is the obvious candidate for the theandric model, as the reference to Christ's glory and excellence suggests (v. 3). Thus the precise character of the eschatological *phusis* of believers is determined by the interpretation of "participation" as a coordinate of the *phusis* of the glorified Christ, rather than phenomenologically or by metaphysical speculation.

Consequently, a Christian theory of human nature necessitates an architectonic role for Christ as proper, and thus perfect, human nature.[94] The eternal Son's election and historical incarnation provides the ontological/protological aspect, his ascension and glorification the teleological aspect, with redeemed humanity's teleological glorified transformation parasitic thereon. By omitting Christology and eschatology, traditional natural law ignores two central elements in Christian theorizing about human *phusis* and restricts itself to speculative rational metaphysics (e.g., participation in eternal reason), or empirical observation (e.g., protological/ontological theories of rationality or teleological theories of self-evident natural inclinations).[95]

---

94. Chalcedonian Christology constitutes Part Three.
95. Derived from φαω (to grow), φυσις takes on a vitalistic and biological tone in

This constitutes a basic lack. In this respect, Augustine's eternal/natural law ethic, despite its lack of explicit Christology, is more adequate due to its strong teleological (eschatological) eudemonistic *agapaism*,[96] which reflects Petrine use.

Both the mundane and eschatological aspects of human nature are coordinated by the double use of *arête*. First, *arête* is coordinate with Christ's ascended glory (v. 3), confirming the moral aspect of eschatological theandric nature. The second use (v. 5) links present existence (v. 5–10) with eschatological transformation (v. 10–11, see also v. 4 and v. 11). Such future hope (the end) determines that present life is shaped through virtue (the means, v. 3, 5–7). Hence the final end/good of participation in the divine nature (v. 4) *necessitates* (τον, v. 5a) the means/virtue practice. This means that the instrumental character of *arête's* practices or acts (love, goodness, kindness, etc.) lies in *arête* belonging to humanity's essential being. The practices internal to our nature serve to realize the *telos* of that nature because our *end* is a function of our *kind*. This *end* of the perfective process of our *kind* is participation in Christ's *arête* because his human nature is perfect. By binding temporal human existence to the eschatological Christ, *arête* makes humanity's intrinsic moral nature christological in character.

In 2 Peter 2:12, to act immorally is to act like irrational animals. Animal *phusis* as irrational and ignorant implies the rational nature of human *phusis*. The vice list (v. 10–15) is an ethically rich exegesis of irrational and ignorant speech (v. 12), suggesting that the opposing virtues constitute rational action. Human *phusis* is thus clearly implied as rational in contrast with non-human non-rational sentient life. *Phusis* here is a species-specific term and provides the basis for criticizing irrational human behavior as ethically cross-species and thus *para phusis*. This species-specific use of *phusis* as "kind" is also found in James 3:7.

Paul and Peter's use of *phusis* does not support a natural law ethic either as wholly rational or as possessing any status extraneous to theological categories. Biblical *phusis* thus provides the basis for a naturalistic ethic that is theologically derivative and provisional. The four Greek psychological terms that primarily bear upon *phusis* are *kardia, synerdēsis, nous,* and *logos,* the latter two providing nature's cognitive and rational aspect. The will weakens all their divinely created but currently flawed powers.

Aristotle. Torrance, *Divine Meaning*, 211.

96. When discussing eternal law, Augustine's dualistic anthropology of ascending value terminates in God: humans are body and soul, the soul is constituted of both animal faculties and reason, and reason is action and (final) contemplation of God "when we shall be like him, for we shall see Him as he is," "Reply to Faustus," XXII. 27, 283.

Thus natural law understood as a wholly rationalistic ethic[97] displays an unacceptably narrow New Testament moral psychology. Theologically rich lexical contexts interpret *phusis* as a provisional and secondary category contingent upon election, divine power, soteriology, eschatology, Christology, and the gospel. Nowhere is human *phusis* equated exclusively with *logos, nous,* or *phronēsis*. The ethically rich lexical contexts (the virtue/vice lists) suggest human *phusis* is inherently ethical and necessitates virtue practice and vice avoidance for its realization. Hence unrighteousness generates irrationality that degrades human nature toward animal nature (2 Pet 2:9–22). As *phusis* must necessarily be invested with external critical content due to its polysemous sense,[98] theological categories are necessary to constitute a natural law theory as Christian. Thus Finnis's statement that "natural law can be understood, assented to, applied, and reflexively analyzed without adverting to the existence of God"[99] is contested. The *kata phusin/para phusin* formula suggests that the virtue lists describe moral reasoning, dispositions, and acts that are properly natural, while the vice lists describe human reason, acts, and dispositions that are improper to human nature. However, because of the human tendency to moral irrationality, infallible claims to knowledge that is *kata phusin* are tempered. Consequently, because *phusis* is coordinated with revelation, Chalcedonian Christology enables a reframing of natural law ethics based upon true human nature, which is pursued later.

4. Conclusion

Chapter 1 has proposed a theory of nature grounded in a three-leveled critical realism (objective reality, epistemology, and semantics), which maintains the naturalistic axiom. It has been argued that the polysemous sense of "nature" necessitates its supplementation by theological terms, and that such an approach is consonant with the New Testament's use of *phusis*. This

---

97. "A rational ethic is based upon rational considerations and is logically consistent . . . A rationalistic ethic, on the other hand, allows only the reason to determine moral theology, at the expense of other human spiritual capabilities and ethical phenomena," Göran Bexell, "Is Grisez's Moral Theology Rationalistic? Free Choice, the Human Condition, and Christian Ethics," in Biggar and Black, *Revival of Natural Law*, 133.

98. "In 'naturalness,' there is always secreted that which is non-natural," Barth, *Romans*, 52, commenting on Rom. 1:25–27.

99. Finnis, *Natural Law and Natural Rights*, 49. That the "standard natural law theory is not essentially theistic shows it is inadequate as a theistic explanation of natural law," Murphy, *God and Moral Law*, 70.

is developed in Part Three. The rationalism of traditional natural law is foreign to the New Testament.

The origin of formal natural law in antiquity reveals a twofold taxonomy: the teleological in Aristotle, and the protological in Cicero. Despite not being exclusive, they provide a useful division for assessing natural law, which is now considered.

2

Protological and Teleological Natural Law Theories

1. Protological Theories

NATURAL LAW HOLDS HUMAN ontology as architectonic, reason as psychologically central, and objectivism as transparent: "[Natural law's] ontological foundations . . . [mean that] the very essence or nature of man as composed of body and spirit appears as a norm of moral behavior and of law. There is an objective order defined by natural law and this in the final basis is based upon 'being.'"[1] Reason is itself called natural law, ordaining that "good be done and evil avoided,"[2] and also a participation in God's own operations and moral agency: "Reason engaged upon the intelligibilities of nature must be seen as God's work."[3]

Because human nature is understood here as essentially rational, acts that are proper to humanity are necessarily rational. Hence "if the natural law is understood as an expression of the principles of action intrinsic to a given kind of nature, then it makes sense to say that the properly human expression of natural law involves acting in accordance with reason, because

---

1. Josef Fuchs, "The Natural Law in the Testimony of the Church," in Curran and McCormick, *Readings in Moral Theology*, 7–8. Contrast Thomas, for whom "being" is a subject for speculative, not practical reasoning, Aquinas, *ST*, Ia2æ, q. 94. 2.

2. Fuchs, "The Natural Law," in Curran and McCormick, *Readings in Moral Theology*, 8. Thomas is stronger "that good is to be done and pursued," *ST*, Ia2æ, q. 94. 2.

3. Fuchs, "The Natural Law," in Curran and McCormick, *Readings in Moral Theology*, 9.

the characteristic expression of human nature *is* to act in accordance with reason."[4] Because "human nature is morally significant,"[5] it is rational to act in ways that realize and express this nature. This makes *phusis and logos/nous* morally apposite. Yet while it is rational to act according to one's nature, one can do so in either a rationalistic or non-rationalistic fashion. At this point the discussion turns to Cicero as a rationalistic theorist before assessing Calvin's non-rationalism. Both affirm the divine origin of natural law, despite their extensive differences.

a. Cicero

Cicero's use of "πολις" to describe his Latin works *The Republic* and *The Laws* indicates his indebtedness to the Hellenistic tradition.[6] His legal concerns are philosophical rather than technical. He attempts to base state law, as an aspect of communal life, in natural law. By stating in *The Republic* that "true law is right reason in agreement with nature; it is of universal application, unchanging and everlasting,"[7] he makes law to be fixed, meta- and pre-positive, anthropologically intrinsic, ubiquitous and eternal. It is also of divine origin and enforcement.[8]

Cicero articulates his philosophy of law most extensively in *The Laws* where he asserts realist grounds for jurisprudence.[9] "Law is the highest reason, implanted by Nature, which commands what ought to be done and forbids the opposite. This reason when firmly fixed and fully implanted in the human mind, is Law."[10] Such a mind resides in the wise man.[11]

Law is a natural force containing justice.[12] Rationality is the foremost quality of both God and humanity,[13] human reason being grounded in God's reason. This shift from humanity to divinity avers law's stability and reliability and provides its metaphysical basis. Nature appears somewhat

---

4. Porter, *Nature as Reason*, 87, 85, italics original.

5. Porter, *Natural and Divine Law*, 26.

6. Jonathan Powell and Niall Rudd, "Introduction," in Cicero, *Cicero: Republic*, xi.

7. Cicero, *DE REPUBLICUS*, 33. *Cicero's Practical Philosophy*, Walter Nicgorski, (Notre Dame, IN: University of Notre Dame Press, 2012) was too late for my consideration.

8. Ibid., 33.

9. Cicero, *DE LEGIBUS*, 63, 315–369.

10. This is how Cicero commences the discussion, *LEGIBUS*, I. v. 1, 8.

11. Ibid., I. v. 18. Stoicism's wise man tames the passions by cognition.

12. Ibid., I. v. 19.

13. Ibid., I. vii. 22—I. ix. 27.

organic and open to rational development through reflecting upon reason, which in turn perfects reason.[14] This is a dialectically perfective relationship between reason and nature as a type of process metaphysics. Nature and reason appear personified, reason being the essence of but not exhausting nature, with "justice [being] inherent in Nature."[15] They are inseparable.[16] Living by natural law is living in "line with the order of the cosmos,"[17] which positive law and the virtues must express if they are to be considered binding and normative.

Law is not of human origin but is eternal and rules the cosmos. Cicero practically hypostatizes it when he describes law as "the *primal* and *ultimate* mind of God, whose reason directs all things."[18] This is problematic, for such rationalism (God is mind/reason and law) contrasts with biblical personalism (God is love), even though divine moral law does express God's moral being. "God is reason" becomes less problematic if interpreted proximally with Johannine *logos* Christology, because his *logos* Christology is embedded in the gospel of love. Moreover, what is *primal* and *ultimate* in Cicero becomes John's *Alpha* and *Omega* (Rev 1:8) and *First* and *Last* (Rev 1:17)—the divine persons of Father and Son—rather than impersonal divine law or reason.[19]

Just positive law is grounded in this divine mind that "is coeval with that God . . . For the divine mind cannot exist without reason, and divine reason cannot but have this power to establish right and wrong."[20] Thus even without written legal proscription rape breaks the eternal Law, for "reason did exist, derived from the Nature of the universe . . . and . . . [became Law] when it first came into existence . . . simultaneously with the divine mind."[21]

---

14. Ibid., I. ix. 27.

15. Ibid., I. xii. 34.

16. Ibid., I. xiii. 35.

17. Pettit, 'Substantive Moral Theory," in Paul et al., *Objectivism*, 1–27, 11; that is, *homologia*, Engberg-Pedersen, *Paul*, 58–59.

18. Cicero, *DE LEGIBUS*, II. iv. 8, discussing state religious law, emphasis added.

19. "Where the Stoics spoke of . . . reason . . . Paul speaks of God and Christ," Engberg-Pedersen, *Paul*, 47. Natural law's nomism rather than agapaism is the basic problem for Brunner: "The Ultimate and Supreme is not a *law* but the generous Divine love," Brunner, *Divine Imperative*, 270, emphasis original. This makes love rather than reason proper to human nature due to the *imago Dei*.

20. Cicero, *DE LEGIBUS*, II. iv. 10.

21. Ibid.

Most precisely: "The divine mind is the supreme Law."[22] What for Nuremberg is a crime against humanity is for Cicero contra the divine mind.

Because Christian ethics has often found natural law a congenial theory, it is arguable that the historicist rejection of Christian ethics is due in part to its confusion with the cold rigidity of Ciceronian divine rationality. Augustine's non-personal doctrine of eternal law shares responsibility here because it displaces the love of God, and the Son and Spirit, by an impersonal transcendent absolute. Unlike such neo-Platonism and neo-Stoicism, John's *Logos* lovingly lives and dies for others (John 3:16), so that the internal rationally of God is redetermined as self-giving love, not the rigid abstraction of unyielding law.

Notwithstanding this, the quest to establish rational justification for jurisprudence in metaphysical realities beyond localized particularities, and the tendency of states to unjust legal positivism originating from unconstrained desire, is laudable. The instability of the Roman state in Cicero's time gave his assertion that persons acquire their true nature through political/social engagement added urgency.[23] While historicism casts suspicion over such metaphysical realism, positivism is unable to match its conviction that, for instance, rape is never a good because such acts are ineradicably, universally, and metaphysically wrong. If positivism prevails, there must be an instance where rape is a good act because it achieves a better end than otherwise. Positivism's instability and Cicero's rigidity are unable to account for the requirement that ethics must be, respectively, both permanent and ineradicable, and personal and loving. Despite frequent citations of *The Laws* and *The Republic*,[24] Calvin's natural law is derived from biblical and Christian texts, and exhibits the warmth of love and mercy of which Stoicism is incapable.

b. Calvin

Reformed natural law is "the idea of an implanted knowledge of morality" that stands in continuity with "an ancient moral and legal tradition that Christian theologians, jurists, and statesmen have amended, supplemented, and assimilated over time to serve moral, political, legal and canon law

---

22. Ibid., II. iv. 11.

23. Natural law "in the Aristotelian and Stoic tradition takes its point of departure in the idea that humans were originally social beings," Bayer, *Freedom in Response*, 249, despite sociality receiving meta-social grounding in Cicero.

24. Primarily regarding civil law, Calvin, *ICR*, IV.ii.

objectives."²⁵ It remained non-controversial in the Reformed tradition until its mid-eighteenth-century rationalist critique, and its later dismissal by Barth.²⁶

Calvin's natural law is epistemic, subjective, morally discriminatory, and primarily juridical, as is evident in his definition: "Natural law is that apprehension of the conscience which distinguishes sufficiently between just and unjust, and which deprives men of the excuse of ignorance, while it proves them guilty by their own testimony."²⁷ It is primarily negative. In identifying natural law's material content as justice, Calvin maintains Thomas's continuity with Aristotle and Cicero.²⁸ However, their variant *post-lapsum* anthropologies (Thomas, deprived of supernatural grace; Calvin, wholly depraved psychologically) produce different assessments of its efficacy.²⁹ Calvin's *Institutes of the Christian Religion* and *New Testament Commentary on Romans* are examined.³⁰

1. Calvin's Institutes of the Christian Religion

Calvin's robust natural theology (Books I and II) constitutes the initial context for his treatment of natural law,³¹ the latter being a function of the former. Book I.iii–v argues that the naturally implanted knowledge of God in the mind is true and "beyond controversy," but insufficient, suppressed

---

25. Grabill, *Rediscovering the Natural Law*, 1–2 and 70–74 regarding Calvin. He argues that wider Reformation tradition inherited and transmitted natural law as "noncontroversial legacies of patristic and scholastic thought," 1. Berkouwer, *General Revelation*, 197, argues that "in the Reformation *natural law* plays an important role," italics original.

26. Grabill, *Rediscovering the Natural Law*, 21–53.

27. "Nec, male hoc modo definetur, Quod sit consientiae agnitio, inter iustum et inistium sufficieter discernetis; ad tollendum hominibus ignorantiae raetextum, dum suo isorum testimonio redarguuntur," Calvin, *ICR*, II.ii.22, 282. The context is knowledge of God the Redeemer. All future references, Battles. "Calvin differs from the Roman jurists and medieval theorists by arguing that the conscience, rather than reason, discerns natural law," Schreiner, *Theatre*, 149, n. 86.

28. On this point, the Reformers and Scholastics agreed, Schreiner, *Theatre*, 77.

29. The deprived/depraved parallel derives from a conversation with Gordon Preece.

30. Calvin, *CNTC*.

31. Calvin, *ICR*, II.viii on the Decalogue, and IV.xx on civil government supplement it.

and distorted *post-lapsum*.[32] It prevents pretentious ignorance and excuse.[33] Acts 17:28 demonstrates that "the secular poets, out of a common feeling . . . called him 'the Father of men.'"[34] "Feeling" suggests intuitionism, not rationalism. Natural knowledge of God leads to condemnation of sin via conscience.[35]

Calvin's natural theology is here juridical: general revelation, though limited materially to God the Creator, functions instrumentally as a prosecutor, voiding excuse. By revealing the right, it indicts the wrong. His transition from natural theology to natural law is seamless and unsurprising as his concern is theology, especially sanctification, not philosophy. Natural law is ethicized natural theology, as two proximal statements demonstrate in their use of anthropological terms. First, of natural theology: "Men of sound *judgment* will always be sure that a *sense* of divinity which can never be effaced is engraved upon men's *minds* . . . *deep within*, as it were in the very *marrow*."[36] Second, of natural law: "For the worm of *conscience*, sharper than any cauterizing iron *gnaws away at them*."[37] Such natural law is primal, ineradicable and consequently unforgettable.

Calvin's protological theory is not without an ends/means dimension, particularly an Augustinian eschatological eudemonism: "If all men are born and live to the end that they may know God . . . it is clear that all those who do not direct every thought and action in their lives to this goal degenerate from the law of their creation."[38] The *telos* of "the law of their creation" is knowing God, the means is "every thought and action." This is a protological/teleological model, as the final human good emerges from its original creation and is realized through a reason/act theory of means. The protological and teleological are dialectical because the law of human creation collapses if cognition fails to progress beyond the bare minimum of acknowledging God as Creator. Moving towards one's proper end realizes

---

32. Calvin's "self-evidence."

33. Calvin, *ICR*, I.xiii.1, 43.

34. Ibid., I.v.3, 55.

35. Ibid., I.iii.1, 44.

36. Ibid., I.iii.3, 45f, emphasis added.

37. Ibid., I.iii.3, 46, emphasis added.

38. Ibid., I.iii.3, 46. Also, "the perfection of blessedness consists in the knowledge of God . . . that none might be excluded from the means of obtaining felicity," *ICR*, I.v.1, 51f. Unlike Calvin, Irenaeus christologizes Adamic creation: "in Jesus Christ there appears the One who possesses everything that man as a creature ought to have," Wingren, *Man and Incarnation*, 85; see Irenaeus, "Against Heresies," in ANF vol. 1, 541.

one's creation: *telos* realizes *phusis*.³⁹ Conversely, failure to acknowledge the Creator courts judgment. For Calvin, the human mind possesses a "universally imprinted nonsalvific knowledge of God" that holds people morally accountable before God, rather than leading them to him.⁴⁰

Thus Calvin's natural theology is the context for natural law and functionally approximates it, for the knowledge of God is the knowledge of a moral being. True knowledge of God is primarily religious and affective, and secondarily rational. However, this basic knowledge is generally inoperative because it is rarely fostered and never ripened.⁴¹ Despite this universal non-realization, such natural knowledge of God is noetic ("deposit in our minds"), eschatological ("perfection of blessedness," the means of "obtaining felicity"), and spiritual ("seed of religion," "heart," "felicity"), if acted upon in faith.⁴² Like Paul's doctrine of law, he affirms the truth but inefficacy of natural revelation.

"Nature" refers to humanity in both its *pre-* and *post-lapsum* states."⁴³ This distinction enables God, the "Author of nature," to be exonerated from any defect that is inherent in (human) nature.⁴⁴ In this defective human nature⁴⁵ "the conscience . . . responds to God's judgment [and] is an undoubted sign of the immortal spirit. For how could a motion without essence penetrate to God's judgment seat?"⁴⁶ It is unclear here whether conscience indicates God's judgment because it belongs to the essence of humanity, or that it belongs to the essence of humanity because it penetrates to God's judgment. What is clear is that conscience is both sign and motion: a sign of humanity's essence as an immortal spirit, and an action that

---

39. Compare Irenaeus's developmental/perfective doctrine of Adam, in "Against Heresies," IV. xxxviii, 521–522. For Irenaeus, "speaking of human τέλος begs a backward reference to human ἀρχη," Holsinger-Freisen, *Irenaeus and Genesis*, 139.

40. Grabill, *Rediscovering the Natural Law*, 71.

41. Calvin, *ICR*, I.iv.1, 47. Calvin uses "heart" not "mind" here, although "mind" is not wholly absent. Such knowledge is the "seed of religion"—possibly alluding to wisdom texts (Psalm 1, Matthew 13:1–23)—demonstrating Calvin's non-rationalistic theology.

42. Ibid., I.v.1, 51f. His non-rationalism is again clear: the noetic deposit brings felicity and blessedness, not understanding.

43. Ibid., I.xv.1, 183, no reference to renewed or perfected nature.

44. Ibid., I.xv.1, 183.

45. Calvin's anthropology consists of body, spirit and soul. Spirit and soul, while distinguished when used together, are synonyms when used singly, I.xv.2, 184. The soul is dualistic, consisting primarily of the understanding and secondarily of the will, I.xv.7, 194.

46. Ibid., I.xv.2, 184.

connects this essence to God's moral determinations. Humanity's subjective conscience corresponds to God's objective judgments because both human essence (spirit) and God are moral in character.

The juridical nature of Calvin's moral epistemology is again evident in his third use of the law, which is that "spiritual insight . . . [for] . . . knowing the rule for the right conduct of life."[47] Natural law sufficiently indicates right standards but because it is not used according to right reason it renders humanity "inexcusable."[48] As this sufficient natural instruction is universally evident, a tendency to conservatism, which privileges social convention over innovation and its perceived propensity to political disorder, is characteristic of Calvin.[49]

Natural law is thus sufficient but fallible: measured by God's law it is in many ways "blind."[50] Natural reason is inadequate regarding knowledge of the Law's First Table but is more reliable regarding the Second Table.[51] Its inconsistent philosophical application and the biblical texts stressing regeneration and petitions for spiritual understanding and fidelity demonstrate its inadequacy.[52] Such compromised efficacy leads Calvin to place *lex divina* over *lex naturae* in his epistemic hierarchy.

However, he maintains the scholastic relation between *lex naturae* and *lex divina*, and between *lex naturae* and *lex certus* (positive law). First, concerning the relation between *lex naturae* and *lex divina*, the *lex divina* is a providential and historic expression of *lex naturae*, necessitated by humanity's *post-lapsum* cognitive impairment and consequent misapprehension of the former.[53] Thomas's statement, "whatever belongs to the natural law is fully contained in (the Law and the Gospel),"[54] compares well with Calvin's account that the "inward law . . . asserts the very same things . . . [as] . . . the two Tables," and that the "written law . . . gives us a clearer witness of

---

47. Ibid., II.ii.22, 281.

48. Ibid., II.ii.22, 281f, on Rom. 2:14f.

49. Schreiner, *Theatre*, 86–89. Calvin tends to conflate natural law and convention regarding civic law.

50. Ibid., II.ii.24, 283.

51. Ibid., II.ii.24, 283f.

52. Ibid., II.ii.27, 287–89.

53. Melanchthon also commences his exegesis of the Decalogue with, "The Ten Commandments . . . contain the most important parts of what is termed the *lex naturalis*." Natural law "is precisely the eternal unchangeable wisdom of God which he proclaimed in the Ten Commandments," Melanchthon, *Christian Doctrine*, 85, 128.

54. Aquinas, *ST*, Ia2æ, q. 94. 4. Also citing Gratian's association of natural and divine law and the Gospel, the latter described as the Golden Rule.

what was too obscure in the natural law."[55] The Decalogue—the "rule of righteousness"—is universally applicable because it conforms to the eternal divine law.[56] Conversely; the natural law conforms to the principal points of the First Table, although natural reason does not. So despite maintaining the scholastic relation between the two laws, Calvin breaks from its optimistic view of reason. Although divine law is perfect (Ps 19:7) and spiritual (Rom 7:14) it shares natural law's inefficacy due to reason's inability and the influence of *sarx*.

Secondly, *lex naturae* as universally noetically engraved constitutes *lex certus*'s grounds: "The entire scheme of this equity [state justice] . . . has been prescribed in [the natural law]."[57] Diversity of national positive law is not incongruent with natural law's ubiquity, so that in respect to theft, perjury, murder, and adultery, "with one voice, they pronounce punishment against those crimes which God's eternal law has condemned . . . But they do not agree on the manner of punishment. Nor is this either necessary or expedient."[58] What matters is that the nations' *lex certus* conforms to the "perpetual rule of love," which is its universal purpose.[59] This concurs with Thomas: "In matters of action, truth or practical rectitude is not the same for all, as to matters of detail, but only as to general principles."[60] This rule of love and social utility is critical in Calvin and expresses his fundamental aversion to social disorder, which *lex naturae* prevents, not unlike Aristotle's view of persons as naturally tending to social peace.[61] Further, by his repeated positive citing of Cicero and Seneca regarding civil law, he demonstrates his belief that *lex naturae* is ubiquitous and universal.[62]

Thus Calvin's three-fold use of the law includes *lex naturae*: theologically, it is partially revelatory; soteriologically, its value lies in conviction of sin; socially and politically, it prevents disorder, but needs supplementation by *lex divina* and prescription in *lex certus*. These are *post-lapsum* deficiencies of its efficacy, not essence. His Romans commentary is complementary.

55. Calvin, *ICR*, II.viii.1, 367–368.

56. Ibid., IV.xx.15, 1503.

57. Ibid., IV.xx.16, 1504.

58. Ibid., IV.xx.16, 1504–1505, regarding the nations besides Israel. Calvin's legal training is evident.

59. Ibid., IV.xx.15, 1503. Calvin's terms apposite to love are social profit, justice, and gentleness.

60. Aquinas, *ST*, Ia2æ, q. 94. 4.

61. Calvin's natural law is a form of providence preventing human barbarism. Here he is darker than Anabaptism, proffering state power as the necessary bridle upon disorder, Schreiner, *Theatre*, 82–87.

62. He also cites OT texts where nature upholds social order. Ibid., 87–90.

II. Calvin's Commentary on Romans

Natural law is partially efficacious epistemologically, but non-efficacious ethically. The discussion is limited to Paul's two relevant uses of *phusis*. On Romans 1:26: "They have reversed the whole order of nature."[63] On Romans 2:14–16: Gentile ideas of justice "which are implanted by nature in the hearts of men," are found in their judiciary.[64] Although Gentile law is contrasted with divine written law, it is identical to "the natural light of righteousness"[65] which is imprinted on their hearts,[66] though not engraved on their wills, which explains its non-efficacy.[67] It is incomplete,[68] and identified with conscience in its positive defense of right action, and negative accusation of evil. Conscience is epistemologically operative now, but juridically affected eschatologically, which prevents its rejection.[69] The gospel confirms the judgment of conscience: "[Paul] adds the expression *according to my gospel* to prove . . . a doctrine which corresponds to the inborn judgment of mankind."[70]

In his Romans commentary, Calvin's juridical natural law accuses and holds people responsible for disobedience to God. All of its many positive qualities—its divine origin, its ubiquity and universal operation in the conscience, its epistemological efficacy and social utility, and its correspondence to the gospel and eschatological validation—serve its primary negative purpose.

Despite this Pauline focus, Calvin exhibits a Ciceronian and Scholastic *duplex* theory of natural law's form and matter. Yet where Cicero is a rationalist because his doctrine of God is rationalistic, Calvin is not a rationalist because his doctrine of God is biblical and personal. Overtones of Cicero are clear in his protological theory of divine origins, and of Augustine in his eudemonistic teleology. Christology does not feature, yet this is unsurprising as Calvin is offering an *apologia* for the catholicity of the Reformation, not attempting to construct a coherent ethical theory. The primary sense is that natural law is ethicized natural theology and general revelation, which,

---

63. Calvin, *CNTC*, vol. 8, 36. " Order of nature" is synonymous with natural law. "Order" reflects his Augustinian neo-Platonism.

64. Calvin, *CNTC*, vol. 8, 48, commenting on v. 14.

65. Ibid., echoing Augustine's doctrine of divine illumination.

66. Ibid., "*Hearts* is . . . (to be taken) . . . simply for the understanding."

67. Ibid., "He does not speak of a power of the will to fulfil the law."

68. Ibid., There are "only . . . some seeds of justice implanted in their nature."

69. Calvin, *CNTC*, vol. 8, 49, commenting on v. 15.

70. Calvin on Romans 2:16, *CNTC*, vol. 8, 49, italics original.

despite being epistemologically trustworthy and underpinning positive law, contains negligible personal benefit. The persistence of lawlessness and sin indicate its limitations. Whereas the natural knowledge of God in natural theology leads to universal awareness of God, natural knowledge of morality in natural law leads to universal culpability before God. The theological/juridical interpretation, that natural law voids personal excuse before God, is his main innovation. Thomas's natural law leads to happiness, Calvin's leads to guilt.

2. Teleological Theories

The neo-Thomist Ashley writes that Aquinas's natural law is "first . . . a true understanding of our *human nature*, our need for happiness, and the elements of a happy life and their relative importance," and second, "a true understanding of the various *means* to this supreme goal and its integrated subordinated goals."[71] Thomas's indebtedness to Aristotle's focus upon earthly human goods and ends is clear, partly because the *Summa* was a Christian *apologia* confronting a revived Aristotelianism. Yet this focus was not without an Augustinian dimension, which affirmed the Trinity as humanity's final good. Nonetheless, his natural law theory remains essentially non-theological. Four teleological theories are considered; Aristotle, Augustine (briefly), Thomas, and the Finnis school.

a. Aristotle

Aristotle's realism is evident from the start of his *Nicomachean Ethics*, where he articulates an understanding of humanity and its activities as the ground for ethics and politics. Persons are essentially political and have happiness as their chief good and final *telos*. Although moral virtues develop by practice and are not inherent in human nature, political justice includes *natural* justice as a moral virtue with definite content, not simply as a potentiality or principle.[72] This means that justice has a *duplex* form, natural *(phusikon)* and legal *(nomikon)*[73] with natural justice providing the inner logic of legal or political justice. Legal justice differs across states but natural justice is

---

71. Benedict M. Ashley, "The Anthropological Foundations of the Natural Law: A Thomistic Engagement with Modern Science," in Goyette et al., *Contemporary Perspectives*, 14, emphasis added.

72. Aristotle, *Nicomachean*, II. 1. 1103a33; V. 7. 1134b18, 124.

73. Ibid., V. 7. 1134b18, 124. Νομικον, possibly also "conventional."

universal, pre-cognitive,[74] and is "unchangeable and has everywhere the same force."[75] Despite this difference, both types of justice can be valid: "A thing is unjust by nature or enactment."[76]

In *Politics*, Aristotle builds on *Nicomachean* by construing the state in the light of the nature of human beings.[77] The state is a single diachronic community of associated villages for the pursuit of humanity's natural end of the good life. This nature is realized when the appropriate end is realized: human *phusis* is a function of arriving at humanity's *telos*. This end is recognized through the natural inclination of speech, which is a uniquely human social capacity for the "perception of good and bad and right and wrong."[78] His argument is thus: speech is a natural inclination and instrumental capacity that enables justice for the realization of social peace, which is humanity's proper end and thus nature. The relationship between natural and conventional/state law is outlined in Table 2.

Aspect	**Natural Law**	**Conventional/State Law**
Origin	*Divine*	*Human*
Matter	*General*	*Particular*
Form	*Unwritten*	*Written*
Character	*Rational*	*Rational*
Scope	*Universal*	*Specific*
Authority	*Primary*	*Secondary*
Role	*Directive*	*Compliant*
Sociality	*Prior*	*Posterior*
Existence	*Eternal*	*Temporal*
Content	*Justice*	*Justice*
Telos	*The Good—Peace*	*The Good—Peace*

74. Ibid., V. 7. 1134b18, 124.

75. Ibid.

76. Aristotle, *Nicomachean*, V. 7. 1135a5, 125.

77. Harris Rackham, "Introduction," xvii, *Nicomachean*. "Our investigation is in a sense the study of Politics," *Nicomachean*, I. ii. 8, 7, Rackham trans. "The city-state is a natural growth, and . . . man is by nature a political animal," Aristotle, *Politics*, I. i. 1253a1, 9. A citiless being is either sub or supra human, animal or god. Calvin concurs: "Man is by nature a social animal, and tends by instinct to foster and preserve society." Universal social order via law is "ample proof" of the ubiquity of human reason, *ICR*, II.xiii.13, 272–273.

78. Aristotle, *Politics*, I. i. 1253a, 15. Δίκαιος (right) and ἄδικος (wrong) are better as "just" and "unjust."

Emotionality	*Unaffected*	*Affected*
Stability	*Invariant*	*Variant*

Table 2: Aristotle's Duplex Scheme of Law

Justice requires law, and law is identical with divine rationality. For the law to govern is for "God and reason alone [to] govern . . . [as] wisdom without desire."[79] Such law is "based upon nature,"[80] unwritten, universally recognized, and antecedent to and independent of human sociality.[81] As such it is privileged over state law.[82]

As the table above indicates, just state law is identical to natural law in its character, content and *telos,* despite its potential for distortion by desire. State/positive law is *techné* and must be rationally constructed to comply with natural law (*phusis*) to be just and socially constructive. When human *techné* is discordant with human *phusis* it distorts social peace. Natural law's theological realism, ubiquity, and immutability limits positive law, thereby proscribing unjust laws that disrupt humanity's proper end: positive law must serve peaceful ends. By interpreting *phusis* as social peace, Aristotle argues that positive law serves just communal life rather than potentially socially disruptive individual rights.[83]

Furthermore, natural law's participation in divine reason possesses social utility by constraining the unruly character of desire. Natural law can constrain a ruler's greed from constructing legal *techné* as forms of *injustice,* thereby preserving social peace and enabling the realization of true human *phusis*. In contrast, the modern concept of individualized *phusis* produces a concept of justice that leads more to individual rights and a thin social contractualism. If justice is a function of divine and human natures as Aristotle affirms, then superior theologies and anthropologies will produce better natural law and justice, and by implication better conventional and state law if such laws are consciously developed from and enacted for the purpose of expressing such prior commitments. Aristotle's realism, and his linkage of nature, justice, and law, anticipates the Chalcedonian model of ethics proposed here, for Chalcedon unites in the one person of Jesus both natures, which are expressed in concrete human acts. Aristotle's divine *nous,* upon

---

79. Aristotle, *Politics.* III. xi. 1287a, God and νους read in apposition.

80. Aristotle, *"Art" of Rhetoric,* I. xiii. 1373b2, "κοινων δε των κατα φυσιν." A more precise translation of κατα with the accusative is "Universal law is the law of nature," *Rhetoric,* 48. Examples cited are human burial and the prohibition on killing.

81. Aristotle, *Rhetoric,* I. x. 1368b8; I. xiii. 1373b5.

82. Aristotle, *Rhetoric,* I. x. 1368b8.

83. *Dikaiōs* as *just* tends to communalism, as *right* tends to individualism.

which his rationality and natural law is predicated, becomes the incarnate *Logos* existing in ineradicable covenant relations with both God and other human beings.

b. Augustine

Augustine initially appears to reflect a platonic-based protological theory, as he defines sin as breaking the natural order required by eternal law.[84] However, this natural order is teleologically oriented, because he understands human nature primarily from the perspective of its final completion. In an ascending order of body to soul to reason he ends at the final contemplation of the greatest object, "The image of God, by which we are renewed through faith to sight."[85] Thus eternal and natural law instrumentally order righteous living, including the virtues, for the end purpose of contemplating the beatific vision.[86]

However, Augustine's realism appears to recede behind a form of voluntarism when he states that natural order and law can be suspended or superseded by the divine will in specific circumstances and still satisfy moral criteria.[87] Stoic type rational-law theology and metaphysical non-personalism is softened here, but questions of arbitrariness are begged.[88]

Despite this moderating effect Augustine remains problematic in this respect, for unlike Irenaeus he fails to identify God's relation with his creation with the Son and the Spirit—God's two hands—so that impersonal transcendence tends to eclipse personal engagement as the primary mode of the relation between God and humanity. As such, God and humanity easily become adversaries.

The teleological nature of Augustine's natural law is clear in his assertion that the order established by natural law serves to create peace. We note this in three contexts. First, peace between various subjects is due proportion, harmony, well-ordered obedience, concord, harmonious enjoyment, and tranquility. "Peace between man and God is the well-ordered obedience

---

84. Augustine, *Faustus*, XXII. 27, 283.

85. Ibid. The identification of law, order and will in God at this point is left hanging.

86. The object of the virtue love is God, "the chief good, the highest wisdom, the perfect harmony," Augustine, "Morals," 25, 48.

87. Augustine, *Faustus*, XXII. 73, 300, regarding the command to Abraham to sacrifice Isaac.

88. Arbitrariness haunts divine command ethics, but for an argument that "God" necessarily includes the complement "good," Adams, *Finite and Infinite Goods*, 249–76. Also, "Will not the judge of all the earth do right?" Genesis 18:25.

of faith to eternal law," and, "the peace of all things is the tranquility of order. Order is the distribution which allots things equal and unequal, each to its own place."[89] Such tranquil peace is natural, which the wicked share partially and the devil shared initially as created by God.[90] Eternal law orders creation to its natural end of peace, achieved through obedience and faith.

Second, despite being discordant with creation, slavery is legitimized by natural law's ordered social prescriptivism. Here natural law includes both the original created moral structure and a contingent *post-lapsum* order serving peace.[91] Sin thus triggers natural law to function unnaturally—that is, contrary to created human relations—to maintain order and peace. Despite an eschatological limit (until "God be all in all"[92]) this remains deeply problematic, and illustrates the hazard of identifying natural law, and what is natural, with convention.

Similarly, he conflates natural law, social convention, and apostolic paraenesis in his exhortation to maintain domestic peace: "For the law of nature and of society gives him readier access to [his own household] . . . hence the apostle says . . . "[93] The "hence" makes the apostolic exhortation a consequence and example of natural law, anticipating the later tradition where *lex divina* is a secondary expression of *lex naturae*. In this it departs from the organizing principle that typifies apostolic moral reasoning, where the gospel stands as the definitive moral adjudicator amongst many other considerations, including social convention and nature.

Third, peace is the eschatological good end: "The supreme good of the city of God is perfect and eternal peace," because it is free from evil. The greatest temporal happiness is to pursue the perfect peace and secure eternity of God. Without this end, Aristotle's social *eudemonia* is "false happiness": with it, peace is experienced in "hope."[94]

Augustine combines the platonic concern for eternal order and infinite goods with an Aristotelian concern for finite goods and temporal order. Although both *kinds* and *ends* are theologically personalized, because there is no christological anchorage, such personalism tends to be obscured by eternal laws and impersonal orders. Only in Christ and the Spirit does

---

89. Augustine, *City of God*, XIX. xiii, 409.

90. Ibid.

91. Ibid., XIX. xv, 411: "But by nature, as God first created us, no one is the slave either of men or of sin. This servitude is, however, penal, and is appointed by that law which enjoins the preservation of the natural order and forbids its disturbance."

92. Ibid., XIX. xv, 411, referring to Paul's admonition to slaves.

93. Ibid., XIX. xiv, 410.

94. Ibid., XIX. xx, 414, all quotes.

theology become suitably personalized in a human fashion, because in the Son's incarnation through the Spirit God shared our personhood. Furthermore, Christ's socially conflicted life (e.g., disputes over identifying *lex divina* with social conventions like Sabbath keeping) due to pursuing God as his final end is an ill fit here. Is Augustine a philosophical theologian, where the concept of ordered peace is a metaphysical reality, a cipher into which theology/ethics is poured?

c. Aquinas

Aquinas mirrors Aristotle's *Nicomachean* by commencing the Prima Secundæ Partis of his *Summa Theologica* with a discussion of humanity's final end, happiness. We limit our treatment of natural law to *ST* Ia2æ, questions 90 to 108, although the *Summa* deals in many places with the character of and relation between nature and grace.[95] The rational nature of law in general is clear: "Law is something pertaining to reason."[96] The existence of eternal law is argued syllogistically: Law is a dictate of a ruler's practical reason; the universe is ruled by the eternal rational God (Prov 8:23); "Therefore it is that this kind of law must be called eternal."[97]

The eternal law "is . . . the type of Divine Wisdom,[98] directing all actions and movements."[99] By associating law and wisdom, congruent with

---

95. For the relationship between natural law and law generally, see Russell Hittinger, "Catholic Moral Theology," in Cromartie, *Preserving Grace*, 1–30, 16. Thomist natural law is a "principle of interpretation" for both the Old and New Laws, and also our lives, argues Hauerwas, *Truthfulness and Tragedy*, 61. On Thomist natural law requiring the virtues (especially prudence) to soften any harsh edge, see Hall, *Narrative*.

96. Aquinas, "Ergo lex est aliquid rationis" *Textum Leoninum Romae*, Question 90. 1, on the essence of law. Law's practical rationality serves the common good, *ST*, Ia2æ, q. 90. 4. Yet the inclination to concupiscence may be called a "law" of the body (Rom. 7:23), for concupiscence rules the body, *ST*, Ia2æ, q. 90. 1.

97. Aquinas, *ST*, Ia2æ, q. 91. 1.

98. "Ratio divinæ sapientia." According to Ford, David Kelsey's *Eccentric Existence: A Theological Anthropology* frames creation as a "wisdom-centred approach . . . being both directly and *indirectly* related to God and having its own integrity quite apart from eschatology or salvation history . . . [which allows] a separate account of creation . . . and engagement . . . with the sciences and other accounts of the 'what' of humanity without reference to eschatology or salvation." Wisdom is "God's *mediated* involvement in ordinary life," emphasis added. However, creation (and law) as wisdom remains too metaphysically hypostasized without Christology. Ford, "Theological Anthropology," 45, 41–54.

99. Aquinas, *ST*, Ia2æ, q. 93. 1. Such direction comes through divine commands for rational creatures, and providence for non-rational creatures, q. 93. 5.

Proverbs 8:23, he personalizes and softens its sharp edge in contrast to Ciceronian divine-mind theology. Yet despite arguing that the eternal law has been promulgated (not just conceived as a divine *ratio*) in the incarnate Word, who expresses the essence, person, and works of God, he does not extend this christological move by citing Christ's life as divine wisdom in the cross (1 Cor 1:8–2:16).[100] This christological lacuna is typical of the natural law tradition as a whole, constituting its basic weakness as a Christian ethic, despite its theological concerns and its relation to *lex divina*.[101]

The relation between the new law (the "Gospel," "law of liberty," "law of faith," "grace of the Spirit") and natural law is complex. Grace and the new law correct natural law's omissions, and are more efficacious than nature, yet the law of nature is more essential and enduring than grace.[102] The natural law points to proper natural human ends, while the new law indicates proper spiritual ends, yet it "added very few precepts to those of the natural law."[103] This is an unwarranted differentiation between the natural and the spiritual, for humanity was created through the Spirit (Gen 2:7). Both forms of law are instilled in the heart, the natural by way of nature, and the new by way of grace.[104] Natural law does incline persons to God as a good,[105] but is powerless to enable its realization, because humanity acts according to nature only by intellect and will, which our final good, God, transcends (1 Cor 2:9).[106] Thus what the natural law intends, human happiness, the new law achieves. The Spirit enables the grace of the incarnate Word's humanity to overflow to us (John 1:14) "like an interior habit," so that we are inclined

---

100. Although all types of law derive from the eternal law (*ST*, Ia2æ, q. 93. 3), and both the natural and new law point to humanity's proper end (God), only the new law enables it, *ST* 1a2æ, q. 106. 1, 2. In contrast to Thomas's Aristotelianism, (God as "end") and Platonism (God as "good") Luther's Paulinism stresses the personal "Word," Zimmermann, *Recovering Theological Hermeneutics*, 47–51. Irenaeus's concept of the Word "shatters the concept of substance, and a functional or dialectical movement between God and men appears instead of the two static natures," Wingren, *Man and Incarnation*, 89. Hence divine wisdom is the union of two dynamic natures in the Incarnation.

101. Porter identifies a threefold scholastic use of Scripture; 1) to justify appeals to natural law; 2) as a key source from which to derive moral content; and 3) its interpretation as a moral document through a natural law framework, *Natural and Divine Law*, 121–85. Christology is still lacking, however.

102. Aquinas, *ST*, Ia2æ, q. 94. 5, 6.

103. Aquinas, *ST*, Ia2æ, q. 107. 4.

104. Aquinas, *ST*, Ia2æ, q. 106. 1, 2.

105. Aquinas, *ST*, Ia2æ, q. 94. 2, 3.

106. Hall, *Narrative*, 69.

"to act aright," like a "second nature."[107] By so acting rightly through the new law, we are enabled to achieve our final and ultimate end, God *simpliciter*. Knowing that God is our final end enables us to properly order life so that the finite goods, indicated by the inclinations of the natural law but improperly perceived as final goods, are subordinated to the infinite good of God, our proper final end.[108]

There appears a clear distinction here between humanity in nature and humanity in grace.[109] Thomas errs when he separates the new law from creation on the basis that the bestowal of the Spirit is contingent upon the irruption of sin.[110] This produces a sense of Deism, for people "in nature" are consistently described as devoid of grace, yet human creation is a gracious act in and by the Spirit (Gen 1:1–2, 26; 2:7; see also Irenaeus's divine hand). Likewise, if natural inclinations indicate our goods in accord with our nature, and our nature is a gift from God, then such goods are also divine gifts. So how can natural law be proper to but insufficient for human nature, if this nature is a gift of grace? The answer appears twofold. Firstly, the irruption of sin distorts natural law's efficacy. But secondly and significantly, because Thomas understands human nature as rational, and the intellect cannot apprehend God, the knot tying human nature and God is cut. Grace and human creation/nature (reason) appear opposed. Thomas's rationalist anthropology is a primary problem. Consequently, natural law needs supplementation by revelation, the new law, not just because of sin, but also because of human nature itself.[111]

Those aspects of the eternal law that are known to all constitute the common principles of the natural law.[112] For instance, natural law "has a share of the Eternal Reason, whereby it has a natural inclination to its proper act and end: and this participation of the eternal law *in* the rational creature is called the natural law."[113] The participative and locative "in" is similar to

---

107. Aquinas, *ST*, Ia2æ, q. 108. 1.

108. Aquinas, *ST*, Ia2æ, q. 108. 4.

109. The old and new law "contain many things . . . above nature," Aquinas, *ST*, Ia2æ, q. 94. 4, citing Gratian.

110. Aquinas, *ST*, Ia2æ, q. 106. 3. The new law is the grace of the Spirit. Thomas argues soteriologically, but the criticism remains valid.

111. Thomas Hibbs, "The Fearful Thoughts of Mortals. Aquinas on Conflict, Self-Knowledge, and the Virtues of Practical Reasoning," in Cunningham, *Intractable Disputes*, 290, sees this relation as an "overlap," with natural law as the new law's "*praeambula fidei*."

112. Aquinas, *ST*, Ia2æ, q. 93. 2, 5. Non-rational creation is subject to eternal law by providence, rational creation by understanding.

113. Aquinas, *ST*, Ia2æ, q. 91. 2, emphasis added.

"Christ in you" (Col 1:27). As Christ is the eternal *Logos*/reason (John 1:1), the law of Christ (Gal 6:2) may easily be substituted for the eternal law, but this Aquinas does not do.[114] Likewise, natural law's ubiquitous "every knowledge of truth"[115] could be christologically redetermined, for in him are "all things" and "all wisdom and knowledge" (Col 1:15–20, 2:3). Aquinas again does not make this move.

By participating in the eternal law, natural law indicates those finite goods that constitute our natural ends, and the precepts necessary for their acquisition. Both its rational character and natural inclinations are proper to humanity, and include the virtues which make persons "good simply"— that is, good as determined by divine justice.[116]

Contemporary historical consciousness considers the realism of such natural law as too static and incommensurable with human freedom and cultural pluralism.[117] However, realism enables a grounded critique of injustice and evil, whether they are embedded in socially prescriptive customary laws or legal positivism, or conversely, when the social ascriptivism characteristic of modern voluntarism separates freedom from rationality and human nature.[118] Voluntarist historicism's rejection of realism may facilitate departure from traditions of objective truthfulness which enable the true good to be rationally discerned. Voluntarism begs the question, "Whose will?" and tends toward emotivist conflict. Citing Psalm 4:6, the "proper act and end" of natural law serves justice through the discernment of good and evil, which is "an imprint on us of the Divine light,"[119] and the "rational creature's participation of the eternal law."[120] Such discernment requires prudence, which, being a virtue about means not ends, implies that "prudence is not from nature" and must be acquired.[121] By indicating only primary principles, natural law requires prudence for its expression through second-

114. See Graham Stanton, "The Law of Christ; A Neglected Theological Gem?" in Ford and Stanton, *Reading Texts*, 169–84.

115. Aquinas, *ST*, Ia2æ, q. 93. 2.

116. Aquinas, *ST*, Ia2æ, q. 92. 1.

117. Porter, "Does the Natural Law Provide a Universal Morality?" in Cunningham, *Intractable Disputes,* argues otherwise, 53–96, responding to MacIntyre, "Intractable Moral Disagreements," 1–52. Porter argues that the *first principles* of Thomas's natural law are too abstract in themselves to provide a universal morality, while criticizing MacIntyre for including *secondary precepts* with first principles when he asserts the opposite, 58.

118. John Paul II, *Veritatis Splendour,* 56–61, where freedom is a function of truth.

119. Echoing Augustine's doctrine of divine illumination.

120. Aquinas, *ST*, Ia2æ, q. 91. 2.

121. Aquinas, *ST*, Ia-Iiæ, q. 47. 15.

ary precepts in situations requiring moral discernment.[122] Such prudential discernment implies a degree of freedom in the application of precepts, which mitigates the perceived stasis and rigidity of natural law.[123]

Thomas formally discusses natural law in *ST* Ia2æ, question 94, providing a six-fold description, noted below. "To the natural law belongs everything to which man is inclined according to his nature."[124] Upon the first principle of law, "That good is to be done and evil is to be avoided . . . all . . . precepts of the natural law are based."[125] This includes the "inclination to good, according to the nature of his reason, which nature is proper to him," as well as the "truth about God."[126] Also, as natural law is humanity's rational participation in the eternal law, it would appear to follow that such participation should include a natural inclination to the final end, God.[127] Yet in contrast with the natural law that is instilled in us by nature, it is the new law (instilled by the grace of the Spirit through Christ) "added on to [our] nature," that enables this end.[128] Hence despite God being humanity's proper end, this end is not proper to people as *rational creatures,* nor apprehended through the natural law, for God cannot be apprehended through the intellect alone. It is unclear here whether God, as our end or good, belongs to the natural law, the new law, or both.

The six-fold description of natural law is clear: it is not a habit,[129] contains multiple precepts,[130] prescribes all the virtues,[131] is ubiquitous

---

122. This is the means of solving quandaries. For corporate discernment in the Spirit, see Acts 13:1–3 and Acts 15.

123. Prudence "perfects the activity of practical reason," Hibbs, "Fearful Thoughts," in Cunningham, *Intractable Disputes*, 290.

124. Aquinas, *ST*, Ia2æ, q. 94. 3.

125. Aquinas, *ST*, Ia2æ, q. 94. 2.

126. Ibid.

127. Ibid.

128. Aquinas, *ST*, Ia2æ, q. 106. 1.

129. Aquinas, *ST*, Ia2æ, q. 94. 1. Compare "Nothing that exists by nature can form a habit contrary to its nature," Aristotle, *Nicomachean*, II. 1. 1103a.

130. Aquinas, *ST*, Ia2æ, q. 94. 2. Including those of biological drives. Catholic theology affirms that "pre-rational aspects of our nature . . . set clear limits on human action in the form of prohibitions against acts that violate the natural teleologies of biological processes," Porter, *Natural and Divine Law*, 29.

131. Aquinas, *ST*, Ia2æ, q. 94. 3.

and uniform in relation to general principles,[132] originates with human creation,[133] and is ineradicable as to its general principles.[134]

Divine law attests to natural law, thus "all were bound to observe the [natural law precepts of] the Old Law . . . because they belonged to the natural law."[135] Thus *lex divina* is secondary to *lex naturae*. These precepts are unspecified, but include the First Table because humanity "has a natural inclination to know God."[136] By so arguing, aspects of special revelation become rationally self-evident. But if self-evident as *lex naturae*, then why necessary as *lex divina*? If necessary due to concupiscence, then self-evidence collapses. If First Table law belongs to rational knowledge of God, seventh-day worship and non-idolatry belong to natural law's universal natural inclinations and self-evidence, which becomes problematic given the universal practice of idolatry, including that of pre-revelation Abraham (Josh 24:2).

Thomas's reasoning has certain attractions, yet empirical evidence for God-directed natural inclinations appears lacking, and natural inclinations in the Aristotelian tradition are universally observable human practices. But is this because modern de-Christianized culture, unlike Thomas's, has fewer socially embedded explicit Christian practices, including public worship? If so, this would make the natural inclination to worship a social convention misinterpreted as a universal reality and law, thus confirming the positivist critique. If, however, natural inclinations are functions of our *pre-lapsum* created nature, the problem of true worship is theoretically eliminated yet empirically persists, because natural inclinations as understood in the Aristotelian sense possess the character of *post-lapsum* universal self-evidence, of which there is no instance, except Christ.[137] Or has worship been irratio-

---

132. Aquinas, *ST*, Ia2æ, q. 94. 4. The gap between invariant first principles and diverse concrete practices is filled with the doctrine of intermediate principles by Finnis: see below. In a sense, he frames the nature of prudence.

133. Aquinas, *ST*, Ia2æ, q. 94. 5, quoting Gratian's Decretals. However, divine law, given later, overrides natural law, hypothetically legitimating both adultery and theft, for God owns all, including another man's wife or property, *ST*, Ia2æ, q. 94. 5.

134. Aquinas, *ST*, Ia2æ, q. 94. 6. "Written in the heart" means ineradicable, that is, "instilled" in the heart by the Spirit, citing Jeremiah 31:31ff; *ST* Ia2æ, q. 106. 1. Secondary details may be removed if reason is hindered due to "concupiscence or some other passion," *ST*, Ia2æ, q. 98. 5, citing Romans 1.

135. Aquinas, *ST*, Ia2æ, q. 98. 5. Hence the *lex divina* possesses the six characteristics of natural law noted above. Calvin and Melanchthon are similar. This appears contra Thomas's assessment about theft and adultery, above, n. 133.

136. Aquinas, *ST*, Ia2æ, q. 94. 2.

137. As the eternal law rules rational creatures through the understanding, Aquinas, *ST*, Ia2æ, q. 93. 2, 5, this would make Christ the eternal law's perfect example.

nally suppressed by concupiscence? If the natural inclination *to* God was replaced by natural awareness *of* God, empirical self-evidence is universal, but this is not what Thomas argues.

Thomas's theoretical reasoning clearly places God as the rational eternal ruler of the universe issuing law as command and prohibition, directed to the good of human flourishing. Such medieval feudal theology fails to identify God as Father, Son and Holy Spirit.[138] His rationalist theology and anthropology makes his natural law substantive and real, and one aspect of divine providence.[139] But two problems remain. First, the relation between God and natural law remains unclear. Second, because natural law is a function of the normative moral significance of human nature, Thomas's rationalist anthropology leads to a non-christological determination of natural law. In this respect, Porter correctly states that natural law presupposes a "framework of speculative belief" about humanity, which could include the doctrine of the *imago Dei*.[140] Yet she also fails to make any christological move here, despite Christ being the express image of God (Col 1: 15). Without such christological determination, natural law remains unable to account for specifically Christian practices such as the love of enemy, humility and self-sacrifice, which remain "unnatural." If natural law is to be accorded Christian status, Christ's acts, and particularly his Passion, must be capable of being described as acts proper to human nature. If not, Christ's actions did not participate in the eternal law of divine Wisdom.[141] That is, as the divine Wisdom and Word, he denied his being, thus undermining Chalcedonian Christology and orthodox trinitarianism.

d. The New Natural Law Theory: Finnis, Grisez and Black

The Finnis school attempts to reconfigure natural law and its attendant moral actions without postulating human nature as a rational soul with a fixed origin, as does Thomas. Rather, it lists seven (Finnis) or eight (Grisez) basic human goods,[142] in two categories (substantive and existential/

---

138. This is Barth's criticism of natural theology and natural law, discussed later.
139. Aquinas, *ST,* Ia2æ, q. 91. 2. So too Calvin, *ICR,* I.xvi.3, 200.
140. Porter, "Universal Morality?" 89, 91.
141. Aquinas, *ST,* Ia2æ, q. 93. 1.
142. Finnis's goods are life, knowledge, play, aesthetic experience, sociability, practical reasonableness and religion, Finnis, *Fundamentals,* 50–51 and *Natural Law,* 85–90. Grisez's goods consist in four existential/reflexive goods (self-integration, practical reasonableness or authenticity, friendship and justice, religion or holiness), three substantive goods (life and bodily well being, knowledge of truth and appreciation of

reflective[143]), which correspond to basic elements of human nature, namely, natural inclinations. These goods and their inclinations act reciprocally. The basic human goods possess six characteristics: they are pre-moral, incommensurable, non-hierarchical, constitutive of human fulfillment, culturally embodied, and self-evident, and are reasons in themselves for acting. Neither pleasure (a neurological phenomenon), nor freedom (having potential for immoral ends) are basic human goods.[144]

The goods are self-evident ends identified by the inclinations, which also enable their attainment. This indicative and instrumental nature of the inclinations provides the key to understanding the moral psychology of the theory. In contrast to Thomas's mono-dimensional anthropology, the theory is septa- or octa-dimensional. Basic inclinations are "innate behavioral dispositions" that set "no definitive limits on 'freedom' and on the human capacity in principle to alter and transcend the antecedent conditions of the human situation . . . [but] . . . designate . . . the place that is the abiding point of departure for the human adventure of self-transcendence and historicity."[145] Such dynamism concurs with the theory's criticism that traditional Thomism's realist/rationalist anthropology diminishes human adventurousness and devalues temporal life by eschatological constraint (hellish horror or heavenly hope), and life-denying legalism.

The quest for fulfillment (achieving basic human goods) is conducted and guided by a graded five-fold test, from general principles to concrete decisions. The first principle is the typical and simple proposition of natural law: "Good is to be done and pursued."[146] Second are ten self-evident basic requirements of practical reasonableness that prevent the distortion of the goods by emotions.[147] Third, choices should never be made against any basic human good. Fourth, developed moral norms must move a person close to, or prevent them moving away from, basic human goods. Finally, concrete decisions are determined by their comportment, and as the basic goods are non-hierarchical, any concrete decision to pursue any comporting good according to the above principles is acceptable. The perceived

---

beauty, and skillful performance and play), and one existential/substantive good (marriage), *Fulfillment*, 56. Also Rufus Black, "Introduction: The New Natural Law Theory," in Biggar and Black, *Revival of Natural Law*, 6–7.

143. Goods not requiring deliberation or choice, and those that do, respectively.

144. Contra Aristotle regarding pleasure, *Nicomachean*, X. 5. 1176a4.

145. Pannenberg, *Anthropology*, 41, citing I. Eibl-Eibesfeldt, 'Stammesgeschichtliche Anpassungen im Verhalten des Menschen,' in *Biologische Anthropologie II*.

146. More simple than Thomas's "Good is to be done and pursued, and evil is to be avoided," Aquinas, *ST*, Ia2æ, q. 94. 2.

147. Finnis, *Natural Law*, 100–133.

lacuna in Thomas between the basic human goods and the derived moral norms that concretely structure them (e.g., scriptural commands), and the need to choose which good to pursue at any one time,[148] is filled by Finnis's ten self-evident basic requirements of practical reasonableness.[149] Practical reasonableness is therefore architectonic (but not by positing reason/*nous* as the substantive essence of human psychology) and its claims are transparent,[150] enabling humans to participate in all the goods well: that is, to flourish. Thus the master principle of practical reasonableness is to "make one's choices open to human fulfillment: i.e., avoid unnecessary limitations of human potentialities," so as to allow one to "remain open to integral human fulfilment."[151]

Human nature is understood in terms of the self-evident basic substantive and existential/reflective human goods, derived from practical moral reasoning, not from metaphysical/ontological categories that are derived from theoretical reasoning. Finnis cites Thomas in support: "Aquinas asserts . . . that the first principles of natural law . . . are *per se nota* (self-evident) and indemonstrable. They are not derived from speculative principles . . . [nor] inferred from facts [or] . . . metaphysical propositions . . . They are underived (though not innate)." Thus the "Principles of right and wrong are . . . derived from these first, non-moral principles of practical reasonableness, and not from any facts . . . metaphysical or otherwise."[152] Similarly, "the study of the nature of a being is . . . a study of the potentialities or capacities of that being": that is, not its essence. These "potentialities or capacities are understood by understanding their corresponding acts (actualizations); and acts or actualisations are in turn to be understood by understanding their objects."[153]

Such actualism also typifies Barth and Bonhoeffer, noted later, although both Barth and Bonhoeffer bring being to the fore more than Finnis in their treatment of acts, and both determine human acts and being christologically. Therefore, practical moral reasoning concerns the internal experience of being human in the relation between inclinations, acts and

---

148. Finnis, *Fundamentals*, 69–70.

149. Ibid., 74–76, where he adds an eleventh.

150. Ibid., 70–71.

151. Ibid., 72, 76.

152. Finnis, *Natural Law*, 33–34. For Aristotle, "practical reasoning is reasoning which reasons out of the good, as theoretical reasoning is reasoning which reasons out of the true," Anthony Kelly, *Aristotle on the Perfect Life*, 1.

153. Finnis, *Fundamentals*, 21, citing Aristotle, *De Anima* II, 4: 415a16–21. Also Aristotle, *Nicomachean*, II. 1. 1103a..

PROTOLOGICAL AND TELEOLOGICAL NATURAL LAW THEORIES   59

external objects.[154] Nature is thus not a static realist/ontological term, but existential, historical, practical and teleological, understood from practical rather than theoretical reasoning.[155]

In both Finnis and Grisez, practical reasonableness (not reason *per se*) is a basic human good and performs the central instrumental role of ordering the natural inclinations towards the basic goods and safeguarding them from disruptive emotions. Does this constitute the theory as a rationalistic theory, seeing that reason *per se* is not included? Bexell argues that the theory is rationalistic in the Aristotelian and Thomist sense (affirming "humankind's ability to act and choose well and rationally") partly because "an ethical system having at its heart freedom of choice, free will, and rational reflection will in most cases end up in the vicinity of rationalism."[156] Thus, despite theoretical reasoning's absence, practical reason's central place in deliberation about and determining the identity of the basic goods, it being a basic good itself, and its regulative role in ordering and safeguarding the inclinations to those goods, constitutes the theory as rationalistic.[157]

A rationalistic theory is not necessarily a law ethic unless rationality is seen as a law. In Finnis, practical rationality's cognitive determination (of self-evident goods), deliberative power (weighing of and free choice from amongst the goods), and regulative role (ordering and governing the emotions), are all normative functions, constituting the theory as one of law.

A central principle of the theory is Aristotle's bifurcated rationality of theoretical and practical reasoning.[158] Consequently, the naturalistic axiom is rejected. The denial of logical deduction from an *is* to an *ought* implies the denial of a logical induction from an *ought* to an *is*. This is problematic, as knowledge, to which Finnis gives the most sustained treatment, is one of his seven basic human goods.[159] Unlike belief (either true or false), knowledge

---

154. Finnis, *Natural Law*, 34. A particular problem with Aristotle's teleology is this tendency to self-enclosure. In Aristotle, A is ordered to A (vegetation is ordered to luxuriant growth), whereas in Plato, A is ordered to B (vegetation is ordered to serve animals), O'Donovan *Resurrection*, 34. Aristotle thus prevents A from being reduced to instrumentality; Plato prevents A from collapsing in on itself.

155. Yet Black contends that Grisez's theory is realist, *Moral Realism*, 114, 166.

156. Göran Bexell, "Is Grisez's Moral Theology Rationalistic?" 134, 133. He contrasts this with Augustinianism's negative assessment of reason's ability to understand the human good.

157. Natural law's precepts are "rational norms, available . . . to the non-Christian," Finnis, *Moral Absolutes*, 10.

158. Finnis, *Fundamentals*, 1–23, conceding the differences are "simply operational," 11. For Thomas, see Aquinas, *ST*, Ia2æ, q. 94. 2, 4.

159. Finnis, *Natural Law*, 59–80. "It would be more accurate to call it 'speculative

(resulting from theoretical reasoning) is invariably true and universal. However, knowledge is one of the seven basic goods corresponding to natural inclinations and accessible to practical reasoning, yet the naturalistic fallacy asserts a barrier between theoretical reasoning about the true and practical reasoning about the good. The *duplex* theory of knowledge (theoretical and practical) necessitates a corresponding *duplex* theory of logically unrelated rationalities, and as practical rationality is central and determinative of the goods, then knowledge *per se* cannot be a basic human good, for theoretical knowledge about truth is excluded. Therefore the knowledge of truth cannot be a basic human good, which is senseless, for theoretical reasoning about existent realities, such as human existence itself, and Grisez's substantive good of the knowledge of truth, are self-evident basic human goods.

A further problem is how its bifurcated rationality can include natural inclinations as objects of practical moral reasoning. These inclinations constitute the major human phenomena in the theory, and as such pre-exist the process of practical moral reasoning: they simply *are*. Yet practical reasoning reasons only out of proposed future acts, not pre-existent realities. It is problematic to limit practical reasoning to future acts, yet maintain inclinations (as intrinsic, pre-existent human orientations) as a major component in such reasoning.

Furthermore, as the basic goods are pre-moral, and as practical moral reasoning is ordered to the future, how can such pre-moral goods be objects of moral reasoning? It appears inconsistent to argue on the one hand that practical moral reasoning is wholly oriented to the future, but that the objects of such reasoning, human goods, are pre-moral—that they exist prior to their appraisal by such reasoning. This includes the basic human good of bodily life, which can hardly be excluded from practical moral reasoning, for instance the life of an unconscious neonate. Finnis upholds the Aristotelian bifurcation as "simply operational differences," because practical and theoretical reasoning have different objectives.[160] But as practical reasoning's objectives are "oughts" and future human actions (not pre-existing realities), such reasoning cannot be directed to the good of bodily life that antedates the act of practical reasoning. The theory thus needs modifying at this point.

Furthermore, as Northcott argues, the theory's anthropocentric "restatement of the natural law tradition . . . seriously disables the tradition as a vehicle for establishing the moral standing of nature and the duties

---

knowledge,'" 59.

160. Finnis, *Fundamentals*, 11.

we owe to the natural world,"[161] by instrumentally debasing non-human entities to serve human goods. Yet as Finnis is concerned with human action, such chiding is somewhat inappropriate, even though it expresses a proper dissatisfaction with traditional ethics' neglect of the wider creation. In contrast, although O'Donovan describes milk as properly food (i.e., a human-oriented good) rather than a commodity, he does so due to its self-evident nature, rather than economic nominalism. Thus things have a "*natural meaning*" and relate to each other in a "given pattern within the order of things." Simply: an entity's existence is its kind, and this kind reveals its purpose.[162] This he calls the "natural generic-teleological order" of kinds and ends;[163] so for example, "speech is ordered to truth, and marriage to fidelity."[164] This contests both a voluntarist determination of an object's end, and a nominalist denial of a particular's genus. In contrast to Finnis's view of natural law's anthropological utility, O'Donovan includes all creation, as well as God's immutability, as that which orders and determines goods for ends other than human use.[165]

O'Donovan's strong realism leads him to criticize Finnis's discussion of the norm of "Feed your child," when the only food available is the flesh of a neighbor's living child. For Finnis, the norm "Feed your child" is non-exceptionless and non-absolute here, being overridden by the greater norm of the prohibition of killing the innocent. For O'Donovan, the norm simply does not apply in this case because "the flesh of my neighbor's child *is not food* . . . There is no food to be given, and that is the end of the story."[166] Human flesh can be deemed food by a voluntarist or nominalist, but not by a realist theory of kinds and ends in respect of both persons and food.

Positively, the Finnis school takes seriously the historicist quest for dynamic openness and human adventure. Its anthropology is richer than Aquinas's rationalism, yet like Aquinas, it remains christologically empty. Its bifurcated rationality appears internally inconsistent, and its rejection of metaphysics/theology renders it anthropologically self-enclosed and thus problematic for Christian ethics. Like Aquinas's *Summa*, which was a

---

161. Michael Northcott, "The Moral Standing of Nature and the New Natural Law," in Biggar and Black, *Revival of Natural Law*, 262.

162. Oliver O'Donovan, "Natural Ethic," in Wright, *Essays*, 22–23, emphasis original.

163. O'Donovan, *Resurrection*, 38.

164. Ibid., 34.

165. Ibid., 38, 45.

166. Oliver O'Donovan, "John Finnis on Moral Absolutes," in Biggar and Black, *Revival of Natural Law*, 115, emphasis original.

Christian *apologia* responding to a revitalized Aristotelianism, Finnis offers a neo-Thomist *apologia* in the face of vigorous Western non-theism.

3. Conclusion

Natural law's realism and universal, rational, self-evident, and substantive character constitutes its central claim and appeal. Protological natural law's antecedent moral realism provides a clear criterion for assessing and orienting practical moral reasoning. Teleological natural law provides ends that are intrinsic to entities and their relations that structure proper practical reasoning, and which are themselves indicated by natural inclinations.[167] Despite both Aristotle's and Cicero's primary concerns with human and divine natures respectively, they are unable to provide an adequate account of the relation between God and humanity so that the valid concerns of both eternal and temporal moral concerns are realized.

Calvin is a protological theorist who applies natural law primarily soteriologically-juridically in personal ethics, and juridically in political contexts. Thomas is a teleological theorist whose natural law orients humanity to its proper good. Despite this difference, both assert that the ubiquity of natural law extends to universally identical basic principles, despite diversity in particulars. In both the Thomist and Reformation forms, divine law is a historically contingent necessary *post-lapsum* witness to, and re-presentation of, ubiquitous and ineradicable natural law, participating in eternal law. There is a marked absence of Christology in the tradition.

This christological lacuna is the primary flaw in natural law, because an ethic must necessarily derive directly or indirectly from Christ to qualify as Christian. This is demonstrated only once in Thomas where he cites Gratian's reference to the Golden Rule, where Christ exemplifies the general principle.[168] Finnis's attempt to overcome Thomism's realist/static limitations omits theology altogether, demonstrating that rationality *per se* does not constitute a theory as either theistic or Christian, even if rationality is understood as a divine *donum*. If reason *per se* constitutes natural law as theistic, rationality shares the divine nature as in Ciceronian theology: "God is reason." The biblical "God is love" justifies Brunner's theological critique of natural law as mistakenly characterized by law rather than love. Further, its rationalism is too anthropologically thin to constitute an adequate moral psychology or criterion of human nature. As such it places one single element

---

167. Schockenhoff, *Natural* Law, 3.

168. General principles displace God's particularity according to Barth, *CD* IV/3.1, 448.

of moral psychology—reason—at the center of human nature, often without theological determination. Yet God's decision to create is more primitive than the created person itself, meaning that the divine-human relation is more primitive than any specific anthropological component. Finally, even if reason is understood as a divine *donum*, it tends to Deism when it is considered sufficient in and of itself without any divine engagement.

Natural inclinations tend towards a reflexive understanding of human nature. For instance, the natural inclination of bodily life (a basic human good in Finnis) in the face of conflict is fight, flight, or freeze, none of which accord with the sapiential tradition to love, do good to and feed one's enemies (Matt 5:43–48; Rom 12:17–21), exemplified in Christ forgiving his crucifiers (Luke 23:34).[169] The natural inclinations appear incapable of including Christ loving his violent enemies. But as such inclinations are considered to be proper to human nature, this implies that Christ acted unnaturally, which negates Chalcedonian Christology and orthodox trinitarianism.

The polysemous and indeterminate character of the material content of *phusis* begs the question of the practical moral reasoning grounded therein.[170] Thus, Paul's rich theological and ethical determination of *phusis* and Thomas's determination of *phusis* as a rational soul produce different material and formal theories of natural law and moral reasoning. O'Donovan's assertion that "Christian ethics must arise from the gospel of Jesus Christ. Otherwise it could not be *Christian* ethics"[171] is negatively illustrated in natural law. This project proposes Chalcedon as a way towards christological natural law, for the fact that "God created reality" means that "all epistemology and interpretation occur at some level within the Logos."[172] To that end, Part Two considers the central place of Christology within Anabaptistic ethics.

---

169. Contrast Nietzsche, who eulogizes the instincts.

170. "We consider something rational because our tradition validates it as such," Zimmermann, *Theological Hermeneutics*, 108. This could be rephrased as extending MacIntyre, "Which *Phusis*, Which Ethic?"

171. O'Donovan, *Resurrection*, 11, emphasis original.

172. Zimmermann, *Theological Hermeneutics*, 104.

Part Two

The Radical Tradition of Christian Ethics

Introduction

PART ONE ARGUED THAT natural law ethics' concern for ubiquitous and universal moral norms, such as its basic tenet of doing good and avoiding evil, is legitimate and proper. Protological theories such as Cicero's doctrine of *spermatikos logos* or divine mind, and Calvin's "law of our creation" both cite theological grounds for natural law. Aristotle and other teleological theorists cite ends that are intrinsic and proper to human nature as grounds for natural law. Yet despite this concern with both divine and human nature, it has been argued that both are inadequate as a Christian ethic due to their lack of Christology.

The purpose of Part Two is to describe and evaluate the radical tradition within Christian ethics. This tradition of ethics sits uneasily with natural law. Yet Part Two is not meant to suggest that natural law simply requires a correction, for the thesis is not about natural law and its deficiencies. Nor is it a defense of christological ethics or the suggestion that it requires a natural law corrective. Nor is it an extensive analysis of any particular authors who represent or inhabit this tradition. Rather, this part serves to describe and evaluate the primary ethical category germane to this tradition. Taken with Part One, it lays the groundwork for Part Three, which attempts the rapprochement of both traditions through Chalcedonian Christology.

The title "The Word Became Flesh" is meant to express the purpose of the thesis: to present a model of ethics based on the incarnation of the eternal Word, as expressed in the double *homoousion* and single *hypostasis*

Christology of Chalcedon, which is sensitive to the primary concerns of both natural law and radical christological ethics. It is the concept of the *flesh*, concrete human existence, which takes center stage in both natural law and radical ethics: human nature generally in natural law, and Christ's humanity specifically in radicalism. Consequently, Part Two concerns the strengths and inadequacies of the christo-ethical radical moral tradition.

The form of reasoning germane to this tradition will be called christological moral reasoning. Three significant characteristics of this tradition are noted: 1) the primary place given to the Gospels and their witness to Jesus' life; 2) its uneasy relationship with the abstract categories preferred by the classical tradition generally, and natural law specifically; and 3) its governance by its concern to faithfully reflect Jesus' life rather than conform to the wider world's thought and practices. These three factors constitute christological moral reasoning as a distinct category and tradition of thought beyond confessional boundaries, although it is a common feature of those groups that could be called Anabaptist.

As used here, Anabaptism describes a Continental movement commencing in the sixteenth century, and the theological/ecclesial groups that emerged from and are in continuity with it. It does not refer to any specific group, such as the Mennonites, even though writers from that confession are frequently cited. The intramural debate about identity and what constitutes the core characteristics of such groups reveals the fluidity of meaning in this term, but this is not a concern here. Yet an analysis of these debates suggests that the defining criteria, or genetic make up, of such groups, are found in various interactions between ecclesiology, discipleship, Christology, and non-violence. In practice, the core identity of any one group is how these genes are spliced together to produce a single organism. Of these four genes, the focus here is Christology and its central role in the moral reasoning of this tradition. When non-Anabaptist Reformation and modern authors are cited, a critical engagement with their broader theology and ethics is not necessarily pursued because the single intention is to demonstrate that they exhibit a consistent christologically-determined ethical focus, and that this focus exists over time and across confessions. Such areas of disagreement that may exist do not mitigate the common christological focus, and are not the concern of the thesis. Indeed, a common focus upon Jesus does not preclude various Christologies with their attendant ethics, as noted later. Rather, the concern here is narrow: to show that Christology functions as the norming principle in such ethics.

Radical, as used here, means an intellectual tradition reflecting the christologically-determined ethics of sixteenth century Anabaptism and their confessional descendants. It is not a confessional term in the narrow sense. Whereas Anabaptist describes *groups* that exhibit this christological moral focus, radical describes a *movement*, or intellectual moral posture, which exhibits the same. It is thus a more global term than Anabaptist: it approximates the adjective "Anabaptistic" or the generic term "anabaptist."[1] However, Anabaptism and radical will often be used interchangeably to describe the sharp christological focus common to both, the context providing the best guide to precise interpretation. This form of ethics is called christological moral reasoning, or christo-ethical radicalism. When writers who are not confessionally Anabaptist are cited, such as Spohn and Barth, it demonstrates that such a christological emphasis is not confined to a narrow confessional band. Consequently, authors are cited not because of their confessional identity, or their agreement, disagreement and interdependence in theological matters generally, but because they demonstrate a common christological determination to their moral reasoning. In this sense they are grouped together as radical.

Consequently, while a valid methodological framing could be around authors, Part Two is methodologically framed around concepts. Its purpose is not to critically engage select writers, even though Yoder is significant, but to attempt to demonstrate a consistent christological focus across many authors over time.[2] The framing is conceptual, not authorial, covering philosophical, biblical, historical, confessional, and ethical matters, as outlined in the contents. Consequently, older writers like Friedmann are also cited when they exhibit the christological moral reasoning that is considered central to this tradition, for a tradition by definition perdures through time.

It will be argued that Christology is the center and framework for such moral reasoning, and that such Christology acts as a hermeneutical lens through which other concerns are viewed. After arguing for the centrality of Jesus, chapter 3 examines four philosophical concerns pertinent to establishing and describing christological moral reasoning, namely: control beliefs, the basis of moral reasoning in reason or practice, the dialectic of the universal and particular, and essentialism. Chapter 4 examines eight theological subjects: trinitarianism, Christ's three-fold office, regeneration, justification, law and gospel, election, violence, and vocation, in an attempt to demonstrate how christo-ethical radicalism ethically reconfigures them.

---

1. Compare McClendon, *Ethics*, 20, who uses "Anabaptist" and "Radicals" synonymously. His use of "baptist" to describe a theological vision is appropriated: "anabaptist" here refers to a christological moral vision.

2. Yoder illustrates a broad expression of christological moral reasoning. Although confessionally a Mennonite, he was also seen as an ecumenical catholic: Michael G. Cartwright, "Radical Reform, Radical Catholicity: John Howard Yoder's Vision of the Faithful Church," in Yoder, *Royal Priesthood*, 1–49.

3

Theological, Textual and Philosophical Considerations

1. The Theological and Textual Center.

a. Christology

THE RADICAL TRADITION IN theology and ethics is formally and materially christological. For instance, Marpeck argues that "the time of the Old Testament before Christ became Man is called yesterday, and the time of the New Testament after the incarnation of Christ, His death, resurrection, and ascension is called today."[1] He writes, "to establish . . . that only today the essence of eternal salvation has come and did not exist yesterday."[2] As essence, Christ constitutes the *actuality* of the norm and substance of all theological and ethical reasoning in Marpeck, so that "the word 'actual' . . . means the things unto eternal life which . . . became reality today . . . (and) that whenever today's actuality is promised yesterday one pays close attention to the words which clearly refer to today and do not concern themselves with the figure itself."[3] As actual succeeds promise, the New Testament prevails over the Old.

---

1. Marbeck, "Preface to the 'Explanation of the Testaments,'" in *Pilgram Marpeck*, 559.

2. Ibid., 565–566, citing Colossians 2:17; Hebrews 19:16 (sic) and Acts 3:18.

3. Ibid., 560.

Similarly the ethical center is "that recorded experience of practical moral reasoning in genuine human form that bears the name of Jesus."[4] Therefore, "the Gospel accounts . . . [of Jesus'] deeds shows a coherent, conscious socio-political character and direction, and that his words are inseparable therefrom."[5] Consequently, Jesus' disciples take his "life and teachings [as] *normative* for them," and "the entire life of Jesus forms the basic norm of Christian ethics."[6] Here, Jesus *in toto*, not simply his teaching, functions as the comprehensive ethical norm: "[Christ] is the formally universal norm of ethical action,"[7] making his socially embedded humanity the formal and material center of Christian ethics, like a hub from which all ethical reasoning radiates. In an Antiochene fashion, "historic Anabaptists often apprehended Jesus' significance from below."[8]

This christological focus is unusual, as Christian ethics is often disengaged from theology and biblical studies.[9] Thus Blough's *theological* statement, "I have yet to meet or read a Christian theologian . . . who does not say that the credibility of his or her theology depends on an ultimate reference to the story of Jesus," contrasts with Yoder's *ethical* statement; "The person concerned with social ethics, [is] accustomed . . . to assume Jesus not to be

---

4. Yoder, "The Hermeneutics of Peoplehood: A Protestant Perspective," in *Priestly Kingdom*, 37. Termed "Jesus-oriented Christians" by Grimsrud, "Anabaptism," 373. "Yoder believed that Jesus is central within the Christian faith, not only for doctrine . . . but also for the moral character of the Christian community," Nation, *Yoder*, 55.

5. Yoder, *Politics of Jesus*, 115. Three Anabaptists are uneasy with Yoder's political focus. Martens accuses him of reducing theology to ethics, particularly politics, (Martens, *Heterodox Yoder*, 3, and throughout text). However, as Yoder's project (social ethics) concerns the *polis*, has he misread a lack of emphasis for an antithesis? Reimer, also a Canadian, criticizes Yoder's apparent historicist minimization of classical-ontological theology, (Reimer, *Mennonites and Classical*, 247–271). Finger is ambivalent in *Contemporary Anabaptist Theology*, while in "Did Yoder Reduce Theology to Ethics?" (in Ollenburger and Koontz, *Patient and Untamed*, 318–339) he is more critical of Yoder's "classical lack," but warmer than Martens. Yoder accepts the Incarnation and the Trinity: *Priestly Kingdom*, 128; *Preface to Theology*, 116, 203. Yoder is discussed here as the dominant contemporary Anabaptist ethicist, but this is not a study of Yoder *per se*.

6. Spohn, *Go and Do Likewise*, 10, 29, italics original.

7. von Balthasar, "Nine Propositions on the Christian Faith," in H. Schurmann *et.al. Principles of Christian Morality*, trans. G. Harrison; (San Francisco, CA: Ignatius Press, 1975), 79.

8. Finger, *Anabaptist Theology*, 365.

9. Spohn cites the dismissal of his project about "Jesus and ethics" by both biblical scholars and theologians in *Go and Do Likewise*, 9. Burridge cites various strategies for removing Jesus from Christian ethics in liberalism and historical and biblical studies (Burridge, *Imitating Jesus*, 1–32). Burridge insists "on the priority of the person of Jesus of Nazareth," 4.

relevant to social issues, or at least not *immediately*."[10] When ethical considerations are discussed, the basic theological claims of Christology seem to recede behind other moral categories.[11] It is this general omission of Christology from ethics that radicalism attempts to redress.

b. Norming the Identity of Jesus for Ethics

It was argued above that anabaptism exhibits a single formal "Jesus principle." However, this single formal criterion readily results in multiple material content, where Jesus is reduced to something like a container into which are poured multiple forms of idealized moral character.[12] Furthermore, this plurality extends to the point of contact between Jesus and persons who see him as morally significant. In Anabaptism, the three key terms in this respect are participation, discipleship, and imitation.[13] For instance, the sixteenth century Radical Reformers' desire for ecclesial restoration "tends to coincide now with the ideal of imitation of Christ."[14] Consequently, "One who claims to belong to Christ must follow the path taken by Christ," thus joining participation ("belonging to") and discipleship ("following the path"), while excluding pietism and mysticism.[15] The singularity of the norm (the life of Jesus) is therefore capable of finding multiple expressions in various Christologies, various modes of association with him, and in their attendant ethics.

This suggests that a more nuanced approach than the biblicism of sixteenth century radicalism is required to establish a proper relation between the single formal criterion, its proper material content, and the form of relation between Jesus and those who find him morally significant. Two approaches are suggested in respect of both Jesus' identity as such, and the

---

10. Blough, *Christ in Our Midst*, 232, and Yoder, *Politics*, 12, italics original.

11. Hauerwas, "Jesus: The Story of the Kingdom," in *Community of Character*, 36–37. Christian identity "comes by learning to follow and be like [Jesus],"*Peaceable Kingdom*, 75.

12. Schweitzer, *Quest*, 396–401. The "historical Jesus" cannot function as a "norm of Christian faith," Spohn, *Go and Do Likewise*, 19.

13. Yoder, *Politics*, 116. Imitation results from pushing back beyond Paul to Jesus according to Bainton in Hershberger, *The Recovery of the Anabaptist Vision*, 106. The new interpretation of Paul's *pistis Jesou Christou* makes Christ's faithfulness to God the object of *imitatio*: Douglas Harink, "The Anabaptist and the Apostle; John Howard Yoder as a Pauline Theologian," in Ollenburger and Koontz, *Patient and Untamed*, 278–81.

14. Bainton in Hershberger, *Recovery*, 106.

15. Augsburger, *Dissident Discipleship*, 27, quoting Hans Denck.

mode of association with Jesus: the analogical imagination and the Chalcedonian Definition.

Regarding the mode of association with Jesus, the place of analogy is suggested. The analogical imagination "bridges the moral reflection of Christians and the words and deeds of Jesus . . . [and provides] the cognitive content for obeying the command 'Go and do likewise.'"[16] Jesus and his context provide the analogate, which "exercises a normative function" by implying "actions and ways of living that are congruent with the prototype."[17]

This analogical imagination contrasts with univocalism, which is a mere repetition, and equivocalism, where worlds are completely unrelated. Unimaginative Anabaptist biblicism is univocal, making the story of Jesus one-dimensional and timeless, while the non-christological moral reasoning of classical moral reasoning is equivocal and tends to downplay the life of Jesus altogether.[18] Thus the term "as" (Kant's "copula of imagination") facilitates a dynamic connection between Jesus and the disciples, enabling them to "love 'just as' Jesus has loved them."[19] The "as" provides the link to the normative pattern in such a fashion that the reader's narrative is shaped by Jesus' narrative. In this way the idealized moral character that typifies the wider world's narrative at any moment, and in which the moral reasoner is immersed, is less likely to be poured into the empty form of Jesus. This analogical imagination has clear biblical warrants: "Forgive as the Lord forgave you," (Col 3:13).

For this analogical imagination to function, the Gospel stories must become and remain compelling and normative, for they give proper access to Jesus' life as the norming principle. The copula "as" means that the analogical imagination protects Jesus' story from *existential* distortion through the believer's experience, because it places Jesus, the analogate, as the primary criterion of moral action.

---

16. Spohn, *Go and Do Likewise*, 50. An "'analogy is the repetition of the same fundamental pattern in two different contexts,'" 54–55, quoting Dorothy Emmet, *The Nature of Metaphysical Thinking*. Notwithstanding other areas of disagreement, Spohn concurs with Yoder that Jesus' life is morally normative, although he uses the language of analogy. This is a Catholic version of the christological ethics of this thesis, and may thus be called radical. The polygenesis theory of Anabaptist origins places their antecedents partly within pre-Reformation Catholic monasticism, of which Spohn may be a contemporary expression. Similarly Blough, *Christ in our Midst*, 287–323 argues for Augustinian, Benedictine, Dominican, and Franciscan antecedents and contributors to Marbeck's *imitatio Christi* ethics.

17. Spohn, *Go and Do Likewise*, 55.

18. Ibid., 55–56.

19. Ibid., 61.

Second, regarding Christology as such, the Gospel stories need to be joined to the substantive Christology of the church's ecumenical traditions, such as Chalcedon, which is taken up in Part Three. These traditions act as historical mediators and patterns of reasoning linking the primitive narrative and the contemporary situation, even though Scripture has the final word.[20] Such ecumenical traditions protect the primitive narrative from being distorted or displaced by non-christological patterns of reasoning located in contemporary ethical and philosophical presuppositions. Moreover, they enable the primitive narrative to be critically engaged with wider concerns without abandoning the original story. This is particularly true of their engagement with classical forms of thought, which is how Chalcedonian Christology is used here. The Christology of these traditions also ensures that the Jesus principle remains ecumenical, orthodox, and ecclesially embedded across the centuries. Chalcedon protects Jesus' story from *philosophical* distortion through the wider world's beliefs.

Consequently, the analogical imagination and Chalcedon function as mutually corrective. First, the analogical imagination ensures that the Gospel's emphasis upon the *practices* of Jesus is not lost under the abstractions of Chalcedon. The Gospels are necessary not only because they are the only texts that make Jesus' life accessible, but also because the classical creeds and definitions are ethically empty, and thus insufficient of themselves to produce the moral life of Jesus in the believer. Second, the abstractions of Chalcedon ensure that the analogical imagination does not isolate the humanity of Jesus from its union with his divinity or deny him as being *homoousios* with the Father. Unless this union, and the high Christology embedded in it, remains central, there are no *theologically* compelling grounds for the morally normative character of Jesus' humanity.

Such a high Christology provides epistemological and axiological justification for christo-ethical radicalism. That is, we *know* more about moral *value* in and through Christ than elsewhere. Because God is wholly knowing and wholly good, Marpeck's eschatology of promise and fulfillment means that Jesus, as the fulfiller of God's promises, is the source of greater moral *knowledge* and truer moral *values* than those that are discernable or discoverable elsewhere. Ethically, what God knows and values is focused in the fulfillment.

But even greater than the concept of fulfillment is the Christology of Chalcedon. Jesus' *divine* consubstantial nature means that he fully shares the moral nature of God as wholly knowing and wholly good, while his *human* consubstantial nature means that such knowledge and values are

---

20. McClendon, *Doctrine*, 265.

revealed and concretized in one person in history. As the incarnate divine Son, Jesus is thus the primary bearer of both moral knowledge (his epistemological significance) and moral values (his axiological significance).[21] Because God is a concept with universal extent, the sum of moral knowledge and goodness is found in that concept, which in Chalcedon is located within the history of this one man Jesus.

Yet without the copula of imagination—the "as"—being applied to the Gospel stories, the historical concreteness of christological moral reasoning tends to dissolve. This is evident in forms of classical moral reasoning that neglect creational realities, and concrete history, due to their aversion to contingency and their preference for timeless abstractions and ideas. Thus while historical ethics can account for classical and abstract categories, and use them in its justification,[22] to wholly restructure historical ethics within classical and abstract categories necessarily voids their particularism and spatio-historical location. Simply, historically-grounded moral reasoning cannot be *reduced* to abstract concepts without resulting in Gnosticism, which in its "rejection of particularity means that Christ himself becomes a vague spiritualized being."[23] Such an anti-materialist Christology results in either an ethereal Christ principle that lacks concrete anchoring and material content, or the replacement of Jesus with abstract moral categories. In the same way that gnostic spirituality is elitist, the escape from particularity into abstractions may constitute an elitist appeal to supra-mundane reasoning accessible only to the sapient.[24] For these reasons both the analogical imagination and Chalcedon maintain a proper balance between historical and classical moral reasoning, and ensure that the identity of Jesus remains ethically normative without either classical abstraction or historical reduction.

c. The New Testament

Marpeck's eschatology of christological fulfillment is typical of Anabaptism. Consequently, it privileges the New Testament over the Old.[25] "The Bible

---

21. Yoder, *Priestly Kingdom*, 11, 62, although Yoder does not cite Chalcedon as the reason.

22. As does O'Donovan in *Resurrection*.

23. Lee, *Protestant Gnostics*, 41–42, 17.

24. Lee, *Protestant Gnostics*, 33–40. An elite governs Plato's state. Such criticism exemplifies the Enlightenment hostility to history as seen in Kant and Lessing.

25. See text on Marbeck, n. 4. Also Conrad Grebel, "We are no longer under the Old Covenant," in Bender, "The Anabaptist Vision," in Hershberger, *Recovery*, 51.

is a story of promise and fulfillment which must be read directionally ... Abraham and Moses are read through Jesus and Paul."[26] This focus does not demonstrate theological or biblical ignorance, as most sixteenth century Anabaptist leaders were schooled in medieval, and in some cases, early Reformation, theology.[27] Rather, it was a refusal to engage in theological or ethical discussion or debate by the formal and material rules established by those who did not hold to the same concept of christological fulfillment. By so doing, they reframed ethical and theological debate on their own discursive grounds.[28] Appealing to authorities other than Scripture, and the New Testament particularly, would have methodologically contradicted their theological stance upon Jesus as the central and final authority, in the same way as would a deontological justification of emotivist ethics.

Because we know more about moral value in and through Christ, the Gospels function as theologico-ethical "identity documents" that shape the moral identity of Jesus' followers.[29] By containing the gospel (Jesus), the Gospels (texts) "rhetorically invite readers to *become* [Jesus'] participating disciples" by imitating his practices embedded in that narrative.[30]

This constitutes Scripture, especially the Gospels, as moral documents, although not exhaustively. This does not mean they simply contain elucidations of the right or the good like a moral handbook, but that they exert moral power over the reader, unlike a mere doctrinal repository. Thus "the mystery of godliness" is wholly christological (1 Tim 3:16) and Scripture is designed for "all good works" (2 Tim 3:16). A proper reading of the Gospels necessitates the moral transformation of the reader into the shape of the person who Jesus is.[31] Likewise, the *Swiss Brethren Confession* (1578) urges Christians to "use the Scriptures for teaching, admonition, for discipline and improvement, and to demonstrate that the foundation of their faith is in harmony with the Scriptures."[32]

Similarly, when the Gospels are understood as "lives of Jesus," the imitation of Christ approximates a normative moral absolute.[33] This is because

---

26. Yoder, *Priestly Kingdom*, 9, and compare Finger, *Anabaptist Theology*, 100.

27. Finger, *Anabaptist Theology*, 192.

28. Biesecker-Mast, *Separation*, 237. Such rhetoric relativized, but did not negate, credal Christianity.

29. McClendon, *Doctrine*, 38, 227.

30. McClendon, *Doctrine*, 228.

31. McClendon, *Ethics*, 332.

32. Koop, Confessions, 50, concluding its first article.

33. Burridge, *Imitating*, 74, citing Reginald White, *Biblical Ethics*. *Imitatio* is the primary biblical foundation of Christian asceticism for Davis, *Anabaptism and*

Jesus, as the divine Son incarnate in perfect humanity, both commands the good and the right as fully divine, and instantiates the good and the right as fully human. The Catholic natural law imperative to be human is thus christologized: "Be human in the way in which Jesus Christ is human."[34] The narrative becomes the vehicle for remembering Jesus, and thus the church's test for conduct.[35] This is a consistent biblical model, found in the call of the Deuteronomic history's foundational exhortation to remember God's acts (Deuteronomy 8), and the *imitatio Dei* of the Holiness Code (Leviticus 19).[36]

This means that the New Testament *imitatio Christi* is not without precedent in the Old Testament *imitatio Dei*. Yet because of the directional reading of the Bible, the emphasis lies unambiguously on the New Testament. For radicalism, the Gospels and christological moral reasoning are intrinsically related so that abandoning one necessarily implies abandoning the other. The ethically normative person is Jesus, who is the center of the normative text, the Gospels.

2. Philosophical Considerations

a. Control Beliefs and Christology

All moral reasoning derives from a center and operates within a boundary. The boundary defines the data, phenomena, or subject matter under consideration, and is explicit. The center comprises the presupposition/s, control beliefs and basic commitments of the theorist, and is usually implicit. To this end, Wolterstorff's theory of theorizing is helpful in articulating christological moral reasoning.[37]

Control beliefs are basic and authentic personal commitments so that changing them changes the theorist and his/her fundamental orientation. They come into play when a theory is weighed or assessed,[38] and become explicit when a theorist is forced to examine their first principles due to con-

---

Asceticism.

34. Spohn, *Go and Do Likewise*, 144.

35. Burridge, *Imitating*, 75. Collinson, *Making Disciples*, sees Christ's example as central to faith.

36. Burridge, *Imitating*, 77. He cites Marcus Borg, *Conflict, Holiness and Politics in the Teachings of Jesus*, who argues that Luke christologically fulfills Leviticus 19 as Jesus' mercy code.

37. Wolterstorff, *Reason*.

38. Ibid., 67.

flict or confusion. They function negatively to reject perceived irreconcilable challenges, and positively to propose solutions to reconcilable challenges in such a fashion that the control beliefs remain intact or modified, yet still determinant.[39]

Anabaptism's central control belief for ethics, Christology, is the "doctrine . . . in which [this] Christian community beholds reality."[40] As "authentic Christian commitment ought to function *internally* to scholarship,"[41] christo-ethical radicalism tends to reject those ethical norms, imperatives and conclusions originating from or expressing non-christological moral reasoning. However, between such outright rejection and the devising of new theories, any fresh challenge may be appropriated by harmonizing, contextualizing, or Christianizing such norms,[42] but only when the basic authentic commitment and the control belief remain uncompromised. If fundamental change occurs, then the control belief has been displaced by another, with a concomitant change of the theorist.

Consequently, Anabaptism's basic commitment to the Jesus of the Gospels overrides competing ethical claims or authorities. For instance in politics, non-coercive exemplarist Christology acted as Anabaptism's control belief in the sixteenth century, whereas non-christological theories of social peace, predicated upon coerced religious conformity, were Magisterial and Catholic control beliefs. In Wolterstorffian theory, christological moral reasoning is one among many conflicting control beliefs in the area of social ethics. The matter for debate is thus not the existence of such control beliefs, but whether they: a) are derived from, internal to, and comport with the discipline of which they are a constituent part; b) are open to engagement with, but not necessarily modification by or conversion to, other beliefs; and c) yield to Christ as a necessary correlate of his universal lordship over all powers, including moral reasoning and the social structures derived therefrom.

Classical Christian moral reasoning consistently applies a) and b), yet tends to resist c). In particular, classical ethics readily maintains a) as its primary criterion, as has already been noted in Part One, but in such a fashion as to negate c), wherever Christology is considered ill fitting. This is partly

---

39. Ibid., 67–68.

40. McGrath, *Scientific Theology*, vol. 3, 28, defining doctrine. McGrath's contention that theory "thins, prunes, distorts and limits," and "systematically truncates," by favoring generalities over particulars, is an apt summary of Anabaptist criticism of classical non-christological moral reasoning, which "*reduces* [Christian] *narrative to formulae,*" 31, emphasis original.

41. Wolterstorff, *Reason*, 81.

42. Ibid.

due to classical moral reasoning often being embedded in cultural institutions and social norms that are theologically supported by non-christological concepts of providence. Such justifications are now rightly criticized on postmodern grounds as ontotheologies.[43] The Anabaptist term "outside the perfection of Christ" becomes a pragmatic rationalization for non-Christian moral practices in a fallen world, rather than a red flag of prohibition.

On the other hand, christological moral reasoning maintains a) because orthodox Christology affirms Christ as the origin and center of all things (Col 1:16–20); and b), by maintaining the internal integrity of each discipline in dynamic relation with, but not yielding to, extraneous forms of reasoning; and c), by affirming the comprehensive lordship of Christ. Only when c) determines both a) and b) is fragmentation avoided and a comprehensive Christian theory of moral reasoning possible. Christo-ethical radicalism maintains that c) must determine, or at the minimum, not be in conflict with, the practical moral reasoning and the attendant practices that are internal to a), otherwise such reasoning and practices are disordered and rebellious, and thus cannot claim a morally norming function. When it comes to practical moral reasoning, it is therefore axiomatic that c) must exercise the primary controlling function over both a) and b) because Christ, as the incarnate fullness of deity (Col 2:9), is himself what is proper to moral reasoning, for God is wholly good in who he is, and wholly right in what he does. Because the Son is the agent of creation and assumed humanity's created nature (Col 1:16; John 1:1–14), moral theorizing as a created ability is christologically framed.

This being so, christological moral reasoning is an example of the consistent application of a control belief beyond its "placing" by classical and secular moral reasoning. In particular, the *lordship* of Christ comports well with the concept of a *control* belief, as both terms imply determination over other powers. Thus while christological moral reasoning is found in socially sectarian Christianity, it is a form of universal moral reasoning due to the universal claims of Christ's lordship. Conversely then, non-christological forms of Christian moral reasoning are theologically sectarian, as they elevate a non-christological norm or entity (e.g., "orders") to the status of control belief in moral reasoning.[44]

One tendency of universal moral reasoning is its transformation into an ontotheology by projecting ideal human ontology, and the dominant

---

43. Ingraffia, *Postmodern Theory*, 6: Because "God . . . fixes human meaning," the Son's incarnation means that non-christological practices cannot express true moral meaning.

44. E.g., Kantian ethics derives from the person of Kant, and "not everyone believes in Kant."

social *mythos* or *nomos*, onto a previously inchoate concept of God. This includes the negative theology of atheist ethics.[45] The christological control belief of Anabaptism was a conscious attempt to strip the legitimacy of such reasoning, and also typifies Barth. The Son is explicit in his incarnation, in contrast to the Father who is inchoate and implicit in creation, and the Spirit who becomes inchoate in mysticism. This explicitness, because it is embedded in a set of actual historical life practices, provides concrete content to theology and ethics, whereas the inchoate moral content of classical moral reasoning's concept of God readily provides space for non-christological moral reasoning to displace Christ as its norming center.

b. Practice or Reason as a Basis for Ethics

If Jesus' life can legitimately function as a normative ethical model, then specific personal *practices* possess universal moral claims in their embodied sociality. In the standard model of ethical theory, personal *rationality* serves the same basis. In both instances, the origin lies with a person, either their whole life practices, or reasoning. The classical model tends to privilege reasoning over practices, whereas the Anabaptist tends to privilege practices over reasoning, or the coordination of both. Thus "the legitimate human concern for rationality is framed by a range of powers of quite another order. It is this larger contingent context which narrative is designed to order in the only manner available to us."[46] Christological moral reasoning places reason within the bounds of christologically exemplified practices.

Consequently, if practical moral reasoning is not embodied in the practices that lie internal to such reasoning, such reasoning loses its ethical character, because ethics deals with practices and actions. To know the good but fail to do it is hypocritical. If theoretical reasoning establishes the proper *telos* of life, and practical moral reasoning establishes the *means* appropriate to that end, not only are both forms of reasoning united, but the practicing of those means (as distinction from articulating those means) is necessary to establish the theory's validity, because only in such practices is a human model of the theory found. The life gives shape to the theory, enabling its assessment. Hauerwas goes further: if human witness to God were unnecessary, Christian theological claims would be incapable of evidential

---

45. Ingraffia, *Postmodern Theory*, 241.

46. Hauerwas with Burrell, "From System to Story: An Alternative Pattern for Rationality in Ethics," in Hauerwas, *Truthfulness and Tragedy*, 26–27. McClendon, *Ethics*, 105, locates virtues in communal practices and stories, and Smith, *Desiring the Kingdom*, in social liturgy, 133–154.

support.[47] As an unlivable moral theory is incoherent, so too is a theology that does not require human testimony, for only in a life lived can theologico-ethical claims be evidentially supported and demonstrated. However, a good practice may exist without an articulated true theory, being performed due to convention, tradition or some other non-cognitive reason. This does not detract from the moral status of the practices. Yet because theoretical and practical moral reasoning are united, claiming truthfulness for a theory is itself a moral practice for it implies a criticism of the contested truthfulness of rival theories of the good. A moral theory itself is a moral claim: the true and the good are ineradicably connected.

Consequently, ethical theory possesses no status that safeguards it from practical and ethical, as well as rational or philosophical, criticism. Hence moral reasoning—say in the tradition of Kant, where the rational will possesses determinative status—is no more defensible than moral reasoning where the concrete practices of an individual life possess determinative status. Both may be rationally explained as well as ethically lived. Furthermore, both reasoning and practices are personal and ethical acts, one located in cognition and reason, the other in sociality and concrete acts. Thus to argue that a reasoned ethical theory possesses greater weight as a groundwork or justification for ethics than a life of ethical practices is unjustified, for both the theory and the acts are personal practices. Human reasoning, as an intellectual/cognitive act, is itself a subset of the category of practice.

Therefore, exemplarist christological ethics is not naïve or philosophically indefensible, as though Christ's ethical normativeness is reducible to volitional acknowledgment by persons attracted to his life practices. If so, rational ethical theory is equally indefensible, for the ethical normativeness of one theorist's moral reasoning is likewise reducible to volitional acknowledgement by persons who happen to find that theory interesting or convincing. Others may not. If a rationally grounded ethical theory is unpracticed by its author, the theorist's moral authority and the theory's rationality and moral weight are diminished. But the reverse is not the case: a consistently enacted set of moral practices that are unable to be rationally explained does not weaken the moral status of the practice in question, even though it does indicate the rational inadequacy of the agent.

In this regard, the christological moral reasoning of Anabaptism affirms Jesus' life as a coherent, consistent and defensible moral practice, coordinate with his teaching. Because early Anabaptists considered the

---

47. Hauerwas, *With the Grain*, 212, n. 12. Citing Barth, Hauerwas suggests that natural theology is a witness to and derived from the greater concerns of revelation, 146. This places him with McGrath as noted in Part One.

Reformers primarily to be theoretical religious thinkers lacking practical obedience, their theology was seen as inadequate.[48] Swiss Anabaptist Christology was "chiefly concerned that Christ be obeyed," both as human but also as risen, even though "Sattler once referred to Christ as the 'of one essence *[eingewesen = homoousios]* true God and Savior.'"[49] Such privileging of Jesus' practices over the practices of others has various justifications: his identity as the incarnate divine Son, his status as Lord, the perfection of his moral life, his ontological status as the perfect human, or his vindication through resurrection. "The Lord of Christian morality is not a principle or an ideal goal or *telos*, but a person whose timely life confronts our stories with his own."[50]

c. The Particular and the Universal

Lessing and Kant typify the Enlightenment concern for the universal, which reduces history to "accidental" events unable to justify rational truth, and where the person's will is valid only if it embodies "a universal law." Because history deals with singular events, it is assumed that historically localized moral acts are antithetical to universal, rational, ethical law, resulting in "an unhistorical account of the moral life."[51] Lessing and Kant express a type of scientifically positivist ethics that purports to discern universal or repeatable patterns which, it is argued, form the only bases of truth, and as such enable predictable futures and right actions. But such universalism disengages persons from their spatio-temporal identity as "a father, a mother, a soldier, or a student,"[52] in the name of universal abstract reason, alienating them from their own decision making by the constraints of publicly determined moral discourse that at any particular moment claims universal assent. The Kantian "Moral Point of View" leads to a "noumenal self . . . without any history" and an "atomistic moral psychology."[53] Kant's objectivist imperative

---

48. Friedmann, *Theology of Anabaptism*, 20.

49. Finger, *Anabaptist Theology*, 367, citing Sattler, *Legacy*, 63.

50. McClendon, *Ethics*, 332. He appropriates MacIntyre's social concept of practice, 166.

51. Katongole, *Beyond Universal Reason*, 29.

52. Ibid., 23, derived from Hauerwas and Burrell, "From System to Story," in *Truthfulness and Tragedy*, 17.

53. Katongole, *Beyond Universal Reason*, 23. Katongole supplements the Moral Point of View with Kant's "Categorical Imperative, Universalizability, Ideal Observer and the View from Nowhere," 32.

is also seen in Descartes's ethics, which is disengaged from the concrete realities of the world.[54]

Once reason was disengaged from history, ethics emerged as a discrete academic discipline, devoid of theology.[55] Kant's uncoupling of the phenomenal subject from the noumenal object, the bifurcation of faith and doctrine, and the subjective displacement of the objective, meant that Christianity was increasingly defined as a moral system without dogmatic determination. By extruding Christian morality from its narrative context, Kant's universal ethic was purchased at the cost of its theological grounding. Consequently, his volitional/categorical imperative appears to hang in thin air like a new Platonic Form or Stoic Eternal Reason.[56] This allowed Christianity to "be included without remainder in the wider wisdom" of the world, for the remainder—that is, its dogmatic determination—had been eliminated.[57] As a unique discipline, ethics was detached from real objects and the order of things, and became teleologically empty.[58] Like Christianity generally, ethics was "placed" by universal secular reason, itself no longer capable of placing other disciplines or believing itself to be a metadiscourse.[59] This Enlightenment project failed because it kept the classical moral language but emptied it of its classical content.[60] Such self-referential moral canons are legitimized within each distinct sphere of human action, so that "every calling is its own norm," rather than Christ, who no longer exercises any reforming or reframing role.[61] Such a theologically stripped view of ethics has been described as a sinful form of moral self-determination.[62]

The thesis is increasingly held that universal reason's repudiation of history and particulars, which appears so natural in contemporary secularism, is itself a particularist viewpoint emerging from the European

---

54. Taylor, *Sources of the Self*, 155. "The standard account" makes "alienation the central moral virtue," Hauerwas and Burrell, "From System to Story," in *Truthfulness and Tragedy*, 23.

55. MacIntyre, *After Virtue*, 39, dating it between 1630 and 1850.

56. See Hauerwas, *Peaceable Kingdom*, 22–24, regarding narrative stripping.

57. Yoder, "Why Ecclesiology is Social Ethics: Gospel Ethics Verses the Wider Wisdom," in *Royal Priesthood*, 111.

58. Katongole, *Beyond Universal Reason*, 25.

59. Milbank, *Theology and Social Theory*, 1.

60. MacIntyre, *After Virtue*, ch. 5. When the matter is eliminated, the form intrinsic to that matter necessarily collapses.

61. Yoder, *Priestly Kingdom* 59.

62. Barth, *CD*, II/2, 518, and Bonhoeffer, *Ethics*, 18. Barth's assessment is explored in detail in Part Three.

Enlightenment.⁶³ Nonetheless, the modern quest for the universal is still the basic form of attack upon christological ethics as sectarian.⁶⁴ This attack is historically disabled, however, because all ethical theory is traced, not to abstract pre-existing ideas, but to theories of the right and the good propounded by historical persons, such as Plato, Aristotle, or Jesus. Thus the negation of christological ethics as sectarian, due to its historically anchored origin in Jesus, is equally applicable to Aristotelianism, unless one can show that Aristotelian ethics is traceable not to him historically but to the pre-existent truth of which he is no more than a cipher. Consequently, if one can negate Christian ethics on the basis of being non-Christian, one can equally negate Aristotelian ethics on the basis of being non-Aristotelian, regardless of the rightness or truthfulness of their ethical reasoning. The negation of christological ethics on grounds of the primacy of universality is unjustified unless applied to all ethical theorists.

On the other hand, post-Enlightenment rationality's affirmation of the particular circumscribes or denies universal claims. Each particular is granted its historical-cultural autonomy and integrity by limiting its claim to that particular spatio-historic location. Innumerable particular minor-narratives are thus placed and circumscribed. Such limitations are determined, however, not from within the rationality inherent in the minor-narratives themselves, but imposed from without, constituting the external rationality as either a meta-narrative, or the illegitimate hegemony of an arrogant minor-narrative, thus being incoherent with its own claims. The claim that universal claims are chimeras is thus either an illegitimate claim of a minor-narrative beyond its assigned spatio-historical location, or a legitimate claim of a meta-narrative, whose existence has been denied, and is thus self-contradictory.

However, it is the nature of truth-claims to be universal simply because truth is a universal category. Strict dualistic reasoning disfigures the relation between the good and the true, because moral claims about the good presuppose theoretical claims about the true. Moral claims amount

---

63. Katongole, *Beyond Universal Reason*, 21. Because science deals with repetitions and universals, and history with singular and particular events, scientific modernism spurned history. The historical location of this move is variously ascribed: for Katongole it is post-reformation European conflict and the emergence of nation-states; for Milbank, it is late-Medieval nominalism, the Protestant Reformation and seventeenth century Augustinianism, *Theology and Social Theory*, 10. For MacIntyre it is Descartes (in "Epistemological Crises, Narrative, and Philosophy of Science," in Hauerwas and Jones, *Why Narrative?*, 138–57), and Kierkegaard, Kant, and Hume (in *After Virtue*, 36–50).

64. Yoder, "Why Ecclesiology is Social Ethics," in *Royal Priesthood*, 111–13.

to truth claims in and of themselves, simply because the good and the right are grounded in the true. Moral claims do not have to conform to external referents such as reason or passion or will. Thus the assertion that christological ethical claims are universal is due to them being simply Jesus' claims, not by their correspondence to any external universal form of being, substance, obligation, right, or good, even though such appeals may constitute aspects of their justification. Thus *particular* persons and their moral claims are capable of bearing *universal* intent. This provides an alternative to any form of dualistic metaphysics, such as Aristotle's, that locates the essential "I" beyond the historical person, and to which the latter must conform to be regarded as rational or universally true.[65]

In respect to the place of universal moral truth, it is worth considering Yoder more extensively. He appears to place Christ's lordship as the basis of the universal claims of his ecclesially located christological ethics.[66] Three traditional claims to Christian universalism are dismissed as leading to three basic miscalculations. First, Constantinianism locates the meaning of history in society, which the church attempts to christologically shape despite Constantinianism's absence of Christian confession and practice. Second, Spiritualism places the locus of universal meaning in the spirit, thus averting social conflict and enabling universally unobjectionable inwardness. Third, Gnosticism dissolves particulars into non-material metaphysics in an attempt to safeguard their undifferentiated essence.[67] Constantinianism denies the inner spirit, Spiritualism denies outward society, and Gnosticism denies their co-inherence. All display dualistic metaphysics, whereas in the believers' church the inner spiritual reality and the external forms and structures "which are expressive of the character of the disciples' fellowship" co-inhere.[68] It is this fellowship that is the locus of history due to Christ's indwelling, as he is the Lord of history. Consequently, Yoder denies that Christian identity can be found outside the concrete community of the

65. Katongole, *Beyond Universal Reason*, 36.

66. If Reimer, *Mennonites and Classical*, 247–71, and Martens, *Heterodox*, 145–146 are correct about Yoder's historicist reduction of Jesus, lordship becomes a political term. Yet *kurios* has a surplus of meaning more than just political in Hellenism, Emperor worship, the LXX, and the New Testament. The ecclesial location of Yoder's christological ethics is critical, and demonstrates the importance of historically embodied practices in his understanding of ethics; see "Why Ecclesiology is Social Ethics," in *Royal Priesthood*, 102–126.

67. Yoder, "A People in the World," 71–72, and "Ecclesiology is Social Ethics," 108–11, in *Royal Priesthood*.

68. Yoder, "People in the World," in *Royal Priesthood*, 72. Reimer, *Mennonites and Classical*, 252, sees Constantinianism as exhibiting "neoplatonic dualism between invisible and visible worldliness."

church, for the church is the only post-resurrection locus of the unity of the inner and the outer, the essence and the actual, the material and the formal, the spiritual and moral existence; that is, Christ the Lord in his people.

Nonetheless, the status of the universal appears ambiguous. Yoder affirms a universal basis of christological moral reasoning in Christ's lordship, yet disavows the universal *per se* with three arguments. First it is dismissed merely as the "the wider world." Second, arguing from anti-foundationalist coherentism, christological reasoning is simply unconcerned about external verification.[69] Third, the form of universal reasoning found in Christian traditions that cite created orders, "station" and vocation, culture, or reason and nature, is described as a psychological defense against the critical impact Jesus.[70] All seek to minimize the effect of Jesus and therefore reject the biblical narrative of election, where God narrows humanity to particular servants—Israel and the church—in contrast with primal religion that sacralizes the entire tribe.[71]

Consequently Yoder dismisses six adaptive strategies for relating Christian ethics to the universal sphere: isolationist fidelity, capitulation and conversion, enlightened pedagogy, apology, adoption of the public metalanguage, and humble fidelity. All six strategies affirm "the priority in truth and value of the meaning system of the world claiming to be wider," which Yoder maintains is itself spatio-temporally provincial.[72] Five New Testament texts dealing with cosmological universals are cited (John 1:1–14; Heb 2:8–9; Colossians; Rev 4:1–5:4 and Philippians 2) as providing methodological warrants for his stance. Each of these texts demonstrate identical christological moves that establish that God's rule, not "the world, culture, [or] civilization . . . is the definitional category." Despite arguing that the universal is a Graeco-Roman "illusion" and that pluralism and relativism is how the world always was and is, Christ's lordship is affirmed, and what "could be more universal than that?"[73] Readers may here be left wonder-

---

69. Yoder, "Ecclesiology is Social Ethics," in *Royal Priesthood*, 113.

70. Ibid. Yoder's term for universal reason is "wider wisdom."

71. Ibid., 114.

72. Yoder, "'But We Do See Jesus': The Particularity of the Incarnation and the Universality of Truth," in *Priestly Kingdom*, 49. First published 1983, sixteen years later than "People in the World." Nation describes this as the "key essay" of the collection, *Yoder*, 56.

73. Yoder, "'But We Do See Jesus,'" in *Priestly Kingdom*, 59. Hauerwas and Burrell place the origin of universal claims later, in Comte's evolutionary theory (from story to metaphysical philosophy to science), itself located within Hegel's historical idealism, "From System to Story," in *Truthfulness and Tragedy*, 25. Spohn refers to Jesus as the "concrete universal," *Go and Do Likewise*, 64.

ing whether Yoder affirms Christ's universal lordship to be real, or merely a strategic New Testament claim, although the former appears to be the case when he affirms that lordship language was the language of deity for the first Christians.[74]

Whatever the case, Christ as universal Lord does not lead to violence, because his commands on enemy love and non-coercion sanction space for unbelief.[75] This contrasts with coercive universalism's establishment *mythos,* including the *mythos* of Constantinian Christianity, which obscures or destroys all particularism and relativism.[76] Thus when Christian ethical reasoning enters any ideological territory, it is the ordinariness of Jesus' humanity, not coercion, that constitutes the "warrant for the generalizablity of his reconciliation."[77] Thus *non-coercive* universal claims of particular moral reasoning legitimize unbelief and *de facto* pluralism and relativism with their divergent universal moral claims.

So does Yoder accept a universal? It is hard to deny that he does, yet it is historically particularist, christological, and legitimizes pluralism. Similar is McClendon: "There is no universal agreement, but only competing claims to universality, one of which is our own."[78] Thoroughgoing christological moral reasoning functions as Yoder's universal reasoning, and will be taken up in the main section of this thesis concerning Chalcedonian Christology. Nonetheless, Yoder's lordship Christology is his ground for dismissing universal claims as illegitimate mythic claims by particular "lordless powers."[79]

However, his earlier *Politics of Jesus* cites Nicene and Chalcedonian christological categories and thus possesses deeper theological resources: if

---

74. Yoder, *Preface to Theology,* 72.

75. In relation to violent nihilism, theology as a master discourse "alone, remains the discourse of non-mastery," Milbank, *Theology and Social Theory,* 6. He argues that the Reformation's displacement of love by faith is "the *gravest imaginable* heresy," in Milbank, "Alternative Protestantism. Radical Orthodoxy and the Reformed Tradition," in Smith and Olthuis, *Radical Orthodoxy,* 33, italics original. Milbank overstates the case, unless it can be shown that post-Reformation history is more violent that its predecessor, and that such violence originated in *sola fide.*

76. Yoder, "'But We Do See Jesus,'" in *Priestly Kingdom,* 59–60. Contrast Gunton, *The One, the Three and the Many,* 106–107, who traces relativism's earliest origins to Protagoras's theory of agnosticism: "the general meaning of Protagoras' . . . [is] that what appears to each individual is the only reality," quoting Guthrie. However, Gunton locates modern relativism in the "rebellion against authoritarian theological homogenisation of culture" where "the Parmenidean God of Christendom is replaced by the dispersed Heraclitean deity of individual human judgment," 122.

77. Yoder, "'But We Do See Jesus,'" in *Priestly Kingdom,* 62.

78. McClendon, *Doctrine,* 43.

79. Barth's term: Barth, *Christian Life,* 213–233.

Jesus is not authoritative and normative, two-nature Christology collapses into either Ebionism (which neglects his divinity) or Gnosticism (which dismisses his humanity).[80] Yet because this is never extensively developed, Yoder is criticized for reducing classical Christology to idealism, or more specifically, to politics.[81] The paradox is that Arian Christology, which critics see as a tendency in Yoder, also possesses no *human* ethical norm, because when the theological universal is deleted from Jesus' particular humanity, the result is merely particularized sage-ethics. This occurs in Ritschl's moral prototype Christology, where Christ's perfection is his "complete dedication to his vocation," or Kant's Christ as the personification of his "ideal of [deontological] moral perfection."[82] By denying Jesus' divinity, Arianism functionally transforms Jesus into a cipher, or an example of the apex of the moral perfection of the *mythos* or *nomos*. Divine-human Christology becomes ideal-human Christology: Jesus' humanity is swallowed by idealism with the awkward aspects of his life textually, historically, or strategically eliminated.[83]

Thus Yoder's consistent focus on Jesus' ordinariness leaves a question mark hanging over the theological character of Jesus' universal claims. While the universal *claim* is clearly stated, the theological *reality* behind the claim appears muted, although not denied.[84] Yet if the humanity of Jesus is not understood within the traditional anhypostatic/enhypostatic couplet that prioritizes the divine person of the Son, Christ's human nature is necessarily joined to its own human hypostasis. This drives out the divine person of the eternal Son as the driving force of Jesus' humanity, so that his humanity becomes self-subsisting within its own hypostasis. The an/enhypostasis couplet is meant to preserve the priority of the pre-incarnate existence of the person and nature of the divine eternal Son, who alone is the hypostatic basis for the humanity of Jesus. Jesus' humanity exists only enhypostatically with the person of the Son. If this is lost, four results may follow. First, the divine Word either enters into a pre-existing person, resulting in two hypostases and two natures. Second and more commonly, the Word adopts the already existing person of Jesus. Third, Jesus somehow absorbs the divine nature, resulting in a form of human monophysitism. Fourth, the divine

80. Yoder, *Politics*, 22. This is maintained later in *Preface to Theology*, 202.

81. Reimer, *Mennonites and Classical*, 273, and Martens, *Heterodox*, 3–4, 70, 145–146.

82. Pannenberg, *Jesus—God and Man*, 44–45.

83. Bonhoeffer, *Christology*, 83–84.

84. While defending the difference between language and substance in classical Christology, and its strategic appropriateness, he criticizes its narrative stripping character, Yoder, *Preface to Theology*, 202.

person and nature are simply lost. None of these comport with orthodox Christology.

While these outcomes are not explicit in Yoder, his focus on Jesus' ordinariness needs to be strengthened by a more vigorous Chalcedonian Christology which foregrounds Jesus' divine nature. This would enable a more robust claim to moral realism and provide a greater basis for the universality of christological moral reasoning, and is developed in Part Three.

d. Essentialism

Essentialism was widespread in the Medieval and Reformation periods, and supplied the logic for Spiritualist, Reformation, and Catholic objections to radical ethics.[85] Anabaptist leaders such as Hubmaier were familiar with such metaphysics through their prior training for the priesthood. Anabaptism's rejection of essentialism is seen in its treatment of baptism, ecclesiology, regeneration, and *sola fide*.

The Anabaptist rejection of paedo-baptism was due to their insistence that inward grace cannot be separated from the outward life of faith, of which infants are incapable. Their rejection of the invisible church (required by Reformation and Catholic territorialism) was similar: the visible church was the spiritual church composed of the regenerate. Their doctrine of regeneration opposed both the Spiritualists' claim to internal essence/experience devoid of external practices such as baptism and communion, and the Catholic doctrine of internal baptismal regeneration devoid of external spiritual life. Finally, Luther's *sola fide* was questioned as it implied a change of legal status without any ontological change or outward renewal.[86]

Radical ethics' rejection of essentialism's dualism was due not so much to philosophical considerations, but to reasoning out of the New Testament texts. Such biblicism produced its own form of dualism where the two kingdoms of the world and Christ were opposed. Radicals considered that essentialism permitted external Christian forms or doctrine to harmoniously co-exist with, or justify, sub-Christian morality: *sola fide* did not appear to improve ethical life in Lutheran territories, despite the transformative

---

85. "A metaphysical theory that objects have essences and that there is a distinction between essential and non-essential or accidental predications," Michael J. Loux, "essentialism" [sic] in Audi, *Cambridge Dictionary of Philosophy*, 241.

86. Noted above in Simons. Luther strongly advocated brotherly love in "Lectures on the Epistle to the Hebrews. 1517–1518," *Early Theological Works*, 242, and good works in "The Freedom of a Christian," *Three Treatises*, 297. Despite such advocacy, the Reformer's violence voided their theology in Anabaptist eyes.

power of Luther's doctrine of vocation; paedo-baptism declared an ontological change without ethical evidence; territorial Christianity legitimized unregenerate "Christian" immorality by minimizing Christ's commands; and Spiritualism neglected love, social obligation and sacramental obedience in favor of inwardness. By rejecting essentialism, Anabaptism insisted on the integration of the true and right, the inner and outer, theoretical and practical reasoning, the spiritual and the embodied, and that the union of Jesus' divine and human nature together consist in the one personal center of theology and ethics.

3. Conclusion

This chapter has argued that the centrality of Christology in Anabaptism and radicalism is seen in at least five key areas. First, it decisively prioritizes the New Testament over the Old. Second, it acts as an explicit control belief. Third, it expresses a coherent set of concrete practices. Fourth, it asserts that these practices, although particular to Jesus, possess universal significance. Finally, it disavows essentialism's metaphysical dualism in favor of the congruence between form and substance.

This christological determination of ethics generally sits uneasily with natural law's moral reasoning. Whereas the former is christologically muted, radicalism is christologically robust. And despite having a preference for the language of lordship, which implies universality, christological moral reasoning tends to be dismissed as sectarian and socially inadequate. Its historical association with a gathered and somewhat exclusionary ecclesiology contributes to this, as seen in both Anabaptist and monastic forms. In this respect, the strong social character of Barth's Chalcedonian Christology enables a more universal Christology that unites the universal concerns of natural law and the christological concerns of radicalism in the one person of Jesus.[87]

---

87. Is Barth's lack of ecclesiology only apparent and hidden underneath the entire matter of the *Church Dogmatics,* which is an extended articulation of proper Christian speech within the church? This would make the *CD* an ecclesial witness, in triune form, to the triune God. The first words of the *CD* describe dogmatics as "the *scientific self-examination of the Christian Church* with respect to the content of its distinctive talk about God," *CD,* 1/1, 3, italics added. The criticism that the *CD* is ecclesially thin is not altogether true: IV/1, §62, IV/2, §67 and IV/3.2, §72 are all explicitly ecclesial. Barth states that "Man will be true man [and] ... realise his humanity ... [in] existence within the community," i.e., church, IV/3.2, 811. Such a community is the subject of gospel witness, i.e., where christocentric speech occurs, 801–12.

The five areas considered in this chapter are all evident in early Anabaptist Confessions, as well as in contemporary christo-ethical radical arguments against mainstream theological moral reasoning. The following chapter examines some early Anabaptist confessions before exploring and describing how such christological moral reasoning functions in respect to a number of basic theological categories.

4

Historical, Confessional and Ethical Considerations

1. Exemplarist Christology In Early Anabaptist Confessions[1]

THIS SECTION EXAMINES THE fourteen texts in *The Confessions of Faith in the Anabaptist Tradition 1527–1660* in an attempt to demonstrate the ethical nature of radical Christianity.[2] Sections of these confessions will be quoted when the example of Jesus is put forward as the basis for moral actions or dispositions. The citing of later interpreters is meant to demonstrate that the moral shape of such confessions perdures through time, and as such constitutes a theological tradition. The citations of Barth demonstrate how this tradition has spilled over confessional boundaries, and anticipates the greater treatment of Barth later. What is particularly noted in the early Anabaptist confessions is how the life of Jesus functions as an ethical norm. Such an approach a) denies the ethical inertness of theology, and b) reasons ethically out of the life of Jesus rather than out of universal concepts such as the good or the right.

---

1. The uncontroversial taxonomy and nomenclature of G. H. Williams, *The Radical Reformation*, (Philadelphia, PA: The Westminster Press, MCMLXII) is adopted. Representatives of his threefold classification are: of the Evangelical Rationalists, Servetus; of the Spiritualists, Schwenckfeld; of the Evangelical Anabaptists, Grebel, Marpeck, Sattler and Simons. The latter group is the concern here.

2. This is a non-exhaustive yet representative collection from north and northwestern Europe.

Contrary to standard criticism, these confessions display classical orthodoxy in the following five areas.³ First, the classical creeds:⁴ the *Confession of Faith* by Jörg Maler of 1554 commences with an extended exposition of the Apostles Creed, while the *Swiss Brethren Confession of Hesse* (1578), the *Thirty Three Articles* (1617), the *Dordrecht Confession* (1632), and the *Prussian Confession* (1660)⁵ all contain explicit echoes of either or both the Apostles and Nicene Creeds in their articles on the Father, Son, and Holy Spirit. Second, ten of the confessions are explicitly trinitarian.⁶ Third, traditional two-nature Christology is affirmed or assumed in eleven of the confessions. Fourth, a substitutionary or representative model of atonement through the death of Christ is explicit in eight confessions. Fifth, the threefold christological office is affirmed in *The Short Confession* (1610), the *Swiss Brethren Confession of Hesse* (1578), and *The Confession of Jans Cents* (1630). Of these five affirmations, trinitarianism in particular warrants Anabaptism as orthodox, as trinitarianism is the defining characteristic of Christian orthodoxy.⁷ The dismissal of Anabaptism as sub-Christian due to alleged Spiritualism mistakenly implies that theories of revelation and inspiration are orthodox-defining criteria, yet such theories are absent from the orthodox-defining ecumenical creeds.⁸ Yet while this orthodoxy locates

---

3. The standard account, which dismissed all sixteenth century Christian radicalism, has been revised due to latter twentieth century English publications of their original works. The old historiography, which still persists, dismissed Anabaptism due to Luther's mistaken identification of it with the *Schwärmer*. Münster was a violent Spiritualist aberration, not an Anabaptist event.

4. "Confidence about the importance of the Apostle's Creed appears to have been widely present in most Anabaptist circles, and producing commentaries on the basis of the Creed was not uncommon," Koop, *Confessions*, 36. "As to the basic doctrines of Christianity . . . they were orthodox, teaching nothing foreign to the Apostle's Creed," Robert Friedmann, "The Doctrine of the Two Worlds," in Hershberger, *Recovery*, 105. The baptismal article of Hubmaier's "A Christian Catechism" (1526) refers to both the Apostles and Nicene Creed: "This is the understanding and decision Christianly issued by the Nicene Council . . . I acknowledge one baptism for the remission of sins." An interrogative form of the Apostle's Creed is included in "A Form of Water Baptism" (1527) in Hubmaier, *Balthasar Hubmaier*, 351, 389.

5. Koop, *Confessions*, 35–44, 47–92, 169–265, 288–310, 314–30, respectively.

6. The most explicit is *The Concept of Cologne* (1591), *Confessions*, 119. The other four neither refer to nor deny the classic doctrine of God.

7. Torrance, *Trinitarian Faith*, 5.

8. If anything, the solitary Nicene third-article affirmation of revelation, "He has spoken through the prophets," possesses a spiritual (not Spiritualist) sense, not a second article *logos* sense, although it would be wrong to fracture the creed's unity by opposing the two.

Anabaptism within the classical tradition, its essential distinctiveness lies elsewhere, in the fields of ecclesiology, ethics, and discipleship.[9]

In contrast with non-Anabaptist confessions, these statements include ethical articles. Formally articled subjects include possessions, mutual admonition, church discipline, diet, politics and government, oaths, marriage, divorce, raising and educating children, alms, work, wealth and usury, clothing, virtue, good works, foot washing, defense and war, and vengeance. This inclusion of ethics in theological confessions constitutes Anabaptist theology as tripolar,[10] and has various explanations: apologetic, catechetical, judicial,[11] or ecclesial.[12] However, these circumstances were not unique to Anabaptism, which suggests that their inclusion was intrinsic to their theology, and were debated for their own sake.[13] Such supplementing of confessional classical orthodoxy with ethical articles demonstrates a concern not only for "logical coherence . . . or doctrinal orthodoxy" but also shows a fundamentally critical attitude to received credal theology, which is considered inadequate to produce true faith by itself.[14]

Incarnational exemplarist Christology clusters around a number of themes. The following are cited from Koop's *Confessions*:

1. Suffering and Persecution.

    a. Whoever will live a sanctified life in Christ must suffer persecution and tribulation . . . Therefore hold fast to the comforting assurance of Christ, your Savior (who also took this path), 43.

    b. Those born of Christ reject all that is visible, customary and transitory in the world, and follow him to the cross where there is oppression, scorn and suffering, as Christ himself speaks and testifies, 100f.

---

9. Denny Weaver affirms sixteenth century Anabaptist orthodoxy yet argues that their ecclesial innovation "which emerged out of a renewed emphasis on Jesus' life and teaching as normative," is their distinctive mark, Denny Weaver, *Anabaptist Theology*, 106.

10. Augsburger, *Dissident Discipleship*, 7–22, develops a threefold spiritual taxonomy of tripolarity (God, self, neighbor), bipolarity (God and self), and monopolarity (self).

11. Not unlike the apologetic, but written explicitly for forensic proceedings.

12. As in The Schleitheim Confession, Sattler, *Legacy*, 35.

13. Yoder, "Radical Reformation Ethics," in *Priestly Kingdom*, 108.

14. Biesecker-Mast, *Separation*, 138, 238, where he describes these confessions as extraorthodox rhetorics. This is not necessarily anti-credal, but extra-credal.

c. Because of these people we must suffer, and also carry all disgrace to our deaths in the same way as our master, Jesus Christ, has gone before us in all suffering, 107.
   d. Concerning the life, suffering, death, resurrection and ascension of Jesus Christ . . . it is confessed that when the Lord Jesus was humiliated in the flesh . . . he set himself up as a holy, divine example for us, 209f.

2. State Authorities, Government, and Defence.
   a. The weapon of the faithful . . . is alone the . . . saving word of God. We take this on in faith . . . and fight with it against the enemy of our souls . . . who with false teaching and human wisdom want to direct us away from Christ and his holy word of life, 107.
   b. With a continuing voice from heaven, they are called to follow his nonresistant life and cross-bearing footsteps for which there is no evidence of worldly government, power or sword, 154.
   c. On the contrary [Christ] urged them to follow the footsteps of his life bearing the cross without weapons, 278.
   d. From this we understand that following the example, life and doctrine of Christ, we may not cause offense or suffering but should seek to promote the welfare and happiness of others, 304.
   e. For this reason you have been called as Christ also suffered for us and left us an example that we are to follow in his footsteps, 326.

3. Foot washing.
   a. Also [we confess] that [all will] receive proper Christian love . . . according to the example of Christ, 133.
   b. When our fellow believers come to visit us . . . we wash their feet according to . . . [the] example of Christ, 277.
   c. We also confess a washing of the saints' feet just as the Lord Jesus instituted and commanded but also exemplified, 302.
   d. We confess that foot washing among the believers is an ordinance of Christ, which he demonstrated among his disciples as an example that is to be followed . . . and that by his example of profound humility we also are to be truly meek and humble toward each other, 322.

4. Regeneration.

HISTORICAL, CONFESSIONAL AND ETHICAL CONSIDERATIONS 95

   a. The new birth is not an empty or hidden thing but requires a new walk and following after Christ, 198.

5. The Christian Life Generally.

   a. We have diligently examined the holy Scriptures, of the prophets, of Christ and his apostles, and have taken cognizance of their teaching, life and behavior, their order [Ordnung], practice and commandments, 50.

   b. We have discussed our apprehensions concerning the growing inclination of the merchant class toward temporal greed and the vanity of ostentatious clothing, which imitate the world rather than displaying the humility of Christ, 121f.

   c. They cause innocent and unlearned persons—who regrettably are more impressed by men of today than by the teaching and life of our Savior Jesus Christ and his beloved apostles—to shy and turn away from it, 289

   d. In order to save us he ... in his human form lived holy and perfect before us, setting us a perfect example, teaching and confirming his teaching with divine miracles, 160.

6. Ecclesiology.

   a. The church of God is known by her character ... putting on the true character of the love of Christ ... They should learn from him how to be humble and meek of heart ... since he, as a humble lamb, did not open his mouth ... And showing himself among his own as a servant ... [in] the same way the members of Christ must learn from him and serve one another out of love, 217f.

7. Baptism and Communion.

   a. Just as Christ ... along with his holy apostles ... neither taught, wrote nor exercised the false practice of child-baptism, 99.

   b. Christ has neither given nor commanded anyone to practice this holy Supper except to his holy and dear disciples alone ... [who] have followed after him the way of the cross, 99.

8. Preaching and Church Teaching.

   a. The doctrine taught by ordained servants ... is the same as Jesus brought from heaven, which he taught by Word and deed (that is, with life and teaching), 151.

9. Oaths.

a. Christ . . . being the only law giver . . . has entirely abolished and forbidden all aforementioned swearing of oaths . . . The high apostles of Christ . . . have also followed the teaching of Christ in this. For this reason, all believers are responsible to follow obediently after this teaching of Christ and the example of the apostles, 239f.

Four observations are noted: First, in traditional nomenclature, exemplarist christological ethics is grounded in both the active (1. c, d) and passive obedience (1. b, d) of Christ.[15] Second, exemplarism is expressed in the *peripateō* language of the New Testament (2. b, c, e; 4. a).[16] Third, exemplarism is identical to conversion and regeneration (4. a).[17] Fourth, exemplarism is christological *phronēsis* (3. c, d).[18] Despite this ethical emphasis, the theological content of these confessions as well as their formal structure reflects the classical Western theological tradition. Exemplarist christological ethics is thus not incompatible either formally or materially with the majority tradition, yet its inclusion in the confessions elevates it to normative status. As such, this inclusion speaks into the ethical silence found in the creeds through their omission of Jesus' life between his birth by Mary and suffering under Pilate.[19]

Interpreters of the tradition also draw out the ethical implications from the more explicit theological articles in these statements, demonstrating the intrinsic ethical dimension of theology. This shows that such Christianity was not theologically pedestrian, simply adding ethical articles to otherwise unchanged theological traditions.[20] There are at least two aspects of their confessional re-working that bear this out: first, the orthodox theological statements are creatively appropriated and re-worked as rationales for their ethics; and second, the ethical inclusions imply that orthodox belief is not in itself a test of true faith. For instance, Riedemann's re-working of

---

15. Soteriology is also thus grounded: Philips, "Concerning the New Birth," in *Early Anabaptist Spirituality*, 201.

16. John 6:66; Romans 8:1; Ephesians 2:2, 5:2; Colossians 3:7; Philippians 3:18; 1 John 1:7, 2:6; 2 John 6. Also, "By this counsel we are all taught [to] . . . follow His footsteps," Simons, "The New Birth," in *Complete Writings*, 92, 100.

17. "All those . . . born of God . . . follow the example of Christ," Ibid., 93.

18. "We are all taught [to] . . . be of the same mind as Christ . . . and follow Him," Ibid., 101.

19. The ethical silence of the creeds is particularly unusual because post-Apostolic writings are replete with moral debates both within and beyond the church. For instance sections 2–6 of *The Didache* deal primarily with moral concerns, Lightfoot, *Didache*. On the creeds' omission of Jesus' life, see Moltmann, *Way of Jesus Christ*, 52.

20. A common criticism of Anabaptism contested by Hauerwas, *Peaceable Kingdom*, 74.

trinitarianism as a basis for ecclesiology, or his insistence that true Christian confessing means living obediently to divine commands, renders "untenable the idea that the Creed represents a core of Christian belief held by all Christians."[21] In so doing Riedemann was judging confessional statements and orthodox doctrine as inert unless ethically interpreted both theoretically and practically. This was more than simple supplementation of theoretical affirmations by practical implications, but the fusion of practical reasoning with theoretical reasoning, so that theological statements became moral statements simultaneously.[22] Such linkage means that theology has a primary role in supporting faithful witness, and cannot be reduced to the task of merely establishing formal doctrinal schemes: "Doctrinal claims are not themselves adequate to produce a life of faith" unless read as intrinsically ethical.[23]

Thus the theoretical claims of doctrine contain within them the practical claims of ethics, similar to the practices of law and medicine. Whereas classical orthodoxy tends to "place emphasis where the New Testament does not . . . as discrete propositions," radicalism sees Christian doctrine as a "regular *practice*."[24]

Such early Anabaptist theological ethics was generally non-speculative. The reasons are multiple: their status as outlaws in both Catholic and Protestant states severed them from universities, libraries, and open theological debate; their pastoral focus; their rejection of territorial Christianity and thus freedom from the requirements of Constantinian Christianity's modes of reasoning, and their own internal disputations. However, in turning from their Catholic classical education to the Bible, like Luther, they turned from speculative texts to a practical text, made all the more urgent because of their precarious social situation. Their theological commitment to gathered—rather than territorial—Christianity lessened the demand to justify their theology and ethics at the bar and in the language of state

21. Biesecker-Mast, *Separation*, 145, on Peter Riedemann's *Account of Our Religion*.

22. Barth exemplifies a Reformed version: "Dogmatics . . . and . . . the Christian doctrine of God, is ethics," *CD*, II/2, 515. The trinitarian structure of ethics in the *CD* exemplifies this. Christian ethics helps us see "how our convictions are in themselves a morality," Hauerwas, *Peaceable Kingdom*, 16. Hauerwas early appreciated Barth's theological ethics, yet criticized his tendency to play down character, *Character and the Christian Life*, 176–177. Biggar *Hastening*, 127–45, defends Barth against Hauerwas's criticism. However, Barth's christological narrative is Nicene-Chalcedonian whereas Hauerwas's is Anabaptist, 143. Hauerwas, *With the Grain*, 194, n. 46 accepts Biggar's criticism.

23. Biesecker-Mast, *Separation*, 238. Yet inadequacy is not identical with heterodoxy.

24. McClendon, *Doctrine*, 28–29, emphasis original.

legal procedures and institutions, but perhaps tended to leave the world to its own Machiavellian ways. Social sectarianism is not constrained by the canons of established reasoning, as it undervalues social propriety.[25] Anabaptism affirmed a type of straightforward historical ethics that had as its central object the human Jesus located within its own substantive text, and consequently minimized the claims of moral reasoning embodied within the grand narrative or *mythos* of any social location.[26] Constantinianism, however, opens itself to the possibility of degrading its theological identity and moral reasoning by uncritically engaging with the intellectual structures, pre-suppositions, and reasoning of the state and culture, in order to maintain its social location. Christian ethical reasoning is here easily demeaned to the status of servant in the palace of the state and attempts to "establish and justify the theologico-ethical inquiry within the framework and on the foundation of the presuppositions and methods of non-theological, of wholly human thinking and language."[27]

2. Christological Moral Reasoning and Classical Moral Reasoning Contrasted

At this point christological moral reasoning will be contrasted with classical Christian moral reasoning, to demonstrate how the life of Jesus is used to criticize the ethical inadequacies of the classical forms of reasoning. Radicalism's *theological* affirmation of classical Christian categories, which makes them orthodox, included an *ethical* affirmation of those categories as morally normative, which makes them extra-orthodox. This unites their theoretical and practical reasoning in a credal and orthodox manner.

---

25. Whereas social sectarianism draws a line between the church and the world, Constantinianism tends to separate priests from people, shielding the latter from discipleship and the counsels of perfection.

26. Reimer, *Mennonites and Classical*, 305–306, criticizes Yoder as being historicist (not historical), and thus avoiding ontological concerns. O'Donovan, *Resurrection*, 58, describes historicist ethics as denying "a universal order of meaning and value . . . given in creation and fulfilled in the Kingdom of God . . . to which action is summoned to conform in its making of history."

27. Barth, *CD*, II/2, 521. For Barth "non-theological" thinking is non-christological, which means that he concurs *at this point* with the christological focus here articulated.

a. Trinitarianism

Peter Reidemann's perichoretic trinitarianism demonstrates that Anabaptism was not just an ethical corrective or supplement to orthodox theology. Whilst their confessions did include explicit ethical articles, they also ethicized pre-existent dogmatic statements. For instance, Reidemann states that

> Community means that those who have this fellowship hold all things in common, no one having anything for oneself, but each sharing things with others. Just so, the Father has nothing for himself, but everything for himself he has, he has with the Son. Likewise, the Son has nothing for himself, but all he has, he has with the Father and with all who have fellowship with him.[28]

Here, perichoretic theology necessarily implies perichoretic sociality and economics if immanent trinitarian relations are understood as ontologically and ethically normative. This can be a dangerous move, due to our sin and creatureliness. Yet the Holy Spirit, who creates the church and imparts to it the mind of Christ, enables the possibility of an anticipatory experience of these relations in the church prior to the eschaton.[29] Furthermore, as the Father and the Son are united, state and church cannot be opposed as realms of the Father's creation and Son's redemption respectively, with each realm sanctioning "contrary behaviors in each," even though they both have differing although complementary trinitarian appropriations and leading roles.[30]

Reidemann's moral reasoning indicates that Anabaptist exemplarist ethics is not limited to Christology, but may emerge from broader theological grounds. Although Christology remains the dominant category, such examples suggest that their ethical reasoning was theologically driven and anchored.

---

28. Biesecker-Mast, *Separation*, 140, citing John Friesen, *Peter Riedemann's Hutterite Confessions of Faith*. Riedemann anticipated twentieth century western social theology, as in Boff, *Trinity and Society*, 11: "The trinity can be seen as a model for any just, egalitarian . . . social organization," 11. Riedemann's *Account* is formally and materially structured around the Apostle's Creed. Volf suggests that humanity's sin and ontic difference from God limits such mimesis mainly to self-donation in *imitatio crucis*, Volf, "'Trinity is our Social Program,'" 404.

29. Finger, *Anabaptist Theology*, 431.

30. Ibid. "'Trinity' did not originally mean . . . that there are three kinds of revelation, the Father speaking through creation and the Spirit through experience, by which the words and example of the Son must be corrected," Yoder, *Politics*, 101.

b. Christ's Three-Fold Office

Protestant orthodoxy's threefold christological office becomes an ethical category in christological radicalism by extending the movement from the Old Testament prophets, priests, and kings, through Christ, to New Testament believers.[31] This constitutes the Christian social stance as prophetic, priestly, and royal witness.[32] Anabaptism often exhibits a preference for Petrine over Pauline theology.[33] The critical Petrine text (1 Pet 2:4–10) concerning this three-fold status is situated within clear ethical *inclusios*: holiness (1:13–25), and honorable deeds while suffering (2:11–17). Negatively, these are the rejection of evil desire, malice, guile, insincerity, envy, slander, and antinomianism; and positively, mutual love, honorable public conduct, acceptance of political authority, and reverence toward and service of God. Significantly, the Christian's three-fold status (2:9) is the theological basis for a sectarian ethic "as aliens and strangers in the world" (2:11).

Except in anti-sacerdotal polemic, classical Protestantism has applied the prophetic and kingly offices to Christian offices more than the priestly. The prophetic is represented in preaching and the kingly by the transfer of rule from the papacy to the secular Christian ruler. However, a standard element in the Anabaptist critique of orthodoxy is its separation of Christ's priestly office (death) from his prophetic office (life), as found in the transition of the second credal article "born of the Virgin Mary, suffered under Pontius Pilate," which ignores the greater part of the gospel narrative and Christ's life.[34] Reformation and classical doctrine is criticized for affirming Christ's death as satisfaction for sin, while avoiding his moral example in matters such as discipleship.[35] Properly, "Christ worked satisfaction for our sins . . . *insofar as* the world . . . follows after Him according to the requirement of faith."[36] Sattler links Christ's priestly and prophetic offices by the moral imperative. He rejects the accusation of fanaticism on trinitarian grounds: if discipleship is fanaticism, then Christ the exemplar must

---

31. We note prophets in Acts and Corinthians, priests and kings in 1 Peter and Revelation, and Paul's priestly apostolic ministry in Romans 15. The Petrine and Apocalypse references are more corporate than individual.

32. 1 Peter 2:9: "But you are a *royal priesthood* . . . that you may *proclaim* the mighty acts of him," NRSV, emphasis added.

33. Friedmann, *Theology of Anabaptism*, 37.

34. The Nicene addition of "became human" strengthens the anti-docetic Christology, yet omits any concrete content.

35. A main concern of Yoder and Denny Weaver; Reimer, *Mennonites and Classical*, 253–59.

36. Sattler, *Legacy*, 116, italics added.

necessarily be a fanatic, and "the Father must also be a fanatic" for he gave his approval to the Son at the transfiguration.[37]

Similar is Yoder's stance: "Christ's perfect obedience is, for orthodox Protestantism, no criterion for the obedience of the believer, but merely the prerequisite to an innocent and therefore vicariously valid death."[38] Therefore the "structural connection between Christ and ethics" in Protestantism is negation because salvation comes from Christ, not good works.[39]

In the above example, Sattler preserves the clear linkage between atonement and exemplarism found in 1 Peter 2: 21–25. The explicit exemplarism ("leaving you an example, that you should follow in his steps," 2:21) is christological, peripatetic and non-retaliatory. Trust is the central disposition of Jesus (2:23). The striking move is the introduction of substitutionary atonement theology (2:24a, "He himself bore our sins"), followed immediately by "therefore" (ἵνα), which introduces ethical, not soteriological, implications ("die to sins and live for righteousness"), which is itself followed by a soteriological affirmation ("By his wounds you are healed").[40] Thus apostolic paraenesis concerning suffering, a central First Peter theme, is predicated upon substitutionary atonement and Christ's priesthood as its exemplar. This makes Petrine theology a seamless integration of classical atonement Christology, exemplarist Christology, and Christian ethical imperatives, so that exemplarism does not imply a subjectivist type of Christology void of objective theological content. Abelard and Anselm are united. The priestly office of Christ in its central soteriological aspect functions as a clear moral exemplar. This is schematized in Diagram 1, over.

---

37. Ibid.

38. Yoder, "Prophetic Dissent," *Recovery*, 99. Forensic interpretations that apply Christ's active obedience vicariously may excuse a believer's obedience on the basis that it is imputed.

39. Yoder, "Prophetic Dissent," *Recovery* 100. This is overstated, for the atonement as expressing God's faithfulness, mercy, and love, is to be exemplified (Rom 15:2–3; Eph 5:25; 1 John 3:16–20). Further, Luther's doctrine of universal Christian priesthood includes ethics and vocation: "a cobbler, a smith, a peasant . . . are all alike consecrated priests and bishops," Luther, "To the Christian Nobility of the German Nation," in *Three Treatises*, 15.

40. The use of ἀνήνεγεν (ἀναφέρω) in 2:24 is "commonly used in the LXX (e.g., Lev. xiv. 20) of bringing a sacrifice to the altar . . . Here, 'bearing sins' means taking the blame," Kelly, *Epistles*, 122–123.

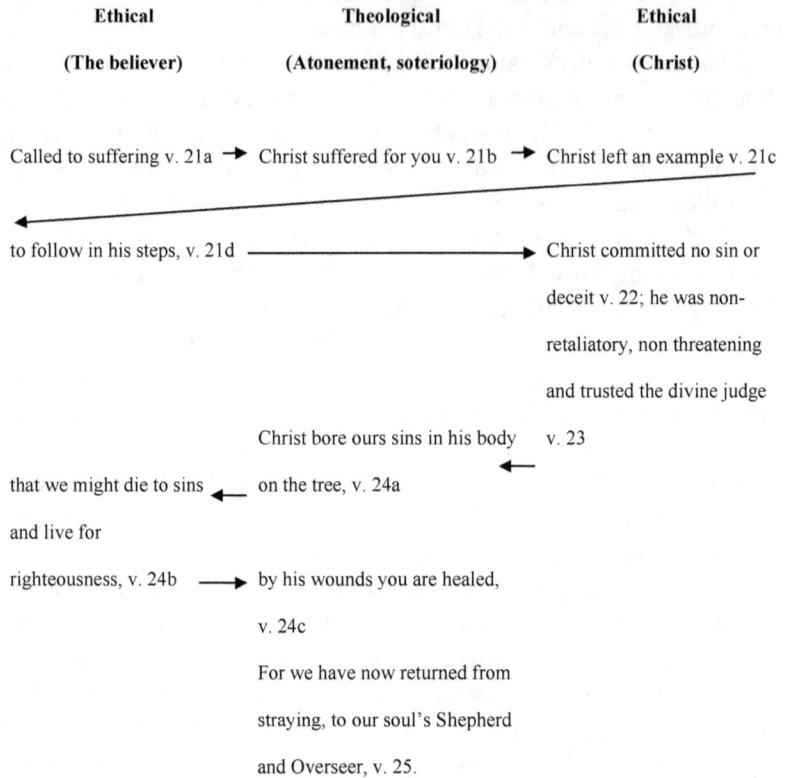

Diagram 1: The Theological and Ethical Structure of 1 Peter 2:21–25

c. Regeneration

Anabaptist moral reasoning is not alone in being dualistic. Constantinian dualism separated the inner faith from the outer life and confession. By emphasizing the latter, it required the concept of the invisible church as the location of the former.[41] Spiritualist dualism was identical, but emphasized the inner and ignored the outer, suggesting "the Spiritualists must be classed

---

41. Yoder, *Priestly Kingdom*, 57. The invisible church is an example of the "aesthetics of disappearance," (Virilio) which permits violence to remain uncontested due to the disappearance of the concrete existence of a peacemaking church following Jesus' example of non-violence; K. Huebner, "Patience, Witness, and the Scattered Body of Christ: Yoder and Virilio on Knowledge, Politics and Speed," in Ollenburger and Koontz, *Patient and Untamed*, 56–74.

... with the mass-church Reformers."[42] As such, it structurally belongs within the classical tradition. Anabaptist dualism however was confessional, ecclesial, and christological: one either did or did not confess Christ as Lord and live inside Christ's perfection in the gathered church.[43] This is illustrated clearly in the Anabaptist response to Spiritualism's Platonizing, world-averting doctrine of regeneration, where external works, ceremonies, and institutions were suspended. Dirk Philips's doctrine of regeneration is examined as illustrative.[44]

The Anabaptist doctrine of living within the perfection of Christ presupposed regeneration. The inward and invisible nature of regeneration as a divine act would make it seem a strange weapon with which to criticize the Spiritualists, but this is what Philips does. After commencing with a repudiation of false claims to regeneration, Philips outlines its biblical warrants (1 Pet 1:23; Jas 1:17–18; Titus 3:5–7; Gal 3:26; John 1:12–13; 1 John 5:1, 4–5) and affirms an orthodox trinitarian anti-Pelagian soteriology: regeneration is a "a work of God in human beings by which one is born again from God through faith in Jesus Christ in the Holy Spirit."[45] In dismissing paedo-regeneration he links the inward and the outward: infants cannot exercise the outward works arising from inward regeneration, thus regeneration is inapplicable to them.[46] Exemplarist Christology is then cited as the defining fruit of regeneration: the Holy Spirit is given for the renewal of the mind in "the explicit likeness of the invisible God, which is Jesus Christ. He is a true example to all Christians and a beginning of God's creation . . . *Therefore*, they ought to be conformed to the image of his only son Jesus Christ, who is the firstborn of many brothers . . . *Therefore* . . ."[47] This is a christological uniting of the inward and outward: the invisible God is seen in the outwardly incarnate Jesus.

---

42. Yoder, "Prophetic Dissent," *Recovery*, 98, n. 7.

43. "Perfection of Christ" was a common Anabaptist term. Anabaptist dualism is variously described. Four examples will suffice: 1) Friedmann's two worlds and two kingdoms in *Theology of Anabaptism*, 36–48 and "The Doctrine of the Two Worlds," in Hershberger, *Recovery*; 2) Bender's two worlds/two kingdoms is similar, cited in Hershberger, *Recovery*, 105f, n.1; 3) McClendon's two realities—"the church is not the world"—which is also existential as "the line between church and world passes right through each Christian heart," *Ethics*, 17; and 4) Yoder's confessional dualism, which "is the divide . . . on which there are those who confess Jesus as Lord and those who don't," in "Ecclesiology is Social Ethics," *Royal Priesthood*, 108.

44. Philips, "Concerning the New Birth," 200–217.

45. Ibid., 203.

46. Ibid., 205.

47. Ibid., 206, emphasis added.

The second "Therefore" above introduces four critical moral affirmations following the New Testament pattern of οὖν. They are: 1) keeping Christ's whole life in mind; 2) Christ as showing the way to follow; 3) Christ's baptism as exemplary of obedience; and 4) Christ's teaching and example. Thus exemplarist Christology is the heuristic device Philips uses to rebut the Spiritualists' repudiation of external works, uniting the inwardness of regeneration and the outwardness of works.

Most critically he affirms, "I have written concerning Christ Jesus, in part . . . to show that we . . . walk in the right way so long as we follow Christ." Here the orthodox Christology, "concerning Christ Jesus," serves the ethical end, "we follow Christ." The Spiritualists' inner/outer separation, on the other hand, rejected dominical teaching and ordinances because they saw themselves so "full of the internal essence of truth."[48]

Thus Philips argued that the Spiritualists' Platonism caused disobedience by disregarding the concrete practices of Christian existence. Modeled upon Christ, however, he does not deny inwardness: the regenerate are washed, changed and renewed inwardly through the Spirit.[49] Contextually, Philips is defending sacramental practice against its suspension by the Spiritualists, but extends his argument to defend all external works using a type of Hebrews 11 catalogue of biblical examples of concrete obedience. Finally he returns to an ontic and ethical exemplarist Christology: "Jesus Christ . . . a reflection of God's glory and an image of God's being, is the example to all Christians, that we might be conformed to him."[50]

This high Christology is not only compatible with exemplarist christological ethics, but is its ground and pattern because godliness, the ethical fruit of regeneration, "is perfectly reflected . . . in him," and regeneration is being "renewed in the image of God," that is, being Christ-like.[51] In criticizing the Spiritualists as being full of the internal *essence* of truth, he acknowledges the classical philosophical tradition of essentialism and accuses them of perpetuating dualistic classical forms of moral reasoning that compromised moral obedience. Philips therefore rejects the distinction between internal essence and external form that legitimized the suspension of the external ethical practice in preference for the inward essence. The inward theoretical category of truth, and outward practical categories of right and good, are united in Jesus, and are thus to be united in Christians.[52]

48. Ibid., 206–8.
49. Ibid., 205.
50. Ibid., 217.
51. Ibid.
52. Although not inevitable, Protestantism's inner/outer dualism may also lead to

Similarly, the foundational baptismal narrative of Anabaptism describes regeneration in exemplarist christological terms, with a glossed Matthew 16:24 the only biblical text cited: "If anyone will come follow me—notice, if anyone wishes or has desire—let him deny himself and take up his cross and follow me."[53] This baptism of January 1525 "began the separation from the world and its evil works," not the world's theology. In this act, they "stand together like Christ and Pilate."[54] Zwingli is condemned for he "shuddered before Christ's cross, shame, and persecution."[55]

A close reading of this narrative demonstrates that its Christology functioned ethically in three areas. First, against Spiritualism, inward regeneration associated with baptism necessitated following the outward example of Christ. Second, against Magisterialism, the Gospels became ethically normative. Third, and consequently, this Christology overturned the dualism between theory and practice as found in the Spiritualist's suspension of outward forms in preference for inner faith, and in Magisterialism's separation of Christ's example (e.g., his non-violence) from orthodox Christology.

By minimizing the importance of the external, Spiritualist moral reasoning and practice are easily shaped by alternative modes of non-christological practical moral reasoning, and thus moral practice. This was the form of moral reasoning Paul confronted in the Corinthian church, which reconfigured power and wisdom in non-christological forms. Such Spiritualism "denies the lordship of Christ and shuts him up in the monastery of the heart"[56] and is Hellenistic to the extent that it considers "the invisible and timeless [as] more real than the visible and historical."[57] Equally, Constantinian moral reasoning, which discards radical christological ethics as utopian or impractical, demonstrates preference for calculable outcomes, and denies obedience or *imitatio* a central place in Christian ethics. Such consequentialism presupposes both reliable human prescience about, and human determination of, outcomes and events, and may thus lapse into idolatry. By seeking to determine calculable outcomes that are broadly socially acceptable, does it mistake a combination of utilitarianism and convention with

---

ethically inert high Christology (dry orthodoxy) or theologically empty high ethics (liberalism); Yoder, "Prophetic Dissent," *Recovery*, 100.

53. "The Beginnings of the Anabaptist Reformation. Reminiscences of George Blaurock," in George Hunston Williams, *Spiritual and Anabaptist Writers*, 42. The gloss indicates the rejection of territorial Christianity.

54. Ibid.

55. Ibid., 45.

56. Yoder, "Hope of the World," *Royal Priesthood*, 217.

57. Yoder, "Prophetic Dissent," Recover, 99.

created orders, natural laws, or providence, so that being shaped by Jesus' example recedes behind a wish for dominion over history?[58]

Thus it is here argued that Anabaptist moral reasoning on the doctrine of regeneration reflects a unitive form of thinking which seeks to unite inner regeneration and outer works, the true and the good, as two sides of the one reality. By applying a consistent exemplarist Christology, Anabaptism criticized the separation of these two spheres in Spiritualism and Constantinianism, both of which it considered to be legitimized sub-Christian forms of ethical life.

d. Justification and Lutheranism

1. FAITH ALONE

Anabaptism generally rejected the Lutheran *sola fide* and "its forensic or 'imputed' justification" and *simul* doctrine that the believer "remains ontologically unchanged,"[59] by coordinating works and faith as equal in status and inherently related. While the *simul* doctrine possesses pastoral merit by explaining the believer's continuing struggle with sin, it was rejected because it was misappropriated as a foil under which unregenerate behavior was excused. Four instances are cited here where works and faith are given equal status.

First, in the *Swiss Brethren Confession of Hesse*, all thirty-eight articles—both theological (matters of faith) or ethical (matters of works)—commence, "We believe, acknowledge and confess."[60] Thus the ethical articles are considered equal to the theological articles as defining what constitutes the Christian faith. Second, the Schleitheim Confession's first article (on baptism) locates the theological material between two ethical conditional statements: "Baptism shall be given to all who have been taught repentance and the amendment of life and [who] believe truly that their sins are taken away through Christ, and to all who desire to walk in the resurrection of Jesus Christ."[61] Third, Simons: "The Lutherans teach . . . that faith alone saves, without any works. They emphasize this doctrine so as to

---

58. Yoder, "Hope of the World," *Royal Priesthood*, 203.

59. Davis, *Anabaptism and Asceticism*, 130.

60. To illustrate both: "We believe, acknowledge and confess God as Lord and Creator of heaven and earth," and, "We believe, acknowledge and confess that children are responsible to follow their biological parents," articles III and XXIX, in *Confessions*, 53, 81 respectively.

61. Sattler, *Legacy*, 36.

make it appear as though works were not necessary . . . that faith is of such a nature that it cannot tolerate any work alongside it."[62] Fourth, Hubmaier: "Mere faith alone is not sufficient for salvation . . . For faith must be active through love . . . people have in so many years not learned better than to say: 'We believe, faith saves us'; while in this age brotherly love and loyalty have grown staler and colder."[63] Both Simons and Hubmaier considered *sola fide* as antinomian because of the perpetuation of widespread immorality in Lutheran states. This is likely because when the *sola* is overstressed, the *fide* is more decisively disengaged from ethical categories. A wholly forensic doctrine of justification may exacerbate this, as noted below. Luther's emphasis was clearly pastorally helpful, given his struggle with late medieval Aristotelian inspired soteriology, where acts produce character; yet the *sola* is absent from the classic text on justification (Rom 1:16–17). Anabaptism on the other hand argued that faith is ineradicably engaged with other soteriological and moral categories, including works of love. Simons argued that it has four essential components: cognition, regeneration, ontological renewal, and behavioral change: "All who can believe this[64] as certain and true are sealed through the Word of God in their spirit, are inwardly changed, and receive the fear and love of God. They bring forth out of their faith righteousness, fruit, power, an *unblamable* life, and a new being."[65] The antecedent christological paragraph is both classical and exemplarist: "He taught us the will and good pleasure of His Father, went before us in an *unblamable* example, and freely offered Himself upon the cross for our sins."[66] Christ's unblamable life serves both the soteriological purpose of enabling his death to be effective, and the ethical purpose of providing a moral example of an unblamable life before God. Not only so, his death enables such a life through the Spirit's inward renewal. Simon's double use of unblamable thus typifies the Anabaptist's exemplarist *imitatio* christological ethics. "If there is a unifying discursive orientation through which Anabaptist practices signify, it is the story of Jesus' life, death, resurrection read as an account of how . . . God . . . acts decisively in the world through costly obedience of

---

62. Simons, "The True Christian Faith," in *Complete Writings*, 333, article III, "The Faith of the Lutherans."

63. Hubmaier, "Apologia," in *Balthasar Hubmaier*, 526–527.

64. The antecedent paragraph on Christology and soteriology.

65. Simons, "The True Christian Faith," *Complete Writings*, 336, article V, emphasis added.

66. Ibid., emphasis added.

disciples . . . Anabaptism [is] an array of christologically oriented historical practices."[67]

Finally, numerous instances of sixteenth century legal and political charges of people being Anabaptists were laid on the basis of the exemplary moral life of the accused.[68] Lutheranism is indicted as giving much "instruction" but possessing a "great lack as regards repentance, conversion, and the true Christian life . . . Changes were made only as concerned external things."[69]

However the question remains whether the problem was actually *sola fide*, or the territorialism it was embedded in, and the double *simul* doctrine. If a whole population is sacralized through enforced confession devoid of inward renewal, and the *simul* doctrine is unhinged from its original pastoral and theological context, it is easy to see how behavior that is sub-Christian is enabled. For early Anabaptists, *sola fide* muted the call to imitate Christ by excusing anti-Christian behavior generally, and justifying violence towards fellow Christians in particular. True *fide*, it was argued, takes Christ as both savior and example. That is, faith is directed not just to the soteriological work of Christ's death, but also towards his exemplary human life. Faith accepts that because Christ's earthly life pleased God, it is normative for proper human experience. Consequently, early Anabaptism expected an affirmative answer to two basic questions: 1) "Do you believe that Christ bore your sins?" and 2) "Do you believe that Jesus' human life, which pleased God, should be copied?"

Consequently christo-ethical reasoning has a unitive soteriological anthropology that does not divide the inner faith and the outer works that

67. Biesecker-Mast, *Separation*, 68–69. He cites A. Friesen, *Erasmus, the Anabaptists, and the Great Commission*, (Grand Rapids, MI: Eerdmans, 1998), 27 that this is partly due to Erasmus's Christocentrism. Friedmann wrongly states that exemplarism is rare in Paul due to his high doctrine of sin, Friedmann, "The Doctrine of the Two Worlds," Hershberger, *Recovery*, 106–107: see 1 Corinthians 11:1 (μιμηταί μου γίνεσθε, καθὼς κἀγὼ Χριστοῦ) and Galatians 4:12; Ephesians 5:1; Philippians 3:17, 4:8; 1 Thessalonians 1:6; 2:14; 2 Thessalonians 3:7.

68. Bender, "Anabaptist Vision," in Hershberger, *Recovery*, 42–47. An inverse example is also included: a Casper Zacher was acquitted of Anabaptism due to his obvious sins, 47. Constantinianism transmuted theological statements into legal statements, so that distinctive Anabaptist doctrines became legal challenges to social-ecclesial power, McGrath, *Scientific Theology*, vol. 3, 72.

69. Bender, "Anabaptist Vision," in Hershberger, *Recovery*, 39, quoting an Anabaptist leader of 1538, taken from an unpublished manuscript in the *Staatarchiv des Kantons Bern*, (*Unnütze Papiere, Bd*. 80), entitled *Acta des Gesprächs zwüschenn predicannten und Toüffbrüderenn* (1538). Copy in the Goshen College Library. A. McGrath, *Iustitia Dei*, 180–88, argues that the Reformation understanding of the *nature* of justification (not its mode) was wholly novel.

appear present in the *sola fide* doctrine. Under the *sola* it detects moral excuse. Yet even if *fide* was *sola*, the object of *fide* included, in a way Lutheranism did not, the life of Jesus. *Fide's* object is the entire gospel story, not just the passion: Jesus' life is proper to ethics and his death is proper to soteriology.

11. Law and Gospel

Like *sola fide*, the distinctive Lutheran Law/Gospel thematic is a pastorally irenic notion that eases the moral conscience, although it would be unfair to dismiss it as no more than a sop for fragile consciences. Yet Thielicke sets up a strong opposition between the Law/Gospel thematic and an ethic of *imitatio*, primarily on pastoral terms. *Imitatio*, he argues, confuses and disfigures both Gospel and Law, and by so doing destabilizes the confidence intrinsic to the Gospel.

Thielicke differentiates evangelical ethics from philosophical ethics in three propositions. First, philosophical ethics begins in concrete human acts, evangelical ethics in "justification as accomplished." Second, in philosophical ethics the concrete act is primary and the "intelligible ego, has merely the significance of a heuristic symbol," whilst in evangelical ethics only "justification has reality; the ensuing ethical acts . . . have symbolic significance." Third, in philosophical ethics, acts are determined by the task immediately presented, whilst in evangelical ethics, acts "are determined by the 'gift' already given."[70] The division is clear: ethical reality is understood as either my own concrete act yet to be done (a legal work), or Christ's concrete act already done (a divine gift). Practical moral reasoning, which is directed towards the imperative future (my act), is thus decisively relegated behind theoretical moral reasoning, which looks to the indicative present, or in his case, the past (Christ's act). Such an approach appears to see such epistemological categories as wholly incommensurable and antithetical rather than related in any way.

Despite this strong opposition, Thielicke can call Christ our exemplar, archetype or model, but not our example. As exemplar, his life becomes ours *de jure*, an alien righteousness, ensuring the priority of justification as the basis of sanctification. Natural ethics, which is detached from this "backward reference to justification," is idolatrous as it attempts to actualize the "blasphemous idea of a 'self-creation of the ego,'" in "opposition to the

---

70. Thielicke, *Ethics*, 51–52.

First Commandment."[71] Yet it is not altogether clear why an archetype or exemplar cannot also be an example.

In particular, *imitatio* leads to despair, for it turns Christ from the gracious *Deus defensor atque revelatus,* into the *Deus accusator atque absconditus.* Hope is found only *coram Deo,* not *coram ipse,* because *imitatio* equates with Law. Consequently, *imitatio* links the Gospel "to certain presuppositions, with certain acts of obedience and sanctification" that obscure its character as gift. The result is permanent problems of doubt.[72]

Without this Law/Gospel thematic, the inner meaning of both Law and Gospel collapse, for if the law is "robbed of its true character ... [as] ... total judgment," then so too is resurrection, which presupposes judgment and death.[73] This is seen in secularized forms of religious *imitatio* ethics that have reduced Christ to a mere illustration of admirable ethical postulates while at the same time denying the sheer gratuity of grace.[74]

What can be said in reply? First, the existential rejection of *imitatio* is largely anachronistic, because the contemporary robust Western conscience is mostly unconcerned with righteousness *coram Dei.*

Second, the radical division between Law and Gospel expresses bifurcated moral reasoning, similar to that found in Aristotle, between the past and the future. As such, a division emerges between what is theologically true (Christ's past acts) and what is anthropologically good (my future acts), so that the relation between God and those justified is reduced to largely forensic categories mediated through the gift of justification. It has already been argued that the New Testament's use of "therefore" renders this approach problematic. However, the gift of Christ cannot be reduced to a merely forensic category, because the gift is the whole *person* of Christ, not the soteriological status of justification (Rom 5:15). God gives the whole person of his Son (John 3:16) as the only morally perfect human, not simply as a legal declaration of innocence. The gift is not so much salvation, but the Savior and Sanctifier himself, who is the human shape of the sanctification intrinsic to salvation (1 Cor 1:30). This is gospel, because the justified person is not left hanging in ethical limbo, or wrestling with abstract ethical concepts that may or may not be internal to a legal fiction, or needing to

---

71. Ibid., 61.

72. Ibid., 96. Thus Luther's "you do take Christ as an example," becomes secondary to taking him as a gift, Zimmermann, *Theological Hermeneutics,* 65, 66.

73. Thielicke, *Ethics,* 116–117. Here the radical *imitatio,* and Calvin's "second use," are rejected.

74. Thielicke, *Ethics,* 185.

bear the burden of moral self creation, but given a concrete expression of what a true moral life looks like.

The Lutheran concern with the divine gift (Rom 5:15-16) is thus extended from soteriology to ethics (Rom 5:17-19, 6:1-4 where baptism into Christ's death and new life has clear ethical implications to cease sinning, 6:5-14). If the whole of Jesus is a gift, this necessarily includes his consubstantial and sinless humanity that provides the moral shape into which humanity is transformed through the perfective process of sanctification.[75] Our mortal bodies (Rom 6:12-23), that is, our concrete historic existence, is to be modeled upon Christ's life. The exemplary nature of this ethic is clear: as Christ died and was raised to new life, so too is the Christian dead to sin and to live a new life (6:4, 6, 11). The fact that Christ's new life is resurrection life (6: 4, 9-10) does not counter this *imitatio* ethic, but forms its gracious grounds. Righteousness cannot be a purely forensic concept here, because its opposite, wickedness (*adikia*, 6:13), is an ethical concept concerning the instrumental use of our bodies. The object of this *imitatio* is Christ's death to sin and life towards God (6:10), which is to be embodied by refusing evil desire (6:12-14). The gift is the whole person of Christ, not simply the forensic status of justification. Both Jesus' life and death show that "God will provide" (Gen 22:8), both ethically and soteriologically.

Consequently the anguish feared by Thielicke occurs when *imitatio* is understood in an Aristotelian fashion, where good works make a person good before God, or through the existential burden emerging from the modern quest for moral self-creation. This fear comes about because Thielicke places the moral meaning of Jesus' humanity in the category of Law, not gift or Gospel. It is as though once Christ has done his work as the objective justifying Gospel, he effectively vanishes from the subjective sanctifying Gospel. Any appearance of Christ's life in the moral life of the justified seems to take on the inappropriate form of Law, not Gospel.

These existential concerns are largely absent in early Anabaptist testimony. The conflict was outward, not inward: "The issue with Luther was

---

75. Bonhoeffer, *Ethics*, prefers the term conformation, of being "drawn into the form of Jesus Christ" by "Christ who shapes men in conformity with Himself," 80-81. This maintains the priority of grace. Spohn, *Go and Do Likewise*, 149-52, overstates it when he argues that Romans 6 expresses Paul's "master paradigm" of *imitatio*, which is his "touchstone for Christian moral discernment," 146, 149. Yet he correctly argues, citing Karl Rahner, *Spiritual Exercises*, that *imitatio* is ontologically grounded because "our humanity . . . has been joined to Christ [and] comes from participation," in him through baptism, 150. Simo Peura, "Christ as Favor and Gift (donum): The Challenge of Luther's Understanding of Justification," claims that Luther sees Christ *himself* as the gift because God gives *himself* with his gifts, and we are united with Christ *himself* in baptism (in Braaten and Jenson, *Union with Christ*, 42-69).

guilt . . . the issue with Anabaptism was . . . physical torture and death."[76] Thus we read, "I go today the way of the prophets, apostles, and martyrs . . . the way which Jesus Christ . . . Himself went."[77] A spirituality of irenic spiritual equilibrium cannot cite Christ as its exemplar given his temptations in the desert and agony in the garden. Such preparedness to imitate Christ's passion in martyrdom evidences confidence *coram Dei*, not an existential fear of his Law. Yet the deeper reality of *imitatio* is that it is more an ontological structure into which people are baptized in Christ, than a simple set of mimetic acts. This places the *humanity* of the disciple and Christ, not just their acts, in a mimetic relation.[78]

Consequently, *imitatio* is not a blasphemous "self-creation of the ego" when it amounts to conformation to Christ's moral humanity. The active moral agency of *imitatio* is the human element in the perfective process of sanctification that responds in gratitude to, rather than procuring, the divine gift. It is the proper response to the gift of Christ's life as the model of perfect and normative humanity. *Imitatio* expresses the belief that an external object or act is admirable and worthy of emulating. When christologically framed, Christ's moral life becomes proper to humanity. A Christian ethic of *imitatio* takes Christ's humanity as God's gift—Gospel—that is normative to our humanity.

e. Calvinism

Calvin himself did not altogether dismiss exemplarist christological ethics. Scripture enjoins us first to "refer our life to God, its author," and "after . . . it also adds Christ . . . [who] has been set before us as an example, whose pattern we ought to express in our life" due to adoption. He sets this against an

---

76. J. Lawrence Burkholder, "The Anabaptist Vision of Discipleship," in Hershberger, *Recovery*, 148.

77. Ibid., 146, quoting Anneken of Rotterdam at her martyrdom. O'Donovan, *Resurrection*, 145, considers that Thielicke's ethics sounds "like a gospel of deliverance *from* the world," and although such gnostic tendencies are held in check, the concreteness of the Incarnation is overlooked. Emphasis original.

78. Slane, *Bonhoeffer as Martyr*, 180. Stauffer and Friedmann understand early Anabaptist martyrdom as a vindication of the "truth" of their faith, because "Christ was . . . crucified because he is the truth" and "truth cannot manifest itself *otherwise than through the loyalty of the confessors*," "Anabaptist Theology of Martyrdom," 179–214, emphasis added. This sounds like Hauerwas's assertion that truth becomes properly evident in practice, and that the epistemological overcoming of theology is misplaced, *With The Grain*, 36.

ethics of virtue grounded in nature.[79] Nonetheless, the matter of state religious coercion escaped such christological reasoning. If Christian identity is determined by election—itself hidden in the unfathomable grace and mystery of God's eternal decrees—and not divine prescience, ethical practice, or sacramental practice, Constantinian Calvinism is inconsistent. Calvinist coercion and judicial punishment for non-conformity stands contrary to its own doctrines of election, sin, and moral bondage. Thus "if it does not depend on the one who wills or runs, but on God's mercy, of what good is the Calvinist sword here? For it is a matter of God's foreknowledge and election, and his mercy."[80] The internal rationality of Calvinism logically necessitates voluntary response, for the state has no knowledge of the elect's identity, nor can they be identified with territorial boundaries. Calvinist coercion expresses essentialism where the outer practice is enforced contrary to the inner renewal of the person: essence and form are non-congruent. It also acts vicariously by taking upon itself God's high sovereignty by enacting his judgment now: it over-realizes the eschatological verdict and legally enacts it.

This is not dissimilar to the "standard account"[81] of morality where the agent's historicity is negated by universal moral determinations such as the categorical imperative. In contrast, exemplarist christological ethics is compatible with Calvinism as it provides space for divine grace to shape the whole person, resulting in the congruence of the inner and outer aspects of life. Government religious coercion makes Christian discipline (a subcategory of discipling, Anabaptism's fourth mark of the church) a state act, not an ecclesial one. This turns Matthew 18:15-20 into a civil text requiring state coercion, rather than an ecclesial text requiring moral persuasion and possible church exclusion. Coercion thus disengages moral agents from their own moral identity, preserving bifurcated moral reasoning that separates theory (confession of faith) from practice (external compliance). It is modern to the extent that it makes alienation a central virtue.

---

79. Calvin, *ICR*, III.vi.3, 686. Adoption's single condition is that "our life express Christ." Failure here is "to abjure our Saviour himself," 687. Mouw, citing Bolt, argues that deemphasizing exemplarist Christology "is not essential to Calvinism" (contra Kuyper), although it "is not pronounced in Reformed ethics," Mouw, *God Who Commands*, 156–157. Mouw offers a Reformed olive branch to Anabaptism in the Foreword to *Royal Priesthood*, vii–ix.

80. Biesecker-Mast, *Separation*, 52, citing Leonard Dax. In sixteenth century Anabaptism the sword symbolized both the internal coercive civic power of magistrates and police, and the external state power of armies in war, including cross-jurisdictional religious conflict.

81. Hauerwas, *Truthfulness and Tragedy*, 16.

f. Violence

For Anabaptism, a central aspect of Jesus' humanity is his non-violence.[82] Historically, the key texts cited were Jesus' adoption of the servant model of leadership, his rejection of the sword in Gethsemane, his willing acceptance of death, and Philippians 2. This was supplemented by his explicit teaching, particularly the Sermon on the Mount. Servant-hood and non-violence are intrinsically linked: servants do not to rise up against, but stoop down to serve. "Christ is the Lamb of God and was led like a lamb to slaughter. A lamb never tears a wolf to pieces."[83]

The Schleitheim Confession cites Christ as justification for the rejection of the sword, motivated by love, in matters concerning punishment of the wicked and the defense of the good. Three gospel incidents are cited as grounds: 1) the woman taken in adultery; 2) Jesus' refusal to pass sentence on dividing an inheritance; and 3) Jesus fleeing from attempts to crown him as king. Each incident is exemplary. Of the first, Jesus' rejection of stoning and showing mercy means "exactly thus should we proceed." Of the second, "therefore, we shall do likewise." Of the third, "Thus shall we do as he did, and follow Him."[84] Christ's mercy, his refusal to act as judge or king, and his subsequent call to obedience, constitute a coherent model for Christian social practices, and provides a counter-rationality to moral reasoning grounded in pragmatic calculation and the concept of orders, where kings were expected to rule, magistrates to decide family conflicts, and adulterers were to be punished by Christian magistrates. The life of Jesus negates the adoption of earthly models of life or vocation where violence is considered normative. Yet this raises the question of divine violence.

It is clear that God's eschatological acts are painted in violent tones. When wedded to state sovereignty, such eschatology readily justifies violence, evident in some forms of imperial theology. On this point, Anabaptism displays a decisively futurist eschatology by refusing to enact now that which is proper only to God later, thus maintaining the balance between the now and the not yet. In the New Testament, Christ's eschatological judgment never stands in a mimetic relation to earthly judicial punishment.

Because it is assumed that force and violence are necessary for the establishment and continuation of states as legal entities, Anabaptism has generally stood outside those state social practices that are considered

---

82. Two others are noteworthy: truth-telling (refusal of oaths) and economic sharing.

83. Biesecker-Mast, *Separation*, 58, citing Riedemann.

84. Koop, *Confessions*, 30.

essential to such state maintenance. Such rejection of coercion, violence, and territorial Christianity in Anabaptism challenged a fundamental category of traditional moral reasoning: that of vocation.

g. Vocation

Anabaptist rejection of the sword instantiates its broader opposition to the doctrine of vocation where "every calling was its own norm," practices, and ends, "known by reason, from creation, despite the Fall."[85] The medieval doctrine of vocation, with its dual spirituality and orders (spiritual and secular), was replaced by the Reformers' multiple secular orders, and single territorial spirituality. Anabaptism however transposed vocation from orders as a formal societal concept, whether religious or secular, to discipleship, which reduced orders as previously understood to provisionality: thus, "the sword is an ordering of God outside the perfection of Christ."[86] The "perfection of Christ" is discipleship, self-denial, cross-bearing, and following Christ's example, which is vocation proper.[87] The general calling to Christ takes priority over the specific calling to work, so that "the Christian . . . has been called away from the world. He has been called never to conform to the world."[88] By hermeneutically privileging Jesus as the primary element in moral reasoning, Anabaptism denied or weakened the normative ethical authority of received societal norms and structures. Their supersessionist biblicism relegated the Old Testament to provisional status, thereby limiting recourse to Israel as a source for appropriate patterns for the church or the state. Anabaptist christological ethics provided a fundamental alternative to received patterns which had de-christologized social possibilities, and thus opened the way for all roles—with their concomitant practices and particular subset of ethical maxims and norms (considered politically, strategically or socially necessary)—to be possible for Christians.[89] Social roles were thus legitimized as spiritual vocations serving God's good order, despite their practices being non-congruent with Jesus. This is a form of situation ethics, where the practices of the socially embedded role become self-legitimizing and not subject to Christ.[90]

85. Yoder, *Priestly Kingdom*, 59.
86. Sattler, *Legacy of Michael Sattler*, 39.
87. Ibid., 40.
88. Friedmann, *Theology of Anabaptism*, 39, citing the Great Article Book of the Hutterites, Section Four, Point 70, (circa 1577).
89. Compare Augustine's defense of slavery as natural/eternal law.
90. Yoder, "Ecclesiology is Social Ethics," in *Royal Priesthood*, 122. The situation is

Christological moral reasoning thus narrows available sources for legitimate definitive moral reasoning, or at minimum limits the normative claims of those sources, taking "every thought captive to obey Christ,"[91] because "all things in heaven and earth were created, whether things visible or invisible . . . dominions or rulers or powers . . . and in him all things hold together."[92] "Things invisible" and "dominions and powers" include intellectual and societal structures and traditions of rationality.[93] This establishes a clear moral hierarchy whereby Christology displaces social positivism, Neibuhrian moral realism, calculable consequentialism, and loose interpretations of general revelation and common grace. Calculable consequentialism is rejected in place of obedience: the Anabaptists had to chose between "living by faith and surviving by alliance," after the promising start of Luther and Zwingli was abandoned for the alliance model.[94] Likewise, Hauerwas criticizes the view that morality means fixing the world, citing Burrell: "We are never enjoined [in Scripture] to *accomplish* anything . . . we are to recount . . . *God's* accomplishments."[95]

In this regard, a recurring feature of Yoder's criticism of Constantinianism is its self-adopted vocation of world-improvement.[96] Under the heading "Anatomy of the Constantinian Temptation," he outlines its two essential features: the belief that the true meaning of history is in the cosmos, not the church, and that Christian assistance and engagement supplements

---

the given "order" or "vocation."

91. 2 Corinthians 10:5, NRSV.

92. Colossians 1:15–17, NRSV. A clear moral hierarchy is clear: Christ as Lord takes priority over all other considerations. But this may tend to ignore rather than prioritize other moral categories: Christ *first* may become Christ *only*.

93. Friedmann argues that "*Kultur* or civilization is a Graeco-Roman and a Renaissance concept, not a Christian one," in "Doctrine of the Two Worlds," Hershberger, *Recovery*, 113. This overstretches it, ignoring the cultural mandate of Genesis 1:26–28. The "powers" may however be disordered orders, or un-mandated mandates, Bonhoeffer, *Ethics*, 207–213.

94. Yoder, "Prophetic Dissent," *Recovery* 103.

95. Hauerwas, *Peaceable Kingdom*, 149, 151, citing David B. Burrell, "Contemplation and Action: Personal Spirituality/World Reality," in *Dimensions of Contemporary Spirituality*, emphasis original. The Catholic social justice movement of Dorothy Day would contest Burrell's Catholic contemplative ethic. Faithfulness and effectiveness are too sharply pitted against each other here: there is both a rest day and work days. The holy day, coming first, elucidates the following six laboring days in Barth, *CD*, III/4, 47–72.

96. Ironically, Martens, *Heterodox*, similarly accuses Yoder of reducing theology to politics.

the world's own self-salvation.[97] Both presuppose that the orders of creation are self-evident and possess their own internal norms, which relegates Jesus to the role of supplement rather than norm. What classical moral reasoning may see as created orders he sees as human constructs. Similarly, secularism "implies that each of the various spheres of life (politics, art, etc.) has its own particular set of laws inherent in the very nature of the matter which is its peculiar concern."[98] In contrast Barth, whose "spheres and relationships" (not orders) is the *location* where the command and will of God is heard concretely, argues that "neither the command of God nor the obedience or disobedience of man *coincides* with these spheres and relationships in which they take place, and therefore cannot be simply read off from them."[99] Thus he criticizes Brunner's theology of orders as being an "abstraction from the revealed Word of God," and as voiding the connection between *credo in unum Deum* and its first article content of Creator and creation, leading to a theologically minimal understanding of orders.[100] But most significantly, by stating that the eternal election of Jesus Christ constitutes him as the "ontic" and "internal" basis of creation, Barth implies that "orders" can only be truthfully interpreted and ethically assessed christologically.[101]

Without such christological reasoning, vocation may be reduced to a pragmatic calculus matched with professional skills, embodying certain Christian virtues in an attempt to achieve their idealized Christianized forms.[102] Such pragmatism presupposes autonomous and reliable human

---

97. Yoder, "Hope of the World," *Royal Priesthood*, 198–203.

98. Thielicke, *Ethics*, 7: a secular perversion of Reformed sphere sovereignty?

99. *CD*, III/4, 29, also 45, emphasis added. He used "orders" earlier, in *Ethics*, 215. He unites the concepts of orders and divine commands: "The Word of God . . . says to man . . . Live under the order of life!" 268. Barth criticized Gogarten for whom "everything was determined by an 'ordinance of creation,'" Busch, *Barth*, 194. When concepts such as orders become primary, the place of obedience, central to both Reformed and Anabaptist ethics, degrades into deontological legalism because an abstract principle displaces Christ and the Spirit. For Kant as a secularized Lutheran exhibiting moralism without grace, see Zimmermann, *Theological Hermeneutics*, 135–59.

100. *CD*, III/4, 37–38.

101. Ibid., 39–40. Yoder acknowledges Barth: "What the Anabaptists spoke of as 'discipleship' was . . . what twentieth-century theologians think is a new insight, when they argue that ethics is an integral part of dogmatics, and that the sole criterion of dogmatics is Christ Himself," in "Prophetic Dissent," *Recovery*, 100.

102. As in some Christian professional associations (e.g., Christian Economists), where the profession may sometimes take precedence over the Profession (of faith). The opposite, where the profession is reduced to a mere sphere of witness for the Profession is simple pragmatism. Both separate creation from redemption and vocation from witness. Christ's life as a divine vocation is a witness: his redemptive Passion

prescience and providence which guarantees the outcomes envisaged: it leads us to "perceive a casual (sic) link between our own obedience and the results we hope for."[103]

Similar to Yoder's concern for faithfulness is Finnis's rejection of consequentialism. Finnis traces the emergence of proportionalism[104] to the Benthamite and Marxist rejection of Christianity's false moral-cultural absolutes, such as property, and their transposition of the Kingdom of God to this world "constructed by enlightenment human planning and providence." Thus "one's ultimate . . . responsibility is to bring about good states of affairs in the world," which necessitates the pursuit of actions that produce the greatest quantity of calculable good outcomes.[105]

Proportionalism is rejected by Finnis for three reasons. First, it "confuses human with divine providence, and human responsibility with God's." Second, it is incorrectly focused on maximizing goods rather than avoidance of wrongs, which shrinks the horizons and narrows the criteria of assessment to non-moral principles of responsibility, exemplified in bureaucratic pro-abortion advice to the poor, and the bombing of Hiroshima. Finally, human reason is incapable of accurately measuring possible future goods.[106]

Proportionalism is seen by Finnis as the chief antagonist to moral absolutes, which though few, are strategic and exceptionless. He argues that it is incompatible with divine providence, reduces morality to pseudotechnical non-moral reasoning, and by measuring the incommensurable produces illusionary outcomes. In contrast, Christian moral absolutes cooperate with God, and *"take into account everything* (the principle demand of proportionalists) *in the only way we can."*[107]

This Catholic argument is not dissimilar to that of Yoder, who rejects consequentialism on the grounds of the inadequacy of human reasoning and its suspect universal claims, Christ's omniscience and providence as Lord, and the exceptionless moral norm of Christian faithfulness and obedience. He rejects human *techné* and its consequentialist calculus, not from the essence, capacity, or end of human nature as such, but from the

---

restores creation.

103. Yoder, "Hope of the World," *Royal Priesthood*, 203. "Casual" read as causal.

104. Finnis's preferred term.

105. Finnis, *Moral Absolutes*, 14. Contrast Hauerwas, who challenges "the very idea that Christian social ethics is primarily an attempt to make the world more peaceable or just" on eschatological grounds, *Peaceable Kingdom*, 99. Is he contesting American messianic exceptionalism? For eschatology as a reason to act now, see 2 Peter 3.

106. Ibid., 16–20.

107. Ibid., 20, emphasis original.

particularity and lordship of Jesus in *his* humanity.[108] Finnis, however, rejects human *techné* and its consequentialist calculus not only on the basis of providence, but also on Aristotelian grounds: a "sound moral theory does not deduce moral norms from some presupposed knowledge of human nature, but rather from an understanding of the basic aspects of human fulfilment."[109]

A further problem with consequentialism is that it easily displaces God as the sovereign of history, despite human sub-agency under God. In particular, by eliminating christological determination from certain autonomous spheres, consequentialism and pragmatism bear no Christian witness to those spheres.[110] When the spheres' autonomy is justified by common grace or providence, or Christian ethics is reduced to supplementing the sphere's own internal norms, Christ's lordship is easily minimized. Yoder sees this dislocation in the Reformers' ceding to the state certain powers and limits of reform of the church, rather than being guided by faithfulness to Christ.[111]

Consequentialism is here contested on two fronts: first, the commonly observed disjunction between its prior calculations and its outcomes due to limitations of human prescience; and second, the incommensurability of the competing outcomes which makes the process of calculation questionable or unsustainable. This second problem can only be avoided if the contested outcomes are elements of a universally acknowledged hierarchy of human goods, itself a type of pre-existing calculus. Social debate indicates otherwise.

Such calculable moral reasoning based on confident claims to both prescience and *techné* stands in contrast to christological ethics that is determined by faithfulness to Christ, as the Lord of history (Revelation 5; the Lamb opens the scrolls). Such christological non-consequentialist moral reasoning is seen in the earliest Anabaptist testimony, when the decision to

---

108. However, the creation mandate (Gen 1:26–31) is recapitulated in Christ's lordship/authority over all creation (Matt 28:16–20), so that *techné* may be used in service for the nations. The three mountains (Matthew 5–7, 28; Exodus 19) weave creation (Matthew 5–7's images of creation suggest "natural law," Bockmuehl, *Jewish Law*, 117–126), Christ's lordship (Matthew 28) and divine commands (Exodus 19) into a single strand of three braids.

109. Finnis, *Moral Absolutes*, 24.

110. O'Donovan's terms, "kinds" and "ends," rather than spheres, are better, being interdependent and God-determined, *Resurrection*, 31–52. Although no things have a *generic* (kinds) relation with God, their *telos* (end) is Christ: *ta panta* are "in him" and "for him," 32f, in love, 245–64.

111. Yoder, "People in the World," *Royal Priesthood*, 88–89, n. 50 contains the relevant quotation. Zwingli feared an uprising: the irony is that Zwingli rose up against the radicals.

accept believer's baptism was received "in the pure fear of God," acknowledging "what they would have to bear and suffer on account of it." The testimony later recounts the drowning of Mantz "because of his . . . true baptism," and Zwingli's decree that persons baptized "should be . . . without trial . . . cast into the water and drowned." From the citation's conclusion ("However, since the work fostered by God cannot be changed and God's counsel lies in the power of no man"), four implications follow.[112] First, by making the act christologically warrantable (citing Matt 16:24), a clear identification is established between divine counsel and Jesus as the source, form, and matter of moral reasoning about politics and social engagement. Second, the dominant universal social *mythos* or *nomos*, represented by Zwingli, is no warrant for ethical action. Third, consequences are non-determinative, as the acceptance of possible martyrdom indicates. Fourth, no human power may alter God's counsel. Thus "the criterion most apt for validating a disposition, a decision, an action, is not the predictable success before it but the resurrection behind it, not manipulation but praise." This does not prevent all consequentialist reasoning, but does expose its inadequacy when the reasoner presumes to read the future as a "closed system" through a type of "reductive quasi-mechanical utility calculus."[113]

A utility or pragmatic calculus may appear sustainable in a qualified sense if applied to eschatological virtue theory, as such weighing of moral practices is done in the context of a divinely promised outcome. To do so however, may strip Christian moral practices of any personal dimension and reduce virtue practice to crass reward seeking.[114] Notwithstanding this possible exception, actions are not guaranteed any pre-eschatological utility, nor is it easy to form a true calculus. For example, concerning the Zurich baptisms cited above, does faithfulness to Christ and subsequent martyrdom outweigh any temporary apostasy followed by later repentance and faithful service, as in Hubmaier's recantations prior to his eventual death? Will martyrdom win more to the faith than the post-apostate ministry?[115]

Radicalism thus denies a central role to the moral calculus of pragmatic consequentialism that supports the internal moral norms of vocations as "laws unto themselves." Nonetheless, historical precedents indicate radicalism has achieved broad social goods, which suggest that it is well capable of

---

112. "The Beginnings," *Spiritual and Anabaptist Writers*, 42–46.

113. Yoder, "To Serve our God and to Rule the World," in *Royal Priesthood*, 137–138.

114. See Finnis's criticism of traditional Catholic natural law's focus on heaven and hell. Cognitive-rationalist hermeneutics, expressed in traditional natural law's rationalism, eclipse Christ himself, Zimmermann, *Biblical Hermeneutics*, 81.

115. Such a crisis confronted Anglican Puritans when considering separatism.

shaping history.¹¹⁶ However, these goods are not calculable as types of warrants for those acts prior to the acts themselves, but are non-calculable and non-guaranteed consequences of Christian faithfulness. Thus two distinct forms of consequentialism are possible: first, the standard account whereby consequences are calculated by universal forms of generalized prescient reasoning internal to a particular vocation; and second, whereby they are the providential outcomes of Christian faithfulness.

This concern for Christian faithlessness over calculable consequences is the object of much criticism. This criticism expresses a number of assumptions. First, that the given orders and *mythos* are genuine social goods worth preserving; second, that human prescience is typically reliable; third, that human *techné* is competent to achieve the calculated ends; fourth, that Christian particularism is socially irresponsible; fifth, that opposing forces do not possess an equal or greater determination to thwart the calculated ends; and sixth, that various competing ends are commensurably calculable, thus ensuring the best end is chosen as the greatest good.

As an instance, we take war, a central Anabaptist subject, outlining responses to the argument above. First, preservation of the given orders and the cultural *mythos* is not absolute, as witnessed by the divinely willed destruction of states in the Old Testament. Second, human prescience is limited, as failed military adventures demonstrates. Third, human *techné* is limited, as seen in the continual obsolescence of military equipment, revision of strategy, and lost battles. Fourth, women have normally not been accused of irresponsibility for being non-combatants. Fifth, opposing forces may cause a greater evil than the conflict seeks to alleviate. Finally, multiple ends are not calculable due to the absence of commensurable denominators.

Thus christological reasoning affirms that Christians "need not rule because Christ is Lord."¹¹⁷ Because in the apocalyptic vision the slain Lamb is the ruling Lion (Revelation 4–5), there is no quasi-mechanical cause and effect between "our faithfulness and the direct triumph of God in human history."¹¹⁸ This attitude of faithfulness and obedience is the key criterion in the christo-ethical moral posture, which in Yoder is parasitic upon a high lordship Christology. Contrary to medieval Christ-pantokrator Christology, where Christ rules coercively through his earthly agents, radicalism's apocalyptic high Christology (the Lion) serves as an eschatological war-

---

116. Yoder, "To Serve our God and Rule the World," *Royal Priesthood*, 136. Methodism, outside established Anglicanism, generated England's eighteenth century moral renewal, *Priestly Kingdom*, 63, although Church of England evangelicals were not uninfluential.

117. Yoder, "Let the Church be the Church," in *Royal Priesthood*, 177.

118. Ibid.

rant for faithful pre-eschatological Christian discipleship, renunciation of violence, and acceptance of suffering (the Lamb). The coercive nature of imperial Christology separates the Lamb from the Lion and adopts the motto, "Christ reigns, so must we," whereas radical high Christology says, "Christ reigns, we need not."[119] Thus Constantinianism, when expressed in the form of imperial theology, is a form of over-realized eschatological and amillennial social ethics. The eschatological reign of Christ never functions in the Bible as a warrant for Christian or ecclesial rule over, or violence towards, other people.

Vocation is thus determined and normed by Christ and located in his social form as church. Preece correctly states this "exclusive ecclesiology of the gathered church can create a vacuum of values in the wider world,"[120] yet this vacuum remains a possibility, not a necessity. Such social disengagement is true only insofar as an exclusive ecclesiology is separated from exemplarist Christology, for Jesus was not socially disengaged, and sent his disciples into the world "as he was sent" (John 17:15–18, 20:21). The point of the debate is the form of engagement, or the mode of relation between the particular and the universal. This relation has differing *primary* modes: for radicalism it is faithful witness, for Constantinianism it is rule, for Spiritualism it is withdrawal, and for the Reformed it is responsibility.[121]

3. Conclusion

It has been argued that for moral reasoning to be properly Christian, it must emerge from Christ. Yet because there are many Christologies, there are many ethics that claim to be Christian. For this reason, Chalcedon is joined

---

119. However, given the dominion mandate of Genesis 1, this may be an overstatement, but there the rule is not over fellow humans. Yoder expresses Anabaptist vocational dualism here, yet Christ's foot washing combines lordship and service. Similarly environmental management is a "servant dominion" over creation.

120. Preece, *Viability*, 316. Preece understands the gathered church *(ecclesia)* and the scattered church to be subsets of the primary biblical concept of the people of God. Consequently if vocation is understood only *ecclesially*, it disengages the Christian from responsible engagement with the wider world. Vocation as a subset of the people of God however includes both ecclesial and worldly engagement: service in the church and in society. Nonetheless, christological moral limits ought to govern the forms of vocation in the wider world. For Yoder, Jesus is one of many particulars in a world of multiple provincial beliefs, and should guide public Christian moral discernment in an unembarrassed way, "Hermeneutics of Peoplehood," in *Priestly Kingdom*, 40–43.

121. Preece notes Barth's Christocentrism ensures that witness plays a central role, *Viability*, 179. Hauerwas, *With the Grain*, 195, argues that ethics is a form of witness in Barth's CD.

to the Gospels so that an ecumenically orthodox Christology prevails. This is evident in early Anabaptism, where christological ethics is theologically parasitic upon classical theological orthodoxy. This model preserves the congruence between theoretical reasoning and practical reasoning: the dogmatic content intrinsically demands certain ethical affirmations that are necessary in order to establish and preserve a coherent form of reasoning. But more than that, the dogmatic content is itself ethical.

Yoder is criticized by Martens for rendering this classical character opaque by emphasizing Jesus' humanity at the cost of his divinity. If the classical tradition tends to a type of divine monophysitism, the radical tends to a human monophysitism. Yet any attenuation of classical theology may be accounted for by understanding that Yoder's project concerned social ethics, and that he sought to redress an equal attenuation of the tradition concerning Jesus' historical humanity.[122] Yet by concentrating so extensively upon Jesus' human ordinariness, Yoder shares a similar anthropological concentration to that of much natural law—albeit the humanity of just one man, rather than the humanity of all.

Thus it is fair to describe Yoder as historical, but not historicist, for despite this lack, he does not deny the classical tradition. Yet without its union with the divine nature, Jesus' humanity, although identical with ours, possesses no theologically compelling reason for being accorded normative status over against the humanity of anyone else. We easily lapse back into voluntarism: Jesus becomes morally normative for those who choose him. This fits well with a gathered ecclesiology where baptism and membership is a result of free choice, but it lacks a rich *theological* purchase upon the moral imagination.

In contrast, it is precisely because of the hypostatic union that Christ's humanity, as against the humanity of any other human, is finally and universally normative. We are to be human in ways analogous to the way Jesus Christ was human, not only due to the consubstantial nature of his humanity with ours, but because his humanity was united to the divine nature and person of the Son. Even though this union was uniquely hypostatic, unlike ours, this humanity nonetheless originated from, was determined by, and tended towards God, and in so being is proper to created humanity. Moreover, as relationships between persons produce a richer life than the life of a socially isolated person, so too the hypostatic relation between the two natures in the Incarnation produces a richer understanding of human

---

122. Strongly argued by Carter, *Politics of the Cross*, 121. He defends Yoder's classical orthodoxy against the charge that he dissolved normative Anabaptism into relativizing historicism, 53.

nature—one that is necessarily related to the divine nature and person. It is this Chalcedonianism that will be explored later, but as an anticipatory comment, it can be said that if Yoder and Barth are compared at this point, we will note that their varying emphases produce different effects on the moral imagination. Yoder's lack of Chalcedonian balance produces an ethic that is more immediately socially and politically imaginative, while Barth's more balanced Chalcedonianism produces an ethic that is more theologically imaginative. If Yoder pushes the reader into the church through Jesus, Barth pushes the reader into humanity through Jesus. Yoder sacralizes the church, Barth sacralizes the whole human tribe.

Thus, while disagreeing with Martens's heterodox assessment of Yoder, we agree that he takes "the story of Jesus . . . as the fundamental 'paradigm' . . . on the basis of which the moral norms ordering human life are to be developed."[123] In this he faithfully expresses early Anabaptism. Yoder appears to be primarily a Sattlerian,[124] continuing the Schleitheim Confession's emphasis upon an ethics of *imitatio Christi*, primarily on separation (article four) and the sword (article six), while remaining tacitly silent on classical theology. Yet Yoder's general silence concerning classical categories, while strategically canny in his dealings with post-metaphysical modernism, amounts more to an inadequacy than a denial of orthodoxy. It is this inadequacy that this thesis seeks to redress.[125] Consequently, "classical dogmatic formulations are essential for assuring an ontological-metaphysical grounding for ethics . . . especially . . . when ethics is defined primarily . . . in terms of free human agency."[126]

Therefore Part Three explores and appropriates Chalcedonian Christology to propose a rapprochement between natural law's universal concerns and radicalism's christocentric ethics. It does so by locating the human nature of Jesus within the person of the divine Word and Son, and by refocusing natural law's view of universal and phenomenal humanity to the particular humanity of Jesus as the second Adam. It also takes up Cicero's concerns with metaphysics through a *Logos* and cosmological Christology.

---

123. Martens, *Heterodox*, 133, citing G. Kaufman.

124. Reimer, *Mennonites and Classical*, 273, sees Yoder's *The Christian Witness to the State* this way.

125. That Yoder was "protecting, declaring and unpacking the claims of classical Christology," Carter, *Politics of the Cross*, 17, and 27, 113–36, is contested by Finger, "Yoder Reduce Theology?" in Ollenburger and Koontz, *Patient and Untamed*, 332.

126. Reimer, *Mennonites and Classical*, 265, and Martens, *Heterodox*, 143: "The problem lies in what [Yoder] excludes."

Part Three

The Word Became Flesh
Chalcedonian Christology and Moral Reasoning

5

Chalcedonian *Logos* Ethics

1. Introduction

PART THREE OF THE thesis will propose and argue that Chalcedonian two-nature and *logos* Christology provides both the theological resources and conceptual structure required to meet the legitimate concerns of both natural law and christo-ethical radicalism, while simultaneously going some way in addressing their primary deficiencies. Part One affirmed that the concern of natural law to establish a universal ethic is legitimate, despite its problematic lack of Christology. Part Two agreed that radicalism's strong ethical Christology is proper, but found its tendency to Christian provincialism and Chalcedonian imbalance problematic.[1] Part Three attempts a rapprochement of these two traditions through Chalcedonian Christology.

It has become commonplace to dismiss Chalcedonian theology as the illegitimate intrusion of Greek ontological language into Christian historical thought forms. Responding to this criticism, Gunton defends Chalcedon as an attempt to look *through* the data of the New Testament and Christian worship, *to* the truth about Jesus Christ, describing the Christology of Chalcedon as an explicit scientific clarification of what is implicit in both sets of data.[2] Its christological "minimalism suggests that the Chalcedonian

---

1. The popular dismissal that "not everyone believes in Jesus" is jejune: the same is true of all historic teachers.

2. Colin Gunton, "The Truth of Christology," in Torrance, *Belief in Science*, 105. Reimer concurs in "Theological Orthodoxy and Jewish Christianity: A Personal Tribute to John Howard Yoder," in *Mennonites and Classical*, 307, sparring with Yoder.

definition is not determined exclusively by soteriological interests (but) is also largely a hermeneutical construct," which establishes it as not only "constitutive but also regulative," while also possessing an "open textured reticence" enabling further fleshing out.³ Following Gunton and Hunsinger, we attempt to look through Chalcedon and *logos* Christology to its regulative significance for Christian ethics.⁴ This approach approximates Athanasius's use of *homoousios*, which, though foreign to the New Testament, enabled and forged a compatible link between Scripture and doctrine.⁵

Although the entire Chalcedonian Definition is significant, there are two precise formulations that concern us. First,

> The same perfect in Godhead,
> the same perfect in manhood,
> of one nature with the Father in respect of his Godhead,
> of one nature with ourselves in respect to his manhood.

This statement is at once metaphysical and ontological, historical and anthropological.⁶ Its double consubstantiality is the core of this thesis. However, while both *homoousion* statements are important, they exist in an asymmetrical relation, with the divine Alexandrian nature existing prior to the human Antiochene nature.⁷

The second formulation is,

> One and the same Son and only-begotten, God the Word,
> our Lord Jesus Christ.⁸

---

3. George Hunsinger, "Karl Barth's Christology. Its Basic Chalcedonian Character," in Webster, *Cambridge Companion to Karl Barth*, 128.

4. This compares with the implications of Nicene theology for cosmology, soteriology and anthropology argued by Ayres, *Nicaea*. He rejects the idea that Nicene theology turned away from earlier *Logos* theology, 302–21.

5. "The New Testament . . . did not simply give rise to it but actually contained [*homoousios*'] meaning," Weinandy, *Athanasius*, 136.

6. Plato's moral order from above and Aristotle's moral order from below are here united.

7. Early Alexandrian theology stressed Jesus' divinity, and early Antiochene theology stressed his humanity. "The divine and human work together . . . [but the] . . . divine is still above the human below," Barth, *CD*, IV/ 2, 116.

8. The "only defensible foundation for . . . ethics [is] grounding the interpretation of reality in the incarnation," because the "personal transcendence of the universal Logos, who became the paradigmatic human being while retaining his nature of eternal Logos, allows for both otherness and sameness . . . individuality and universality, the elements crucial for hermeneutics and ethics," Zimmermann, *Theological Hermeneutics*, 144.

This *logos* Christology includes both double consubstantial assertions. That is, the Chalcedonian "God the Word" is read in conjunction with the Johannine formula "the Word became flesh." In reading the Chalcedonian statements traditionally, divine nature is predicated to the *Son/Word*, human nature to the *sarx*, without diminution of either, united in the one *hypostasis*.

To anticipate the argument: the divine consubstantiabilty of the Word relates primarily but not exhaustively to metaphysical moral realism, whilst the human consubstantiabilty relates primarily but not exhaustively to anti-real historicism. In this fashion we will argue that natural law, whether in its protological or teleological forms, cannot be separated from Christology without it lapsing into a form of moral Deism.[9] Conversely, christological ethics cannot be reduced to anti-realism through its historical expression in the humanity of Jesus without lapsing either into a form of moral two-person Nestorianism, which displaces the divine person in favor of the human Jesus, or into Schleiermachian or Ritschlian ideal-man Christology, which minimizes the divine nature. The mimetic relation between true thought and speech, and the eternal forms of the real world, as in Hellenism, suggest that the *Logos ensarkos,* which is the concrete human Word, instantiates the eternal *Logos asarkos,* which is the eternal divine Word. If this mimetic relation does not exist, clear knowledge of God's eternal realities remains uncertain. Two implications follow: 1) God is either incapable of or unwilling to clearly express himself to his creation; or 2) humanity is incapable of or unwilling to clearly understand God. The first implication impinges upon God's power and love, while the second impinges upon humanity's cognitive or moral capacities. Yet these human incapacities, real as they are, do not thwart God's power and love to communicate himself by assuming humanity. Thus by affirming the double *homoousion*, the *Logos ensarkos* maintains its ontological anchorage in the divine nature that enables real and proper knowledge of God. Without this anchorage, Jesus is reduced to one of many possible *logoi*, stripped of any divine and substantial moral meaning.[10]

Consequently, this chapter leaves behind much of the vocabulary of Part Two, and partly returns to a focus upon specific authors, as did sections of Part One. The act/being thematic of Barth and Bonhoeffer is explored because by forcing together act and being they offer a means of uniting being (realism) and act (history) in both the divine person (Barth) and the human person (Bonhoeffer). When united, the differences between realism

---

9. It is ethics "making traitorous use of 'natural' theology," Barth, *CD*, I/1, 523.
10. Torrance, *Divine Meaning*, 379.

and history tend to dissolve, or become more manageable; for the acts reveal the being, and being is found in its acts. Thus Barth enables a discussion of theological ethics and Bonhoeffer a discussion of anthropological ethics that are christological and orthodox: that is, as the Word made flesh.

The rest of this chapter explores *logos* Christology more explicitly in relation to Chalcedon, rationality, and the prologue of John's Gospel.

2. Being and Act in Barth and Bonhoeffer as Heuristic Ethical Tools

a. Barthian Act and Being in Church Dogmatics

Barth's main discussion of God's act and being is in *CD*, II/1, 257–321, the Doctrine of God. But this act and being is itself ethical, for the Doctrine of God is ethical.[11] He rejects both German idealism's term "spirit," and Greek metaphysics' term "essence," as separating God's being and life from his act and revelation.[12] By bringing the immanent and economic trinities into the closest possible relation through his act/being thematic, Barth safeguards the immanent Trinity from metaphysical or speculative reasoning that is ungrounded in the concrete act of Christ, for the question "Who or what is God?" is answered only by "God's act in His revelation."[13] Hence Barth's act and being theme continues his reversal of liberal philosophical method: the concepts of divine being and act are determined and defined by God as Father, Son, and Holy Spirit, in his overflow of love towards his creation in a specific act, not through pre-theological philosophical concepts.[14] In this act, God gives himself lovingly as a necessity in himself, but not as a necessity grounded in love's object.[15] "God is" means "God loves."[16] This could be extended: Father, Son, and Holy Spirit love because they are love, and this loving is freely manifested towards humanity in the triune act of creation,

---

11. Barth, *CD*, II/2, §36, "Ethics as a Task of the Doctrine of God."

12. Barth, *CD*, II/2, 265–266. For a discussion of Barth and German Idealism, see McDowell, "One Person, Many Persons?" Like Athanasius, Barth "objects to a subordinationism that separates God from the revelatory event," 9.

13. Barth, *CD*, II/2, 261. In Barth, "God is what he does, and does what he is," Gunton, *Act and Being*, 76. Torrance argues that Athanasius was the first to elucidate the implications of the act/being thematic, *Ground and Grammar*, 67.

14. Liberalism is accused of deducing the doctrine of the Trinity from the premises of formal logic, *CD*, II/2, 261.

15. Ibid., 280.

16. *CD*, II/I, 283.

reconciliation, and redemption. Thus, "What God is as God . . . the *essentia* or 'essence' of God . . . we shall encounter at the place where God deals with us as Lord and Saviour, or not at all."[17]

Barth defends such non-abstract and personal language against the accusation that it may be "childish," a criticism that is similar to the criticism that Anabaptist ethics and theology is jejune.[18] By this language, he rejects the theological copula "God and . . . " because it opposes the concept of *Deus non est in genere,* if and when the copula reduces God to a *genere*.[19] Nonetheless, aseity does not preclude an infinite variation in forms of divine immanence and action *ad extra*, but expresses the "overwhelming richness of distinctions within His being," which in turn is safeguarded from lapsing into disorder or speculation through affirming that their center, crown, and apex is the hypostatic union, "the principle and basis of all divine immanence."[20]

Whilst traditional classical theology has shown a predilection towards God's being, Barth's act/being thematic includes the actuality and events of God within his being, so that God *ad intra* is identical with God *ad extra*. Such a divine actualist ontology leads McDowell to suggest three conclusions:

1. God is not imprisoned in a form of stasis as an object of human speculation, but always remains as Subject,
2. It undermines the Kantian noumena-phenomena dualism, and
3. It prevents revelation from being construed purely as a past event.[21]

Point three need not concern us here. However, points one and two lead to the following two comments about natural law ethics and Christology.

First, the concern that metaphysical natural law is static and leads to non-dynamic moral agency overlooks the reality of God as active Subject, author, and end. Protological natural law can be argued as static when God is understood as the Uncaused Cause, or deistically, or as a variation of Stoic *spermatikos logos,* but not when the being of God is actualist. The

---

17. Ibid., 261, simply because God's being is a being in act, 284. However, this identity can threaten God's freedom if understood in a non-Chalcedonian fashion: "The revealing power that comes from the Word and is not transferred to Jesus' humanity will be merged with history and then become dependent upon it," Molnar, *Divine Freedom,* 70.

18. Barth, *CD,* II/1, 286.

19. Ibid., 310, an error he finds in Thomism.

20. Ibid., 316–317.

21. McDowell, "One Person, Many Persons?" 12–13.

christological apex of God's historical actualism denies all stasis to God, and hence any sense that divine natural law, as an expression of his being and nature, is static or rigid. Whilst such actualism can lead to occasionalism and hence a soft form of Deism (punctiliar moments of divine engagement in an otherwise deistic world), this is not a necessity, and is safeguarded by the non-variable constant of the *imitatio Christi* of radical ethics. God's acts are not a mélange of variables or a series of unconnected dots on a line, but form the constant line of Christ's singular life. That is, the actualist nature of the divine Subject, crowned in the Incarnation, serves as the mode and model of an actualist human-nature ethic.

Teleological natural law is also safeguarded from a rigid stasis, for Christ is the end of creation, towards which all creation moves as its final goal and purpose. As the being and act of God are identical and find their apex in Christ, the eschatological Christ as the glorified person in his historically assumed humanity maintains this actualist ontology as archetypical of the *telos* of human life. Teleological natural law thus moves towards a fulfillment that is not static, but dynamic and actualist, maintaining active agency as intrinsic to the human subject.

Second, the Kantian dualism is overcome in the act/being thematic. The phenomenal God of Kant is one of the idols of Athens; the noumenal God of Kant is the unknown God of Athens.[22] Contra Kant, the *ad intra* noumenal and *ad extra* phenomenal coalesce in Christ without confusion, change, division, or separation.[23] In respect of natural law, the phenomenal *ad extra* act of God in Christ is the noumenal *ad intra* being of God, such that Christ's acts and life are eternal law in and of themselves, without diminution or remainder. As natural law is the divine law of our creation (Calvin) the Chalcedonian Definition makes this law christologically precise because "all of God's acts take their beginning in the Father, are *put into effect through the Son* and reach their completion in the Spirit."[24] Furthermore, *imitatio* is not reducible to Kant's categorical imperative (Christ is the best example and teacher of the Golden Rule, therefore I ought to will that this rule becomes a universal law) within the act/being thematic, because the act of Christ in his life and teaching is an *ad extra* form of the divine *ad intra*, and hence expressive of the divine being. Thus radical ethics' *imitatio*

---

22. Acts 17:23.

23. This is Chalcedon's apophaticism: the hypostatic union is ἀσυγχύτως, ἀτρέπτος, ἀδιαιρέτως, and ἀχωρίστως (unconfused, immutable, indivisible, and inseparable). It rejects Hellenism's dualism of ideas and sensibility, Torrance, *Divine Meaning*, 45.

24. Gunton, *Act and Being*, 77, italics added.

is "a useable concept, certainly, but only if grounded in a transcendental Christology," otherwise it is reduced to naïve sage ethics.[25]

Augustine grounds moral law in eternal law, itself grounded in God. Moral law's first use in Calvinism is to reveal the character of God. This grounding and character is revealed in Christ's person and acts as the apex of God's multiple acts of immanent actuality, but also, as the second Adam, in recapitulating proper human obedience to these moral laws that express God's character.[26] Thus the actuality of the Incarnation reveals both the being and moral character of God (eternal law), and the shape of proper human moral nature corresponding to it (natural law). Hence the act/being thematic provides the epistemological means of overcoming two basic problems. First, it overcomes the tendency to immanent and self-enclosed ethical historicism to which radical ethics tends due to its focus upon the historical Jesus, because his divine nature means that the actuality of Jesus is non-reducible to his human nature without participation in the being of God. Consequently natural law's anthropological focus (human nature) is also given a broader and truer account by enhypostasia, so that by union with the divine nature, human nature is understood not self-referentially, but through its association with the origin of its own existence in the divine being. Because Jesus' human nature is *homoousios*, it enables an understanding of humanity to escape self-enclosure and self-determination because this human nature exists only in relation to the divine nature and person of the Son. Without this divine reference, the human I is unable to move beyond itself so that natural law, when based exclusively upon human nature as a self-subsisting entity, becomes theologically attenuated.

Second, it overcomes speculative metaphysical natural law by affirming that the being of God is actualized in the history of Jesus, not reducible to reason *qua* reason, nor diffused non-personally as in Stoic *spermatikos logos*.

However, an over-emphasis upon the divine act as constituting the divine being may lead to a distorted immanent Trinity and a crude historicizing of God which threatens his freedom, so that God and humanity impinge upon and determine each other, as in process theology or historicist-experiential theology.[27] Hence while the divine *act* is a *divine* act, it is not such

25. John Webster, "The Ethics of Reconciliation," in Gunton, *Theology of Reconciliation*, 115. Henriksen, *Desire, Gift, and Recognition*, 255, argues that Girard makes the object of imitation not another person, but the other person's *desire* of an object. If so, it wrongly turns *imitatio Christi* into a competition between two desires, Christ's and the believer's.

26. Irenaeus, "Against Heresies," III. xvi. 6, 443.

27. The central concern of Molnar's *Divine Freedom* is the threat to the doctrine

that the act creates or shapes the divine being. There is a need to maintain the distinction between the eternal election of Christ to be incarnate, and the historic occurrence of the Incarnation. Without this distinction we may be led to understand God's being as historically determined, falling prey again to the mere historicizing and historical self-enclosure of God. Such an outcome would somewhat reflect the Aristotelian concept of virtue or character (nature and being) formation through acts. In this understanding, God's being is act-created and act-constituted, as though his being was deficient and requiring of the acts for development, formation, or perfection. Hence Aristotle's teleological ethics whereby virtues are created and shaped by acts is theologically contestable regarding God and, furthermore, contestable through Christ's Incarnation.[28] In both God and Christ, the acts are wholly congruent with the being so that the acts fully reveal the being and the being fully expresses itself in the acts, yet without the acts creating or forming the being.[29]

Barth's act/being exposition of Chalcedon's double *homoousion* provides significant means for a rapprochement of natural law and christological ethics, for the metaphysical/theological concerns of protological natural law and the anthropological concerns of teleological natural law are united in Christ's hypostatic union. This also theologically thickens christo-ethical radicalism and prevents its reduction to mere sage ethics.

b. Bonhoeffer

In *Act and Being* Bonhoeffer attempts to recast Heidegger's individualistic existential concept of existence—*Dasein*—in christo-sociological terms. *Dasein* for Heidegger was the mode of being of human beings, into which he succeeded in "forcing together act and being."[30] Bonhoeffer argues that the transcendental (being) and ontological (act) are only resolvable and in-

---

of the immanent Trinity when it is situated within human experience: "If our knowledge of God is not grounded in the very being of God himself . . . then it is in fact nothing more than our own religious or irreligious speculation grounded in our self-experience," 15. "Rahner's Rule," where the economic Trinity is the immanent Trinity, and vice versa, may lead to similar outcomes if the economic Trinity is read existentially. These are simply other ways of warning against ontotheology.

28. Christ "becoming perfect" (*telos*) in Hebrews 5:8 concerns soteriology and is not apposite.

29. Contra Byzantine theology that separates God's *energia* from his *ousia*, Ware, *Orthodox Church*, 232.

30. Bonhoeffer, *Act and Being*, 167, quoted in the editor's afterword to the German edition. *Act and Being* always capitalises the word *Dasein*.

terpretable sociologically in the church, the locus of revelation. Nonetheless, the church is not reducible to a mere sociological concept, for it is the place of "final revelation, as 'Christ existing as community' . . . as the δεύτερος ἄνθρωπος."[31] But the decisive difference is that unlike the first Adam, Christ the second Adam acted as a vicarious representative. Yet both acts were representative and brought corporate outcomes to sin or communion with God respectively. It is because Christ's representative action is vicarious that his action in being for others makes our "being-for-each-other" a basic form of humanity and ethics in communion with him.[32] This sociological emphasis means that the I and *Dasein* are irresolvable self-referentially, and can only be encountered and placed into the truth of Christ, through revelation and faith.[33] "It is clear . . . that on its own, the I cannot move beyond itself. It is imprisoned in itself . . . it basically does not understand itself."[34]

The relation between act and being is dialectical, for whilst being precedes acting, being acted upon—that is, being created—precedes being and leads to acting. The order is then: being acted upon, being, and acting.[35] For Bonhoeffer, act and being are cognitively, but not substantively, separable. Furthermore, the passive—being acted upon again—removes act and being from self-enclosure and immanent self-reference and places the I within theological and social contexts through which the I is more comprehensively understood and shaped by matters external to itself. Although Bonhoeffer understands act as always related to an individual person, he avoids the individualism of existentialism by predicating being to humanity generally, and as the person is a "synthesis of act and being," act is lifted out of individualistic self-enclosure.[36]

However, it is through Christology that Bonhoeffer forces together human *Dasein* and human sociality, for Christ is not only the second Adam but also constitutes the corporate nature of the church. This second Adam Christology means Bonhoeffer rejects the traditional *analogia entis* concept as an illegitimate ontology, for it grounds being in the first Adam and thus

---

31. Ibid., 112. He decisively argues this in *Sanctorum Communio*.

32. Bonhoeffer, *Sanctorum Communio*, 146, 184. "Vicarious representative action" is one of his "recurrent theological leitmotifs," J. von Soosten, "Editor's Afterword to the German Edition," 303.

33. Bonhoeffer, *Act and Being*, 114, 138. The Delphic oracle "γνωθι σεαυτόν, seeks to establish the ultimate self-justification of human beings," 138.

34. Ibid., 45. "Dasein . . . is not in itself self-subsistent," 38.

35. Ibid., 116, citing Luther.

36. Ibid., 120. Consequently "the nature of being must essentially be known before one can know how to act in an existential moment," Anderson, *On Being Human*, 58.

in sin, from which it attempts to produce a pure metaphysics of being. This constitutes a form of self-idolatry, of humanity becoming its own creator, unless it permits revelation to drive it into the sphere of the church.[37] This is exacerbated by conscience attempting to "limit sin to the act," and thus exonerating being from sinfulness.[38]

Bonhoeffer thus recasts act and being as explicit christological and ecclesial concepts. This has the triple effect of 1) removing it from immanent self-referentialism to a sociological/relational understanding; 2) excising it from the sin of the first Adam to the purity of the second Adam; and 3) affirming that *Dasein* cannot be understood properly apart from faith.[39] In this understanding of *Dasein*, Bonhoeffer anticipates Yoder's later christo-ecclesial ethic.

In terms of natural law, Bonhoeffer asserts that "creation is unable to provide a basis for the ontological definition of the human being in Christ" because "the world of entity is transcended and qualified by this personal being," God, so that "Christ sets Dasein free."[40] Here is a strong critique of a theologically neutral protological natural law because human being and act is always in either the first or second Adam. This is not simply a christological assertion but also a sociological one, for the being of persons is social, such that any attempt to understand being in a self-enclosed atomistic manner reduces true human nature. The social identity of being and act is determined by their connection with either the first or second Adam—they are thus not neutral, ubiquitous, or universal of themselves.

Even though Bonhoeffer appears to move in the opposite hermeneutical direction to Barth, from human existence to the divine,[41] the outcome nonetheless contests, like Barth, the notion that human nature (being and act) can be determined self-evidently by either reason or observation of natural inclinations. For Bonhoeffer, the common way to understand *Dasein* is non-christologically: that is, as being in the first Adam, and hence sinful and dysfunctional. This is the Heideggerian method and conclusions he dismisses.

---

37. Bonhoeffer, *Act and Being*, 138. In Adam, human beings "seek themselves in themselves," 139, citing Luther. Bonhoeffer's ecclesial determination of *Dasein* approximates Hauerwasian social/ecclesial formation of character, *Community of Character*, 83–86.

38. Bonhoeffer, *Act and Being*, 145.

39. Metaphysical answers are "surrendered by revelation," i.e., disclosed by it; Ibid., 153.

40. Ibid. For Bonhoeffer, "reality is conceptualised Christology," Dannals, *Aspects*, 151.

41. This is unsurprising, as he engages Heidegger.

Typical of this is existentialism's assertion that the essence of being results from a heroic act of self-creation out of mere existence, a parody of God's "Let there be . . ." (Gen 1:3). In this it places a premium value on the future, identical to the future focus of traditional moral reasoning. Yet there is "a genuine future only through Christ and the reality created anew through Christ" in faith, uniting creation, soteriology, and eschatology.[42] The dialectic of act and being occurs in the future as the "human being 'is' in the future of Christ—that is, never in being without act." Thus, while natural law's teleology might provide some clues about natural inclinations at a basic level such as nutrition, human relationships, and sexuality, and some clues about human goods through reason, it is not able to rise beyond either self-enclosed observable phenomena or self-referencing reason. Love of enemies is deeply problematic here. Even the Augustinian argument that the *summum bonum* is God by virtue of reason founders at this point, for reason as such is unable to give any moral or theological content to God as Father, Son, and Holy Spirit. Hence natural theology concepts of God cannot construct an adequate Christian teleological theory of natural law—even though they may serve an apologetic function—for they lack christological determination. Christological moral reasoning however unites the present with the future because Christ is both the Creator and the first fruits of the new creation (1 Cor 15:23).

This christological focus is maintained when Bonhoeffer later moves from considering *Dasein* itself to ethics proper. Because moral deliberation—questions about my being and my acts—concerns matters that are considered to be ultimate, ethics cannot finally be about my being good or doing good (being and act) because such an approach presupposes a view of reality that excludes God in Christ as that ultimate reality.[43] If moral deliberation is not placed within the framework of such ultimate reality, ethical reasoning is wholly reduced to the penultimate. Yet the ultimate (God) cannot displace the penultimate (humanity) by denying the goodness of creation and humanity, for this results in Gnosticism and pietism. The proper relation between the ultimate and penultimate is christological, for the Son is not only the Creator of time and the penultimate, but also the Redeemer of that penultimate for eternity and the ultimate. But the ultimate always takes precedence because, first, the Son is the Creator and Redeemer of the penultimate, and second, in his Incarnation, his divine nature takes priority over his human nature. Yet in his *being* and *work* Christ is both the ulti-

---

42. Bonhoeffer, *Act and Being*, 157.

43. Bonhoeffer, *Ethics*, 188–95. "All concepts of reality that do not take account of [Jesus Christ] are abstraction," 194.

mate and the penultimate: the ultimate as God the Creator and Redeemer, and the penultimate as created incarnate human nature.[44] Only by placing ethical deliberation within Jesus Christ, who perfectly unites the ultimate and the penultimate, can justice be done to both the final eternal concerns and the immediate temporal concerns that confront human *Dasein*. Finite and infinite goods are christologically determined.

Both Barth and Bonhoeffer provide, in different ways, heuristic tools to join the metaphysical/theological concerns of natural law with the historical focus of radical ethics through the being and act of God in the Incarnation, which through the enhypostasia of Christ's humanity also affects the being and act of human persons. Regarding natural law, if the being of God is in his acts and his acts inhere in his being, then the metaphysical concerns of natural law are revealed historically in Christ because of the consubstantiality of his divine nature with the Father, and the anthropological concerns of natural law are also revealed because of the consubstantiality of his human nature with ours. Regarding radical ethics, if the acts of Jesus cohere in the divine being, then the provincialism and voluntarism with which christo-radical ethics is charged dissolves under his divine nature.

As it has been argued that the being and the act of both God and humanity are united and revealed in Christ, a further fruitful avenue to pursue is the *Logos* Christology of John's Gospel and Chalcedon. Because the *Logos* is both God and flesh (John 1:1–2, 14), this anchors moral reasoning in that which is proper to both God and humanity.

3. The Logos Christology of Chalcedon

Chalcedon's affirmation that the only begotten Son is "God the Word, our Lord Jesus Christ" unites John 1:1 and 1:14 under a particular name. By becoming flesh, the *Logos* did not change into *sarx*, nor enter pre-existing *sarx* as either a visceral experience or a shop-front display, but assumed *sarx* as that which was proper to it for the purposes of redemption and re-creation. The movement is from the *Logos* to the *sarx*, but in such a way that the *sarx* illuminates and expresses the fullness of the *Logos*. Yet by anchoring both *Logos* and *sarx* in the personal name of Jesus Christ, Chalcedon prevents any abstractions that avoid the concrete life of Jesus as recorded in the Gospels.

In contrast, the tradition of seeking the rationale and basis for ethics in a speculative understanding of divine nature, as in Cicero, easily falls prey to

---

44. Ibid., 125–33. While I have argued that Bonhoeffer's christo-ecclesial understanding of ethics anticipates Yoder, he would likely dismiss Yoder as a "radical" whose binary view pits the ultimate against the penultimate, 127.

an ontotheology serving the will, and has been adequately critiqued by Nietzsche, Marx, and Feuerbach. As previously noted, Augustine's justification of slavery by eternal law indicates this tendency, partly because it replaces God's trinitarian personhood with the abstract concept of law. Similar, by starting from phenomenological anthropology in developing his doctrine of the Trinity, he tends to overlook God's act and being in the Incarnation. This method of *vestgium trinitati* constitutes a genuine form of *analogia entis*.[45] The problem with the *analogia entis*, or any other form of *analogia humanitas* that is de-christologized, is that it readily produces an inchoate concept of God or spirit invested with the forms of idealized social *mythoi* or *nomoi*. That is, the *humanitas* is itself an idealized concept determined by the reasoning of the wider world. God becomes a super-sized I. It is because of this that theology and ethics must be anchored in the life of Jesus in order to avoid the justifiable critique of suspicion and remain faithful to the being of God revealed in his own act.

By doing so, the reconfiguration of the *"vestigum trinitatis in creatura"* through the Incarnation[46] corresponds to Byzantine theology, which rejects psychological analogies as the means of knowing God and the *imago Dei*, and rather commences "from the idea of God in whose image man has been created."[47] Thus the Feuerbachian criticism is valid when the divine nature is de-christologized through the projection of forms of the *analogia entis*, in the same way that the "historical Jesus" became an empty cipher for liberal ideals. Barth's Antiochene method, whereby the divine nature is apprehended through its actuality in Christ, is not a naïve Christology and process, but rather the placing of the being and act of God in a coherent dialectical relation.[48] The act of God in the Incarnation avoids theological speculation because God's being is found "only from the Word of God, as it has already occurred and has been given to us in the Word of God."[49] Here the divine being or nature is actualist, because the Word that is both "in the beginning" and "was God" is also "the Word made flesh."[50] Chalcedon implies that "we do not know in the abstract what 'Deity' and 'humanity' really mean, but we

---

45. Augustine, *Holy Trinity*, 1–128. Barth rejects *vesitgia trinitatis* as well meaning but idolatrous, CD, I/1, 336–38.

46. Barth, CD, I/1, 346f.

47. Lossky, *Mystical*, 115.

48. Barth, CD, II/1, 257–321. God "does not exist in His divine being and perfections without Jesus Christ, in whom He is both very God and man," CD, II/2, 509. "Only in radical historicity is transcendence found," because abstract truth distorts biblical personalist reality, Zimmermann, *Theological Hermeneutics*, 49, 50.

49. Ibid., 261.

50. John 1:1, 14.

must learn to understand them in the light of the Incarnation, which first shows us what true Deity and humanity really are in their fullness, rather than the reverse."[51]

It thus follows that arguments about the divine nature must operate within an incarnational christological control belief, as does radical ethics, described in Part Two. Non-christological theology not only allows an inchoate concept of God and spirit, but also, by separating God's being from his act, drives a wedge between God's *potentia absoluta* and *potentia ordinata*, giving rise to the possibility of a wholly hidden and inscrutable God.[52] While conceptually these two categories are interesting, and seek to preserve the freedom and sovereignty of God (he has the power to do either A, B, or C, but actually did C), they effectively cut the knot between immanent (being) and economic (act) trinitarian theology, so that revelation concerning God's essence is not necessarily epistemologically trustworthy. This high voluntarism leads to four problems: first, the problem of arbitrariness in divine command theory; second, the exaltation of divine power over divine love;[53] third, the positing of the concepts of being or nature as antecedent entities in which God himself participates for existence;[54] and fourth, the human determination of divine nature which may legitimize non-ethical behavior and the use of violence by avoiding the example of Christ's acts, as per the Feuerbachian critique.

In contrast, following the Chalcedonian double *homoousios*, we propose to interpret the divine being and nature christologically, so that the concrete act of revelation precedes epistemologically, but not ontologically, the divine person and nature. Thus the epistemological priority of the actuality of the Incarnation over speculative concepts of divine being and nature inverts the asymmetrical relationship of Christ's two natures, where the divine takes precedence over the human whilst never diminishing it. This means that the enhypostasia of Christ's human nature—that it exists only in its relation to the divine nature in the one person, having no independent existence as a generic type—preserves the *ontological* priority of the divine nature, yet ensures that the human nature of Christ as the revelatory act of God takes *epistemological* priority. Hence there is cognitive access to the personal divine nature only through Christ's human nature in its concrete

---

51. Hunsinger, "Karl Barth's Christology," 132, reflecting Bonhoeffer and Barth.

52. Not to be confused with Luther's benign *Deus absconditus*.

53. "God is power" or "God is will" are foreign to Christian theology.

54. For example, see the existential concept of God as "being," approximating a verb, in John Macquarrie, *Principles*, 94–110. "The understanding of God as being rather than *a* being will bring new intelligibility." Being [is] the "*incomparable* that *lets-be* and is *present-and-manifest*," 107, 105, italics original.

acts: christological *acts* give access to the divine *nature* and *being*. In this method, the historical *sarx* of John 1:14 exegetes the eternal *Logos* of John 1:1. While the *Logos* exists eternally, Jesus Christ only exists through the *Logos's* apophatic and enhypostatic union with created human nature.[55] This means that the union of two natures includes the union of Christ's acts with the divine nature, for acts exist only in their natures, which themselves only exist hypostatically. The act is an act of the nature, and the nature is of the person, for there is no human nature without a human person, because nature only exists hypostatically. That is, *hypostasis* takes conceptual priority over *phusis* or *ousia*, and internal to the meaning of *ousia* and *phusis* is the act. Consequently, the union of Christ's two natures enables an understanding of the divine person through an analysis of the moral acts and life of Jesus. It is this that the *Logos* theology of Chalcedon encapsulates in "God the Word, our Lord Jesus Christ."

Such an approach preserves the asymmetry of the divine and the human natures, and the asymmetry between revelation and speculation, with the first of the pairs taking precedence in both cases. As the Incarnation is both an act by and about the divine being, access to the divine being is affected through that act. Natural law theory grounded in the divine nature, which bypasses the Incarnation as its commencement point, form, or substance, necessarily becomes speculative non-christological moral reasoning, and is thus unable to be properly accorded the descriptor "Christian."[56]

Furthermore, protological natural law, which locates the rationale for ethics in the eternal entities of God or the Good, implies an asymmetrical yet dependent relation between God and the world. This relation is variously understood: God is the reason, creator, orderer, or ground of the world, and the world is an emanation, image, or reflection of God, or divinely ordered pre-existent matter, or a divine creation.[57] Regarding this relationship,

---

55. Extending the rather static Patristic concern with Christ's two natures of Chalcedon, the Reformers introduced more dynamic concepts, including the *communicatio operationum* of Christ as well as the *communio naturarum*: Torrance, *Incarnation*, 221–32. Barth deepened this emphasis.

56. "The first and third articles of the creed can be understood only from the second," Barth, *CD*, III/4, 33. Luther: "to seek God outside Jesus is the Devil," in Ebeling, *Luther*, 235.

57. MacKenzie describes Laudian Church of England thought as being a social, political and ecclesial theory grounded in the order of the immanent Trinity, which regulates the divine economy as expressive of his being. This ordered economy is christological in that "the mind is to be held by Christ, and objectively ordered according to who and what He is—the Word made flesh, God in all His Goodness," MacKenzie, *God's Order*, 32. Yet because "the concept of 'order' undergirds [their] theology," 37, it is unclear whether order is the presupposition or result of the theology.

Athanasius's affirmation of creation *ex nihilo* necessarily implies a radical discontinuity between God and the world, between uncreated Creator and the created, between the necessary and the contingent.[58] In Hellenistic categories, God is being (unchanging, immaterial) whilst the world is becoming (visible, sensible, material, changeable), yet their relation is not one of emanation, competition, or synergism, but one of becoming's contingent creation through its election by the divine being. This high sovereignty is however not deistic, as God's election to be Creator includes his election to be creation's provider, covenant partner, and savior, through the Incarnation.[59] When read through Chalcedon's *logos* Christology, the natural law of our creation means that human nature is a created and contingent reality that is disclosed through the humanity of Jesus.

Conversely, when radical christological ethics fails to progress from the acts of Jesus to his divine nature it suffers a type of arrested hermeneutical development, failing to draw out the implications of the enhypostatic character of Christ's human nature and acts. With this tendency the divine nature is erased or eclipsed, resulting in an ethic which is adoptionist, liberal, or Ritschlian, with Christ's "'divinity' (being) more nearly adjectival than substantive, not intrinsic but participatory."[60] Because Christ's human nature only exists enhypostatically, it is incomprehensible and incoherent unless understood in relation to the divine hypostasis, the *Logos*, which was "in the beginning" and through which it is enhypostatized. Conversely, only through the life of Jesus do we properly learn what it means to utter the word "*Logos*", and subsequently what is proper moral reasoning (*dialogismos*) about the natures of both humanity and God.

---

58. "The creation of the world is not a truth of a philosophical order, but rather an article of faith," Lossky, *Mystical Theology*, 91, and Barth, *CD*, III/I, 3–22. "None of the world-views . . . has attained to the concept of creation by following to the end the way from noetics to ontology and genesiology, but has usually remained stuck either in noetics or at most in ontology," 340.

59. Anatolios, *Athanasius*. He argues that in *De Incarnation* and *Contra Gentes*, God is outside creation by his essence (*in se*) but inside creation by his power and love (*ad extra*), 38–47, but that it "belongs to God's goodness to overcome this ontological distance between himself and creation," 42. Thus the divine economy like the divine immanence includes his moral attributes such as mercy, grace, lovingkindness etc. MacDonald suggests that God became the Creator through his self-determination to be the Creator, not by determining (making) the creation itself, *Metaphysics*, 24–43. Thus "the creation of the world irreducibly and sufficiently pertains to God's own 'being,'" not just his act, 48.

60. Hunsinger, "Karl Barth's Christology," 130.

4. *Logos* Christology and the Problem of Reason

Traditional natural law's affirmation that human nature is transparent to unaided reason is problematic due to the conflicting nature of moral claims. If such transparency were evident, moral conclusions would be largely unarguable and non-controversial. Such contestability of the concept of nature causes McGrath to propose a new natural theology, and a threefold criticism of the received approach: first, reasoning is itself a culturally learned activity; second, "nature" is a constructed notion; and third and consequently, natural theology is therefore as equally bound by dogma as is revealed theology. "None of the multiplicity of interpretive frameworks that are brought to bear upon nature can be regarded as being authorised or legitimised by nature itself." McGrath thus proposes a distinctly Christian natural theology, grounded in John's *logos* Christology.[61]

Do these problems of natural law and reason lie in the definition of reason itself, the manipulation of reason by the will, or the defeat of reason by the emotions? Whatever the case, conflicting moral claims demonstrate that reason *qua* reason cannot be isolated from the rest of human moral psychology as a type of independent infallible umpire directing the rules of the game.

The opposition of reason and desire in traditional natural law suggests that emotions are invariably disruptive of reason. This implies that reason is essentially cool, detached and objective. So Boethius:

> Rid yourself
> Of joy and fear,
> Put hope to flight,
> And banish grief.
> The mind is clouded
> And bound in chains
> Where these hold sway.[62]

Here, Philosophy[63] argues that both the positive emotions of joy and hope, and the negative emotions of fear and grief all cloud the mind, even

---

61. McGrath, *Open Secret*. 169, 172–174.

62. Boethius, *Consolations of Philosophy*, Book I, vii, 21, from a poem by Lady Philosophy. She had previously declared that the Muses of Poetry, "these hysterical sluts ... slay the rich and fruitful harvest of Reason with the barren thorns of Passion," I, i, 4. Henriksen, *Desire, Gift, and Recognition*, 33–38, rehabilitates desire christologically: in Jesus' divine nature, God desires humanity; in Jesus' human nature, humanity desires God.

63. The capitalisation follows Boethius's feminine personification.

though "happiness is the highest good of rational nature," which cannot be taken away by Fortune if reason prevails.[64] However, emotions are not necessarily disruptive of reason, unless one defines reason as cool, tranquil objectivity. In fact, passions may inspire reason, as when deep feelings of injustice give rise to rational plans to right such wrongs, or when deep evil inspires horror which in turn leads to plans of social justice.

That reason is able to be manipulated by the will is unarguable, as demonstrated in the politicization of "truth," and tendentious legal arguments that plead innocence in the face of overwhelming evidence of guilt. Yet the will may also be empowered by virtue or faith to act according to reason in the face of overwhelmingly negative emotions, as found in the early Christian martyrs: based upon the belief in resurrection, such actions of faithfulness are reasonable.

Therefore, while emotions and volition may well disrupt reason, such disruption remains a possibility but not an invariant necessity or rule. This leads us to query the nature of reason itself. The Aristotelian split between practical and theoretical reason has been dismissed as not finally meaningful, although epistemologically interesting and even analytically helpful, for reason *qua* reason is non-existent: what exists are people who think. In its understanding of reason Christian natural law is confronted with a fundamental challenge, for its basic assertion that created human moral nature is rational and observable curiously tends to avoid the historically observable person of Jesus (1 John 1:1–3) who is the incarnate eternal *Logos* (John 1:1, 14) and the agent of creation (John 1:3). But as the Creator of his own created humanity, The Word hypostatically instantiates as Jesus what is morally true and good about divine and human natures. So it follows trivially that if the Word is the agent of creation, and natural law is a law of our creation, then Christ's created enhypostatic humanity would express natural law most fully. By ignoring such Christology, creation ethics tends towards moral Deism as it shifts the Creator out of the foreground, substituting him with creation itself. This distal location of God engenders an autonomous grounding of moral reasoning and consequently a conflict model of divine-human relations. In contrast, Chalcedonian Christology moves creation into the closest possible relation with the Creator because the created humanity of Jesus only exists through its assumption by and relation to the person of the divine Word and Son, so that christological moral reasoning and creation ethics become identical.[65]

---

64. Boethius, *Consolations*, II, iv, 31.

65. The basic concern of Anatolios, *Athanasius*, is precisely this relation. Chalcedon is the final determination of this relation in its most precise and focused location,

Without incarnational Christology, the nature and reasons (*logoi*) of creation are uncoupled from the nature and reason (*Logos*) of the Creator. Natural law looses its anchorage in the divine person and approximates a form of universal Creator-creation moral intermediary, tending to a view of reason and ethics that is non-personalist, static, and cold. It is this ubiquitous and transparent view of reason that, like McGrath, MacIntyre contests.[66] In respect to the multiple goods which confront human choosing, he suggests that in Aristotle's account "the individual human being confronts an alternative set of ways of life from a standpoint external to them all . . . [without] as yet *ex hypothesi* no commitment . . . [thus] such an individual has been deprived of the possibility of rational evaluation and rational choice." That is, the person is elevated above any historical anchorage, as a type of detached meta-moral agent. Yet because humans need to choose and act "*qua* rational beings . . . [they] cannot be understood in detachment from their necessary social context, that setting within which alone rationality can be exercised."[67] Justice and rationality are dialectically related and set within "some larger . . . overall view of human life and of its place in nature," whether in Aristotle's *polis,* Aquinas's complex integrated society, or Hume's Anglicizing society of ordered "mutualities and reciprocities of passion and interest." MacIntyre tends to an historicist anti-real understanding of reason and its claims to justice, for their social contexts "are not accidental or peripheral" to their philosophy.[68]

MacIntyre's rejection of the received account of practical rationality— "that there are standards of rationality adequate for the evaluation of rival answers to [moral] questions, equally available . . . to all persons"—suggests, like McGrath, the possibility of a specific Christian form of reason and practical rationality. MacIntyre's own primary interlocutors are the pre-Christian Greeks, Augustine, Aquinas, Hume, and liberalism. What he tends to miss is the practical rationality of the Hebrew tradition generally, and Christ in particular.[69] Curiously, while he uses "Christian," particularly when discussing Augustinianism and Thomism, he fails to mention Christ,

---

the one person of Jesus.

66. Particularly in *Whose Justice?* and *Three Rival Versions.*

67. MacIntyre, *Whose Justice?,* 133, describing Aristotle. Finnis's proposal that all basic goods are equal so that choosing between them is morally inert compounds the problem, for choice between competing goods is often fraught with difficulties, necessitating some type of center, base commitment or higher criterion which can guide such choice.

68. Ibid., 389.

69. Under "The Augustinian Alternative," he surveys the Old Testament and Paul, but doesn't mention Christ, Ibid., 147–63.

as though such tradition(s) of enquiry are themselves unembedded in their particular history stemming from Jesus.[70] Here he appears to fall foul of his own critique by de-historicizing claims of practical moral rationality: Jesus is stripped from his own narrative. Augustine is painted as a thinker who combines Plato and Scripture, and Thomas as synthesizing Augustine, Scripture, and Aristotle. Beyond occasional references to Paul, and a few Old Testament redactors, it is as though Scripture exists as a moral depository independently of its writers, in a curious form of quasi-dictation theory.[71] That anything like an Augustinian or Thomist tradition, as we have it, could arise without Christ, is as counter-rational as them arising without Plato or Aristotle respectively.

Despite this lack, MacIntyre opens up the possibility of a distinctive Christian understanding of reason, although he does not pursue it. MacIntyre offers a form of pre-critical realistic Scripture reading where "subject matter and depiction are one," in contradistinction to the modern hermeneutic which reduces the narrative to an extra-biblical referent. Such a referent, whether it be "a moral virtue, the religious self-conscious, or the fulfilment of history" and its attendant theory, served as "something of a foundation upon which the results of exegesis finally depended for their intelligibility."[72] With echoes of MacIntyre, the "ethical dimension of culture is not founded in a universal moral or historical self-consciousness . . . [but] must be seen as a product of the specific ethical practice through which a minority of ethical athletes have shaped a relation to the self as the subject of moral action."[73] Thus an intellectual is someone "who enacts in the form of a *vocation* the demand that we must attempt to be ethically responsible before the truth; in the terms . . . [of] Vaclav Havel, *to live in truth* . . . a life existentially devoted to the truth." However, by citing Havel's example of a grocer refusing to put the sign of support for the totalitarian Czech regime in his shop window as the prime example, such living in the truth is no longer an elitist phenomena.[74] Such an example of living or "*being in the*

---

70. "Jesus" or "Christ" have no index entry in any of his three main works, *After Virtue, Whose Justice?* and *Three Rival Versions*.

71. A "reader discovers him or herself inside the Scriptures" by interpreting the text in obedient trust and humility, the paradigmatic record being Augustine's *Confessions*, MacIntyre, *Three Rival Versions*, 82–83.

72. Thiel, *Nonfoundationalism*, 68, 69–70, indebted to Frei.

73. I. Hunter, *Culture and Government: Emergence of Literary Education*, (London: Macmillan, 1988), quoted by Osborne, *Aspects of Enlightenment*, 88–89.

74. Osborne, *Aspects of Enlightenment*, 169, italics original. Citing this incident, Vardy states that such action is counter the "human need to belong . . . [which] naturally leads to anti-realism or to constructivism in psychology," Vardy, *What is truth?*

truth is an existentialist expression of [the] coherentist idea," and "truth as coherence . . . has this . . . astonishing implication: that existence is made conditional on truth."[75]

Hence the MacIntyrian proposal coheres with Frei's text-narrative theory, so that the Bible as the source of Christian ethics is irreducible to any extra-biblical referent or abstraction. Following Hunter and Osborne, the exemplarist nature of Jesus' moral practice as found in Scripture functions normatively, despite not being elitist or heroic. Following Havel, Christ's moral life is understood as living the truth, based on his claim of being the truth (John 14:6). This establishes Jesus, as depicted in the Gospels, as the proper center and norm of moral reasoning, without reduction to abstract conceptuality, yet not without comportability with forms of abstraction which are consonant with the subject matter of the narrative. In Johannine terms, Christ the *Logos* determines the human *logos* of moral reasoning. Practical moral reasoning *(dialogismos)* is thus anchored to the *Logos*, both eternal and incarnate, so that through the history of Jesus we have access to proper human and divine nature, and what constitutes normative moral reasoning and natural law.

When discussing the idea of reason, the word *logos* is used here in a threefold fashion. First, it refers to the Johannine and Chalcedonian *Logos* that became incarnate. This preserves the pre-critical and non-reductionist identity of Jesus Christ as narrated in the Gospels without reduction to liberal human ideals or projection, while maintaining philosophical connection with the Chalcedonian tradition. Second, it refers to the divinely originated meaning and internally embedded rationality, form, and order of all contingent created entities, including their genus or kind, their operations, and their end, purpose, or goal. Third, it refers to human reasoning. Yet the basic conceptuality of reason and rational speech is maintained throughout all three uses, so that even when *logos* is translated "word," or "Word" as in John's Gospel, the sense of rationality is not excluded, for speech which is reliable is truthful, rational and coherent. That is, there is a direct relation between semantics and rationality so that speech, when truthful, exhibits the rationality that is proper and internal to those things that are the object of that speech.

As a first aspect of this Christian form of reasoning, we explore Christ as divine *Logos* in the prologue of John's Gospel and what that means for the ubiquitous and universal claims of natural law. The following chapter

---

157. The point is that communal "traditions of truth" can be lies.

75. Weissman, *Truth's Debt*, 77, contra those, e.g., Kant, Fichte, Hegel, who see truth as a function of the value-directed will.

explores *logos* cosmology and reasoning as found in representative writers of both the classical and radical theological traditions, and the meaning for ethics that can be extracted from them.

5. The Johannine *Logos*

a. Christ as Eternal Divine Logos Incarnate

Chalcedonian Christology can be understood as an exegesis of the second article of the Nicene Creed, formulated in response to aberrant psychological incarnational theologies concerning the relation between the divine and the created.[76] These proposals either separated or fused that which was to be related and united yet distinct. This debate was a particularly focused example of the enduring concern of the relation of the divine to the nondivine. This relation shapes protological natural law theory, which grounds reason or order in God's eternal essence or will and proposes a relationship between God and creation through the media of divine reason and law.

One promising avenue is Johannine *Logos* theology, which shows "that the eternal divine Logos cannot be found and known elsewhere than in this man Jesus," who, as incarnate and not just eternal, is included in the inner-trinitarian circle of God's glory.[77] Jesus is the *Logos* within both the immanent and economic Trinity, and the interior thought and external speech of God.[78] However, the initial concern of the Johannine *Logos* is not "the Word became flesh" but "the Word was God"—John 1:1 precedes John 1:14—so that any understanding of reason and *Logos* is defined firstly by *theos,* but through *sarx*. The asymmetrical relation between God and humanity is reflected in the asymmetrical relationship between Jesus' divine and human natures: his divine nature is eternal, whilst his human nature is assumed, and exists only enhypostatically with his divine personhood. Human reason cannot commence with itself—ascending speculatively to God and then descending to itself in self-determination and definition—but must commence with the eternal *Logos* as manifested in the Incarnation. The initial material content of the *Logos* is "the Word was God," and its epistemological entry point is "the Word became flesh."

---

76. Particularly Nestorian dualism and Eutychian monphysitism.

77. Barth, *CD*, III/2, 66, 65.

78. Of being God's speech: "if the eternal Logos is the Word in which God speaks with Himself . . . then in its identity with the man Jesus it is the Word in which God thinks the cosmos . . . and imparts to the cosmos the consciousness of its God," Barth, *CD*, III/2, 147.

b. Logos in John 1:1–18

The following descriptions of the *Logos* are clear:

1. Pre-temporal eternity, v. 1a, 2, (*archē*).
2. Divine relationship, v. 1b, 2, (*pros*).
3. Divine identity, v. 1c, (*ēn*).
4. Agent of creation, v. 3, (*dia*).
5. Locus of all life, v. 4a, (*ēn*).
6. Locus of universal human enlightenment, v. 4b–5, (*ēn*).

The use of *ēn* in v. 1–2, 4 means that the *Logos* existed pre-temporally, and was the source and locus of life, while the use of the preposition of agency (*dia*, v. 3, 10) makes the *Logos* the agent of creation. The clear association with Genesis 1:1 strengthens it as the divine source of creation.

The source of light is life (v. 4),[79] constituting enlightenment as a living personal entity. Darkness is thus death or non-being, by implication.

The term "the true light" (v. 9) implies that contradictory claims to human enlightenment are false and keep humanity in darkness (v. 5) and non-life (v. 10). This light is self-authenticating (v. 5, 9), yet not without human witness (v. 6–8). Combined with non-reception (v. 11) and unbelief (v. 12, implied), darkness and non-life constitutes John's negative understanding of the *cosmos* (v. 10b). Consequently, theological/metaphysical and human reasoning, including moral reasoning, is inadequate in proportion to its non-*Logos* character.

The Johannine *Logos* empowers those who receive and believe in him to be born of God (v. 12). This *Logos*-generated birth is contrasted with birth from human blood, flesh and will (v. 13). Here John's dualism is anthropological in respect to human origins. *Logos* reception brings divine birth; *Logos* rejection perpetuates purely human birth.

Most significantly, contrary to the immanent Stoic *spermatikos Logos*, John refers to the *ensarkos Logos* (v. 14). The use of *egenetō* implies that such *ensarkos Logos* was previously *asarkos Logos*. The use of *aletheias* in v. 14 (repeated from v. 9) focuses truth upon a particular historical manifestation of *sarx*. In contrast to the impossibility of humanity becoming God's children though being *born of sarx* the *Logos* becomes *sarx* (v. 13), so that the *sarx* reveals the person of the *Logos*.[80]

---

79. "The words light and life are among the most characteristic of the gospel," Barrett, *The Gospel According to John*. 131.

80. Σάρξ here means "humanity over against God," i.e., distinct from God,

1. Egenetō and ēn

Of particular significance in John's prologue is the contrast between the aorist indicative *egenetō* (became) and the imperfect *ēn* (was). We note first the use of *egenetō*.

- All things *egenetō* through the *Logos*, v. 3.
- The witness *egenetō* from God, v. 6.
- The cosmos *egenetō*, v. 10.
- The *Logos egenetō sarx*, v. 14.
- Grace and truth *egenetō*, through the *Logos*, v. 17.

The whole creation, including humanity, which never *ēn*, *egenetō* absolutely, whereas the singular *Logos* which *ēn*, *egenetō* flesh, grace and truth, one becoming among others. The be*coming* of the cosmos is grounded in the *being* of the *Logos* through a purposeful creative act, not by emanation or pan(en)theistic participation. It is this *becoming* of the *Logos* as *sarx* that is so significant for Christian ethics, for it instantiates and localizes the reason, graciousness and true nature of divine reality that underlies protological natural law. The *Logos's* assumption of human nature is no less an act of divine creation as was the beginning of the cosmos. What is impersonal and diffuse in Stoicism is specific and personal in John, for the "*Logos's ēn*" takes on individual human existence by "*egenetō sarx*." Stoic rationalism, fatalism and *apatheia* are replaced by the humanity, graciousness and life of John's *Logos*. The *egenetō* historically and personally anchors the *Logos*.

Second, particular significance is attached to the use of the imperfect *ēn*. We note the following:

- The *Logos ēn* pre-temporal, with God, and as God, v. 1.
- The *Logos ēn* pre-temporally with God, v. 2.
- The *Logos ēn* the light and the life of humanity, v. 4.
- The witness to the *Logos ēn* not the light, v. 8.
- The pre-temporal *Logos,* as light, *ēn* coming into the world, v. 9.
- The *Logos* as light *ēn* in the world, v. 10.
- The witness testifies to the *Logos's* pre-temporal existence and temporal priority: the *Logos ēn*, v. 15.

The use of *ēn* is limited to the *Logos* himself: it is explicitly denied to the witness, and absent from the *cosmos* and *ta panta*. The being of the *Logos*

---

equivalent to the OT "flesh and blood," Barrett, *John*, 137.

is eternal, divine, life-giving, illuminating, present in the world, and precedes human rationality. It enters visibly into the cosmos, as distinct from its being the cause of the cosmos, by becoming *sarx*. The *Logos's egenetō* thus provides access for the world to the *Logos's ēn*.[81] In respect to the *Logos*, the *egenetō* humanly reveals its *ēn*, while the *ēn* divinises its *egenetō*. This suggests, and will be taken up later, that moral realism can only be articulated through concrete history, as the latter not only provides the epistemological handle to grasp the real, but also is itself the manifestation of the eternally real. *Logos ensarkos* thus unites the rational and the empirical (1 John 1:1–4), eternal forms and the objects that participate in them, and the Good, and the good.

II. Natural Law and Universal Enlightenment

For our purposes, a crucial interpretive question concerns v. 9b (the enlightenment of all people), and v. 10a (who was in the world): does the *Logos* enlighten humanity as *asarkos, ensarkos,* or both? The self-evidence of natural law implies universal moral enlightenment. If v. 9b refers to human enlightenment as *asarkos*, we have a cosmological principle of universal moral enlightenment and self-evidence as aspects of general revelation without necessitating the Incarnation.[82] If v. 9b is understood as *ensarkos* alone, we have an incarnation of the light that was not manifested previously, implying universal darkness prior to the Incarnation. In the former, universal enlightenment is pre-incarnational as well as incarnational: if the latter, it is incarnational alone. The first use of *phōs* (v. 4–5) suggests enlightenment is coterminous with the existence of *zōē* and the creation of *anthrōpos*. The parallels with Genesis 1:1–3 are clear: the bursting forth of light in the first word of creation (Gen 1: 3) banishes the darkness of all things (John 1:3, 5). *Egenetō* (v. 9c, pres. mid. part.) suggests that while the *Logos* enlightened all humanity *asarkos*, by becoming *ensarkos* this light became personally focused. Verse 9b anticipates the *Logos ensarkos* of v. 10 and the consequent manifestation of the divine life, glory, grace, and truth. Because the one *Logos* is both *asarkos* and *ensarkos*, pre-incarnational universal human enlightenment is a christological concept. However, due to the world's darkness (v. 5, 10b), *Logos asarkic* moral enlightenment is

---

81. "He was, *ēn*, beyond all *egeneto*," K. Barth, *Witness to the Word*, 20, n.13.

82. The christological statement of Hebrews 1:1–3, which affirms pre-christological, although non-perfect divine revelation, is supportive. "Perfect" is understood here in Hebrews' focused sense of christological fulfillment and supersession of previous revelatory acts.

ambiguous, non-exhaustive, and partial. If otherwise, the *Logos ensarkos* becomes epistemologically redundant.

Does such pre-incarnational enlightenment run the danger of naïvely baptizing the Stoic *spermatikos logos*? It would if the *Logos* was quarantined from the Incarnation and remained an abstract universal immanent *nous asarkos*. It is for this reason that *asarkos* is better substituted by *presarkos*, as "*presarkos*" provides the temporal aspect essential to a Christian theory of reality, and also implies the later *ensarkos*.[83]

The internal rationality of the *cosmos* and *ta panta* is derived from the *Logos,* for creation necessarily contains the rationality of he from whom it was created. Without this recognition, moral reasoning looses its anchorage in the Christian tradition and becomes speculative. When detached from the *Logos ensarkos*, moral reasoning loses its Jesus-oriented nature. When detached from the *Logos asarkos*, it loses its classical and credal nature. The split between the positive (v. 10ab) and negative use of *cosmos* (v. 10c) is determined by its relation to the *Logos*. *Logos* creation constitutes the *cosmos* as good, yet non-recognition of the *Logos* by the *cosmos* (v. 10c, 11b) constitutes darkness. For reasoning moral agents, receiving or rejecting the *Logos* gives true or false moral apprehension respectively.

When *Logos asarkos* moral enlightenment is detached from its *ensarkos* instantiation, eternal moral laws that perdure through time become metaphysically and ontologically oppressive, as in Augustine's doctrine of eternal law, or speculative, as in Stoicism. Such speculation detaches the *being*ness of creation from its *becoming*ness through the *Logos's* direct personal act, so that its *being*ness becomes self-subsistent, self-referentially cognizant, and internally sustaining and inhering. It is also severed from the moral determinations of the *Logos ensarkos* itself. For instance, Thomistic natural law lacks significant christological *Logos ensarkos* determination.[84] The solution is to interpret John 1:9b by the *into the cosmos* of v. 9c. This *into* is given temporal significance and content by: 1) the *Logos egenetō sarx*, and tabernacling among us (v. 14); 2), the concrete historical actuality of this *ēn*

---

83. *Logos presarkos* and *Logos asarkos* will be used synonymously, yet the *presarkos* meaning is to the fore and always implied by the latter term. *Presarkos* does not imply time as a non-created essence of God's, or the Word's, being.

84. McGrath argues that Luther's problem with his Catholic inheritance was its non-christological character, not metaphysics as such, which he saw as "appropriate when it represents a considered *a posteriori* response to the biblical narrative; what is unacceptable . . . is the theological deployment of an *a priori* metaphysical framework which is determined in advance of and independent of the narrative," *Scientific Theology*, vol. 3, 284–285. Luther's binary categories of the theology of cross and theology of the glory represented metaphysics *a posteriori* and *a priori* respectively, McGrath, *Luther's Theology*, 136–41.

(v. 15b); and 3), the name Jesus Christ (v. 17). In particular, this *ēn* (v. 15b) ties the present with the pre-existent, as further clarified in v. 15c. Hence the highly specific *houtos* (this, v. 15b) *Logos ensarkos,* Jesus Christ, provides the historical handle for grasping the metaphysical eternal *Logos asarkos ēn.* The temporal *this* is the eternal *was.* As such it provides true understanding of *ta panta* which *egenetō* and where not *ēn.*

Consequently, when the *cosmos, ta panta* or *phusis* are understood in ways that are incongruent with the localized and concrete *Logos ensarkos egenetō,* their be*coming* is readily misunderstood as *being.* This may occur synthetically, when each entity is understood in its cosmological context without reference to the *Logos,* or analytically, when each entity is understood in its self-enclosed internal existence. Either way, their *logos* is determined in a *non-Logos* manner. In contrast, it is argued here that each aspect of the *cosmos* or *ta panta* is a *being* from a be*coming,* with their be*coming* grounded in the eternal divine *being* of the *Logos* which assumed concrete human existence in the *Logos's* be*coming.*[85] All *egenetō* is a creation by and understood from the *Logos's* eternal *ēn,* which is noetically grasped in his temporal incarnate *egenetō.*

Consequently, a Christian understanding of cosmology and reality is shaped in a personal, contingent, and historical fashion because the agent of creation is the *Logos presarkos* who becomes *ensarkos* in time and space. This means that, 1), the *being* of the *Logos presarkos* is known, and known to be personal; 2), the *being* of the *cosmos* is understood as a definite and temporal be*coming*; and 3), the moral rationality of the *cosmos's* temporal *being* is accessible in and through its relation to the *Logos.* John 1:1–18 leads to a theory of cosmological moral reasoning which is christological, non-speculative, concrete and historical. Because human nature is the pinnacle of the creation of *ta panta* (Genesis 1), and was assumed by the eternal Word in such a way that neither the human or divine natures were reduced, cosmological moral reasoning—reasoning about *ta panta*—is properly christological. The Incarnation of the eternal Word is the means by which that which is morally proper to humanity is discerned. Natural law's practical moral reasoning about what is proper to humanity, and christological moral reasoning, are twin aspects of the one reality. Yet because the *Logos* precedes the creation of human moral reasoning (*dialogismos*) and is its cause, any

---

85. It may be schematised temporally: divine *Logos presarkos being* à created *logos* be*coming* and *being* à divine *Logos ensarkos* be*coming* à created *logos being* understood though the divine *Logos ensarkos* be*coming.* The be*coming* and the *being* of the created *logos* are sustained providentially by the *Logos,* otherwise they lapse back into non-*being.*

determination of what is morally proper to human nature is attenuated to the extent of its christological lack.

6. Conclusion

This chapter has outlined an understanding of *logos* and reason grounded in Chalcedon's double *homoousion* and John's prologue. Barth's act/being thematic enables a determination of the being of God in the act of the Incarnation, so that the *theological* concerns of protological and metaphysical natural law become non-speculative and historically focused in Jesus. Bonhoeffer's act/being thematic enables a determination of the being and acts of humanity such that the *anthropological* concerns of natural law are likewise non-speculatively determined christologically within the sphere of the church.

Consequently, two-nature Christology functions as a control belief that determines the proper acts and nature of both God and humanity, which are the focal concerns of natural law. Further, Chalcedon's *logos* Christology enables a Christian theory of moral reasoning *(dialogismos)* which is determined by the life of Jesus. Here the subject of reasoning and the practice of reasoning co-inhere, because the *Logos* as his own subject reveals what constitutes proper *dialogismos* as a practice. The *Logos* expresses proper *dialogismos,* so that Jesus' moral reasoning and life is proper both theologically/metaphysically and anthropologically/historically. Consequently, the Incarnation methodologically frames and expresses both classical and historical forms of moral *dialogismos*: the classical, because he is the eternal *Logos presarkos,* and the historical, because he is the historical *Logos ensarkos.* If Christ's humanity theologically matters, then its morality also matters and expresses the proper moral shape of humanity's historical character. Because morality is a highly contested area of reasoning, such a statement will be controversial. Yet if the theology of Chalcedon stands, the eternal *Logos,* who became historical in assuming human nature, enables a form of moral reasoning which is proper to *ta panta,* as noted in John's prologue. This means that Christ's own practical moral reasoning is the focal instance of true moral reasoning and may lay claim to universal scope.

6

Logos Cosmology and Christological Ethical Reasoning

1. Introduction

NATURAL LAW PURPORTS TO be a rationally defensible account of intrinsic moral principles and ends universally inherent in human nature. As human nature is a constituent element of empirical reality, this locates natural law within the wider traditions of science—as demonstrated for instance in Aristotle, who places natural law within the sphere of physics (natural philosophy). On this understanding, natural law is a moral subset of the laws of nature.

In a sense, this is also the approach of Cicero, whose metaphysical *spermatikos logos* is immanent throughout creation. This universally embedded divine rational law is the means of discerning the fixed compass points for both morality and law. Because of the unity of the cosmos, this moral compass transcends historical and cultural particulars, and is accessible to all, even though it is especially available to the sage. The overtones of pantheism are clear. The problem, as outlined earlier, is that Cicero's *spermatikos logos* is impersonal, static, and coldly rational, and there is no real handle with which to grasp it.

Nonetheless, Cicero's concern to ground morality and law in transcendent realties is reasonable, despite the Kantian objections, and enables criticism of unjust positive law from a more stable perspective than social exigencies or voluntarist quests for power. Despite the tendency to downplay ubiquitous moral order in the social sciences, it is clear from the hard sciences that there are universal structures and laws that govern how the cosmos functions at various levels. Despite the popular embrace of empiricism, rationalism still resides in the heart of science and mathematics, as in their prediction of sub-atomic particles prior to their empirical measurement. And demands for retributive justice for universally condemned actions constitute a claim for meta-historical moral balance. While Cicero's *spermatikos logos* is inadequate as an ethic, it lies behind this chapter in its attempt to ground natural law as a human and moral dimension of those rational laws that are embedded within the wider cosmos. Hence Cicero's concerns about cosmological natural law serve as this chapter's starting point.

However, two critical aspects for a Christian approach to Cicero's concerns are acknowledged. First, Cicero's impersonal rationality is given a human face in the Incarnation of the eternal Word. Unlike Stoicism's impersonal and cold *logos,* the incarnate Word of the Gospel is fully human, essentially relational, forgiving, and self-giving. Christological natural law is more wet cement than concrete. But it also has more shape and structure than the formless gas of relativistic postmodernism. Second, this Word, as the agent of creation, has imbued creation with a rationality which reflects his own. Thus the laws of the universe and natural law are not internally coherent, stable, and universal because they are self-subsistent in and of themselves, but because the personal and eternal Word created them. This unites the Word himself, the cosmos, and the laws of nature in such a fashion that natural law is unable to be properly understood without reference to both the Word and the cosmos. This means that there is, conceptually, a double determination of natural law. First, natural law is conceptually determined by the personal Word: without the eternal *Logos*, there would be no proper natural law or moral *logos*. Second, natural law is conceptually determined by creation: without creation there would be no laws of nature and thus no natural law. It is therefore not possible to engage conceptually with natural law without also engaging with both the eternal Word and the creation of which natural law is a constituent part. As such, the scientific and cosmological discussion that follows is essential.

Notwithstanding this conceptuality, in its actuality natural law is inherent in creation, not laid over it as a type of accretion or an extra layer. Its predictable, reliable, and norming qualities are gifts from the Word to the cosmos in the act of creation, which enable it to function in an orderly manner. And because the Word never abandons his creation, natural law does not take on a deistic sense, which would re-route us back to Cicero, but is a manifestation of continual providence. But even stronger—because the Word became part of the creation, this Word not only remains gracious and personally engaged with creation, but is itself accessible historically. That is, the eternally rational Word takes into his own person the created rationality of the cosmos, which as his own creation is wholly congruent with the rationality that is his own. Here there can be no disassociation between the rationality of the Word and the rationality of the cosmos: in the one person they coexist harmoniously. In traditional theological language, this can be expressed as saying that natural law is the mind of Christ.

However, since Kant, ethics has increasingly been reduced to a form of practical reasoning about the phenomenal, particularly the self, disconnected from theoretical reasoning of the noumenal.[1] Consequently, ethics has increasingly turned from metaphysics, resulting in an ethically inert universe.[2] If practical moral reasoning is wholly about the future and severed from the present, then current existence cannot function as a resource for moral reasoning.

In contrast, it is argued here that moral reasoning is necessarily realist because the universe's intrinsic morality is non-illusory and ineradicably grounded in the moral nature of God its Creator; that this moral nature is particularly focused in human nature in accordance with the anthropic principle of science;[3] and that this nature is seen most perfectly in the enhypostatic humanity of the incarnate eternal Word of God. This makes the moral life of Jesus—his words, relations and acts—normative for all persons, who by virtue of their origin, are created and modeled upon him as their archetype. Thus "ethical knowledge is logically related to knowledge about the way the world is as well as to knowledge of transcendent reality."[4]

Four theorists representing the two traditions constituting this thesis will be considered. From the classical tradition, Maximus the Confessor and T. F. Torrance are evaluated. From the radical tradition, Nancey Murphy and George Ellis are examined. By considering these, a rapprochement between christo-ethical radicalism and natural law is explored. The classical approach best represents what Ellis calls top-down reasoning, while the radical approach best represents what he describes as bottom-up reasoning,

---

1. T. Peters, in Pannenberg, *Theology of Nature*, 2.

2. Murphy and Ellis, *Moral Nature*, 104. Is Kant's dualism a strategy to secure human freedom from the rigid determinism of Newtonian mechanics?

3. Most simply, it is "the idea . . . that the universe exists so that human beings can exist," Stephen May, "Introduction," in Rae et al., *Science and Theology*, 9. The Weak Anthropic Principle describes the possibilities and conditions for the intelligible observation of the universe, whereas the Strong Anthropic Principle describes the necessity of intelligible life in the universe, Murphy and Ellis *Moral Nature*, 52–53.

4. Murphy and Ellis, *Moral Nature*, 6.

although neither can be exhaustively so described.[5] Top-down reasoning rejects the idea that exhaustive explanatory causation for both events and entities inhere in the entities or events themselves, arguing that a true account of causation necessarily requires more complex upper levels. This eliminates simple reductionism, and is coarse-grained. Bottom-up reasoning examines the processes of causation, whereby the whole, as a more complex entity or event than its parts, is determined by its constituent parts, and is fine-grained.[6] That top-down and bottom-up reasoning are often pitted against each other lies less in their incommensurability than in the lack of moral imagination and integration that a *Logos* Christology enables.

2. Maximus the Confessor's Doctrine of the *Logos*

Maximus the Confessor was a strong Nicene/Chalcedonian theologian who developed a *logos* theology of creation grounded in God's rationality expressed in the Incarnation.[7] Three elements of Maximus's thought will be considered: 1) his *Logos/logoi* thematic; 2) his *logos/tropos* doctrine; and 3) and his doctrine of laws, before 4) drawing out their ethical significance.[8]

a. Maximus's Logos/Logoi Thematic

Countering the Hellenistic concepts of divine impassibility and motionlessness, Maximus's *Logos* doctrine is dynamic, for he maintains that motion is both inherent in the impassability of God by virtue of his inner-trinitarian relations of love, as well as his free decision to act *ad extra*. Motion is consequently inherent in the nature of the things which God, who is himself dynamic, creates.[9] In contrast, *apatheia* in a positive sense is found in the neo-Origenist Evagrius, one of Maximus's primary interlocutors. Evagrius argued that theological *apatheia*, once realized in this life, enabled contemplation of the *logoi* that lie behind the natural order, which are "the principles in accordance with which everything in the cosmos was created

---

5. Ellis, *Universe of Ethics*, 14, 32.

6. For the former, see Ellis, *Universe of Ethics,* 16; for both, see Murphy and Ellis, *Moral Nature,* 20.

7. "A typical exponent of extreme top-down neo-Chalcedonism," Bathrellos, *Byzantine Christ*, 112.

8. Maximus uses many Aristotelian terms: *logos* is the focus here. *Tropos* means mode.

9. Thunberg, *Man and the Cosmos*, 31–32.

through the Word of God, the *Logos*."[10] *Apatheia* is necessary because the Fall has rendered the *logoi*, especially the human *logos*, opaque, conflicted and unstable. In particular, the Fall is understood by Evagrius in a neo-Origenist fashion as motion and movement, the opposite of God's complete impassability. Apprehending the *logoi* is a sequential threefold process: first, successful *apathetic* contemplation of the *logos* of one's soul; second, the perception of the *logoi* of the wider creation; and then finally ascending to God, the true *Logos*, in prayer *(theologia)*. This is not dissimilar to the *analogia entis* of the Western tradition, and Augustine's *vestgium trinitatis*, which follows an inductive method, moving from the creation to the Creator.[11]

Maximus reverses this order by placing perception of Christ the *Logos* as the first step in the epistemological process. The incarnate Christ "took upon himself our human nature . . . without change, diminution or division; he maintained it inalterably, by its own essential principle and definition."[12] This apophaticism means that Christ's human nature exhibited perfect creational intention and character, so that access to human perfection is revealed in the incarnate Christ. Consequently, Maximus's Chalcedonian apophaticism—that Christ's two natures are ἀσυψχυύτως, ἀτρέπτος, ἀδιαιρέτως and ἀχωρίστως—implies that their cataphatic opposites indicate the rupture of creation: "Confusion, change, division and separation almost invariably carry negative connotations with Maximus" and describe the effects of the Fall on human beings, so that even though the *logoi* of created natures are not fundamentally altered, their apprehension is distorted.[13] The Fall has divided and separated the *tropoi* (modes) from their *logoi*, and confused and changed their relation, even though it has not eradicated or altered God's purposes for the nature, character and ends of anything he has created. As the *logoi* are the divine determinations inherent in creation by virtue of God's creative will and power, they are ineradicable but are "are obscured by the *tropoi* (modes or idioms) that the natures assume" as a

---

10. Louth, *Maximus the Confessor*, 37. Louth argues that Maximus inverted Evagrius's approach, especially his Origenist metaphysics, 37–38.

11. Thunberg, *Man and the Cosmos*, 35, suggests this major feature of Latin theology in rejected by Orthodoxy. The Trinity "left no trace whatsoever to be comprehended . . . for it does not belong to the nature of created order to contain the Uncreated, nor can the Infinite be embraced by finite beings," Maximus, "Ambiguum 10," in Thunberg, *Man and the Cosmos*, 44.

12. Maximus, "Ambiguum 42," in *Cosmic Mystery*, 84. Maximus's anthropology is a "fruit of [his] reflection on . . . Chalcedon . . . [and] Constantinople," Thunberg, *Microcosm and Mediator*, 19.

13. Louth, *Maximus*, 50.

result of the Fall.[14] Thus for Maximus, all the *logoi post-lapsum* are epistemologically opaque. Only in the Word becoming flesh is any *logos* found truly, because his *logos* is not hidden behind a disordered *tropos*. Consequently, a proper cognitive relationship to the *Logos* is the necessary commencement point for a proper understanding of the *logoi* of all created entities. Thus Maximus reverses Evagrius's method. Any incipient neo-Platonism that appears in his affirmation that the *logoi* participate in the *Logos* is blunted because such participation is causal and relational, not substantial as in the Platonic Form or Good.[15] The *logoi* are created by, in, and for the *Logos* (Col 1:16–17). In this sense, Calvin later concurs with Maximus when he asserts that natural law itself is stable, yet regarding natural reason "we . . . find in how many respects it is blind."[16] Thus the intelligibility inherent in creation is not accurately apprehensible without the *Logos* because not only does he determine and interpret the creation's *logoi*, but in becoming human assumed the proper *logos* of creation's apex.

Maximus's metaphysical/theological concept of *logoi* thus places human nature and acts within the broader realities of creation, both being ordered by the *Logos*. Orthodoxy tends to have a greater cosmological dimension than the West, although it is a function of soteriology.[17] Maximus exemplifies the "Eastern tradition [which] knows nothing of 'pure nature' to which grace is added . . . there is no natural or 'normal' state, since grace in implied in the act of creation itself."[18] However, the doctrine of humanity as a microcosm, whilst significant in Eastern and Maximian theology, is secondary to humanity's theological determination.[19] So while the *logos* of humanity is set within, and united and coordinate with, the *logoi* of the cosmos, its primary relation is with the *Logos* as the Creator and Sustainer of all *logoi*: the human *logos*/divine *Logos* relation takes precedence over that of the human *logos*/cosmological *logos*. Thus, "the many *logoi* are the one Logos to whom all things are related and who exists in himself without

---

14. Ibid., 58. This distinction is similar to the dualism of essentialism, noted in Part Two, but is a result of sin rather than being proper to human existence.

15. He "rejects the negative, pessimistic, Platonic-Origenistic view according to which, before coming into existence, the beings pre-existed, substantially united with the divine Logos," Bahrim, "Anthropic Cosmology," 13.

16. Calvin, *ICR*, II.ii.24, 282–283, although Calvin was clearly not dependent upon Maximus.

17. "The cosmology of revelation is essentially geocentric," i.e., human focused, Lossky, *Mystical Theology*, 105.

18. Ibid., 101.

19. Bahrim, "Anthropic Cosmology," 28–31, discusses the anthropic principle in Maximus and science.

confusion . . . the one God, the Logos of the Father." Although this sounds pantheistic, it is in fact a doctrine of participation and recapitulation based on Ephesians 1:10, which consists not in substance but in intellect, reason, sense-perception, vital motion, or fittingness.[20] A *logos* is not an *ousia* or *phusis*, but the divine origin and purpose of an *ousia* that is yet to be embodied or created according to the divine will and purpose.[21] Furthermore, each *logoi* is not confused with other *logoi*, for apophatic affirmations are also found between them: "each is unmistakably unique in itself and its identity remains distinct in relation to other things."[22]

At a simple level, Maximus's *logoi* are "the ideas and wills of God according to which he creates all things" and constitute each creature's nature, constitutive difference, causal and rational account, limit, and purpose.[23] These *logoi* are divinely implanted so that "God comes to be present in each creature as its determination," and "all the logoi are uniformly contained in the universal Logos."[24] This concept of participation is causal and rational, not substantial. Hence the *logoi* constitute each creature's unity in the one, or universal (God), as well as their differentiation and mutual relation in the many particulars (as separate creatures), and pre-exist in God prior to their actual creation.[25]

Consequently, moral reasoning is proper only when determined by the *Logos*, because the *logoi*—God's will and purpose—of humanity exist through their participation in the *Logos*. And as the *logoi* of all created things is ineradicable, the nature (kinds) and purpose (ends) of human life, as particular focal instances of these *logoi*, are also permanent. But they are also dynamic, in the same way as the *Logos*, in which they participate, is dynamic. And because these *logoi* are common to all people, the ubiquitous character of natural law is maintained.

Although Maximus does not provide an account of the practical means of arriving at such moral knowledge, his reversal of Evagrius suggests that contemplation of Christ would be the likely starting point. Yet to avoid falling into mystical inchoateness by simply inverting the direction of

20. Maximus, "Ambiguum 7," *Cosmic Mystery*, 54–55.
21. Bahrim, "Anthropic Cosmology," 14f.
22. Maximus, "Ambiguum 7," *Cosmic Mystery*, 54.
23. Perl, *Methexis*, 147–150.
24. Ibid., 151.

25. Ibid., 152, who sees Maximus as exhibiting the influence of Neoplatonism, Origen and Evagrius, 171–172. On this matter, von Balthasar describes Maximus as inheriting the Christian adaptation of Pseudo-Dionysius, expanding that of Gregory of Nyssa, whilst avoiding all neo-Platonic pantheism; von Balthasar, *Cosmic Liturgy*, 116.

Evagrius's mysticism, contemplation of Christ needs to be anchored in the Gospels because they are the only objective sources of the *Logos*. This redirects ethics back to christo-ethical radicalism's focus upon Jesus, yet with a richer metaphysical and theological framework. Contemplation thus yields to reading, but the reading is lifted out of any historical imprisonment and into the eternal *Logos* who is both the creator and Incarnation of humanity's *logos*. The human *logos* of the narrative is the Creator *Logos* (John 1:1). The compelling moral character of Jesus expresses and articulates the *logos* that is internal to sinless human nature and to that nature's intrinsic moral reasoning as determined and created by the *Logos*.

Such sinlessness means that the *logos* and the *tropos* of Christ's humanity remained creationally intact. And as creation is itself an act of grace, Christ's created human nature means there is no distinction between humanity's created *logos* and its redeemed *tropos*. The human *tropos* is redeemed when it is brought into harmony with its *logos*. This enables human nature to return to the laws of its creation. Only when moral reasoning (as a focal instance of a rational *tropos*) participates in the moral reasoning of the incarnate *Logos* does it become congruent with its own *logos,* which as its creational intent is also its redeemed possibility. Maximus explores this in his *logos/tropos* thematic.

b. Maximus's Logos/Tropos Couplet and the Problem of the Will

Associated with his *Logos/logoi* thematic is Maximus's *logos/tropos* couplet. This concept is derived from Maximus's concept of God who is single in respect of his *logos* but multiple/triadic in respect to his *tropos* (mode).[26] It is only through God's economy that we know this triadic movement or *tropos*. In respect to creation, the *logos/tropos* couplet—idea of nature/mode of existence—implies that *tropos* and *logos* cohere, but that sin has caused their disruption. *Logoi* and *tropoi* are now disordered and cataphatic in relation to each other. Humanity now exists in such a way that its mode is neither properly congruent nor simultaneous with its hypostasis. This is his way of explaining sin and evil. Thus the assertion that it is "impossible for beings to exist without their mode of existence" is a problematic interpretation of Maximus.[27] In Maximus, a *logos* is God's pre-determination of what any created thing will be, and is prior to the actual creation of that which a

---

26. Thunberg, *Man and the Cosmos*, 38. "Mode" is not used in a Sabellian fashion.

27. Nicolaos Loudovicos, *A Eucharistic Ontology: Maximus the Confessor's Eschatological Ontology of Being As Dialogical Reciprocity*, cited by Bathrellos, *Byzantine Christ*, 103.

logos becomes, so that even though its *tropos* likewise exists in God's mind, the *tropos* is only manifested in the actualizsation of the *logos* itself. But as already noted, *tropos* is not identical with *logos*, for unlike the *logos*, the *tropos* is now distorted by sin. Despite, then, the *tropos* of existence and *logos* of nature existing simultaneously and congruently in both God's mind and in their original actuality, the *post-lapsum* actuality of the *tropos* is non-congruent with its *logos*, which renders direct and accurate knowledge of the *logos* from the *tropos* problematic. Hence moral life, as one mode of fallen human actuality, is "out of nature," and now exists and functions discordantly with its divinely created *logos*, being co-determined by the *tropos* of sinful existence. Not only so, but because practical moral reasoning is a mode (*tropos*) of human existence, ethics is itself discordant with its own proper *logos*. Moral *dialogismos* shares in humanity's disordered *tropos*.

It is clearly an easier matter to discern a *logos* from its *tropos* in non-sentient entities, yet even there the clouded *tropos* of the knower's reason still inhibits complete clarity. In respect to human nature and natural law, it is evident that discerning the *logos* of one's own creation is distorted not only because of the opaque nature of the *tropos* of reason, but also due to the *tropos* of the human will being driven into "unnatural passions," the decaying *tropos* of the body, and the total trajectory of the human person towards non-being due to its disengagement from the *Logos* of its creation.[28] This discordant character of moral reasoning extends to the character of the human will.

Maximus considers the will a critical aspect of the human *tropos*. He writes of two human wills: the original *pre-lapsum* natural good will, and the *post-lapsum* deliberative or gnomic will. This gnomic will, coupled with the natural passions, is driven by evil into the corruption of unnatural passions and consequently vacillates and deliberates rather than obeys God. It is through these passions that evil powers have "hidden their activities clandestinely under the law of human nature," and assaulted Christ in the temptations of both the desert and the crucifixion.[29] In the desert, Christ's victory freed the gnomic will from its natural inclination "towards wicked pleasure," whilst on the cross he remained "impervious to his sufferings." In these two victories Christ healed and freed human nature, first of the passion connected with pleasure, and second of the passion connected with

---

28. Maximus, "Ad Thalassium 21," *Cosmic Mystery*, 110.

29. Ibid., 111. Gnomic: from γνώμη, deliberative and thus vacillating. Yet the woman deliberated, through desire, before her fall, suggesting that deliberation is not wholly evil (Gen 3:6).

pain.[30] Thus the gnomic will was defeated by and in Christ's human nature, enabling human nature and volition to be restored to its natural *pre-lapsum* state. This constitutes a form of Adamic recapitulation anthropology.[31]

The ethical implications of this are clear when we consider Maximus's strong Chalcedonianism. As Christ's humanity was consubstantial with ours, these two victories demonstrate that the *tropos* of his human will was in harmony with both its own *logos*[32] and his divine will. Classical christological dyothelitism (literally, two wills, divine and human in the one person) thus suggests that the perfect congruence of the two natures and wills in one hypostasis reveals and exemplifies three normative relations of the human will. First, it shows what is the proper relation between the will and nature of a human *person*. Here the one *hypostasis* of Jesus is the conceptual center of the human will and human nature of which the will is a constituent part. Second, it demonstrates what is the proper relation between the volitions of divine and human *natures* in the one person, Jesus Christ. Here also the one *hypostasis* of Jesus is the conceptual center of the two wills, the divine and the human, which, while remaining distinct, are always congruent. Third, it exemplifies the normative relation between the volitions of divine and human *hypostases*, the Son and the Father. Here the begetting of the Son from the Father, that is, the immanent Trinity, is the conceptual center. Two conclusions therefore follow regarding Christ's human will. First, the human will (as a *tropos*) of the incarnate Word was wholly congruent with that Word's assumed enhypostatic and perfect human nature (his *logos*), so that his human nature and will recapitulated Adam's *pre-lapsum* nature and agnomic will: the *tropos* of that will was congruent with its *logos*. Second, the human will was in perfect alignment with the divine will,[33] exemplifying the proper mode and function of human nature and will. As any human nature or will that does not subsist in its relation with God in a *Logos*-determined fashion is fallen, the comportment of Christ's human will with his divine will exemplifies the proper *logos* and *tropos* of human nature and will.

This christologizes the will as a morally determining mode of human existence in the strongest possible fashion, without falling victim to voluntarism, because the human will of Christ functions in a wholly congruent fashion with both the *logos* of its own creation and the divine will in the one

---

30. Ibid., 112, 113.

31. Ibid., 111. It also suggests that his strong dyotheletism was agnomic in respect to Christ's human will, Bathrellos, *Byzantine Christ*, 155.

32. The union of two natures is extended: each nature was itself united and undivided.

33. Matthew 26:39, John 4:34, and Hebrews 10:7.

person. It is also congruent with the will of the Father through the obedience of the Son.

Is this human will unique to Christ, or is it meant to be exemplary? It would be hard to deny its exemplary nature, given that Maximus was such a strong Chalcedonian, for such Christology necessarily implies exemplarism through its affirmation of human consubstantiability. Chalcedon affirms that the whole of created human nature, without reduction, was assumed by the Son. Yet this humanity (as in Irenaean Adam Christology) pre-exists as a *logos* of the Son prior to Adam's creation, so that Adam's created actuality is after the image of the later-to-be incarnate Word.[34] That is, the *logos* and *tropos* of Adamic human nature are modeled on the humanity of the Son. Christ's human nature and life therefore function not only as an example to follow but also as the archetype of human creation. It is impossible to sever the humanity of the incarnate Son from the humanity of Adam, as both humanities have their being and creation by that self-same Word, with the Adamic modeled upon the christological archetype. Combining Irenaean and Maximian thought, exemplarism can be described as bringing one's *tropos* into congruence with one's *logos,* which is itself patterned on the archetype of the moral *tropos* of the incarnate *Logos,* who logically antedates but historically postdates and recapitulates Adam through his Incarnation. Such reasoning implies purpose and teleology because the created *logoi* are created through grace, by, for, and in Christ, and cannot be read off an entity without christological coordination (weakly) or determination (strongly). Simply put, we are to live out the same moral mode as Jesus if we are to live true human lives.

Maximus's understanding of the will as a *tropos* can be read through modern eyes and applied to modern concerns: "The creature is no more its own goal and purpose than its own ground and beginning. There is no inherent reason for the creature's existence and nature, no independent teleology of the creature introduced with its creation and made its own."[35] Conversely, the modern denial of the teleology of entities and the volun-

---

34. This bears no resemblance to certain sixteenth century doctrines of Christ's celestial flesh. It is essential here to avoid the genetic fallacy that confuses validity and logical order with origin and temporal order. In Irenaean Christology, the Incarnation and thus humanity logically but not temporally preceded Adam's creation.

35. Barth, *CD,* III/1, 94. Being made in God's image means "to be created as a being which has its ground and possibility in the fact that it is in 'us,' i.e., in God's own sphere and being," 183. Being created by God in love means that, "nothing that happens from the side of God . . . can be foreign [to creation and humanity. For its] nature is simply its equipment for grace," 231. I do not pretend that Barth has any dependence upon Maximus's *logos* theology. I simply mean that the modern Barth and the ancient Maximus share a Chalcedonian determination of created existence, nature and teleology.

tarist determination of ends has loosened human *phusis* and *tropos* from *logos*. For instance the sense of vocation, broadly understood as an external determination of human nature and its ends, tends to become opaque, rendering persons malleable to voluntarist determination and existential decenteredness. Here the *phusis* and *tropos* are bent by the human will to any desirable end, which is problematic because desire, as a passion, may tend towards irrationality and unintelligibility. Such historicist voluntarism, when coordinate with *techné*, produces pragmatic ends that are not necessarily divinely determined. Morally, this has allowed human action an unlimited range of self-determination and self-creation. The received self is morally minimal and pliable to self-determined ends for human existence is simply an indeterminate fact requiring personal decisions to create its essence. For example, in the sphere of sexual ethics, consent has become the primary determination of behavioral good: the will alone determines the moral good and right.[36] Such separation of will from person leads to a divided self, just as the objectification of the "I" alienates the self from its history and location.[37] Such voluntarism is considered to be conducive to adventurous creativity and possibilities denied to non-imaginative realism by opening up possible unknown dimensions of human existence.[38] In a parallel to Aristotle, where virtuous acts create virtuous character, voluntary choices are deemed to create human nature itself. The will becomes wholly identified with Maximus's gnomic will so that humanity is understood to be essentially deliberative and volitional in nature. Such voluntarism means that a far broader range of willed human behaviors and dispositions are considered proper than what is considered natural and normal in other sentient creatures. Such a pliable and decentered self however is unable to give a rational and substantial moral account of itself, because the denial of any pre-praxis human essence means that the will remains ungrounded and thus non-moral, merely a formal property without material and moral

---

36. A caveat is necessary: adult consensual sex which is incestuous or between a superior and a dependent (e.g., teacher and student) are both considered unacceptable. Also, note the replacement of "sex," an anatomical given, with "gender," a psychosexual self-determination. Thus Storkey, *Created or Constructed?*, 37: "Postmodernity began to argue that . . . all identity, indeed sexuality itself, was constructed," 37.

37. Thielicke sees dualist anthropology in non-Christian attitudes to death (division into a continuing authentic and terminating inauthentic aspects), and in promiscuous sexual behavior (the objectification of the body from the wider self); *Living With Death*, 63–82, and *Ethics of Sex*, 20–26, respectively.

38. Some secularized forms of the Reformed cultural mandate may misapply this for environmental exploitation, where creation is manipulated for purely human, and usually economic ends.

content.³⁹ Hence, any self-creation through the exercise of the will is problematic because the will, as materially empty, is unable to account for the content of any choice made.

Yet conversely, naïve realism, where human nature or essence is wholly transparent, is also problematic because of humanity's sinfulness. The Western tradition since Augustine plays some part in this process through a form of the *analogia entis*, which sought to move from what it perceived as the uniquely human—the *imago Dei* in creation—to the divine. Yet the *analogia entis* can only be maintained theologically if the analogate, God's being, remains. But since God is removed in modern ethics, the human *entis* has no divine analogate to which it can be analogous, which has rendered the *analogia entis* theologically redundant and produced a self-enclosed understanding of human *entis*. The human self is now perceived to be fully comprehensible without any theological determination. In contrast, the Eastern tradition, instanced in Gregory of Nyssa, "starts with what revelation tells us of God, in order to discover what it is in man which corresponds to the divine image [in God]."⁴⁰ This is close to Barth's *analogia fidei*, yet with a stronger emphasis upon the Subject of revelation rather than the knowing subject, and may be termed *analogia Dei*. It also reflects Irenaeus's recapitulation hermeneutic, except that it concerns God the Son.⁴¹ Thus the actuality of the Incarnation is taken as both the ontological and epistemological starting point, and as the form and matter of human nature, ends and action. This is what Bonhoeffer was driving at when he recast Heidegger's understanding of *Dasein* in christo-ecclesial categories: "Revelation, which places the I into truth, i.e., gives understanding of God and the self, is a contingent occurrence . . . received as a reality—but not elicited from speculations about human existence as such. It is an occurrence with its basis in the freedom of God."⁴² Here the "I" is a derivative concept understood through revelation, not self-referentially, which means that both its proper *logos* and proper *tropos* requires christo-ethical placement in order to become properly comprehensible. Being "in Christ" is the location, or the relation, that enables correct human moral reasoning about the self.

In summary, Maximus's *logos/tropos* couplet means that the modes of human existence function properly when they are brought into conformity

---

39. As in existentialism, noted above.

40. Lossky, *Mystical Theology*, 115. Also note Maximus's reversal of Evagrius, above.

41. Irenaeus's Adam-Christ Christology is especially significant.

42. Bonhoeffer, *Act and Being*, 80, argues that God's freedom is expressed particularly in the Incarnation.

with their *Logos*-determined *logos*. In particular, Maximus's focus upon the will implies that our vacillating response to God is overcome through Christ's victories over temptation, where the gnomic will was defeated by the good will of his created humanity. Neither the gnomic nor the good created will are formally empty properties waiting to be materially filled with moral content. Because the gnomic will as a mode is disordered through its disengagement from its created purpose and determination, the emphasis upon voluntary response in radical ethics is insufficient of itself to account for a Christian ethic properly grounded in the *Logos*. It is not proper to the moral will, as a mode of human nature, to either vacillate before, or decide against its origin, the *Logos*. To do so elevates the gnomic will over the *Logos* of its creation, as well as its own *logos*. For the moral will to function in its creationally intended way, it must be re-engaged with its own proper created purpose. This is seen in Christ's created humanity, and enabled for us through Christ's redemption. The gnomic will must be pressed into the created will. In Maximus, the will is a particularly focused instance of the necessity of the modes (*tropoi*) of human existence needing to be conformed to their proper shape—that is, their own *logos*. This is both christologically exemplified and enabled.

c. Maximus's Doctrine of Universal Laws

Maximus expounds his doctrine of universal law in his exegesis of Jonah.[43] His threefold taxonomy of law is illustrated in Table 3, below. This taxonomy is fluid, for Maximus can describe the natural and the written laws as the same, but also adds the law of grace as a third. All three are one in Christ the *Logos*, for "the meaning of every single natural thing . . . and the meaning of every positive law and commandment . . . is . . . an incarnation of the one divine Logos."[44]

Type of law	Mode	Form of godly life: appropriate discipline/disposition of the will and ethical conduct
Natural Law	Natural reason controlling the senses.	Embracing common human nature as per the Golden Rule (Matt 7:12).

43. Maximus, "Ad Thalassium 64," *Cosmic Mystery*, 167–9.

44. von Balthasar, *Cosmic Liturgy*, 294. Maximus identifies natural law with scriptural law if the latter is translated wisely, and written law expresses natural law if holy people conceive it, "Ambigua," PG 91, 1152A, in Ibid., 295.

Scriptural Law	Natural reason (as above) acquiring spiritual desire.	Starting with fear of punishment, it progresses first to a sense of justice, then to a desire to do good, and finally to love (of neighbor, Matt 5:43).
Spiritual Law or Law of Grace	Supernatural reason transforms nature (*theosis*), leading to direct imitation of God who gave his life for us.	Neighbor love transformed into laying down one's life for others modeled upon Christ, the supernatural and super-essential Archetype of human nature (John 15:13).

Table 3: Maximus's Threefold Taxonomy of Law.

As all *logoi* participate in the *Logos,* Maximus proposes a type of triple embodiment[45] of the *Logos* in the mode of law. The *Logos* is present in 1) creation as natural law; 2) Scripture as written law; and 3) definitive humanity properly embodied as spiritual law.[46] "The content of each law is . . . the Logos . . . The difference between the three laws lies in the intensity of the presence of the Logos."[47] Christ embodies the spiritual law that includes the natural and the written law, so that natural law is seen in its most concentrated expression in the Incarnation of the *Logos*. Both the natural and written law are different *tropoi* of the divine way of life for human beings, which together with Christ constitute a "single law which converges . . . in Christ who as creator . . . is the author of the natural law, and as provider and lawgiver . . . is the giver of the written law."[48] Real natural law, positive written law, and Christ as historical law take part in one another in the sense that the *logoi* of the natural law and the written law participate in him as their proper *logos*. This participation is demonstrated in the transfiguration when Christ's human nature bridges the gap between the invisible and visible orders.[49] As this historically accessible flesh transcends the sensible world by means of the hypostatic union it is also "the means by which we too may transcend the limited realm of the material and finite."[50]

Maximus clearly means that the human nature of Christ is revelatory of natural and written law in a way that the evangelical tradition tends to

45. But not Incarnation, against von Balthasar.
46. Bahrim, "Anthropic Cosmology," 33.
47. Ibid., 120.
48. Cooper, *Body*, 37, referencing Q. *Thal.* 64.
49. The transfiguration is "for Maximus paradigmatic of the totality of God's economic engagement with the creation," Cooper, "Maximus the Confessor," 161–86.
50. Cooper, *Body*, 38–39.

overlook. This is curious, as Reformed approaches tend to see written divine law as the second edition of unwritten natural law, necessitated by human sin, and its covenantal biblical theology associates divine law with its fulfillment in Christ, yet the christological association with, and fulfillment of, natural law is commonly neglected. Maximus would therefore lead us to see Christ as the embodied expression and fulfillment not only of written law, but also of natural law, in his human nature. So in Maximian terms, natural law is the moral *tropos* of the human *logos* assumed and perfectly exemplified by incarnate *Logos*, and reflects a similar christo-ethical determination of human creation as found in Athanasius.

In his discussion of the Incarnation, Athanasius notes that because of the failure of creation's witness to preserve or restore humanity to God, the Word who "gives movement to all things in creation" was "teaching men concerning the Father . . . [and] could renew this same teaching as well."[51] This means that Christ is the proper source of knowledge about God and creation because he is himself the full and proper union of the uncreated divine Word and created human nature. What he reveals theologically and anthropologically—God and humanity—*is* his actuality and history, because there is no distinction between what he teaches and what he is. When he teaches about God, he is that about which he teaches: God the incarnate Son. When he teaches about creation, he is that about which he teaches: created human nature. He himself is the content of his teaching, noted in the "I am" sayings of John's Gospel. Like Maximus, Athanasius links creation's order (natural law), the Father's will (divine law) and Christ (the Incarnation, spiritual law).[52] All moral law is concentrated in Christ so that law is no longer coldly non-personal or deistic, but lovingly divine and lovingly human. Thus the greatest commandments or laws (Matt 22:34–40) concern love. *Logos* moral reasoning, including Maximus's *Logos* view of laws, is not reducible to a form of deontological moral imperatives hanging in mid air as an idealized moral form. Christ's life cannot be nominalized out of his own history (turning his acts—verbs—into abstract nouns) and into an objective rule or an idealized value without a commensurate reduction in his divine or human personal natures. As such, the life of Jesus remains the center of all understanding of moral laws.

Because Maximus's account of laws is christologically framed, *imitatio Christi* becomes compatible with natural law ethics. His taxonomy of law

---

51. Athanasius, "On the Incarnation of the Word," *NPNF* vol. 4, 44. "This same teaching" means the understanding of creation.

52. von Balthasar sees the third spiritual law as hidden within the first two, *Cosmic Liturgy*, 294.

expresses his dynamic model of human life, with the final point of movement being the return to one's origin in God the *Logos*. Only at that point is human rest, a fulfilled Sabbath, achieved. In this model of laws, the crucified incarnate *Logos* is described as *exemplary* love for others, rather than atonement. Thus natural law and *imitatio Christi* are not antithetical, but different aspects of the single moral movement of one's *tropos* towards the *Logos*, such that one's *logos* returns to its proper end and rest in God. The clarity of this argument is explicit in Maximus's Chalcedonian Christology: the human nature of Christ remained undiminished and preserved without change in the hypostatic union, so that though by essence God, the *Logos* displayed "in himself the very goal for which his creatures manifestly received the beginning of their existence."[53] Thus the incarnate Christ is the beginning, middle and end of all ages, such that both eternal and natural law cohere in him as humanity's origin and goal.[54] Christ's origin, purpose and ends are not exclusively his *in respect to his humanity*, but have a surplus of application to humanity generally. That Christ came from God, albeit differently, is also true of John the Baptist (John 1:6); that he is sanctified for the Father is also true of the disciples (John 17:17–19); and that he came to glorify the Father is reflected in their glorifying of him (John 17:1, 10). Christ lived in accordance with that which is proper to human nature in its divine origin from, determination by, and direction to God. The Incarnation reveals humanity living on the basis of the laws proper to its creation.

When Maximus affirms that the *logoi* pre-exist actual creation, there are echoes of the Augustinian concept of eternal election in the will or mind of God, for "the *logoi* of all things known by God before their creation are securely fixed in God . . . and each acquired concrete existence in itself."[55] Maximus comes close here to a necessitarian rather than contingent view of creation, yet is saved by his insistence that the actual concrete creation of the *logoi* is an act of God's free decision. The laws of creation are therefore acts of grace that are contingent upon God's good will for their actuality. He sounds pantheistic when he writes that each *logos* is a "portion of God," and the "one Logos is many *logoi*, and that the many *logoi* are One."[56] Yet this participatory language applies to the non-substantial *logos* and their *tropoi*,

53. Maximus, "Ad Thalassium 60," *Cosmic Liturgy*, 125.

54. Ibid., 117.

55. Maximus, "Ambiguum 7," *Cosmic Mystery*, 56, citing Dionysius the Areopagite and Clement as teaching that the *logoi* are products of the divine will, 61. The human *logos* is "the cardinal causal principle . . . of humanity's creaturely origin," "Ambiguum 42," 82.

56. Maximus "Ambiguum 7," *Cosmic Mystery*, 57–58. He later clarifies: "Portion means member . . . a part of the body," 71.

both of which pre-exist in God's mind—eternal wisdom and election. God himself does not participate in a cosmic *logos* principle, as though he derives his own rationality from it. The common rationality of natural law, divine law, and God himself is not a universal principle in which all participate, but the overflow of God's gracious love and will in creation (natural law) and in revelation (divine law). Divine law is not a burden laid upon humanity but is one with the *logos* of natural law, as both participate in God prior to their actuality in creation or redemption.

Moreover, because each *logos* possesses its own particular created actuality in the *tropoi* appropriate to it, such creation is the external context of all other *logoi* and hence the limits of them all.[57] We picture something like a matrix or coherent web of intelligible and sensible creations and their relations with each other. According to *Ambiguum 15*, the *logos* of each being provides stability, while the matrix of other *logoi* and inter-*logoi* relations provides a degree of movement and a strong corporate dimension to created reality.[58] All created *logoi* are the context of every other *logos*, which makes all laws related. This means that natural law is one part of a greater whole and related to other parts of that whole. As such, any proper understanding of natural law must take into account this wider reality. This disables its tendency to anthropocentric self-enclosure in a world of environmental and ecological concerns. But because all *logoi* participate in the one *Logos*, natural law is also not opposed to divine law, or to Christ. Consequently, natural law's moral reasoning is not properly rational unless it takes into account both divine law and the life of the incarnate *Logos*.

In God's mind, each *logos* "participates" in its own concretion within the context of all other *logoi*. God has set each thing in relation with all others. Such a theory of participation is constituted by two elements: first, having one's being created by and in God according to its pre-existing *logos*; and second, the practice of godly virtues.[59] "Slipping down from God" is an irrational departure from the purpose of one's *logos*, and a corruption of one's *tropos* through ungodly vices. Maximus clearly does not separate nature and virtues, being and act, *logoi* and proper *tropoi* in any way as to cause any fundamental human dualism. While the human *logos* participates in the *Logos* by virtue of its divine creation, the human *tropos* participates properly in the *Logos* only when the will is so changed and oriented that the *Logos* becomes its fundamental exemplar and goal. It is then also congruent with the *logos* of its own creation. Because all the laws are differing "modes" or

---

57. Ibid., 57.
58. Cited in ibid., 57, n. 34.
59. Cooper, *Body*, 95.

expressions of the will of the one *Logos*, they all move a person back towards their origin in that *Logos* as their true goal. Thus the gospel removes errant human nature (which inclines toward evil in its subservience to the senses) from its reign over humanity, just as Jonah persuaded Nineveh to disrobe and mourn in sackcloth (mortification) and ashes (poverty of spirit).[60]

It is this *Logos*-ordered *logos* which renders problematic the Aristotelian/Thomist view that natural inclinations transparently express the proper ends and purposes inherent in the nature of any object. Using Maximian terms, Aristotelian ends and purposes are conceptually an instance of a being's *logos* and are self-evident through their *tropoi*. Yet their christological determination is minimal due to an optimistic view of the capacities of the *tropos* of moral reasoning that tends to enclose such reasoning within its own subject matter. Such self-enclosure is criticized when Maximus asserts that nothing that comes into being can be its own end as it is not self-caused.[61] "The eternal determinations of the 'divine Counsel,' the divine ideas cannot really be made to correspond with the 'essences' of things which are postulated in the so-called natural philosophy of Aristotle ... whose experience reaches only to nature in its fallen state."[62] Aristotle's theory of self-evident natural properties—heat as proper to fire—possesses some cogency regarding both non-sentient and inert objects and human appetitive and endocrinological drives (but even here the passions can distort them), but becomes problematic in respect of the ego-directed human will. In its transparent view of natural inclinations, human nature and self-evident ends, the Aristotelian/Thomist model expresses a view of natural reason disengaged from its own origin and end in the *Logos*. In Maximian terms, it affirms that human and natural *logoi* are transparent in a non-*Logos* fashion, despite their corrupt *tropoi*.

Maximus's doctrine of laws is thus wholly christological. His participatory language is not pantheistic or Stoic, for it refers to the presence of the divine determination and purpose of things rather than their substance. By seeing natural law, divine law and spiritual law (Christ) as all manifesting the laws of creation—the difference between them being of the intensity of the presence of the *Logos*—he opens up the possibility for a wholly christological determination of natural law and the reasoning that is proper to it.

This being so, there can be no natural law justification for any act or disposition that cannot be coordinated with or determined by Christ. If

---

60. Maximus, "Ambiguum 7," *Cosmic Mystery*, 153.

61. Ibid., 48.

62. Lossky, *Mystical Theology*, 101. This is clearly demonstrated by the non-theistic doctrine of natural law in Finnis.

the *logos* of all natural and divine laws is the divine *Logos*, who as Jesus Christ expresses all properly creaturely *tropoi*, then the christological moral reasoning typified in christo-ethical radicalism is proper to natural law. Hence Jesus' life is not unnatural, but is wholly natural, and corresponds to humanity's divine determination. Jesus is the content and the moral limits of natural law.

d. Maximus's Logos and Natural Law.

Maximus argues that the origin, natural good, and end of each *logos* exists through its participation in the *Logos*. The origin of each *logos* in God constitutes its inner logic and end. Because natural power is movement towards a proper end, and the end of each *logos* is also its origin, each *logos* is naturally inclined back to God.[63] Deviation from God constitutes an irrational departure from one's *logos* that pre-existed in God, and thus amounts to dissolution and non-being. This occurs when the gnomic will is driven by unnatural passions into itself, rather than the *Logos*. If purpose is a function of origin, and through volitional dysfunction a person moves away from the *logos* of their creation in the *Logos*, then they fail to achieve their true nature in proportion to their separation from the *Logos*. Conversely, the closer a person remains to or moves towards the *logos* of their creation in and by the *Logos*, then the truer their final end and the greater their experience of being.[64]

However, as the *tropoi* of each *logoi* is distorted through sin, humanity is incapable of rendering a true account of its own *logos*. Maximus's escape from opaque speculation is his doctrine of the Incarnation that elevates "man to God" and "brings God down to man," so that "man is made God by divinization and God is made man by humanization." Most saliently, and beautifully, "the Word of God and God wills always and in all things to accomplish the mystery of his embodiment."[65] True human *logos* is revealed in the incarnate *Logos's* consubstantial human *logos*. Such an embodiment provides access to perfect humanity, so that through imitation by ascetic practice and moral virtues persons move toward their true end in God. *Imitatio Christi* is a christological expression of natural law in an ontological sense, where one's moral nature is brought into correspondence with Christ's moral nature.

63. Maximus, "Ambiguum 7," *Cosmic Mystery*, 59, 54.
64. "A creature has well-being or ill-being in so far as it moves 'with' (πρός) or 'against' (παρά) the logos according to which it is," Perl, *Methexis*, 152.
65. Maximus, "Ambiguum 7," *Cosmic Mystery*, 60.

Hence an empirical Christology grounded in the life of Jesus provides the means by which the true *logos* of humanity may be determined because the *Logos* incarnate did not share the distorted *tropoi* of all other creatures: "Human renewal was only realized when a wholly new way of being human appeared."[66] Without Chalcedonian Christology, a substantial and true account of the natural and moral laws is impossible because a proper example of human nature is unattainable. But Christ as the new Adam did not share the distorted *tropoi* of *post-lapsum* Adam, but assumed the *pre-lapsum* Adam's impeccability and natural passion to sinfulness, yet without sin.[67] Thus he "created our nature anew and returned it to its primordial dignity of incorruptibility through his holy flesh, born of our flesh and animated by a rational soul," and "maintained it inalterably, by its own essential principle and definition."[68] This approximates Irenaean recapitulation Christology, which becomes explicit when Maximus compares Christ's birth from a virgin to Adam's creation from undefiled earth.[69] The eternal *Logos*, wrapped and enfleshed in proper humanity, shows the natural order and end of humanity's created intention.

Maximus's doctrine of incarnational salvation possesses strong ethical dimensions. Fallen humanity's corruption exhibits animalistic desire evidenced in ignorance, decay via the passions, deceit, and wickedness. Through Christ wrapping these in swaddling clothes, they are returned to their primordial incorruptibility and beauty, with desire transformed into its proper procreative good, washed in knowledge through grace, given back its true natural operation, and cleansed from and inoculated against decayed passions.[70] Hence *Ambiguum 7*, entitled *On the Beginning and End of Rational Creatures*, describes the state of human fallenness as having slipped down from God, with the return to God being effected through christological grace and the subsequent practice of virtues such as chastity, steadfastness, contemplation, devotion, and acceptance of revealed truth.[71] These moral practices reverse the movement of personal dissolution, internal division and tendency to non-being, and re-orient the person to God. Thus Abraham saw God by "restoring himself to nature's *Logos* of being, or reason [*logos*] to himself . . . [and] through this being given back to God."

66. Maximus, "Ambiguum 7," *Cosmic Mystery*, 70.
67. Maximus, "Ambiguum 42," *Cosmic Mystery*, 81.
68. Ibid., 83–84. He asserts this more strongly using Chalcedon's apophaticism, 84.
69. Ibid., 88. Although Adam's and Christ's birth are both associated with the Spirit, Maximus's pneumatology is muted.
70. Ibid., 85, exegeting Ezekiel 16:3–7.
71. Maximus, "Ambiguum 7," *Cosmic Mystery*, 63, 66, 70.

This restoration brings peace, for those who practice virtue are "radiantly established as one, having the one *logos* of being within themselves, utterly single in nature and inclination."[72] For Maximus, loss of grace causes fragmentation rather than human unity in love, which is the "first and most excellent good" and foremost inclination that draws people to God and neighbor. Such love is "the inward universal relationship to the first good connected with the universal purpose of our natural kind."[73]

Spatially, Maximus's *Logos/logos* theorizing could be illustrated as a wheel. Christ the *Logos* is the hub from which all rational creatures originate and possess being, like spokes. While the *logos* of each person remains in Christ, the persons themselves in their *tropoi* are either proximal or distal from the hub according to their christological renewal and the practices of faith, love, and the virtues. Both reason and moral practices are essentially christological and cannot find their being, origin, or end in themselves, as no caused or created entity possesses final self-determination.

Consequently, the more congruent one's *tropos* is to one's *logos*, the closer one is to the hub, and the greater one's well-being. This flourishing is also relational, in that such movement brings each creature into a closer relation to all others.[74] As the human *logos* participates in the *Logos* by virtue of its determinations, it follows that proximity to the *Logos* not only creates greater well-being, but also christologically shapes the *tropoi*, that is, the concrete acts of the person. Thus the *tropoi* of each person is shaped by the *tropoi* of Christ in proportion to his or her proximity to the *Logos*. In traditional moral language, this constitutes individual and corporate growth in and towards Christ-likeness, through virtue practice. People become more morally human the closer their moral practices approximate Christ's moral practices.

Because the *logoi* cannot be altered by sin, only the *tropoi* are renewed. The *logoi* is being, and approximates the image of God, while the *tropoi* is act, and approximate the likeness of God.[75] The *logoi* is existence as body and soul, the *tropoi* exist as multiple acts. Hence miracles affect the *tropoi*, not the *logoi*. Thus only the likeness of God needs restoration to its original *pre-lapsum* Adamic state, which is exemplified in Jesus Christ, the second Adam, the icon and example of *logos/tropos* harmony and integration.

---

72. Maximus, "Letter 2: On Love," 400 C, B in Louth, *Maximus*, 89, 88.

73. Ibid., 90.

74. The plural "you" (ὑμεῖς), which dominates NT paraenesis, is lost in modern English Bibles.

75. "Ambiguum 42," 90. His erroneous exegesis of Genesis 1:26 (image and likeness) does not negate the substance of his argument.

LOGOS COSMOLOGY AND CHRISTOLOGICAL ETHICAL REASONING 177

Maximian Chalcedonianism means that, as Christ is the *Logos* in which the *logoi* exist by virtue of their determination and creation, the enhypostatic human nature of Christ constitutes the exemplar of each human *logos*, and the moral goal towards which humanity creationally and properly tends.[76] A goal is not necessarily identical with an example or model, as in a race. But ethically it is identical, for the goal towards which one moves is the *Logos*, the creator of one's *logos*, and ground of one's being.[77] This is a dynamic model of human participation, flourishing, and ethical action, because the human *logos* both originates from and is determined by its orientation and return to the *Logos*.

When a person acts according to natural law, they flourish, because human flourishing is natural to humanity. Flourishing—or *shalom* in the Old Testament—is the graced end of proper natural human life. Human nature *is* its capacity for the grace of flourishing. Yet for such flourishing to be fully-grown and not stillborn, Christ must be the goal towards which one moves. So if "to use something correctly is to use it according to its true nature or *logos*—a fact determined by its divinely given, teleologically directed *skopos*—then the *skopos* of all things is itself determined by their consummation in 'perfect love.'"[78] Such love, the spiritual law, is Christ, who laid down his life for others. For this reason Paul asserts that love is the fulfillment of the law, which in Maximus includes natural law.[79]

Love is the highest of the Maximian virtues, which as a *tropos*-act moves a person towards the *Logos*. This participatory theosis is being "'shaped' and 'impressed' from without, by God, with the marks (γνωρίσματα or ἰδιώματα) which belong properly to God."[80] The greatest mark is love. Such "participation" in God is the goal towards which moral practices (as *tropoi*) shape the person in a *Logos* fashion. This means that theosis includes exhibiting the moral *tropoi* of God, revealed in his incarnate "mode" of love. Because humanity will "participate" in God whose love (as a *tropos*) inheres in his being, loving (as *tropoi*) God and others as exemplified by the incarnate *Logos* moves a person closer to the moral *logos* of their humanity—theosis.

---

76. This exemplarism extends also to the Father who gave himself in Christ, Thunberg, *Man and the Cosmos*, 40.
77. Tillich's term, *Systematic Theology*.
78. Cooper, *Body*, 240. *Skopos* means God's "purpose," 240.
79. Romans 13:10.
80. Perl, *Methexis*, 197.

e. Conclusion

Maximus's strong Chalcedonianism provides theological resources for moral reasoning that unites radicalism's christological focus and natural law's concern with reason. By insisting that the objects of reasoning (the *logos* of the self, the *logoi* of the world, the *logoi* of laws, and the *tropoi* of moral reasoning and practices) must be determined by and coordinate with the *Logos*, Maximus offers an alternative to the Aristotelian/Thomist concepts of transparent self-evidence and natural law. Yet he also elevates the moral life of Christ from its provincial or historical imprisonment through his cosmological *Logos/logos* thematic.

For Maximus, there is no proper apprehension of humanity's *logos* or *tropos* without the *Logos*. Such moral reasoning is a necessary consequence of his cosmological Christology of participation, and elevates human nature and natural law from its phenomenological enclosure. Both Aristotelian natural law and radical ethics tend to be restricted to observable human acts: natural law to universal acts of human flourishing without Christology, and much contemporary radical ethics to Jesus' historical acts disengaged from moral realism and classical theology. Because of the metaphysical richness of Maximus's Christology, Christ's consubstantial human flesh provides not just a moral example, but also a clear instance of true human being, and thus natural law.[81] Radicalism's *imitatio Christi* can therefore be established on a deeper ontological basis, muting the criticism that it is either provincial, or legalistic because it reads Jesus' commands as non-personal deontological rules wrapped in the authoritarian language of lordship. Yet Maximus's highest virtue of love does comport with radicalism's focus upon Christ's love of enemies. As a mode of existence, love is only true to its own *logos* when "forced" back into the *Logos*, Christ, who loved both God and his enemies.

Despite Maximus's language appearing anachronistic and strange, his *logos* Christology has clear biblical and theological warrants in John's Gospel, the Apologists and Chalcedon, and a philosophical antecedent in Cicero. By using the *logos* concept to draw together Christology, creation, human nature, natural law, and divine law, he forged a strongly non-Aristotelian understanding of natural law that is deeply christological. It is the surfeit of meaning that he forced into the term *logos* that enables this rapprochement.

---

81. Twentieth century Latin theology has appropriated trinitarianism as exemplary for social relations: Boff, *Trinity and Society*, and Broughton Knox, *The Everlasting God*, are Liberationist and Reformed examples.

3. Moral Reasoning and the Theological Science of T. F. Torrance

a. Introduction

The work of T. F. Torrance provides a rich resource for ethical reasoning, despite it being primarily about theology and the philosophy of science.[82] Like Maximus, Torrance articulates a strong Athanasian theology that locates him within the Nicene/Chalcedonian tradition both cosmologically and theologically.[83] It is this integration of science and theology that enables his work to be appropriated for the ethical project offered here. In particular, his scientific theology enables christological ethics to be lifted above the historicism of which it is accused, and natural law above its concern with human nature without metaphysics/theology. His wide scientific vision is considered here because, like Cicero, basic metaphysical/theological realities inform his reasoning about the cosmos.

b. From Newton to Einstein.

Whilst acknowledging Newton and the mechanists as presenting a concept of God as the regulator of the universe, Torrance criticizes such mechanism as laying the ground for Deism via a chain of efficient causes removed from God's personal being and providential acts.[84] Such a doctrine of inviolable natural law and rigid determinism compromised both divine and human freedom. In contrast, Einsteinian and quantum physics have revealed the relational, dynamic and fluid nature of the universe, so that divine intervention is not contrary to what the mechanists understood as the laws of nature, which operate in ways unknown to Newton. This approach liberated "nature from the unwarranted imposition upon it of human abstractions so that it was allowed to disclose itself in its own natural or intrinsic order which is of an open, contingent kind, with variables which we are unable to tame by our idealized or mechanical patterns of thought."[85]

---

82. I have previously noted Torrance's critical realism in Part One.

83. Torrance, *Divine and Contingent Order*, 1-8.

84. "Despite the religious motivations of the seventeenth-century natural philosophers who developed the concept, the idea of laws of nature inevitably led to a view of the world in which God was no longer needed," Aldridge, "Should a Christian Believe?," 9.

85. Torrance, *Divine and Contingent Order*, 15. He contrasts genuine objective thought with objectifying or projecting thought, *Divine Meaning*, 380. Compare Cicero's "'*homologia*,' (*convenientia* in Cicero's Latin) . . . which is conformity of the human

Not unlike Maximus, Torrance affirms that there is "one pervasive rational order throughout the universe, so that we do not believe we are really in touch with reality if we come up with results in one aspect of the universe which conflict with those that derive elsewhere."[86] This is not dissimilar to Pannenberg's project of theology and science integration: "If the God of the Bible is the creator of the universe, then it is not possible to understand fully or even appropriately the processes of nature without any reference to that God."[87] Such a coherent concept of nature does not imply that all aspects of nature are somehow in flux, synthetic and mutually indistinguishable, unable to be understood in and of themselves; but rather that all aspects, including laws of nature, must be placed within the context of the whole of reality, which includes God, in order for a true and exhaustive understanding. This is a coherentist epistemology, where the whole must be referenced when considering the part.[88]

In this respect, Torrance proposes a fourfold taxonomy, or four modes of the created order which are distinct yet interactive: number, *logos*, organic form, and aesthetic form.[89] He suggests that these modes possess order and a relative freedom grounded in their rational comportment with God and contingency upon the freedom and grace of God in creation. In contrast to classical and Newtonian models, contingency is understood as God's gift to creation, so that meaning is found in a top-down direction from God to creation, not from a bottom-up direction from creation to God.[90] Thus autonomous ethics are inadequate and unable to rise above themselves because their rationality is self-enclosed within their subject matter, in a way reminiscent of Aristotelian physics that imprisoned laws within the subject matter of which they were explanations.[91] This is not to deny subject-determined forms of rational explanation, but to suggest that at the level of ethics, subjects do not contain their own explanatory or teleological intelligibility in an exhaustive manner.

---

mind . . . to the way things actually are in the world . . . the state in which the *logos* is shaped in accordance with *(homo-)* the world," Engberg-Pedersen, *Paul*, 58–59, citing Cicero, *De Finibus*, 3. 21.

86. Torrance, *Divine and Contingent Order*, 17.

87. Pannenberg, *Theology of Nature*, 16.

88. Compare the ecological doctrine of creation of Peters, *God—The World's Future*, 133–134.

89. Torrance, *Divine and Contingent Order*, 17.

90. This is similar to Maximus.

91. "Meta-scientific reference of our thought cannot be avoided if the intelligibility of the universe is to be sustained in our belief," Torrance, *Divine and Contingent Order*, 28.

Consequently, the creation of the universe *ex nihilo* implies that creation's intelligence, far from being either internally necessary or arbitrary, is both inherently contingent as an expression of grace,[92] and possesses a form of necessity, in that it originates in God's determination to be what it is.[93] Consequently the dualist mode of thinking that splits creation from grace is fundamentally misplaced, and only sustainable in deistic or Newtonian models of theology and science respectively, which imprison the cosmos within its own self-enclosure and self-determination, free from any dynamism or externality.

This being so, natural law cannot provide a proper ethical model if it is concerned wholly with human nature, for then it is imprisoned within its own subject matter. Furthermore, it becomes problematic if understood rigidly and inflexibly, as though the ethical nature of persons amounted to no more than one aspect of the invariable laws of nature, in a sort of mechanistic fashion.[94] It is this concern that underlies much secular objection to Catholic natural law theory, to which Finnis and Grisez have responded. Torrance, agreeing with Pannenberg, affirms that the Einsteinian and quantum understanding of the universe frees science from the rigid determinism of classical, medieval, and mechanistic views, and is consonant with the biblical concepts of providence, covenant, and revelation. Pannenberg also sees the Hebrew concept of history as expressing contingency not simply in human acts, but, from an historical point of view, also in divine actions in history: God does new and unexpected things.[95]

Natural law as an element of the laws of nature is now open to growth and dynamism, without breaking free from its contingent and graced intelligibility. This intelligibility is grounded in the being and act of God and revealed most sharply and completely in the Incarnation as an act of God's expressive, relational and dynamic being. Athanasius was the first to develop such a fluid concept of natural law, which was open-textured and "broke free from the necessitarian or deterministic notions that had prevailed in Greece," being grounded in the dynamism of the Word of God.[96] Natural

---

92. The contingent nature of the universe does not conflict with the anthropic principle, discussed below when considering Murphy and Ellis.

93. Torrance, *Space, Time and Incarnation*, 67.

94. Pannenberg, "Contingency and Natural Law," in *Theology of Nature*, 78, 83, suggests that laws of nature contain certain "preliminariness" as mere approximations, because a) as quantum science has shown, they are limited "in time and space in their field of application"; and b) all future events "throw new light on earlier occurrences," i.e., laws of nature are only exhaustively understood eschatologically.

95. Pannenberg, "Contingency and Natural Law," *Theology of Nature*, 76–81.

96. Torrance, *Trinitarian Faith*, 104. Likewise, Athenagoras links together νόμος

law/s, while themselves contingent, possess reliability due to the faithfulness of God, not by an innate self-enclosed impassability or *stasis*. Appropriating Barth's dialectical language, the stability of natural law is due to its *divine* contingency, while its dynamism is due to its divine *contingency*.

Contrary to this contingent and graced grounding of creation, we note three alternatives that create intellectual difficulties in any discussion of nature and its laws. First, Stoicism's *spermatikos logos* tends to place an interdiction upon empirical science by diffusing and imprisoning divine nature throughout creation. Such sacralizing arrests science by rendering nature too holy for investigation.[97] Second, Greek dualism's distinction between ideal and empirical realities tends to arrest science due to the relative unimportance of the empirical world in relation to the ideal. Third, mechanism's empirical self-imprisoned laws of nature led to either a radical immanentism or Deism. All three tend to a dualistic view of reality, emphasizing or neglecting one side or the other, in contrast to the orthodox Nicene view which, while maintaining the distinction between God and creation and the ideal and the empirical, preserves their integration through grace, divine freedom, contingency, and covenant. Yet such integration is most acutely focused in the Incarnation, which is the "chosen path of God's rationality in which he interacts with the world," and "sets up . . . a co-ordinate system between two horizontal dimensions, space and time, and one vertical dimension, relation to God." Hence divine reason was spatialized and temporalized, and a human person was "divinized." History became the theatre where the "eternal rationality of God" was displayed in perfect humanity.[98]

c. The Incarnation and Creation

Because quantum and Einsteinian science have reconfigured our understanding of the universe as a dynamic reality, the relation between creation and God can no longer be understood in a closed and mechanistic fashion. Such dynamic openness reflects God's own dynamic yet rational character. And because created realities inhere in God's created order in an open textured manner, the Incarnation is both consistent with and expressive of the divine order and contingency of creation. The Incarnation as a top-down

---

φύσεως, φυσικὸς λόγος and θεῖος λόγος, for the laws regulating physical and human reality and behaviour have a common rationality (λόγος, λόγισμος) . . . under the creative power of God's Word," Torrance, *Divine Meaning*, 49, citing *Presbeia*, 3.3; 24.2–3.

97. As does pantheism, and some expressions of romanticism, atavism, and nature primitivism.

98. Torrance, *Space, Time and Incarnation*, 67, 72, 73.

movement of the creator *Logos* assuming human nature provides the supreme model for top-down reasoning, so that human reasoning has access to both its origin and end by attending to this divine act. It is not possible in this model to understand the Incarnation as discordant with either the nature of God, the nature of the universe, or the nature of human beings. If the perfection of God's eternal rationality was incarnate in his Word, then that rationality is now historically open and accessible, like all human acts. It is by attending to this life that the rationality of God can be non-speculatively understood, simply because it was a human event. It was this Incarnation that provided the apostolic response to the metaphysical/theological speculations of Gnosticism, as noted in the anti-docetic and anti-gnostic texts of Colossians and 1 John.

Hence the Incarnation demonstrates the way in which God himself inhabits his own contingent creation in ways that are compatible with its own rationality. That is, God does not inhabit his creation in ways that are contrary to the rationality with which he has imbued it. This means that Jesus' moral practices and words do not disrupt the rational moral order inherent in human nature, but are its proper expression. When conducted in the key of Jesus Christ, practical moral reasoning is not discordant with the harmonics of the wider creation, but provides the primary melody that unites human moral reasoning with the wider creation of which it is a part. The different timbres of Christ and creation produce a single harmony, yet Christ remains the first instrument. Consequently, Chalcedon's double *homoousios* unites Creator and creation in such a fashion that the observable ordered laws of nature, and thus the natural laws of human nature, are only properly appreciated if heard within their wider theological—that is, christological—melody. The segue from Christ to creation is smooth.

Despite being a unique event, the Incarnation was the apex of God's constant faithfulness to his creation since its beginning. Such ordered care does not inhere in creation like Stoic divine participation or the universal embodiment of a metaphysical ideal, but expresses divine covenantal preservation.[99] The "continuity, stability, and uniformity of the natural world [is] grounded beyond itself in the constancy, faithfulness and reliability of God its Creator and Preserver."[100] This Judaic view was further radicalized because, first, God though his "*Logos* has impressed upon the cosmos its natural law"; and second, the relation of God to the world was reconfigured through the "incarnation of God's Word in Jesus Christ within the

---

99. This is unlike the Greek concept of participation found in Maximus, but like Barth.

100. Torrance, *Divine and Contingent Order*, 33.

spatio-temporal realities and intelligibilities of contingent existence in this world."[101] Because this act was a particular, personal, and historical embodiment, it provides, as the Stoic concept did not, *a posteriori* event of the eternal *Logos*: "That which we have seen with our own eyes, what we have looked at and touched with our hands."[102] This makes the Incarnation accessible not only to the sapient or elite, but to all, for the Intelligible lives as the intelligible, knowable through common human knowing.

d. The Reconfiguration of Natural Theology and Natural Law in the Incarnation.

Because the Incarnation so radically reconfigures how God and the creation are related, the traditional understanding of natural theology and natural law as disciplines that stand without recourse to theology, especially revelation, is disabled. Whereas the classical and Stoic methods were unable to hold together the real and the ideal, reason and experience, the metaphysical and the historical, the Incarnation demands a unique understanding of the nature of the relations between Creator and the creation, and of the creation itself.[103] Hence the Incarnation implies two related but separate matters. First, by God's "economic condescension" in assuming a part of creation, the metaphysically real does not disrupt creation but lives within it as an integral part, perfectly exemplifying its creational intentions and ends, and wholly restoring it to its original created purposes. The incarnational theology of Chalcedon reveals the being and acts of human life as congruent with its essential nature: Jesus Christ is "Man of man." Second, the hypostatic union (the "ontological counterpart" of the economic condescension) provides true knowledge of God, for the incarnate Son is in himself what he is antecedently and eternally with the Father: Jesus Christ is "God of God." If the Christology of Nicaea and Chalcedon is denied, Jesus is reduced to no more than a socio-moral or judicial transaction between God and humanity, as noted in liberalism and antinomianism respectively.[104] The Incarnation perfectly reflects post-Newtonian science, with space and time conceived as contingent; hence, natural theology and revealed theology are

---

101. Torrance, *Divine Meaning*, 45, citing Athenagoras, *Presbeia*, 3ff, 6ff, 10ff, 15f, 30f; and *Divine and Contingent Order*, 33.

102. 1 John 1:1, NRSV.

103. Torrance, *Space, Time and Incarnation*, 55.

104. Ibid., 79–80.

conceptually related.[105] In terms of natural law an extended quote from Torrance is salient:

> Natural theology cannot be undertaken apart from the actual knowledge of the living God as a prior conceptual system on its own, or be developed as an independent philosophical examination of rational forms phenomenologically abstracted from their material content, all antecedent to positive theology... In this fusion, 'natural theology' will suffer a dimensional change and will be made natural to the proper subject-matter of theology... it will function... to articulate the inner material logic of knowledge of God as it is mediated within the organized field of space-time.[106]

Here Torrance concurs with McGrath's proposal that the contestability of nature sanctions its qualification by Christian theology and revelation.[107] Thus the term "nature" can be expanded to mean that which is proper to anything in its own being, acts, and relations. Consequently it includes God and his relations in its semantic range. This means that the terms "natural theology" includes what is natural to God, and cannot be set in opposition to revelation, or be understood in a non-theological fashion. It also means that non-theological understandings of human nature and natural law cannot be exhaustive because, despite humanity's sinful breaking of the covenant with God, humanity is still related to God by virtue of being God's creation and the object of his love and condescension, just as a child cannot not be the offspring of its mother. It is natural—proper—for God to create, reveal and pledge himself in covenantal relations (Gen 1:1–2:3), and natural—proper—for human beings in their createdness to hear and receive God in his revealing covenantal love (Gen. 3:8–9). Hence natural theology possesses an expanded semantic range to include theology that is natural and proper to God in his revealedness, and natural law possesses an expanded semantic range to include moral law as found in this revealedness. As such, they cannot be in opposition to revealed theology or revealed law or any form of the revelation of God himself, but include within them revelation as

---

105. Ibid., 69. The implication is that natural theology is the inner *logos* of revealed theology, as geometry is the inner *logos* of physics. Thus historical revealed theology, and realist natural theology exemplify a model of "unitary theory" and semantic coordination, 81.

106. Ibid., 70. For Irenaeus, the *Logos* created the inner logic of things, while the Spirit created their material adornment, Torrance, *Divine Meaning*, 71.

107. McGrath, *Open Secret*, 167–170.

that which is proper to God's being and activity. It is not unnatural to God to reveal, nor unnatural to humanity to respond positively to God.

Consequently, a simple line of reasoning suggests itself: natural law is to be informed by natural theology, which in turn is to be informed by revealed theology. Here all non-theological understandings of human nature are disabled. As natural law deals with the intrinsic morality of the humanity that the incarnate Word assumed, then his humanity as theologically determined must control and inform the content of natural law.

Moreover, natural law on this understanding becomes the inner logic of the moral nature of human persons, and the discipline of ethics itself takes on a scientific character as the inner logic that justifies and articulates the good and the right that is to be done. Natural law does not, however, simply articulate the material content of the good and the right, but also locates the formal property of the good and the right in the actual human person. That is, there can be no proper human person without his or her simultaneous moral nature and norms. Morality is not a foreign burden on human nature. What is right and good is not imposed upon or alien to humanity, but is an ineradicable constituent of its existence. But it is not inherent as a formal property without theological determination, for then we lapse back into a mechanistic and deistic form of natural law. Nor is it accessible in a properly transparent fashion without the Incarnation, for only in the Incarnation is perfected and proper human nature revealed. The formal property of human morality possesses christological contours and shape, as does the material content of what constitutes the good and the right.

This fusion of natural and revealed theology disables three models of the relationship between divine and created natures and rationality. First, the Aristotelian/Thomist/Lutheran approach, which sees God as entering into creation as into a container; second, the Newtonian model which sees God as the container of the universe and thus intrinsically part of it; and third, the Origenist view whereby creation has been imbued with its own rationality and is somehow coterminous with God. Rather, the Patristic model (Anselm, Scotus, Pascal, Barth) affirms that "the structure of space and time are created forms of rationality to be distinguished from the eternal rationality of God," so that God is free and the creation is contingent, yet the Incarnation of "the Son of God in the realm of space and time means that He assumes created truth and rationality and makes them His own although he is distinct from them."[108] Jesus' enhypostatic humanity is the divinely created form of human nature and rationality that is assumed by the eternal *Logos presarkos*. However, soteriological rather than ethical concerns

---

108. Torrance, *Space, Time and Incarnation*, 65.

are traditionally prominent in christological anthropology, so that any part of human nature that is left unassumed is left unhealed. Such traditional soteriology displays a type of component anthropology,[109] whereas ethics is a dimension of the whole person in all their "components:" there is no ethical "part" of persons isolated from their other "parts."[110] Because morality is not a distinct part but an ineradicable property of human nature, it is a defining characteristic of that nature. This makes reason, as a function of that nature, an accompanying characteristic of human nature. Hence the "created truth and rationality" that the eternal Son assumed is embedded in the moral nature of his humanity, otherwise a form of Docetism results. Christ's anhypostatic human nature includes its own created rationality that is different to God's eternal rationality but which is given singular concretion in its union with the *Logos*. Yet there are not two rationalities that are opposed, but two rationalities that are apophatically united. Consequently, the Incarnation is dyologist, with Christ's human *logos* (reason) created and existing in perfect congruence with the divine *logos* (reason) of the incarnate *Logos* in the one hypostasis.[111]

This being the case, moral reasoning and natural law cannot be de-christologized without a severe compromise of traditional Christology. To do so suggests that Christ's form of moral reasoning is non-normative for human reasoning, which threatens Chalcedonian human consubstantiability. If practical moral reasoning is inherent in humanity *per se*, and such moral reasoning is not exemplified in Christ, then his human consubstantiability is necessarily compromised. Or, if Christ's human reason was suspended in favor of the divine reason, his humanity becomes functionally dualist, divided into functional and non-functional components, which not only threatens his perfect humanity (i.e., one psychological element being permanently dormant), but also compromises soteriology.[112] On the contrary, if Christ's enhypostatic human mind exists only by virtue of its assumption by the eternal *Logos* as an act of creation, then such a mind must exhibit the truth and rationality of human nature as divinely intended if Chalcedonian

---

109. For example, bi- or tri-parte theories that posit discrete components such as soul, mind, body, etc.

110. In Barth's actualist ethics —"What am I to do?"—the "I" is the total person.

111. Similar to dyothelitism, dyologism affirms the presence of two proper minds—the human and the divine—in the incarnate Son, if the two natures are to be sustained properly yet apophatically as in Chalcedon. The human *logos* (mind) is not a duplication of the *Logos presarkos*, however: there is one incarnate *Logos* (person) with two *logoi* (minds). Dyologism expresses double consubstantial rationality.

112. If the human mind assumed in the Incarnation was functionally shelved, then it was not healed, and the Incarnation itself is voided.

consubstantiability is to stand. It is for this reason the *Logos* gospel of the Incarnation is also the gospel most concerned with truth.[113]

It has been already argued that the universal enlightenment of John 1:9 includes human cognition temporally but not logically prior to the Incarnation. However, given the temporality of the Incarnation, such universal enlightenment is given explicit and historical expression and grounding in the person of Christ. In his embodiment, the eternal *Logos* wholly assumed and revealed his own *presarkic* moral determinations for humanity. One such moral determination includes the form of practical moral reasoning proper to human nature so that such reasoning is *Logos*-determined and congruent with his divine nature. What he was in himself *presarkic*, the *Logos* was in himself *ensarkic*, in relation to his moral nature, such that there is no disconnection between the moral reasoning and determinations of eternity and time. The hypostatic union means that the moral reasoning of God and humanity are united in the one person, even though there are two such rationalities: the *Logos* does not overwhelm human moral *dialogismos* in a type of ethical Apollinarianism.

Protological theories of natural law, such as Calvin's, which do not cite such incarnational dimensions, are deficient at this point. Created rationality is not simply derived from God, but is incarnate in Jesus. Because Jesus' own will was united with that of his Father's ("Not my will, but yours be done," Luke 22:42), we have a single person instantiating the full coordination of and congruence between the moral reasoning (*dilogismos*) of two *persons*, the divine and human: the moral determinations of the Father and of Jesus are united. But further, the moral reasoning of each *nature* is found in the one *Logos* so that two *natures* are also morally united: the wills of the divine and human natures are united. Traditional natural law's practical reasoning is deficient here, for other than the Golden Rule it cites Jesus' life or teaching only negligibly.[114] However, when it is cited, it is usually because it exemplifies the natural law's first principle of doing good and avoiding evil, reducing Jesus to an instance of a pre-existing rational norm.[115] As such, he

---

113. Note "truth/true" in John 1:9, 14; 4:23–24; 5:33; 8:14, 16f, 26, 32, 40, 45–46; 14:6, 17; 15:26; 16:7, 13; 17:17, 19; 18:37; 21:24.

114. The Golden Rule (Matt 7:12) is frequently understood as an example of natural law's first principle (doing good and avoiding evil). It is part of the textual *inclusios* of the law and prophets (5:17, 7:12). This suggests that the Sermon on the Mount, including love of enemies and non-retaliation (5:38–48) expresses natural law, contrary to popular interpretation.

115. Barth correctly opposes making a moral or theological predicate into a subject for it reduces God to a participating predicate.

is no longer understood primarily as the incarnate divine *Logos*, but a sage who articulates a universal moral ideal.

However, in Chalcedonian Christology, all ideal moral principles recede behind one real moral person—the *Logos*—who is and does good, both eternally and temporally. Proper moral reasoning does not participate in eternal forms of meta-rationality, but corresponds to the moral reasoning of the *Logos ensarkos* and the *Logos presarkos*.

Hence Chalcedonian Christology implies that when Jesus' moral reasoning is considered from a purely human point of view, it is proper to created humanity. What are heard and seen in Christ's moral words and actions are the external expressions of the internal moral reasoning of normative humanity. He recapitulates as the second Adam natural and proper human moral reasoning. Here the moral reasoning of Christ becomes the internal logic and intelligence of created human nature in its moral form, in the same way that Torrance relates geometry and physics. Yet this inner logic was theologically shaped because such reasoning, as a constituent part of the human nature, only existed by its assumption by the eternal Word and union with his divine nature.

Torrance's patristic model comports well with his critical realism, where the object of thought determines the epistemological and hermeneutical approach and method of its investigation. Extending Polanyi, and against Kant, he affirms that although the rationality of nature objectively transcends our experience of it, we do have real knowledge of it by its self-disclosure when we conform our own rationality to that reality. For instance, he argues that the crystalline formations in rocks impose upon our minds geometric patterns, to which we respond "by an act of acknowledgement."[116]

By extension, in "theology we have knowledge of an objective reality in which we hear a word, encounter a *logos*, from beyond our subjective experience ... which guides us to ever deepening understanding of the objective reality."[117] Thus even though God is not an aspect of created rationality, our apprehension of his rationality is, in a methodological sense, like empirical science to the extent that both created reality and God's reality disclose themselves to our minds in ways that are object-determined, yet humanly apprehensible. Here faith is transformed from a purely religious concept to an intellectual virtue, because the objective reality of God, like all realities, exercises a type of coercive power over the mind, which then humbly

---

116. Torrance, "The Framework of Belief," in *Belief in Science*, 12.

117. Torrance, *Theological Science*, 30, italics original. His disclosure model is expressed with clarity: "The Truth is something over which we have no control," *Ground and Grammar*, 114. Torrance's debt to Barth here is worthy of pursuit elsewhere, despite their differences about natural theology.

acknowledges his truth. "I know" is also "I believe," the Anselmian *credo in-verto*. Theology and ethics, and empirical science, are thus disclosure, rather than impositional models of knowledge. Disclosure does not imply passive methodologies, but being teachable and receptive to the realities disclosed. Nor does it yield a world of Newtonian stasis, but one of multiplicity, variation, and surprise.[118] This element of uncertainty and surprise is found in the ethics of Christian discipleship in the book of Hebrews: pilgrimage towards a defined *telos* does not preclude ambiguity, but requires faith as the appropriate intelligible response to God as the author and perfector of life. Hebrews demonstrates a model of constancy and providential care combined with uncertainty and surprise that Torrance affirms in his doctrine of intelligible creation. This suggests that nature and supernature, creation and grace are apposite not opposite, such that the constancy/surprise model of ethics is consonant with the constancy/surprise model of natural science. Hence the moral life of faith in response to God's rationality and call is not unnatural or irrational, but comports with the intelligibility of divine creation and providence. This forces together the disciplines of theology, ethics, and science, as well as the doctrines of creation, Christology, and soteriology. By being responsive to divinely created forms of truth, rationality, and order, ethics becomes a natural science in the older dogmatic sense that included the divine nature.[119] It follows that Christology must necessarily be included in natural law because his double consubstantiality means that the divine nature is expressed in creation and that his enhypostatic human nature, as one aspect of that creation, discloses that divine nature. The hypostatic union is thus the *unique and personal* example of all proper relations between God and creation, particularly humanity: created reality is fashioned by, related and oriented to, and sustained by, God. Creation and grace are twin aspects of the one relation.

This disclosure method is akin to Calvin's concept of revelation: "God alone is a fit witness of himself in his Word," so that "the Spirit . . . must penetrate into our hearts to persuade us" to "truly rest upon Scripture."[120] Here the direction is from God as active subject to human as active subjective receiver. Submitting Scripture to proof is illegitimate, argue Calvin, as Scripture itself carries its own authenticating power through the Spirit. Here is a

---

118. Noted regularly in scientific breakthroughs and discoveries in both the micro and macro levels.

119. The modern use of "nature" as equivalent to "creation" loses its traditional sense that included both divine and created natures.

120. Calvin, *ICR*, I.vi.4, 79–80. The provenance of the assertion that only God can make God known is Irenaeus, "Against Heresies," 4.II.1–5 according to Torrance, *Trinitarian Faith*, 54.

clear distinction between two forms of knowledge: respect for Scripture due to its own bare majesty, and its efficacy according to its own subject matter, i.e., the power of God himself. Scripture is not a repository of abstract theological knowledge, but the means of enabling divine-human encounters, inflaming obedience. Citing the Nicene Fathers, Torrance likewise suggests that "trinitarian worship and trinitarian faith provide the explicit controlling ground for . . . understanding the Mind of Christ."[121] This brings both reason and empirical experience together, neither being intelligible without the other. If worship is the control experience enabling proper understanding of Christ's mind (*lex orandi, lex credendi*), by extension discipleship to Christ in exemplary ethics is the control experience that enables proper understanding of natural law (*lex imitatio, lex naturae*). Yet neither is fully informed without mutual understanding.

e. Conclusion

Torrencian theological science provides an heuristic tool for ethics by providing a conceptual framework that relates the laws of nature to natural law as an aspect of divine intelligible creation, manifested in the Incarnation.[122] Natural law's moral reasoning about humanity is one expression of wider reasoning about the "laws of nature." Natural law's first principle—do good and avoid evil—expresses a universal rationality similar to empirical science's first principle—seek truth and avoid falsehood—because both principles are wholly internal to their subjects. Yet natural law is the more complex of the two for it deals with sentient and volitional human life in its theological relations, whereas laws of nature traditionally describe non-volitional entities and their relationships.[123] Consequently, even though human reason can function "in an indefinite multiplicity of ways" such as logic, mathematics, and abstraction, natural law rejects the voluntarism which bends reason to "attribute to human action a condition that we would not dare attribute to natural processes."[124] If then the deterministic mechanism of Newtonian laws of nature is incapable of richly explaining created reality, traditional natural law likewise shares that incapacity by its limited scope, tendency to a non-theological anthropology, traditionally

---

121. Torrance, *Trinitarian Faith*, 64, echoing Wolterstorffian control beliefs.

122. This stands despite his project not being ethical in nature.

123. This complexity is found particularly in human volition's capacity to disengage from the contingent order of which it is a created part: see Ellis and Murphy below.

124. Simon, *Tradition*, 80. Voluntarism does this by disengaging will from reason.

static and questionable concept of nature, and its somewhat rational and material self-enclosure.[125] This is observed particularly when natural law is erroneously identified with convention to justify traditionalism. Thus the natural law theory of some Catholic scholars—who limit natural law to the narrow scope of the first principle of practical reasoning, and first principles of morality—is insightful, as it leaves scope for the dynamic development of those first principles.[126] Its potential weakness is its self-enclosure within the confines of practical reasoning and its non-theological character, thereby disengaging itself from metaphysics, the wider natural world, and particularly Christology.

Latent in Torrancian nature and creation is a natural law which is fluid and dynamic, affirms creativity, comports with and is a constituent element of the contingent graced intelligibility and rationality of the universe, and expresses God's rationality in the Incarnation through the Jesus' enhypostatic humanity. Natural law is reframed as the moral law of the universe: it is the graced, intelligible, and contingent moral form and matter of creation, and participates in God's eternal intelligibility by virtue of its creation by him, and its assumption by him in the Incarnation. It shares in God's rationality because the human mind is one element of humanity created in God's image. Nicene/Chalcedonian Christology means therefore that the Incarnation "involves the full reality and integrity of human and creaturely being in space and time."[127]

4. The Kenotic Moral Theory of Murphy and Ellis

a. Introduction

It is a central argument of this thesis that ethics must be determined by both human and divine natures and persons to remain intelligibly Christian. If it is severed from the divine nature, and particularly Christology, ethics fails any test of Christian identity. It also reduces to anti-realist voluntarism. If it is severed from human nature, it remains an extrinsic imposition upon

---

125. At the sub-atomic level self-enclosed mechanism fails, replaced by quantum mechanics.

126. See Hittinger, where he describes Grisez's first principle of practical reasoning as "a grasp upon the necessary relationship in existential reality between human goods and appropriate action bearing upon these goods," so that the moral agent acts according to the first principle of morality, which is "to choose and otherwise will those and only those possibilities whose willing is compatible with a will towards integral human fulfillment." Hittinger, *Critique*, 31, 50.

127. Torrance, *Trinitarian Faith*, 151.

humanity, and thus incongruent with the doctrines of creation and the Incarnation. It also enlarges to oppressive ontotheology. It is for this reason that the two-nature Christology of Chalcedon is central. Thus while not being explicitly Chalcedonian, Murphy/Ellis provide a model of radical ethics that enables a Chalcedonian interpretation which unites the historical and the cosmological/metaphysical.

b. The Structure of Reality and its Attendant Disciplines

Central to the Murphy/Ellis theory is a hierarchical model of reality, knowledge and intellectual disciplines. Bottom level sciences are fine-grained and microscopic, while top-level disciplines are coarse-grained or broadly encompassing wholes. In arguing that "the concepts needed for describing and explaining the higher-level entities are not reducible (i.e., translatable without remainder) into concepts of the lower level," the necessity of top-down causation and explanation is maintained over against one-directional bottom-up reductionism and causality.[128] Modern anti-metaphysical epistemology, enclosed as it is in bottom-up human sciences, is inadequate and incomplete because theology "ought to be . . . the highest level of description to which we aspire rather than the down-trodden poor relations of modern scholarship," for the meaning of every level is "found in the level immediately above it."[129]

Murphy and Ellis propose that moral obligation is an essential component of any account of reality because moral obligation is non-illusory. They place ethics as the top-level discipline of the human sciences because it deals with the most complex entities and relationships, namely, human beings as sentient, relational, moral, and volitional beings. It "is necessary to have an answer to the question of the ultimate meaning [and] . . . final purpose or *telos* of human life," which affirms the intrinsic connection between ethics, objective knowledge, and rational adjudication, without recourse to voluntarism or subjectivism.[130] Being at the top of this hierarchy, ethical *action* always includes a dimension of intention because the will inheres intrinsi-

128. Murphy and Ellis, *Moral Nature*, 15–16. Traditional metaphysical top-level explanations have been rejected in the modern period for bottom-up explanations in psychology, sociology and now in biology/genetics, *Moral Nature*, 225.

129. Puddefoot, "The relationship of natural order to divine truth and will," in Murray Rae, et al., *Science and Theology*, 154, and Vysheslavtsev, *Eternal*, 109. Scientific concepts must be "open at both ends," the transcendent and empirical, Torrance, *Theological Science*, 277.

130. Murphy and Ellis, *Moral Nature*, 87, and 105, referring to MacIntyre, no source.

cally in human beings and God.[131] This necessarily excludes any claim that avolitional lower levels are exhaustive explanations. Immediately above the top level (ethics) of the human sciences lies metaphysics/theology, the apex of both hard and human sciences. Top-down reasoning, which commences at this absolute apex (metaphysics/theology), produces metaphysical theories that are contestable, leading in turn to contestable cosmologies and their attendant ethical theories, which possess varying degrees of comportment with bottom-up reasoning. Murphy and Ellis argue that the Christian doctrine of creation, as one top-down theological/metaphysical explanation, offers a coherent and scientific explanation of, and coherence with, fine-grained bottom-up scientific reasoning. In particular, they argue that bottom-up human sciences must be reattached to top-down metaphysics/theology, for only then can they and their attendant ethics avoid relativism and remain coherent.[132]

c. The Kenotic Nature of Humanity.

At the core of the Murphy/Ellis ethical theory is a simple account of human flourishing: "self-renunciation for the sake of others is humankind's highest good."[133] This is grounded not in empirical science but in God's self-renunciation in his act of creation. In respect to moral action, this means renouncing material possessions, rewards, and the harming of others, and practicing non-violence, acceptance of suffering, and submission to God.[134] These are kenotic practices based upon a kenotic doctrine of God.[135]

Creation as an act of divine self-renunciation, however, does not square with the received tradition of creation and God. The question is begged, "What does God renounce by creating a perfect creation?" A strong doctrine of divine impassibility may suggest that he renounces rest or poise, but such a doctrine of impassibility is more Hellenistic and speculative rather than biblical, and as Maximus argues, divine impassibility does not exclude divine movement in the act of creation. As nothing existed prior to creation but God, then the only object of renunciation by God in creation can be some element or dimension of himself. Weil is cited in support, "God

---

131. Ibid., 31, emphasis original.

132. Ibid., 107–108, citing John Milbank, *Theology and Social Theory*, who argues that the social sciences are intrinsically "theologies or anti-theologies in disguise."

133. Murphy and Ellis, *Moral Nature*, 118.

134. Ibid., 119–120, citing Simone Weil, *Gravity and Grace*.

135. Ibid., 119, 173–178.

renounces being everything... He emptied himself of his divinity."[136] However, the complement "divinity" is included in "God" the subject, making the statement nonsensical.

"Being everything" does not constitute a defining characteristic of "divinity," nor does ceasing to be everything constitute renunciation, for the act of creation establishes loving covenant relations (Barth), and enables divine and human *methexis*/participation (Maximus and Milbank). Metaphysically, God cannot diminish through self-giving as he is inexhaustible, eternal, and infinite. Weil's concept of divine self-emptying in the act of creation is deeply problematic and fits poorly with orthodox Nicene-Chalcedonian theology.

Murphy and Ellis are on firmer ground when they associate self-emptying with the christological text, Philippians 2:5–11: "The best explanation of a kenotic ethic is a kenotic doctrine of God... such a way of life is imitation, reflection of the character of God."[137] This provides the metaphysical/theological ground, which they claim is necessary for ethical coherence, i.e., a top-down explanation, yet they argue that the christological act of kenosis is not metaphysical, against traditional interpretation,[138] but socio-political. Philippians 2:5–11 is understood as a recapitulation of creation where Christ as second Adam does not grasp the serpentine offer of being like God, but self-renounces such aggrandizement in the wilderness temptations.[139] The hymn's introduction in corporate language[140] implies that Paul's christologically exemplarist paraenesis (Phil 2:5), grounded upon the teaching of Jesus (Phil 2:3–4, 7; Mark 10:45), supports Yoder's socio-political interpretation that is the theoretical base of the Ellis/Murphy thesis. That the kenosis of Jesus Christ is meant as the basis for practical moral reasoning is explicit in Paul's use of *phroneîte* (v. 5, repeated from v. 2, *phronête*).

In particular, they cite Yoder's assertion that Incarnation means, not the sacralizing of nature as a source of revelation, but rather the opposite, "that God broke through the borders of our standard definition of what is human, and gave it a new, formative definition in Jesus."[141] This expresses a key Chalcedonian concept: "the *divinity and unity of the Son with the Father* are the guarantees that no other claims can be more binding on humankind

---

136. Ibid., 119. See also Moltmann, *God in Creation*.

137. Murphy and Ellis, *Moral Nature*, 174.

138. See A. Oepke, "κενός, κενόω, κενόδοξος, κενοδοδιζα," in TDNT, vol. 3, 660–662.

139. Attributed to Moltmann, McClendon, Yoder, Dunn et al., Murphy and Ellis, *Moral Nature*, 175–178.

140. Philippians 2:1 is plural, ὑμῖν.

141. Murphy and Ellis, *Moral Nature*, 183, quoting Yoder's *Politics*, 2nd edition, 99.

than those of Jesus."[142] Not only so, but christological kenosis demonstrates that humanity's proper posture before God is humility.[143]

The final argument in their theory is the evidence for a kenotic universe that reflects their kenotic metaphysics/theology. They find this in: 1) divine providence evidenced in the laws of nature, which act impartially in respect to moral desert;[144] 2) the divinely determined epistemic distance between God and humanity, which permits human unbelief rather than coerced belief in God; and 3) the suffering and pathos of creation, which gives way to greater forms of life through recycling, stellar renewal through the dissipated elements of other dying stars, and human genetic richness received from previous generations. Thus "all living things must participate not only in the taking of life in order to live but also in the painful *giving* of their lives that others might live."[145] Such *giving* of life qualifies the strict *taking* of life in traditional Darwinism.[146]

If we associate both these scientific and theological affirmations of Murphy and Ellis, we can affirm their kenotic ethic more robustly. Scientifically, the anthropic principle, that "intelligent life must exist in the universe: it is a necessity,"[147] can be reframed theologically as the outworking of the christological archetype and creation of humanity, in an Irenaean sense. Here, human creation is determined by and predicated on the logical (not temporal) precedence of the Incarnation as its archetype. However, as archetype, the Incarnation is not restricted to the simple matter of enfleshment, but includes the specific form of Christ's whole incarnate life, culminating in his self-giving in crucifixion as a servant. Thus the basic anthropic principle, grounded christologically, becomes a principle of giving life through death, that life may appear. If the christological human archetype is kenotic, then the anthropic principle is necessarily kenotic. The anthropic principle can also be seen in the developing stages of creation in Genesis 1, where the acts of each day's creation lead ultimately to the creation of intelligible humanity as its apex.[148] That is, lower levels precede and enable the possibil-

---

142. Ibid., 183, emphasis added.

143. Ibid., 194–196.

144. God did not make a universe where "survival [is] dependent on obedience to God," Ibid., 209.

145. Ibid., 208–13, 213, emphasis original.

146. Ibid., 213.

147. Ibid., 52.

148. The Sabbath is not an aspect of creation in the narrow sense. God "blessed it and made it holy," (Gen 2:3), yet is not described as creating it, nor affirmed as being "good" like the first six days.

ity of higher levels. While Murphy and Ellis do not make these moves, it lies implicit in their theory and provides another level of theological support for their kenotic ethic.

Yet a difficulty arises. By preferring a second Adam reading of Philippians 2, Murphy and Ellis make the text anthropological, not metaphysical/theological in the strict sense. This makes problematic their affirmation that the metaphysical/theological apex of their hierarchy is kenotic, which would be better served by the traditional reading of Philippians 2. In effect, they have removed their ethic's metaphysical justification by a social reading of the Christology of Philippians 2. Yet Chalcedon enables an integration of both the metaphysical/theological and social interpretations of self-emptying: the concept of Incarnation necessarily implies pre-existence and thus theological/divine kenosis, while Jesus' historical refusal to imitate Adam is anthropologically kenotic. The eternal Son's theological kenosis in the Incarnation was matched by Jesus' social/political kenosis in his death. Here the kenotic *theology* of the Incarnation determines the kenotic *anthropology* of incarnate life, due to the hypostatic union of the two moral natures, and because the conceptuality and semantics of the higher levels determine and shape the conceptuality and semantics of the lower levels.

Because ethics as a second order discipline cannot be adequately described within the parameters of a human self-referential discipline without reference to the top level of metaphysics/theology, both traditional natural law (the human sciences) and the traditional laws of nature (the hard sciences) share that limitation. True causal explanation lies at the interdisciplinary boundaries if naïve reductionist or one-dimensional thinking is to be avoided. Utilizing the Murphy/Ellis structure, the upper level of metaphysics/theology is the eternal *Logos*, while the lower level of the human sciences is the life of Jesus. The eternal *Logos presarkos* constitutes the metaphysical/ theological apex immediately above ethics, while the historical *Logos ensarkos* constitutes the empirical realities of human life in the level below ethics, so that ethics is framed from both above and below not by two independent natures which are unrelated, but by their union in the one person. The conceptual coordination of both levels is the one person of Jesus Christ. This is illustrated in Table 4, where the Murphy/Ellis hierarchy is supplemented by christological counterparts.

Therefore the modern project of disengaging ethics primarily from top-level metaphysics/theology, but also from lower-level science is overcome by "restoring the bonds between moral knowledge and the human sciences,"[149] and by affirming that "metaphysics and moral systems cannot be characterized or evaluated in isolation from each other."[150]

Murphy/Ellis Disciplinary levels	Christological *Logos* content
Metaphysics/theology	*Logos presarkos*
Ethics	Natural law and Christological moral reasoning
Social science	*Logos ensarkos*

Table 4: The Murphy/Ellis Classification of Disciplines with Christological Natural Law Implications.

Chalcedonian Christology provides both of these levels. At the top metaphysical level is the Son's divine consubstantiabilty. At the lower social sciences level is the Son's human consubstantiability. At the top level we have coarse-grained traditional metaphysical and theological reasoning. At the bottom level we have fine-grained disciplines such as history, gospel criticism, and the sociology of the church as the living communal witness to Jesus. At the top level, metaphysical reasoning affords cogent reasons for ethical realism through the doctrine of the contingent nature of the universe as a free act of God, who as light and truth embeds the created universe with the inherent rationality of his own being, and who as love and fellowship permits his creation to participate in his ongoing work of creation and the unfolding of the universe's inherent potential. At the bottom level, christological moral reasoning reasons out of the human moral perfections of Jesus—who was seen, touched and heard—that are universally accessible through written witnesses.

It is thus at the boundaries of the higher level metaphysics/theology and the lower level social science of history that an adequate ethical model is found. The opposition between realism and historicism is overcome through this model, for the real divine consubstantiability of the Son is united perfectly and apophatically with the historic consubstantial humanity of the Son in one hypostasis. Here, ethics must *look both ways, up and down* to be comprehensive and adequate.[151] Therefore natural law ethics must look up to theology/metaphysics and down to anthropology and natural inclinations to avoid becoming christologically void, and radical ethics must look up to Christ's divine nature as well as down to his human nature in history, if

149. Ibid., 107.
150. Ibid., 110.
151. Yoder states that John's *Logos* "affirms identity at both ends," i.e., God and human, *Preface*, 186.

it is to avoid being reduced to naïve fideism and being too theologically thin to command wide assent. Looking both ways is achieved by seeing Jesus (Heb 2:9) through Chalcedon's prism. This is a decisive turning from the Kantian skepticism that caused Christianity to be reduced, first to bourgeois European ethics, and later to one ethic amongst the global many, where the ethical core is distilled from its alleged dogmatic impurities.

In contrast, this "look both ways, up and down" model ensures that the metaphysical and historical are united in the one person and provides a thick account of christological ethics that avoids reductionism. If the *one person* of the Word is the united interdisciplinary focus of metaphysical/theological and social scientific ethical reasoning, then the *two natures* of Jesus constitutes the two focal instances of each of these two forms of reasoning. At their interdisciplinary union in the one person, ethics remains focused and binocular.

Notwithstanding this, there are two weaknesses in the Murphy/Ellis position. First, as previously stated, because Philippians 2 is read as an anthropological second Adam text, the metaphysical basis of their ethic is christologically eroded. Yet as previously argued, the kenotic text (Phil 2:5–8) can carry both an incarnational and second Adam interpretation. As the divine Son *presarkos* he emptied himself by becoming incarnate, and as the *ensarkic* second Adam Jesus, he renounced the quest for life outside the will of God. Here *kenosis* (v. 7a) governs both the Incarnation (taking on Adam's likeness, v. 7c, 8a), and the socio/political posture of servanthood (refusing Adam's grasping, v. 7b, 8bc).

Second, their argument moves from a kenotic ethic to a kenotic theology. They ask, "What is it that confirms the *moral rightness* of this way of life?" but also affirm that "an ethical core theory *qua* ethics can only be confirmed *from above* in that it follows from a theological or metaphysical conception of ultimate reality."[152] How is it that an ethic needs *confirmation* from above but also *follows* from above? When they articulate their theology after their ethic, they softly cite Nietzsche and the deconstructionists' argument that ethics is logically prior to epistemology and the key to orthodoxy.[153] Schweitzer's critique of the liberal Protestant life of Jesus, where an ethical ideal finds it justification in theology, is apposite here. The question

---

152. Murphy and Ellis, *Moral Nature*, 173–174, italics original. These statements come under the heading "The Need for a Related Theology," 173, i.e., a theological rationale for their ethic.

153. Ibid., 139. Their "Ethics and Theories of God" (ch. 8) follows their "Ethical Core" (ch. 6). Yet this core cites Jesus (his self-renouncing ethic, Luke 17:33) only once in passing, 121. Yoder also bends theology to ethics according to Martens, *Heterodox*, 142.

is begged: Has their inductive methodology, where a theology is constructed from an ethic, created an ontotheology rather than a theology, thereby turning a metaphysical *basis* into an *a posteriori* metaphysical *justification* after the fact?

Despite these two problems, the basic structure of their hierarchy of disciplines provides a compelling model because ethics becomes the focal point where both theology (God) and social science (humanity) converge. By being explanation-eligible at both the higher-level reasoning of metaphysics/theology and the lower-level reasoning of social sciences and empirical observation, natural law is capable of possessing a properly basic character. If it remains enclosed in the moral subject itself, any claim to universal explanatory status vanishes because universal explanation necessarily includes aspects of reality that are greater than the subject. The question "Why act so and so?" begs a theoretical/realist answer such that metaphysical and theological concerns are ethically non-illusory and ineradicable. Expressly, human flourishing includes factors such as God, inter-human relationships, and human ideals that are considered greater than any one moral subject. For instance, it is generally agreed that non-violence, growth in scientific knowledge, the placing of human life in origin, time and space, as well as a greater-than-the-self life-purpose are intrinsic human goods.[154] One such good in Finnis is religion, yet by isolating lower-level reasoning about the good from upper-level reasoning about the true, he drives a wedge between practical moral reasoning itself and one of his key human goods (religion/God) to which such reasoning points.

The methodological and christological problems of the Murphy/Ellis kenotic ethic are somewhat similar to the "classical lack" Reimer notes in Yoder. This is unsurprising as Yoder is a key source for their thesis. Yet if this lack is overcome by a twofold understanding of *kenosis* (Incarnation and second Adam) the Chalcedonian character of a kenotic ethic is strengthened. One particularly fruitful area of exploration here is the begetting of the Son and procession of the Spirit, understood within the Eastern priority of divine hypostasis/persons rather than divine nature or *ousia* or *substantia*.

---

154. For instance, arguments about biological human origins possess ethical conclusions: theists argue that eternal human value and significance is derived from divine creation, atheists argue the need for courage and moral self-creation in the face of theological emptiness.

d. Kenosis and Divine Hypostasis

Eastern trinitarian theology places the unity of the Trinity in the monarchy of the Father, as this privileges the concept of person above that of nature, which they consider to have been uncritically taken over from philosophy by the West.[155] The critically important Christian move was "*the identification of the 'hypostasis' with the 'person,'*" which gave an "ontological content to each person of the Holy Trinity" without jeopardizing either monotheism or the independence of God from the world.[156] Two significant conclusions follow. First, the "person is no longer an adjunct to being . . . (but) *is itself the hypostasis of being*"; and second, persons "no longer trace their being to being itself . . . but to the person . . . [who is]. . . simultaneously. . . *the constitutive element . . .* of being."[157] This disengaged creation from necessity, and identified God's being with his person, so that the being of the one God is no longer identified with a shared substance of divinity but with the Father from whom the Son is begotten and the Spirit proceeds. "Thus God as person—as the hypostasis of the Father—makes the one divine substance to be that which it is: the one God."[158]

Consequently, the Son's divinity with the Father consists not so much in being con-*substantial* with the Father, although that is not denied, but in the Son's begetting from the Father as a divine person. This leads to a somewhat actualist but decisively personal understanding of God because the eternal begetting of the Son is from the *person* of Father, not through some participation of the Son in the divine nature in which the Father himself consists in order to be God. The same holds true for the proceeding of the Spirit from the person of the Father through the person of the Son. Because the Father's person takes priority over the Father's substance, the *equality* of the Son and the Spirit are functions of the Father's person not his substance. But such a priority of the Father's person also means that the Son's *begetting* and the Spirit's *sending* are also of the Father's person. The divine substance

155. See the discussion in Zizioulas, *Being as Communion*, 27–65.

156. Zizioulas, *Being as Communion*, 36–37, italics original. So too Alexei V. Nesteruk: "The Greek patristics proposed a shift in understanding . . . ontology, such that the old Greek *substance* (Gr. *ousia*) was replaced by the relational notion of *hypostasis* and of *person*." Thus a person "shares the same *logos* of the incarnate Logos of God, that is, Christ," in "Design in the Universe and the Logos of Creation," in Gregersen and Görman, *Design and Disorder*, 174.

157. Zizioulas, *Being as Communion*, 39, italics original.

158. Ibid., 41. Despite avowing a change from the ancient philosophy of being, we have already noted in Part One that Aristotle (Categoriae c. 5) asserts that forms or universals are neither antecedent nor posterior to particulars, but "only realized in particular subjects."

is not some type of Platonic Form or abstraction in which the Father, Son, and Spirit participate and from which they derive their divinity, begetting, and sending, but that which is inherent in each person or hypostasis as a person or hypostasis. God's existence as a person *is* his nature, his being, his substance, and his divinity.

Ethically, this places the hypostasis/person of the Son as *Logos presarkos* in a privileged position over against discussion of *phusis* or *ousia*, so that the personhood of the *Logos ensarkos*, as one hypostasis in two natures, is located only in the eternal Son's personhood. This is the doctrine of anhypostasis/enhypostasis: that Jesus' human *nature* exists only in its assumption by the divine *person* of the Son. By bringing the two natures apophatically together in the one person, Chalcedonian Christology places the hypostasis of the Son, rather than the two natures, central to Christology. Hence when the humanity of Jesus is considered, as in the Murphy/Ellis kenotic Christology, we have necessarily to do with one person (hypostasis) of the Son, for his human nature exists only enhypostatically. Without the Son's eternal pre-existence as a divine person, there would be no human Jesus as such, for his humanity is wholly a function of the hypostasis of the Son. Consequently, a kenotic metaphysics/theology is intrinsically involved whenever the life Jesus is considered, as kenosis describes the hypostasis of the Son, not just his humanity. With this focus upon hypostasis, the "*person* can know God from the world created by the Logos of God; for this *person*, being ontologically distinct from God, shares the same *logos* of the incarnate Logos of God, that is, Christ, who is the ground for the World and Man."[159] While this clearly provides a solid ground for natural theology, the opposite inference can also be drawn: the *logos* of the incarnate *Logos*/Son provides the basic ground for understanding humanity and ethics. Ethical knowledge consists in understanding the hypostatic character of ontological reality, because the incarnate Christ is identical with his hypostasis and not reducible to religious ideals as found in some naïve models of *imitatio Christi*, but in his embodiment is the ontological reality of the person in which he consists, the eternal *Logos presarkos*.

Chalcedon therefore opens up the possibility of a double epistemology, well captured by Puddefoot: the Incarnation offers "the hope and reassurance that God does in a sense know as man knows, and that man can in some sense know as God knows."[160] If natural law is an ineradicable,

---

159. Nesteruk, "Design in the Universe," in Gregersen and Görman, *Design and Disorder*, 174, italics original. He combines an Athanasian *logos* theology, a Maximian *Logos/logoi* thematic, and Zizioulas, to propose an argument for design.

160. Puddefoot, "Natural order to divine truth and will," *Science and Theology*, 153. Also Barth: "the knowledge of man as such includes and implies the knowledge of

ubiquitous, divinely determined reality, it necessarily means that Jesus, as the man who knows as God knows, taught and lived natural law in his humanity. Conversely, if God knows as humans know, the life of Christ is the divinely sanctioned exemplary moral form of humanity. It also means that natural inclinations are experienced by the Son and ordered according to his perfections. That is, God experiences our sensory connection with and responses to the world,[161] so that Christ's teaching and acts take on the status of properly ordered natural inclinations.[162] Jesus' acts and teaching therefore historically exemplify metaphysical/theological natural law, which is kenotic in character. A kenotic Christology is therefore grounded not in the human nature of Jesus but in his divine personhood, because kenosis, as the self-emptying renunciation of the *Logos ensarkos*, is an act of the whole person of the Son, for the hypostasis of the *Logos* is given priority over his modes of *presarkos* and *ensarkos*. Approximating Barth, the historical act of the *Logos ensarkos* inheres in the being of the *Logos presarkos*, so that the human *nature* of Jesus recedes behind the single whole *person* of the Son. Hence the human *nature* and kenotic life of Jesus—becoming a servant and dying for others as the ethical example—is properly understood from the perspective of the *person* of the Son. And as the person of the Son is begotten of the Father, kenosis lies in the personhood of the Father, not in Weil's sense above, but in the Father's eternal begetting of the Son to live and die kenotically. That is, the kenotic hypostatic Son, as begotten by the hypostasis of the Father, implies the kenotic hypostasis of the Father. This provides a richer and deeper metaphysical/theological account of kenosis than that offered by Murphy/Ellis.

This begs the question: Of what did the Father empty himself in the Incarnation and death of the Son? That is, what does the kenotic economy indicate about the immanent Trinity? If we follow Barth and affirm that the act and being of God co-inhere, then the act of kenosis must reveal something of the kenotic being of God, and therefore the being of the Father. And as we have agreed with Zizioulas that person takes priority over nature/being, to affect the being implies affecting the person of the Father, for being cannot exist without person. So the question is not so much whether kenosis lies in an act of the Father, but whether the Father, and the Trinity, is kenotic in person/s and thus also nature. This is what Murphy/Ellis

---

God; and again, that the knowledge of man is possible and attainable only from the standpoint of the knowledge of God," *CD*, III/2, 72–73, summarizing Calvin's introductory epistemology in the *ICR*.

161. Puddefoot, "Natural order to divine truth and will," *Science and Theology,* 159.

162. Christ's teaching in the Sermon on the Mount includes the key natural law text of Matthew 7:12.

attempt, but their Weilian doctrine of God's renunciation of his divinity is non-Chalcedonian.

Because God's acts inhere in his being, and as being exists only hypostatically, the Father's act of sending his Son means the Father is hypostatically kenotic. Yet kenosis does not necessarily characterize each particular act of God. For example, God is personally kind, but kindness does not inhere fully in his acts of judgment in the biblical narrative, or in eschatological judgment. Likewise, God's kenotic nature does not lie in his self-renunciation in the act of creation, against Weil, but in the divine decision of the Father, and in the Son's act, of becoming incarnate.

This provides a realist and metaphysical doctrine of divine kenosis, revealed in the Incarnation. God is thus kenotic in that he gives of himself, his *person*, in servant-love, not disdaining the virgin's womb,[163] as well as granting his creation free determination through grace and love. However, given the specific Christology of Philippians 2:5–11, and the Yoderian trajectory of Murphy/Ellis, it is unsurprising that they argue that kenosis is most significantly embodied in pacifism.[164] Although they recognize this as controversial, it follows trivially from an ethic that is grounded, first, in the example and words of Jesus, and second, in a realist doctrine of God where his being coheres in his acts, and the central act of his person is self-giving love towards his enemies, leading to death. A realist ethic, grounded as it is in real metaphysics, necessarily means that if ethics is to be coherent and comport with its metaphysical grounding, it must socially and morally embody the nature of that reality. As God is not, in a realist sense, violent in his immanent triune self, then a realist divine ethic must also eschew violence. Further, if natural law as a realist ethic is metaphysically grounded in divine *nature* that only exists *hypostatically*, then violence cannot be argued on metaphysical/theological natural law grounds.

This extension of the Murphy/Ellis thesis provides a richer metaphysical grounding of their radical kenotic ethic. By utilizing the Barthian act/being thematic and the Orthodox priority of hypostasis over *ousia*, it is possible to articulate kenotic non-violence as a natural law ethic grounded in both their top-level concerns of metaphysics/theology, and in their bottom-level social science concerns of the historical life of Jesus as the Word who assumed proper human nature.

---

163. The *Te Deum*.
164. Murphy and Ellis, *Moral Nature*, 250, regarding both personal and state violence.

e. Conclusion

Despite the two criticisms of Murphy/Ellis already mentioned, their primary contribution to this project is their scientific understanding of reality and its attendant disciplines, and their focus upon kenosis as proper to creation. By arguing that the person of the begetting Father is kenotic, I have tried to show that kenosis is also proper to the person of the begotten Son as both *Logos asarkos and Logos ensarkos*. Because the Incarnation of the Son and the humiliation and crucifixion of Jesus are both kenotic acts, kenosis is proper to both God and humanity. Thus Jesus' kenotic servanthood and love of enemies, so central in radical ethics, can no longer be considered unnatural, but is proper to the self-giving nature of God and created humanity.

Thus the Murphy/Ellis approach suggests a model of reality and its attendant disciplines that enables a simple Chalcedonian framing of ethics. If ethics must be framed from above by theology/metaphysics, and framed from below by history and the social sciences, then the one person of Christ in two natures offers the focused concentration of this framing. Theology and history are united apophatically in Christ. As such, ethics undergoes a change of category: it is no longer a discipline, but is the person of Christ in his hypostatic union of the right and good which are proper to both theology and history in the one person of Jesus. Jesus is the good and the right that is proper to both God and humanity.

5. Conclusion

This chapter has examined the cosmological reasoning of the classical and radical traditions as represented by four writers. Each enables a christological framing of moral reasoning. By doing so, creation and Creator are united through creation's contingent and graced existence as a good act of the Word who assumed the nature of human creation. The Word who was eternally good assumed one element of his own good work—Adamic humanity.

The explicit christo-*logos* theology of Maximus reframes cosmology, anthropology, and natural law by pressing the human *logos* and *tropos* into the *Logos*. Only then can they be read correctly without lapsing into non-theological and improper apprehension. The *tropos* of human existence, and moral reasoning as one of those modes, is properly recoverable not from disordered human phenomena, but through the eternal *Logos ensarkos*. By being pressed into the *Logos ensarkos* who assumed and inhabited humanity's time and space, proper creaturely moral reasoning is lifted out of sin and becomes properly human. What is humanly right and good finds it proper location in the time of the first century and in the space of Palestine.

Natural law reasoning is thus changed at an elemental level into a christological practice, such that the practical moral reasoning that is a proper mode of human existence becomes christological moral reasoning. The mode of moral reasoning that is proper to human existence must itself be pressed into the contours of the practical moral reasoning exhibited by the *Logos ensarkos*. How Jesus went about reasoning is itself proper to humanity, and thus takes on an exemplary status.

Torrance's theological science stresses that the rational structure of the world is contingent upon and reflective of the rationality of its divine creator, who maintains it in covenant faithfulness. All knowledge of this world is properly understood as disclosed and object determined. As such, moral reasoning is placed within the broader context of the laws of nature, for morality is an intrinsic and non-illusory aspect of the cosmos. Natural law is the moral dimension of the laws of nature, and like the laws of nature is embedded through grace. Laws of nature are framed by natural theology, which is itself the inner logic of revealed theology. By arguing that there can be no forms of knowing which are finally antithetical to each other, Torrance's coherentist epistemology means that natural law and christological ethics are inadequate explanations of the one moral reality if not informed by each other. This thesis argues that their apparent differences are finally not real, and that Christ's human consubstantiality (Chalcedon) must be interpreted through the Gospel narrative typical of christo-ethical radicalism, without minimizing his divine consubstantiality.

Murphy/Ellis understand that the moral nature of the universe is non-illusory and kenotic. While disagreeing with two aspects of their thesis, their radical kenotic Christology is not incompatible with the classical tradition. In particular, it is only by looking both ways, at Christ's divine and human natures, that a coherent ethic is enabled which does justice to the historical event of Jesus' life and the metaphysical reality incarnate in that life. Christ is the only focal instance where history and theology/metaphysics meet in one hypostasis. Because Christ's two natures are united apophatically— unconfused, unchanged, indivisible, and inseparable—so too history and metaphysics/theology are apophatically united. The one person of Christ is the single place where ethics must stand in order to be proper both to humanity's historicalness and to God's eternity. Chalcedon's two-nature Christology suggests that the apparent incommensurability of natural law and christo-ethical radicalism are really two traditions of moral enquiry and two semantic fields which are united apophatically, and describe the one reality.

Both traditions and their semantics are inadequate without each other, yet together inform the practical moral reasoning which is proper to humanity.

All four theorists enable a reconfiguration of moral law as a non-illusory element of the cosmos that is contingent upon its divine creator. Practical moral reasoning is a creationally intended activity proper to human existence in its creaturely mode, and set within the broader creation as a whole. Moral reasoning understood as a *logos* of human existence is best situated within the wider *logoi* of the cosmos itself, but more importantly, in relation to the *Logos* himself (John 1:1–5). Yet because this *Logos* became flesh (John 1:14), cosmological moral reasoning as a *logos* of humanity is non-speculatively grounded in the time and space of first century Palestine (1 John 1:1–4).

Consequently, the rational nature of creation, and human reasoning about the right and the good of creation, are *Logos* determined. Reasoning *about* the good and the right must derive from reasoning *from* the good and the right, which finds its normative form and matter in the reasoning and life of the incarnate Word.

7

The Christological Redetermination of Natural Law Ethics Through Barth's *Church Dogmatics*

1. Introduction

THIS CHAPTER WILL SEEK to develop the previous Chalcedonian emphasis by examining selected parts of Barth's theology and Christology as it bears upon this thesis. The previous discussions of Maximus, Torrance, and Murphy/Ellis focused upon the greater-than-human considerations that are present in the cosmological and creational concerns of the natural law tradition, as in Cicero and Calvin, and attempted a redetermination of these concerns through Christology. In this discussion the focus is more upon anthropology, which for Barth is primarily understood christologically. But because his Christology is so deeply Chalcedonian, it is not possible to deal with his understanding of what constitutes humanity and human nature without doing so theologically. To that end, this chapter necessarily also deals with Barth's doctrine of God.

Barth is also chosen because, like christo-ethical radicalism, he exhibits a strong christological emphasis. Yoder's veiled reference to Barth, already noted in Part One, is apposite: "What the Anabaptists spoke of as 'discipleship' was . . . what twentieth-century theologians think is a new insight, when they argue that ethics is an integral part of dogmatics, and that the sole criterion of dogmatics is Christ Himself."[1] This places Barth

---

1. "Prophetic Dissent," *Recovery*, 100.

within the christological sphere of the thesis. Yet because this Christology is strongly Chalcedonian—that is, it is consubstantial with both divine and human natures—it is capable of being used to reframe natural law because natural law deals with what is proper to divine and human natures. Thus *Church Dogmatics* provides an adequate source for an attempted rapprochement of christo-radical ethics and natural law. The concept of properness, such as "What is proper to human nature?," is a common natural law concept and will thus be frequent in this chapter.

Consequently, the criterion that determines what aspects of Barth's *Dogmatics* are examined is whether they have potential to draw christo-ethic radicalism and natural law into a closer relationship. This chapter therefore is not, a) primarily an examination of Barth's ethics; b) an extensive exploration of his christological anthropology as such; c) an assessment of the development of his thought, even though some works other than *Church Dogmatics* are cited; or d) an examination of any perceived weaknesses in Barth's project, such as ecclesiology. Nor is it a comparison of Barth and other writers, such as Yoder. Rather, this chapter has the narrower scope of exploring how selected parts of Barth's Chalcedonian Christology may offer possibilities that enable a rapprochement of radical and natural law ethics as previously described.

Citing Barth in developing a natural law ethic would appear incongruous, given his antipathy to the concept—yet as McGrath notes, natural law is such a polysemous term that it is capable of a distinctive Christian determination which Barth himself does not explore. His aversion may have many reasons, but it is within the range of possibilities that one reason for this hostility is because "nature" and "natural" are often understood in non-theological and non-christological ways, which is a form of reasoning that Barth forbids. Yet I will attempt to show that Barth's christological reasoning about anthropology, including what is natural, contains within it the latent possibility of that which this thesis attempts. That is, the rapprochement this thesis advocates is in part the development of an unrealized possibility in Barth's Christology. Just as Barth offered an alternative to Calvin's doctrine of election through Chalcedonian Christology, this chapter offers a reworking of Barth's Christology to reconfigure natural law and thus offer a rapprochement between it and christo-ethical radicalism. Yet the burden of the thesis does not fall upon Barth, for this chapter's focus upon anthropological natural law complements Part Three's earlier discussion of cosmological natural law.

After an outline of the structure of Barth's ethics in *Church Dogmatics*, three matters will be examined. First, the criticism that his ethics demonstrates a lack of active human agency is discussed. Second, Barth's doctrine of election and the doctrine of God are considered. Third, his anthropology and his understanding of the basic form of humanity are examined.

2. The Structure of Ethics in Church Dogmatics

Barth's theological ethics follows his three-fold dogmatic structure as the command of God understood as an event in Christ. Ethics never stands as an independent category or discipline but consists materially as the gospel of Christ in the form of divine commands. This christological model prevents theological ethics from being reduced to general theory, abstract concepts of law, or being determined by a static concept of being.[2] This christological model of ethics as the Word of God in three forms is outlined in Table 5.[3] This christological model of humanity (created, pardoned, heir-apparent) demonstrates that ethics is derived from the event of God in Christ, for only that occurrence could yield such a structure or understanding of human existence and ethics.[4] In Barth, to think of ethics is to think of God incarnate in Christ.

The one command of the Son in three spheres as...	...the Word of God in Creation	...the Word of God in Reconciliation	...the Word of God in Redemption
Kingdom of	Nature	Grace	Glory
Revelation of God's eternity	Pre-temporal eternity	Co-temporal eternity	Post-temporal eternity
Human telos	Determined for God	Determined to God	Perfection in God
Christological determination of humanity	Creation: Son of Adam/David created in God's image	Crucifixion: sinful, condemned, yet loved and preserved	Resurrection: realization of the divine image, glory
Church Dogmatics	III/4, XII, §52—§56 The Command of God the Creator	IV/4, XVII, §74—§78 The Command of God the Reconciler	NA (In outline, CD §36, §52, §74, *Ethics*, §15—§18)

Table 5: The Structure of Barth's Ethics in *Church Dogmatics*. The Perichoretic Act of the One God in His one Command in Jesus Christ in Three Spheres

    2. Barth, *CD*, II/2, 548. Command is specific personal utterance, whereas law is impersonal general rule: Biggar, *Hastening*, 14.

    3. Barth, *CD*, II/2, 548–551. The three-fold structure is the epistemological *form* of the one command of God. *CD*, II/2, VIII, The Command of God, §36–§39 introduces ethics where Barth dismisses alternative approaches (§36.1) before describing its christological base (§36.2). The threefold *material* content follows as the claim, decision and judgment of God (§37–§39). See also Biggar, *Hastening*, 46–96.

    4. The history of theological ethics demonstrates conflicts between the alternatives of creation, reconciliation and redemption, Barth, *CD*, II/2, 550.

The Christological Redetermination of Natural Law 211

3. An Ethics of Action

Because Chalcedonian Christology means that God "does not exist in His divine being and perfections without Jesus Christ, in whom He is very God and man," the doctrine of God necessarily includes ethics because ethics inquires about what constitutes good and right *human* action.[5] But it also means that autonomous or non-theological ethics is denied, because ethics is a function of theology. For Barth, to do ethics properly is to do it theologically—that is, christologically. This strong christological emphasis of *CD* has led many to criticize Barth as having little or no place for human moral agency, and if he has no place for human agency, then any development of natural law from his theology becomes problematic because natural law presupposes a strong doctrine of human moral agency. However, such minimizing of human action is only apparent and expresses his greater concern to deny real and true human action any *independent* moral status outside of Christ, as an element of his greater argument with liberalism. Independent action is sinful, and so untrue to human nature.

Barth's ethical model (first found in *CD* II/2) describes humanity as a *being in will and action*. His definition clearly includes human *action*: "The ethical question is . . . what is the good in and over every so-called good human *action*."[6] Each person has his existence in his actions, because "to *exist* as a man means to *act*."[7] This action "means *choosing, deciding*. What is the right *choice*?"[8] The answer to this fundamental ethical problem is "the revelation and work of the electing grace of God," for election claims man for God and places him under God's command.[9] Proper human action is action that is determined by the divine command, for no human actions

---

5. Barth, *CD*, II/2, 509, 512. This sits uneasily with Finnis's non-theism. Barth sees a complete disjunction between Christian and other ethics, II/2, 518–20, the latter being a form of natural theology to be conquered, 513. Theological ethics cannot be reduced to the spiritual sentiments of Neo-Protestant liberalism due to Christ's lordship, II/2, 525ff. Nor can it be coordinated with Catholicism's moral philosophy where the metaphysics of *being* (*analogia entis*) displaces the divine *act* of the Incarnation so that human *being* is understood non-christologically, *CD*, II/2, 528 –34.

6. Ibid., 516, emphases added. The focus on action is maintained in II/2, 645–661; III/4, 3; IV/4, 3; *The Christian Life*, 3, and in *The Humanity of God*, 84. The basic moral question, "What ought we to do" is an exposition of Acts 2:37–38. This focus upon action appears as early as 1922 in *Word of God*, 171, and his 1928 *Ethics*, 67–73.

7. Barth, *CD*, II/2, 535, emphasis added.

8. Ibid., emphasis added.

9. Ibid., 516. Election is not arbitrary but "an obedient reckoning with the One whom Jesus Christ called Father," 24–25. Obedience is the fourth item in the process of election, silence and hearing, 30.

are neutral, but stand under God's command viewed from the perspective of election. Human ethical action is not rejected, but denied independence outside of God. It is autonomous human action that Barth rejects, not active agency itself. Action that is proper to humanity is action that is determined theologically, because the non-theological self is an impossible reality. Self-determination is only truly human when it acknowledges its divine determination, for God wills our wills into existence for the purpose of freely willing his good will. This means that willful sinful action is improper to being human, and thus cannot qualify as being true *human* action because it is determined by sin and trends towards death and dissolution. As such, willful sinful action is untrue to God's intention that humanity flourishes and lives. Nor can it, as sinful action, function as a source for natural law because in itself it is not natural, that is, true to what created realties are in their theologically determined nature.[10] Sinful nature is not true nature and thus cannot function as a sufficient or suitable source for determining what is true human life and action, and hence ethics, except possibly by way of contrast.

This strong theological determination of human action in Barth is the source of the criticism that he has no place for genuine human action. By so doing, it confuses action itself with the origin and character of human action. The thesis that moral action must be self-originating if it is to be genuine has become commonplace since Kant, and has rendered the theological determination of true human action problematic. Ironically, as the Copernican revolution replaced a geocentric planetary system with a heliocentric one (the solar system), the Kantian revolution replaced a theocentric ethic with an anthropocentric one (the autonomous ethic). Copernicus displaced the *geo* by the *helio*, while Kant displaced the *theo* by the *ego*. In both cases, theological determinations receded in the popular imagination: in Copernicus, due to the diminution of humanity as a unique creature central to God's cosmos, and in Kant, due to the exaltation of humanity as central to its own moral purposes. Copernicus's decentering of humanity and Kant's centering of humanity both compromised the theological and christological determination of creation.

The autonomy that subsequently set the human subject as the first and final criterion of ethics has since degraded to a thin voluntarism: "I choose therefore I am." This modern autonomous consciousness makes obedience to divine commands appear oppressive rather than a joyous embrace of one's

---

10. Barth, *Christ and Adam*, 6. The *formal* parallelism of Adam Christ contains the *material* priority of Christ. Originally published in 1952, it post-dates *CD* III/4 (1951) The Command of God the Creator.

own proper humanity. The same can be said for social relations where the other becomes a constraint upon the self-directed I. As noted later, Barth replaces this autonomous "I" by the social "I-Thou" determination of humanity in glad and willing encounter. This theological and social understanding of humanity expresses the two-fold covenantal relations of the Law and the Synoptic love command (Mark 12:29–31). This covenantal form expresses a similar tripolar view of theology as in radicalism, noted in Part Two, where the self, the other, and God are inextricably united.

While *CD* may give an impression that the self as an active moral agent is minimized, such a sentiment is brought about by the modern autonomous self reacting against its theological determination. As such, it is more cultural than real, because the modern autonomous consciousness is itself a social construct.[11] While this does not necessarily mean that it is untrue, it does moderate any claim that the modern view of moral autonomy is definitive or normative, or that autonomy amounts to a defining criterion of moral agency. Consequently, Barth's extensive discussion of human freedom is set within the four creaturely limitations of God, human fellowship, vital life, and time (*CD* III/4), which describe humanity as God's creature (*CD* III/2). Human freedom exists only within its proper creaturely limitations.

Consequently, Barth's rejection of natural law expresses his general aversion to human moral agency as autonomous, self-sufficient, and determined by non-theological reasoning. However, if Christology is used to reframe natural law, it is possible to rehabilitate it within Barth's own theology. This is not to say that a positive view of natural law is latent within *CD* and only needs to be discovered, or that there is an inevitability that *CD* somehow leads to a natural law that Barth himself did not see. Rather, I will attempt to argue that *CD* possesses the resources to enable a rapprochement between natural law and radical christological ethics, and as such is an unrealized possibility of his Christology.[12]

---

11. See Schneewind, *Invention of Autonomy*. By "invention," Schneewind argues that autonomy is not a reality that perdures through time, but a Prussian cultural creation. I have previously suggested that Kant's work in this regard may be a reaction against Newtonian mechanism that imprisoned the self within universal rigid determinations. If Laplace had no need for the "hypothesis" of God to explain the universe, Kant believed the same for ethics.

12. Trainor, *Christ*, 473–526, argues that Barth's rejection of natural law is both rhetorical and substantial in his earlier work, but only rhetorical in his later work. Barth's understanding of God's re-creative work as universally operative in all humanity approximates a "natural law," 493. Biggar, *Hastening*, 55–56 argues that Barth rejected natural law early partly due to its susceptibility to appropriation by Nazism.

4. The Doctrines of Election and God

a. *The Chalcedonian Doctrine of Election as the Presupposition and Content of Ethics*

Barth's reconfiguration of election is a function of his Chalcedonian Christology. It informs both divine and human nature and lends itself to a reconsideration of natural law in these two spheres. He criticizes the traditional doctrine for defining the electing God by abstract concepts of freedom, mystery, and righteousness, instead of by Jesus Christ, in whom freedom becomes loving grace, mystery becomes God's will for salvation, and divine righteousness becomes judgment upon sin through forgiveness.[13] This christological reconfiguration will be explored as it bears upon the nature of ethics.

I. Jesus Christ the Electing God, the Elected Human, and Ethics

Barth's Chalcedonian christological doctrine of election is centered upon Jesus Christ as the electing God and elected (and rejected) human.[14] Because God's first electing act is his self-election, the doctrine of election belongs with the doctrine of God.[15] Yet because this divine self-election includes the determination to never not assume human nature as Jesus Christ, the doctrine of election includes the nature of humanity along with the nature of God in covenantal relations. Election's fundamental Chalcedonian character is critical at this point for two reasons.

First, because Jesus is the elected *human*, and "the elected . . . Jesus is . . . the *destiny* of human nature,"[16] the *telos* of human nature is reshaped in a radically christological direction. One person becomes the true end or "eschatype" of human nature, which elevates humanity above its social enclosure, as found in Aristotle. But furthermore, because "the *ontological* determination of humanity is grounded in the fact that one man among all others is the man Jesus Christ,"[17] the nature of human existence itself is determined by the eternal election of the Son's incarnation, which is its

---

13. Barth, *CD*, II/2, 24ff. Abstractly, freedom becomes caprice, mystery becomes caprice's blindness, and righteousness mere assertion, 27–34.
14. Ibid., 54–76.
15. Ibid., 89. For ethics as intrinsic to the doctrine of God, see 512.
16. Ibid.,118, italics added.
17. Barth, *CD*, III/2, 132, italics added.

archetype. Consequently, what is natural to humanity—both its origin and ends—is no longer determined by observable human inclinations ("the phenomena of man") but by the elected humanity of Jesus.[18] The generic "human" is determined by the specific "Jesus." Consequently, ethical self-evidence gained through general observation can no longer stand as an adequate predicate of either human nature or ends in the Aristotelian/Thomist sense, as such observations are inadequate by excluding the christological archetype and eschatype *(telos)*. Because Jesus Christ is humanity's *being*, he is also its *destiny*. Because he is our *kind*, he demonstrates our *end*, so that natural law's *telos*—that humanity is to flourish—takes on a distinct christological flavor. This flourishing is both structurally and materially covenantal, for Barth understands the covenant as the internal basis or reason for the creation that God elected into being. God elected to create in order to establish his covenant, and this creation has its primary expression in Christ's real humanity in its covenantal relations. Thus human flourishing—a central natural law concept—occurs to the extent that it maintains covenantal faithfulness in the two basic relations to God and others as exemplified in Christ. Because Christ's humanity is consubstantial with ours, both our being (kind) and destiny (end)—the ontological and teleological determinations of our humanity—are established by the type of person Jesus Christ was elected to be.

Second, because Jesus is the electing *God*, Barth shifts the doctrine of the incarnation into the sphere of God's eternal election, thus providing a non-speculative grounding for divinely determined natural law, because the Incarnation is the *a posteriori* epistemological access to the divine being and election. The somewhat speculative theology of Stoicism has some *formal* similarities with Kant's dualism between God and humanity and eternity and time, for in both the precise character of God is unclear or unknowable. By accepting such indeterminate knowledge of God, liberalism lapsed into forms of post-Kantian idealism that transposed theology into the key of anthropology and ethics in an attempt to secure God as the bearer of ideal values. As such it became a bourgeois ontotheology. Yet Kant also lurks in the background of Barth in his criticism of liberalism through the radical discontinuity between God and humanity, the noumenal and the phenomenal. Whereas liberalism stressed the human subject, Barth stressed the divine object (who for him remained forever the real Subject). How did Barth

---

18. Ibid., 133. Barth argues that people are ignorant of their own nature "in and of themselves," according to W. Krökte, "The humanity of the human person in Karl Barth's anthropology," in Webster, *Cambridge Companion to Karl Barth*, 160. Christ is the "fundamental presupposition" of creaturely existence who "encloses . . . humanity within himself," Neder, *Participation*, 17.

overcome this apparent incommensurability? Only in the actual given-ness of God's revelation in Christ, that is, the hypostatic union, or more particularly, the an/enhypostatic doctrine.[19] Barth rejected Kantian-inspired idealism and liberalism by affirming that God as a real object-in-itself is knowable through his actuality in the Incarnation.[20] God is not a concept for discussion, but an event for knowing. Whereas Cicero sees the *Logos* as non-personal divine reason, Barth understands the *Logos* as personal divine being, revealed in Jesus. While natural law is criticized in *CD* (contra his earlier *Ethics*, 209, 247, 263, 270), its realist divine grounding, as in Stoicism, is not without a reasonable justification in that it seeks to provide a *meta* and pre-positive basis for morality above the vicissitudes of positive law, arbitrary voluntarism, and self-referentialism. Consequently, Barth's doctrine of divine self-election enables natural law's metaphysical concerns to be located within the divine reality of God's eternal self-election to never not be incarnate in Jesus Christ. This makes the unknown and unknowable God of Kant and Cicero humanly knowable as the metaphysical/theological basis of ethics. The metaphysical universal Being becomes the historical singular person Jesus Christ.

Consequently, whether we consider either the divine or the human bases of natural law, both are embodied in Christ. The two different bases for natural law, the divine mind and nature, and human nature and ends, can both be absorbed into Barth's dynamic Chalcedonian doctrine of election.

The double consubstantiabilty of the incarnate Word as both the electing God and elected human therefore enables: 1) direct and historical access to divine nature and reason; and 2) direct and historical access to human nature and ends in its eternally elected form. Barth's doctrine of election means that the single life of Jesus constitutes in his two natures the proper being and destiny of humanity, which is Aristotle's concern, and the proper expression of the divine nature and reason, which is Cicero's concern. Furthermore, the act/being thematic, or the *ad extra/ad intra* identity, means that the concrete ethics of Jesus is coterminous with divine ethical realism—and conversely, that the inner reality of God's moral being and nature is revealed in Jesus. While such a strong emphasis on election at this point may imply divine voluntarism, the act/being thematic would suggest a form of ethical realism, for the act of election co-exists with the divine being.

---

19. Hauerwas, *With the Grain*, 159–62.

20. La Montagne, *Barth and Rationality*, argues that Barth's dialectical *theology* expresses his understanding of the dialectical *reality* of the relationship between God (what is *real*, God's revelation) and human knowledge (theology's *critical* nature). Dialectics as a form of critical realism thus describes both the semantics and substance of Barth's work.

Because the act/being couplet means God's act of self-election is an eternal reality of God himself, God's being *is* his act of self-election. Appropriating Barth's dialectical semantics, his ethics could be described as *real* voluntarism, or *voluntarist* realism.[21]

This Chalcedonian christological doctrine of election has four consequences for Barth. (1) Epistemologically, the electing God and the elected human are no longer unknowable or unknown. (2) Historically, the eternal election is identical with its historical revelation. (3) Materially, the self-giving of God in Christ is double predestination: the divine Yes to humanity and the divine No to humanity's sin. (4) Relationally, God's act, because it is in Christ, is an encounter between God and humanity.[22] From each of these, four ethical conclusions can be drawn.

First, the speculative character of metaphysical moral realism becomes redundant, as the electing God's nature, as well as his elected will for humanity, are known. Stoicism's unknown God is replaced by the known God, Jesus Christ, so that what is eternally moral is historically disclosed. What for Cicero is unknown and impersonal divine reason (*Logos*), manifested as law, is in Christ the personal incarnate Word (*Logos*), manifested as love. Just as the physical world discloses itself to human minds in patterns that are appropriate to that which is disclosed, so God's moral nature is knowable in the Incarnation in a way that is appropriate to human knowing.

This means, second, that the moral acts of Jesus in their historical specificity are neither culturally reducible, nor dismissible as those values that Christians happen to find inspiring, but truly refer to the electing God's moral nature as well as the moral nature of elected humanity. Because the electing Word is morally identical with the elected Jesus, christo-ethical radicalism does not reduce to historicism, provincialism, or sectarianism, but truly refers to the divine nature. Thus the eternal Word, not just the human Jesus, is the proper subject of radical ethics. Yet because of the priority of the divine over the human nature (the eternal divine Word created Jesus' temporal humanity), the divine nature functions as a control belief over any disproportionate emphasis upon Jesus' humanity. The primary sources of christo-ethical radicalism (the Gospels) are thus twin narratives describing two natures in the one person, and cannot be reduced to historicist ethics stripped of metaphysical/theological realism. This arrests the tendency of radicalism to disproportionately focus upon the life of Jesus and thus reduce to historicism, a tendency possibly due to its preference for the Synoptic

---

21. Barth's dismissal of many traditional categories likely renders the problem redundant.

22. Barth, *CD*, II/2, 145–94.

Gospels over John. The high Christology of John, which drives this thesis, implies that Jesus as the norm of ethics miscarries if it does not truly refer to God's moral nature—that is, theologically real ethics.

Third, this ethic contains both command and prohibition: a Yes and a No. The moral Yes of command is evident in the obedience of Jesus Christ to his Father's will by maintaining his covenant relationships with both God and others. The moral No of prohibition is evident in Jesus' refusal to act in ways outside his covenantal relationships with both God and his fellows. Furthermore, because Jesus is the electing God, his word is the *imperative* divine command and prohibition; and because he is the elected human, his life is the *indicative* obedience that corresponds to that divine command and prohibition.

Fourth, this ethic is revealed in: a) the relationship between Jesus' two natures, because his elected human nature is always properly determined by his divine electing nature; and b) Jesus' obedient covenant relationship with his Father, which displaces abstract moral principles.[23] There must be a constant holding together of these two relationships, the hypostatic relation between the two natures (the divine and human), and the personal relation between the two persons (the incarnate Son and the Father), in order to properly grasp the meaning of ethics as determined by election. This is because Christ's human *nature* only exists because of the Word's election to become incarnate as the *person* of Jesus. Chalcedonian Christology implies that Jesus reveals both human nature in right relation to the divine nature, and human personhood in right relation to divine personhood. Thus the proper moral relation between God and humanity finds a double determination; first, in the relation of Christ's human nature to his divine nature; and second, in his obedience as the incarnate (human) Son to the Father. Only in these christologically elected relations does humanity hear the divine truth, pledge, promise, and assurance of its own actuality as the basis for its own life.[24] Christ's election is the "eternal basis, the exterior anterior reality, the eternal presupposition of the existence of those who may live as the elect," transcending all other created realities.[25] Consequently, all the considerations of divine and human natural law naturally follow on from

---

23. "The Lord of Christian morality is not a principle or an ideal goal or a *telos*, but a person whose timely life confronts our stories with his own," McClendon, *Ethics*, 323–324. Here Anabaptism's anti narrative stripping character is evident. Contra Kant, whose "practical reasoning . . . employs no criterion external to itself," MacIntyre, *After Virtue*, 45.

24. Barth, *CD*, II/2, 233.

25. Ibid., 321.

Christ's election and the moral shape of his life, because "the being of the elected person is indeed in the being of Jesus Christ."[26]

Barth's Chalcedonian doctrine of christological election means that theological real ethics and radical historical ethics converge in the one person of the eternal electing Son, incarnate as the temporal elected Jesus. What is morally true of the absolute divine *Logos* is manifested in his election to inhabit his creation as a single human creature.

II. Election and Moral Reasoning

This Chalcedonian doctrine of election suggests a possible reconfiguration of two concerns of moral reasoning relevant to this project: classical and historical reasoning, and the naturalistic axiom.

First, the speculative ontological reasoning favored by the classical tradition, where discussions of being and substance dominate, is refracted through Barth's christologically actualist doctrine of election. Yet his Chalcedonianism means that ontological (and Hellenistic) matters never recede completely.[27] Ontology is read through Christ's election, which is historically actualized in Jesus' life. Human nature exists, or "is," only through its election in Christ manifested in this history. Because all of God's acts, including the Incarnation, are eternally elected, the Incarnation can reframe the relationship between the eternal and the historical, between the classical concerns of *being* and the modern interest in *acts*. The historical actuality of the human Jesus (John 1:10) is the manifestation of the eternal being of God (John 1:1) and as such is both the eternal determination of humanity and the historical disclosure of the eternal (John 1:14).

Such a christological recasting of election suggests that the ontological concerns of traditional classical and Catholic theology (with its focus on *being*, and the *is*), and the relational and dynamic concerns of Protestant theology (with its focus on the *act*, and the *ought*), are somewhat merged.[28] Despite these not being absolute opposites, they possess distinct central tendencies. Classical theology tends to be concerned with those ontological properties that are believed to perdure unchanged, and which enable ethics to be anchored in an invariant and stable understanding of humanity. Conse-

---

26. Ibid., 323.

27. Like Barth, Jenson, *Systematic Theology*, 10, judges philosophy to be the theology of Olympian-Parmenidean religion, not to be taken seriously, 21. Barth's use of philosophy, particularly Kantian idealism, is "conditioned at every point by theological requirements and theological purposes," La Montagne, *Barth and Rationality*, 109.

28. Trainor, *Christ*, 505–511.

quently, human *being* is accorded a greater value than human acts, with acts understood as enabling the flourishing of being. For instance, specific acts and practices (such as habits) create the virtues and enable the maximizing of those individual and social goods believed to be intrinsic to good human existence and its true end. That is, acts serve being. On the other hand, Protestant theology's greater interest in the dynamic and relational dimensions of humanity means that human *acts* are given a greater theological value. Consequently, human action is also accorded a greater moral value, with ethics focusing upon concrete activities and choices that are considered to be good and right in achieving the specific outcome of enabling or maintaining proper relationships with God and others. While Barth's emphasis upon action in his "What am I to do?" is clearly a Protestant and modern question, his concern with the nature of humanity as eternally elected in Christ partly expresses the ontological concerns of Catholicism, or at least of the classical and patristic tradition. Thus, being elected in Christ means that the ontological *being* and the relational *act* cannot be separated from each other, for the being of Christ as the elected person is expressed in his specific acts of love. Barth's "God is" as "God loves" expresses a modern theological classicism which somewhat unites the real and the historical, the being and the act, because "God is love" is manifested as "God becomes" human.

This means, second, that the naturalistic axiom can be reframed through Barth's christological doctrine of election, because "God is" as "God loves"[29] transforms into "God becomes"—a human person in Christ (1 John 4:9–10). Hence both the traditional axiom and its fallacious recasting by Hume presuppose a static ontology that is contested by Barth's actualism. Because "God is" is "God loves," the *is* becomes an *ought*, because love, as a divine existing reality, is necessarily a moral action towards another. "God is" as "God loves" are united in "God becomes" incarnate in Christ, for such becoming is an act of God's own love (John 3:16). Barth's theological actualism means that God's being is itself a moral activity, expressed and known in his election to become human. The electing loving Son is the *is*, and the elected Jesus is the *ought* internal to that love, united in the Word who *became* flesh. Yet this *ought* is contained in the *is* of God's own loving being and not called forth by any external factor as though God is under any obligation to another. This love is the wellspring of the entire doctrine of the electing God who becomes the elected human. Consequently the indicative/imperative merge in Barth's actualist/event doctrine of God and election, for

---

29. Barth, *CD*, II/I, 283. The ontological verb "to be" is replaced by the actualist verb "to love."

both the *is* and the *ought* co-exist in God's eternal loving election (the *is*) which becomes historical as the act of love in the Incarnation (the *ought*). As love is the supreme moral act, and ethics concerns future acts determined by practical moral reasoning, "God is" as "God loves"—united as "God becomes"—disables Hume's argument, because he assumes a static view of being and a form of practical reasoning that actualist ontology contests. By merging act and being in God's actualist being, which is the context of the doctrine of election, the *is* and the *ought* necessarily co-exist: Barth "denies that the distinction between the 'theoretical' and 'practical' makes sense."[30] Thus theology as a descriptive-indicative discipline becomes ethical, and ethics as a prescriptive-imperative discipline becomes metaphysical/theological. "God is" as "God loves" is also "God becomes" incarnate in Christ, who is the actuality of the eternal election.

III. Christ's Acts: Proper Human Acts in Correspondence to God.

If at this point Barth's actualism is applied to Christ's acts as the *Logos ensarkos*, it is possible to establish that such acts, as proper to both God and humans, provide the epistemological entry to the concepts of being and reason. This is because Barth's act/being motif means that such acts inhere in and express the being of both God and humanity, and because such acts are historically accessible. Part Two argued that practice is of greater significance than reason as a basis for ethics, for it includes reason as an intellectual practice. Moreover, practices embody certain virtues, not least intellectual ones such as truth seeking.[31] Consequently the practices of Jesus cannot be reduced to the embodiment of ancient Jewish virtues in a naïve Antiochene sense, for when read through Chalcedon such practices embody the virtues or moral nature of the eternal Word and divine nature. From his epistemological start in Christ's act, Barth moves to the divine ontology of God's being, to arrive at his Chalcedonian actualism. Radicalism often stays put at Antioch; classicism often remains in Alexandria. Barth travels back and forth between them via Chalcedon. Thus the moral practices of the temporal Jesus are internal to his being as the eternal Word, such that any discrepancy between his being and practices would render not only Chalcedon's one-person Christology problematic, but also the identity between the

---

30. Hauerwas, *With the Grain*, 176, n. 5, citing *CD*, 1/2, 787. "The truth of the evangelical indicative ... becomes itself an imperative," *CD*, III/2, 512.

31. McClendon, *Ethics*, 105.

act and being of God untenable. This means that the moral practices of Jesus are the concrete actuality and form of the divine moral being.

This union between act and being reflects the Anabaptist rejection of essentialism, because there is no distinction between the inner reality of God (*ad intra*) and his outward acts (*ad extra*) in Christ. The concept of *imitatio Christi* therefore becomes metaphysically placed within the moral nature of God, and conversely, the moral nature of God is non-speculatively ascertained in the life of Jesus. Put simply, morally copying Jesus is copying the divine moral reason and being *in a way that is appropriate and proper to humanity*, because that divine nature is united to the humanity of Christ, which is consubstantial with ours. If the hypostatic union is ruptured, Jesus' humanity would give no access to, nor reveal, the divine moral nature. And if his humanity was not consubstantial with our natures, it could not exemplify what is proper to our moral nature.

Not only do Christ's moral acts reflect the moral being of God, but they also correspond to the divine election of humanity. They are normative for human moral action because all human actions must correspond and be true to the elected humanity to which they belong, if they are to be natural and thus moral. Part Two examined the Anabaptist critique of vocation which replaces "every calling its own ethical norm" with a christological determination of each norm. Barth's question about the determination of human nature is similar. Opposing the free and arbitrary possibilities of human self-determination in both voluntarism and autonomy, where each person is their own norm, the proper determination of both the content and purpose of human nature is found in its election to "be the kind of man for whom Jesus Christ is."[32] Being this "kind of man" consists in a) allowing oneself to be loved and blessed by God; b) responding in gratitude; c) proclaiming this grace as a joyful witness; and d) engaging in the reconciling work of Christ.[33] Gratitude, the first of our actions, or active responses to election, is living and acting in ways that correspond to this election and thus represent and illustrate God's glory. The purpose of election is to be God's "creaturely image, His imitator" which "corresponds" to God's grace through gratitude.[34] *Imitatio* is thus equated with God's creaturely image in Christ. The argument is simple: the true image of God is Christ, humanity shares that image, thus living in accord with Christ as God's image is

---

32. Barth, *CD*, II/2, 410. Barth argues that "Jesus . . . alone establishes . . . human nature," Neder, *Participation*, 29. Barth rejects Brunner's doctrine of orders as dividing the one God and one command, *CD*, III/4, 32–46. Orders separate humanity from its Orderer, II/2, 676, yet note the trinitarian order of *CD*.

33. Barth, *CD*, II/2, 411–19. These are all found in Christ as the object of imitation.

34. Ibid., 413. "The only answer to χάρις is εὐχαριστία," IV/1, 41.

imitatio.³⁵ Jesus' life represents and illustrates the way that human gratitude correctly corresponds to God's glory and grace.³⁶ This correspondence is explicitly described as "imitation"³⁷—the gratitude of Jesus imitates, or corresponds to, God's grace. Gratitude is, in human nature, what imitates or corresponds to grace in divine nature. Jesus is the prototype, the "original" of this four-fold human response to election, because he allowed himself to be loved by God, responded in gratitude, proclaimed God's grace, and engaged in God's reconciling work. As the prototype, Christ "is the reality and revelation of the life-content of the elect," so that *imitatio* follows trivially as the reproduction of Christ's grateful and joyous imitation of God's work.³⁸ By imitating Christ, our moral life corresponds and conforms to Jesus' life as the prototype of the elect. This makes receiving God's love, practicing gratitude, proclaiming the gospel, and doing God's reconciling work, all natural human actions because they replicate Christ's actions, which correspond to the electing God's determination of created humanity. Thus *imitatio* does not describe a pietistic spirituality, but a life that corresponds to Jesus' own correspondence to God's grace in these four actions. Because Christ is the prototype of the elect, his humanity correctly exemplifies and determines the moral shape and contours of our humanity in its correspondence to God's grace.

Barth's Chalcedonian doctrine of election here provides two grounds for an *imitatio* ethic based upon divine and human natures. First, regarding humanity, "teleologically, the election of the man Jesus carries within itself the election of a creation which is good according to the positive will of God and of man as fashioned after the divine image."³⁹ Jesus is the human form and content of creation's goodness, and because this goodness consti-

---

35. Teleologically, Jesus' election contains "the election of a creation which is good . . . and of man as *fashioned after the divine image and foreordained to the divine likeness*," Barth, *CD*, II/2, 122, italics added. "By knowing and loving God," humanity attains its true end, which "imitates by 'similitude' God's reality insofar as every creature is inclined to the full actualisation of its nature," Hall, *Narrative*, 66, citing Thomas, *ST* 1a 2æQ, 8. As God is a fully actualized being, full human actualization is Barth's *imitatio Christi*.

36. Jesus is the elect "incarnate gratitude of the creature [and] the original of this representation and illustration of the gracious God . . . the true imitator of His work," Barth, *CD*, II/2, 413–414.

37. Ibid., 413.

38. Ibid., 421. Webster argues that in *The Christian Life* invocation also "constitutes human persons as agents, and furnishes a prototype to which human action corresponds and in which correspondence its goodness is found," *Barth's Moral Theology*, 177.

39. Barth, *CD*, II/2, 122.

tutes God's image, Jesus is the moral archetype of humanity that is created and elected in him. The natural law thesis—to do and pursue good—is thus christologized: Jesus' life embodies the content and contours of the good that God elected for humanity, so that being and doing good amounts to being and doing the good found in Jesus. To act and live in ways that correspond to Jesus' own correspondence to God constitutes the natural good of elected humanity.

Second, Barth's doctrine of election also concerns God's self-election to be incarnate, and this emptying of the Word's "divine form of being" (Phil 2:6)—but not the divine nature itself—was into the form of a human servant.[40] The change from being in the form of God to the form of a servant (Phil 2:6–7)[41] makes servanthood the specific divine dimension Paul cites as the object of *imitatio* (Phil 2:5). This means that God's self-election as the incarnate Son to suffer and die functions as the moral exemplar. Despite our sin and the ontological distance between God and us, there is one aspect of the divine person and nature that is appropriate for human imitation—*kenosis*. As the elect are elected in the Elect, their rejection is rejected in the Rejected as the "head and in the place of all other men."[42] The double set, that Christ is both the Elect/elect, and the elected/rejected, serve as moral structures: as the Elect, the Son elects to live obediently as the elected, and to suffer and die as the rejected. Both sets are contained within the kenotic text, which has a three-fold introductory appeal to practical moral reasoning, (*phronête,* Phil 2:2, 5). Such reasoning contains specific moral content in the form of a vice and virtue list: love and mercy (v 1), joy and love (v. 2), and humility and other-esteem (v. 3) are urged; whilst strife, vainglory (v. 3), and self-centeredness (v. 4) are rejected.

Consequently the incarnation of the eternal Son is the primary analogate to be emulated.[43] The incarnation of the Word is the divine act that humanity is to replicate in order to express its elected nature as being in

---

40. Barth, *CD*, II/2, 122, John 1:14 read with Philippians 2:6. Barth interprets Philippians 2 metaphysically.

41. The Lord is the servant, and is directly revealed as a particular kind of moral person, not simply through commands, Linda Zagzebski, "The Incarnation and Virtue Ethics," in Davis et al., *Incarnation*, 317. Any harsh edge in Barth's divine command ethic is softened by it supervening upon his doctrines of God and election of humanity to freedom, *CD*, III/4, §53–§56. Commanded freedom is "life in accordance with creaturely nature," Biggar, *Hastening*, 89.

42. Barth, *CD*, II/2, 126.

43. It is primary because the hymn is primitive, Hawthorne, *Philippians*, 76. Such primitivism comports with Anabaptism's rejection of speculative moral reasoning in favor of Biblicism.

the image of the Son. This act anticipates Barth's social "I-Thou" doctrine of humanity, discussed later, but here it is worth noting that it establishes radicalism's ethical emphasis on Christ-like humble service on the theologically robust footing of the Son's eternal self-election, rather than on the voluntarist basis of a human decision to follow Jesus.

Such moral qualities as noted above provide the content of God's commands, which are themselves conceptually determined by and coordinate with election. Because election is actualized in the divine commands, and Jesus Christ embodies these commands as the elected human, the moral shape of elected humanity is no longer speculative, but historically graspable.[44] As the divine Word, Jesus constitutes these commands, and as the historical person embodies obedience to these commands. Jesus' life is the lived obedience to divine commands, which themselves embody God's eternal election of humanity. Thus Jesus embodies humanity's elected moral nature, form and matter, not just its moral capacity or potentialities, for the incarnate Son is the "representative of the whole people that hastens towards this man and derives from him."[45] As humanity is derived from Jesus, he is its genesis (*Was*), and as hastening towards him he is its end (*Is to Come*), and both are given concreteness is his historic life (*Is*), so that election is not a speculative doctrine but has the specific moral shape of Jesus' humanity.[46] Election is into Christ's moral shape (Eph 1:4, 4:24, 5:2). Both God's command and the obedience correlate to it are found in Jesus as the Elect and the elect respectively. So Christ is not the representative human because he embodies ethical ideals, but because he is God's self-election to become human, for the sake of and as the pattern for all others. Hence "it is only in that one man that a human determination corresponds to the divine determination."[47] It thus follows trivially that the moral practices and dispositions of Jesus are included in the divine election of his humanity, as no aspect of his humanity can be excised without compromising Chalcedonian

44. Barth, *CD*, II/2, 632, "The divine command is witness to this will." "Will" here refers to God's eternal election in Christ. Barth's first discussion of ethics as the Command of God follows the Election of God in II/2. Barth rejects *a priori* theology in favor of *a posteriori* actualism: all dogmatics (and hence ethics) is done after the event of Christ, C. E. Gunton, *The Barth Lectures*, P. H. Brazier, (London: T & T Clark, 2007), 90.

45. Ibid., 53. The concept of divine determination—God's self-determination and humanity's God-determination—is a feature of Barth. The determinations are free but determined by the perfection of divine love.

46. Ibid., 38–41. Regarding election, Calvin notes the diversity of Gospel responses, *ICR*, III.xxi.1, 920f, although he cautions against speculation, III. xxi, 2, 923.

47. Barth, *CD*, II/2, 43, dismissing the philosophical concern of the "abstract concept of man," 53.

Christology.[48] Consequently if the Incarnation reveals both the a) moral nature of the temporal elected human, and the b) moral nature of the eternal electing Word, then the theological/metaphysical basis of natural law and goodness is manifested in Jesus' life. The creator *Logos* elected to become a creature that corresponded to and manifested his own moral nature and acts without diminution, surplus, or remainder.

IV. Conclusion

Barth's discussion of election provides clear warrants for a christological determination of human moral life because: 1) Christ's election is the solid ground for all dogmatics; 2) election is coterminous with God himself; 3) the doctrine of God includes ethics,[49] and 4) Christ's life is proper to and exemplary of the divine determination of human moral nature and acts. Further, Barth's initial discussion of the command of God provides identical warrants for humanity's determination, as the command of God is coterminous with the doctrine of God that includes election.[50]

Consequently, Barth's dynamic Chalcedonian recasting of election enables the following ethical syllogism:

> If God has eternally elected never to be God except as Jesus Christ,
>
> And as God has elected to creation all persons in Jesus Christ, in whose enhypostatic humanity lie all good and right moral perfections,
>
> Then Jesus' moral life is proper, normative, and exemplary for all persons as elected, created, and determined by him.

---

48. "In Christ, the Triune God and humanity are both fully represented and fully reconciled," Richardson, *Reading Karl Barth*, 161. Early christological heresies tended to excise a discrete anthropological *part* such as will, yet an equivalent result occurs when the moral *dimension* of Jesus is excised.

49. Barth, *CD*, II/2, 59, especially 76–93. Election is also the basis for vocation, IV/3.2, 484. In respect to natural law: "There is no such thing as a created nature which has its purpose, being or continuance except through grace," i.e., though election, 92. For Barth, "only the grace of God provides the answer to the ethical problem," Hauerwas, *Character and the Christian Life*, 139. *Church Dogmatics* is moral theology, Webster, *Barth's Moral Theology*, 1.

50. The latter half of *CD*, II/2.

b. *The Doctrine of God and Ethics*[51]

Barth places the doctrine of election and divine commands within the conceptual framework of the covenant,[52] just as God elected Israel as his covenant partner and commanded her obedience to his laws. The connection between natural law and Barth's association of election, commands, and covenant is simple: because natural law is the law of our creation, and creation is the external basis of the covenant to which people are elected and in which they are commanded, natural law itself is one aspect of the external basis of the covenant. Humanity was created with natural morality fitting to it as God's covenant partner. This natural morality was given secondary expression in the divine commands that serve the same covenantal purpose. The internal purpose of natural law as the law of our creation is the divine-human covenant. We are created for and elected to the covenant where God is our partner, our true end, our commander and enabler. God is the purpose of our natural and moral creatureliness. In this regard, two matters will be discussed: God as the commanding enabler of moral action, and the relationship between God and freedom.

1. Human Action and God's Enabling

Because humanity exists in a covenantal relationship with God, its existence is determined by divine election and divine commands. Because "ethics belongs . . . to the doctrine of God" the "doctrine of God must be expressly defined and developed as . . . *ethics.*"[53] Furthermore, election as God's ultimate "determination of man" and "rule over man" takes the form of commands.[54] Consequently, human "action is good because the divine address which is an eternal and temporal event in Jesus Christ is good . . . The good of human action consists in the fact that it is determined by the divine command."[55] Thus "[Theological ethics'] matter is the Word and

---

51. Barth, *CD*, II/2, §36–§39 discusses this as the Command of God.

52. Ibid., 510.

53. Ibid., 513, italics original. On ethics and doctrine (Christology) being inseparable, Nancey Murphy asks, "What is about Jesus that makes *his* life normative? What is *about* his life that is normative?" in "Using MacIntyre's Method in Christian Ethics," in *Virtues*, 2, n.1.

54. Barth, *CD*, II/2, 510.

55. Ibid., 547. On this matter, Barth's strength lies in his christological determination of goodness. Plato's impersonal idea of the Good as a moral exemplar is left hanging in "metaphysical limbo" if there is no objective good mind, that is, God, to which it corresponds. Equally, if there is no subjective mind to know the Good, then the Good

work of God in Jesus Christ, in which the right action of man has already been performed and therefore waits only to be confirmed by our action."[56] It is these types of statements that provoke the criticism that Barth negates human moral agency. Yet such criticism confuses the determination and demonstration of the material content of ethics, and its enabling, with its enactment by human moral agents.

The determination and demonstration of ethics is God's actuality in Jesus Christ, not his power or his conformity to an abstract concept of the good.[57] This determination is an act of grace.[58] Two conclusions follow. First, this grace is the presupposition and possibility of obedience, which does not negate human action but enables it, for it is only in and through Christ that human obedience can be fulfilled and human life sanctified. Because sin renders proper moral action beyond human possibilities, it must be made possible by the divine enabling. Yet neither is such human action a *pre-lapsum* created possibility in and of itself without theological determination, because created humanity is an act of grace and cannot be understood "in itself," as noted previously in Bonhoeffer. When grace is separated from nature, including human nature, it implies that anthropology and thus ethics can be properly understood non-theologically. This occurs when grace is understood solely as a soteriological category, as in the term "sin and grace." Yet because creation and providence are acts of God's loving goodwill (grace), human existence is itself gracious. Creation brought humanity graciously into being *ex nihilo* and providence graciously prevents its slide *ad nihilo*. Adam's *pre-lapsum* humanity was upheld through the divine presence and Spirit, not by his own intrinsic power as a Promethean moral hero. Eden was not a static deistic paradise where human goodness would perdure without divine sustaining. So even if we push back behind sin to creation, we see that grace enables good action because good action is only internal to humanity by virtue of it being God's good creature sustained by the Spirit. The human capacity to *do* good is a function of it *being* good, and being good is a divinely created reality, known through God's proclamation (Gen 1:3) and enabled by grace. This is christological because Christ is humanity's eternally elected presupposition, his created human-

---

in meaningless because concepts are philosophically parasitic upon mind, Rist, *Real Ethics*, 40. Augustine's replacement of the hypostatic Good with a personal God did not take the necessary christological next step like Barth, which made the historical Christ a concrete moral exemplar. Similarly, Adams, "God as the Good," in *Finite and Infinite Goods*, 13–49, remains christologically empty.

56. Barth, *CD*, II/2, 543.
57. Ibid., 552–565.
58. Ibid., 559.

ity is consubstantial with ours, he is the second Adam who recapitulates the first Adam's *pre-lapsum* life, and he is our archetype and representative. Despite the formal symmetry, the material asymmetry of the Adam/Christ couplet of Romans 5 means that Adam's humanity is only a "provisional copy of the real humanity that is in Christ."[59]

Second, not only does God determine and enable the human actions appropriate to the divine-human covenant, he also exemplifies them,[60] and their concrete form, in Christ.[61] Consequently it follows that Christology becomes ethically exemplarist: "[Christ] *is* the answer to the ethical question put by God's grace," and as such is "primary and original and exemplary for all other men." Consequently, his obedience to God "is a valid model for the general relationship of man to the will of God."[62] Ethical action that corresponds to this grace is *mimesis*.[63] Such *mimesis* is explicit: "The content of the divine demand on man is that he should do in *his* circle . . . that which God does by Christ in His circle."[64] As God in Christ witnesses and attests to himself, *mimesis* is our acceptance, attestation, and witness to this grace in love, joy, and obedience, leaving aside any sense of threat in the face of God's self-attestation of what is good.[65] This means that the creative powers

59. Barth, *Christ and Adam*, 10.

60. Barth, *CD*, II/2, 566. This content is elucidated, 566–83.

61. *CD*, II/2, 566–67. He has earlier outlined a second Adam Christology in discussing God's "No" to ethics understood as human determination of good and evil (the sin of Adam), with its dialectical counterpoint "Yes" to human determination (Christ's) to live under God's obedience, II/2, 517. At II/2, 566–67 there is no second Adam theology, but Christ does contradict humanity's self-chosen telos as a "child of Adam." Sin is "never in itself anything human," Wingren, *Man and Incarnation*, 86. The divine No, which shatters humanity's Adamic sin, is followed by the divine Yes in Christ that gathers up the shards and refashion them into the image of true covenantal faithfulness to God: Trainor, *Christ, Society and State*, 492.

62. Ibid., 517, 561–562, italics original. As the content and example of the divine command (ὑπογτσμμος, 1 Pet 2:21) Christ's life is the form or blueprint that is to be followed (Mark1:17).

63. Barth, *CD*, II/2, 576–577. This does not deny the singular character of the cross, II/2, 578. Referencing *CD*, II/2, 576, "Our action corresponds in kind to God's actions," Mott, *Biblical Ethics*, 28.

64. Barth, *CD*, II/2, 579, italics original. The first biblical text quoted in his general ethics (the doctrine of God) is Matthew 5:48; "'Be ye . . . perfect . . . as . . . your Father' . . . becomes itself an imperative," suggesting that the *mimetic* analogate includes the Father, not just the Son, *CD*, II/2, 512.

65. Ibid., 579. However Barth appears to eliminate *mimesis* regarding faith: we believe in but not *like* Jesus Christ, due to his divinity, *CD*, II/2, 583. Here is a retreat from *mimesis*, Christ being the object not the model of faith. This predates the current debate about *pistis Christou*.

of humanity must be expressed in actions and dispositions that correspond to Jesus' actions and dispositions. In the language of natural law, such human actions and dispositions have the goal of enabling and maintaining (with grace) the basic human good of covenantal faithfulness with God and others as humanity's chief goods. Because Christ is the form of the divine command, not only does "this identity become normative for what is demanded of us," it also embodies the required obedience, so that *mimesis* naturally follows.[66]

Therefore—and this is critical in defending both human action and *imitatio* in Barth's theological account of ethics—the statement that introduces his ethics, that "the right action of man has already been performed and therefore waits only to be confirmed by our action,"[67] must be understood so that "already been performed" in Christ is the divine presupposition, determination, possibility, and demonstration of the material content of right action, and "confirmed by our action" is our concrete enactment of such right action. God's good action in Christ, and Christ's good actions, model and enable our good action. This constitutes Barth as an exemplarist christological moral reasoner, for if the determination, presupposition, demonstration, and possibility of human action is Christ's own action already done for us, then our action is, conceptually at least, emulating what Christ has already achieved. Christ's action *determines* and *enables* our action, but it is his action still. Our action *confirms* his action, but it is our action nonetheless. Hence Christ's action "for us" cannot here be taken in a substitutionary sense, for that would render our action unnecessary. That this "for us" must be confirmed by "our action" means that it functions mimetically, not substitutionally. God's election, rule, determination, and command coalesce in the person of Jesus Christ, who is the presupposition and enabling power of human action and response. In this way God enables the moral life because Christ lived the "right action of man" as the model of that proper moral life.

However, there does appears a certain passivity in the human response when the content of the divine claim is described as the *acceptance* of God's gracious action as right, to "'acquiesce in' . . . or 'respect'" it.[68] Nonetheless, Barth's exegesis of the relevant New Testament passages highlights the

---

66. Ibid., 606. Divine commands are always ethically normative, III/4, 25.

67. Barth, *CD*, II/2, 543, noted above.

68. Barth, *CD*, II/2, 579. Compare Calvin's sentiment that Scripture carries its own proofs and that the Spirit causes us to "*subject* our judgment . . . to [Scripture] as to a thing beyond any guesswork!" *ICR*, I/vii. 5, 80. Humility is "unfeigned submission of our hearts," I/ xx.5, 760.

Pauline and Petrine imperatives of *mimesis*,[69] so that acceptance means that "our *action* should be brought into conformity with his action."[70] Conformation, *imitatio*, and *mimesis* all refer to a similar concept at this point: an active and rational *acknowledgement* that the shape and contours of Jesus' moral life are proper to our humanity, and subsequent *action* corresponding to his life. The issue is not action or inaction, but the determination of what or who defines and provides the basis and content of our good action, and how this action is enabled. This determination is given a five-fold form by Barth: 1) displaying the image of God, not self-deification; 2) receiving this determination in contentment, joyful participation, and obedience, not in hostility, non-participation, indifference, superiority, or self-will; 3) acknowledgement of not belonging to oneself; 4) living under God's mercy and grace; and 5) recognizing that our righteousness is Christ's.[71] The five participles—displaying, receiving, acknowledging, living, and recognizing —are a mix of passive and active.

Yet it is important to understand that human moral action is important in Barth's theological ethics precisely *because* it is christologically enabled and exemplified. A non-christological understanding of God does tend to compromise human agency, because is sets humanity outside of and against God and his determination of the good. But Chalcedon means that theological ethics includes human action for the eternal Word lived as a human moral agent in the divine-human covenant. Bare theonomous ethics is rejected because it places an abstract good prior to a christological doctrine of God.[72] Whereas Finnis sees God as *unnecessary* to the determination of what is good, and Kant sees God as *unbearable* to the determination of what is good, Barth sees a non-christological concept of God as *expressing* a wholly human idea of what is good by making our fancies about our own good to be God's good, and thus not good at all.[73]

Consequently, Calvin's natural law as the "law of our creation" is problematic because it lacks Christology. When Finnis argues for a non-theological determination of natural law, he comes close to the Kantian identification of active ethical agency with autonomy, because he argues that human goods and ends are wholly determined by the natural inclinations of human nature without theological reference. Such a modern concept of autonomy finds the concept of double agency, where God works through

---

69. Barth, *CD*, II/2, 576–577.
70. Ibid., 577, emphasis added.
71. Ibid., 577–578, 579–580, 580–581, 581–582, 582–583, respectively.
72. Ibid., 565.
73. Ibid.

and with secondary causes, including human action, to be problematic. It is the central assumption that moral agency is identical with autonomy, not the place of human action itself, which Barth denies.[74] This is important because natural law implies a strong concept of human moral agency, and if it could be demonstrated that Barth rejected such agency, it would be difficult or impossible to develop a form of natural law from his theology. But as I have argued that his theological ethics concern genuine human action precisely because of his Chalcedonianism, developing a natural law ethic from his Christology is possible. By assuming his created humanity, the eternal Word inhabited and evoked real human moral action. Here Barth concurs with the Eastern tradition that humanity is not determined by reason unaided by revelation, nor is it transparent to reason, but is only determined, understood, and enabled theologically. The method of Evagrius (Maximus's interlocutor) was to move from the *logos* of one's soul, through the *logoi* of the wider creation, before finally arriving at God as the true *Logos*. Whereas this required passive *apatheia*, Kant demanded active autonomy, despite God being unknowable. Both purport to ascertain the final good from non-theological psycho-moral starting points. Both Maximus and Barth reverse this process: the *Logos ensarkos* determines the human moral *logos,* whether such a *logos* is understood primarily in the language of the soul (Evagrius) or the will (Kant). God enables true agency because such agency is a graced element of our created humanity that is properly exemplified in the moral action of Jesus, to which our actions are to correspond if they are to be truly human—that is, free—actions.

II. God, Human Freedom and Moral Agency

Since Kant's emphasis upon the autonomous will as the base criterion of what constitutes human moral action, theologically determined ethics has been understood as inimical to human freedom. This concerns natural law because freedom of the will is currently assumed to be a defining criterion of human nature and as such becomes a focal concern of natural law. Thus it is appropriate to pursue the concept of freedom and autonomy at this point.

The contemporary emphasis on freedom, when combined with the Lockean concept of persons possessing inalienable property rights over themselves, means that moral choices tend to orbit around and be determined by the single center of the self in its free determination. As such, freedom constitutes the essence of human nature: to be human is to be

---

74. Barth also consistently rejects "divine sole causality," Webster, *Barth's Moral Theology*, 173, 177.

free. In contrast, Barth's theologically grounded ethics takes the form of an ellipse, orbiting around the two foci of freedom and obligation. Freedom avoids legalism, while its elliptical counterpoint, obligation, avoids lawlessness. Freedom is the content of the divine claim and gift, which despite its outward form of law, is gospel.[75] The proclamation of the gospel is the command to be free. Theological ethics *command* freedom as law, and *enable* freedom as gospel. Freedom is the content of the divine command to live true human lives, approximating the Catholic concept of Christian ethics as the imperative to be fully human. Yet because freedom is misunderstood as lawlessness, obligation is freedom's necessary counterpoint.

Such a command, however, which enables the free realization of our true humanity, appears as oppressive law in the *post-lapsum* situation. What is joyfully internal to our created humanity is perceived as fearfully alien due to our estrangement from God and our real selves (Rom 7:10–12). It is this epistemological disorder that makes obligation the necessary counterpoint to true freedom and prevents freedom from degenerating into the lawless dissolution of one's humanity. Because sin turns proper freedom into improper license, obligation is freedom's necessary counterpoint in a fallen world.

This epistemological disorder is partly caused by a false view of divine sovereignty that sets up a clash of wills between God and humanity. The Incarnation eliminates this clash because human freedom and obligation to divine commands coalesce: "No-one takes [my life] from me, but I lay it down of *my own accord*. I have authority to lay it down . . . this *command* I have received from my Father," (John 10:18). Christ lays down his life *freely* in *obedience* to the divine command. Jesus' life and non-violent death constitutes the focal instance of this ethic of freedom and obligation and concurs with the center of christo-ethical radicalism. The full moral agency of Jesus is expressed through his free obedience to the divine command because God is internal rather than alien to human nature and human freedom. This means that moral agency itself needs to be reframed away from a materially empty formal property or capacity to include the materially moral dimension of human nature itself. Moral agency consequently takes on the character of the graced human capacity to freely obey God. It functions naturally, that is, humanly, when in free obedience it maintains the covenantal relations with God and others for which it was made.

Because all human capacities are divine gifts of creation, moral agency—the ability to choose the right and the good—is also a gift. The

---

75. When understood as autonomy, freedom is a deceitful tyrant, Barth, *CD*, II/2, 585–94.

first principle of natural law—to do and pursue good—is thus a gifted human capacity to extend the creation's created goodness (Gen 1:26–31). And because creation is the external basis of the covenant, natural law's first principle maintains creation's basic covenantal character. Moral agency is the gifted capacity to do and pursue the right and the good contained in the divine-human covenant. And because Christ properly did this, he is the model of true moral agency. Refusing the good breaks the covenant and wounds creation (Genesis 3; Rom 8:22–25). What is meant by the image of God in its ethical aspect is the human endowment to freely obey God as its good, which reflects God's being and actions as good. Consequently, moral agency is not simply a formal property without material content (as in voluntarism), or determined by the self (as in autonomy), but the human capacity to be and act in ways that are covenantally—that is, creationally—right and good. The right and good being chosen and pursued must therefore actually be right and good—not just perceived to be so, yet actually wrong and evil. Moral agency contains ontological and epistemological dimensions: to be appropriate, it must be informed by a true apprehension of an objective moral rightness and goodness. Because *action* that is wrong and evil diminishes one's humanity, *choosing* (itself an action) wrong and evil diminishes one's moral agency because moral agency is a dimension of humanity. The more the wrong and the bad are chosen, the more one's humanity diminishes, and as such, one's human moral agency diminishes proportionately. Conversely, the more that the right and the good are done and pursued—natural law's first principle—the more a person's humanity and moral agency flourishes. The humanity of persons grows or diminishes in proportion to the objective goodness and rightness of their moral choice. And as choice itself is an act of the person as a moral agent, the rightness or otherwise of their choices grow or diminish in proportion to the sum of their previous choices. Hence the ability to choose the right and good over the wrong and evil is never static, but grows or diminishes. This approximates Aristotle's argument that actions are prior to and shape the person. The more that choices are right and good, the more likely it is that future choices will be right and good. This is training in righteousness (2 Tim 3:16) through continual use (Heb 5:14). And conversely, the more that choices are wrong and bad, the more likely it is that future choices will be wrong and bad. This is slavery to sin (Rom 6:19; note "ever *increasing* wickedness"). Moral agency diminishes or grows in proportion to the moral content being chosen. The more that autonomy is claimed against God, who is wholly good, the more the moral agent becomes heteronomously determined by sin, and their agency withers. This is seen in the moral pathology of those who become incapable of choosing the right and good because of a history of choosing the bad. That is, their agency is compromised in proportion to their slide into sin and death: agency becomes slavery. It is this that Jesus refused when he freely chose obedience to his Father (John 10:18), but that which Judas chose in his slide to suicide. The free choice of the right and the good—maintaining the covenant by obeying God's commands—increases a person's humanity and their moral agency. Thus the flourishing of human nature, which is a central concern of natural law, occurs when moral choices correspond to Jesus' moral agency in his free obedience to God (John 10:18). If Barth is mined for unrealized possibilities regarding natural law at this point, he reflects Calvin in affirming that good human action is both theologically determined and enabled. But he also stands with christo-ethical radicalism by arguing that such goodness is exemplified in Jesus' obedience to God's commands, so that "man . . . should do in *his* circle . . . that which God does by Christ in His circle."[76]

Moral agency thus finds its focal instance in Jesus' free obedience to God. Moral agency increases in proportion to its correspondence to the human good, as determined and enabled by the divine command toward freedom, exemplified in Jesus. It is through Christology that Barth argues that God both shapes and enables ethics in a way that is internal to humanity. Moreover, because christological moral reasoning is theological reasoning, christo-ethical radicalism is elevated out of any alleged sectarianism, because God is a universal reality. In the *Logos ensarkos* we find morally good actions that are proper to both God and humanity: the good divinity of the Word determines and enables the good humanity of the Word that is exemplary for all people as consubstantial with him. As the divine Word, Jesus is the material content of the command. As human, he is the free obedience to the command. In *imitatio*, human obedience replicates his obedience to the divine commands that bring about human flourishing.

III. Conclusion

Because divine commands are functions of the covenant, they enable human flourishing—for the covenant is the internal basis, or reason, for human creation. Yet because election and commands are understood christologically, God not only determines and enables (as elector and creator) but also exemplifies (as elected and created) natural human goodness in its covenantal relation to God. Human moral agency functions correctly when human actions correspond to Christ's actions, because in the Incarnation God took into himself the created freedom to obey and fulfill the obligations of the

---

76. Ibid., 579.

covenant. In Christ's consubstantial humanity, God created, inhabited, and exemplified true human freedom and moral agency as his faithful covenant partner. As such, natural law is the free law of our creation to fulfill human covenantal obligations that are exemplified in Christ. Human action is free, natural, and good when it corresponds to God's enabling command that is exemplified in Jesus' obedient covenant relation with God.

5. Anthropology and Ethics

a. The Doctrine of Humanity and Ethics

At the most basic level, natural law describes an object's essential nature, internal ends, and the actions appropriate to achieving those ends. By way of example, the correct use of milk is food: it is not essentially a commodity that can be dumped to protect the dairy industry.[77] A rock has a natural use in the ground to harbor insect life: it is not right to throw it into someone's face, although such a use is possible. Natural law pertains to all things. When applied to humanity, it attempts to determine what is *morally* proper to humanity. Hence all anthropologies have a natural law implicitly embedded in them, often as an unrealized possibility. A materialist anthropology will likely understand that which is proper to humanity as its endocrinological and appetitive drives, which enable reproduction and species survival. This reduces humanity to its biological elements and is ethically inadequate.

This means that Barth's Christology is capable of delivering a theory of natural law because its Chalcedonian character affirms that Christ's humanity is consubstantial with ours. Barth unwittingly suggests such a possibility when he writes that "the *special* anthropology of Jesus Christ . . . constitutes the secret of 'Adam' also, and so is the *norm* of *all* anthropology."[78] Moreover, because his Chalcedonian Christology is so global, it also enables a reconstruction of cosmological natural law, which will be briefly considered before turning to anthropology.

I. ANTHROPOLOGY AND COSMOLOGY

The theological and anthropological character of the cosmos is made clear when Barth describes creation as the external basis and context of the divine-human covenant—the conjunction of God's being and action in

---

77. O'Donovan, "The Natural Ethic" in Wright, *Essays*, 21.
78. Barth, *Christ and Adam*, 5, italics original.

The Christological Redetermination of Natural Law

heaven with humanity's being and action on earth.[79] Cosmology as such has no dogmatic status except as the creational enabling of the covenant between God and humanity: the laws of the cosmos are properly described as God's will.[80] Because humanity is the apex of the cosmos, the cosmos is only properly understood through God's relationship with humanity.[81] And because this relation is christological, cosmological natural law shares this christological character.[82] So because "the man Jesus is . . . the source of our knowledge of the nature of man as created by God,"[83] he is also the source of our knowledge of the cosmos as created by God. Accordingly, because moral reasoning about humanity *kata phusin* becomes *kata Christon*, moral reasoning about the cosmos *kata phusin* becomes *kata Logon*, as in the high Christology of John 1:1–5, 10; 1 Corinthians 15:24–28, 45–49; Hebrews 1:1–4, 10–12, and Colossians 1:15–20.[84]

Consequently, the idea of natural law as one element of the laws of nature becomes problematic if separated from Christology, for the eternal Word is not only the origin and *telos* of the created world, but also, by assuming created humanity, the example and means of determining creation's proper meaning. What then of natural law as one aspect of the laws of nature? If by the laws of nature we mean the observable, measurable, and quantifiable regularities operating within the creation, there clearly are laws of nature, and hence natural law. The problem for Barth, however, is not the existence of such patterns, but their inclusion within traditional natural theology: "The cosmos does not follow an intrinsic law, but the will and work of its Creator" so that knowledge of creation is in "indissoluble connection with the covenant."[85] It is non-trinitarian metaphysical realism and semantics that Barth contests, not the concept of an ordered cosmos itself.

By placing cosmology within anthropology, similar to the scientific anthropological principle, the possibility of a non-speculative understanding of cosmological natural law is enabled. This reverses the normal understanding of *microcosmos*, where humanity is understood as a small example

---

79. Barth, *CD*, III/2, 11f: the concept of humanity as *microcosmos* is rejected, 15.

80. Ibid., 17–18; *Ethics*, 210.

81. Barth, *CD*, III/2, 18–19: Humanity "is the point in the cosmos where . . . its relation to God is illuminated." The covenant reveals God's plans "representatively for the whole cosmos."

82. Ibid., 132.

83. Ibid., 41.

84. The τὰ πάντα of John 1, Colossians 1 and Hebrews 1 is discussed briefly in *CD*, III/2, 137.

85. Ibid., 16, 11. "That there are these inner relationships, even exact science cannot deny," 17.

of the wider cosmos, as in Maximus.[86] The *microcosmos* view of humanity is inverted to a *macroanthropos* view of the cosmos. Yet humanity as such is also inadequate due to the corrupting reality of sin, which renders both speculative and "exact science" inadequate.[87] Sin distorts science by concealing accurate knowledge of human nature (its epistemological effect), and by being included as an essential element in human nature (its ontic effect). Nonetheless, sin does not eradicate human nature, which is created to be the covenant partner with God and recipient of grace.[88] This leaves open the correct means of determining human nature.

The answer to this is that human nature is determined by the sum of the original created relationships between God and humanity. Consequently, the laws of nature—that is, the structure, inner reality, and *telos* of the cosmos—is a function of the divine human covenant. This is what Barth means by arguing that creation is the external basis of the covenant and that the covenant is the internal basis of creation. The cosmos' internal covenantal character means that cosmological natural law cannot be antithetical to the natural law of humanity as God's covenant partner, but rather provides its setting and creational enabling. The way into this understanding is not by penetrating the inner meaning of the cosmos in and of itself, but by penetrating into the form and structure of humanity. And as this is christological, the covenantal relationship between the incarnate Son and the Father reveals the covenantal and relational meaning of the cosmos. The Stoic concern to live truly—that is, true to the laws of nature and the universe—is not to live rationally as in Cicero, but to live covenantally in Christ. This is both human and cosmic: Christians, who are "in Christ" (Eph 1:2b), will share in the cosmos' eschatological renewal "in Christ" (Eph 1:9–10): "If *anyone* is in Christ, he is a new *creation*," (2 Cor 5:17). Because "the eschatologically awaited world-redemption has an anticipated reality already in existence," this anticipated ontological reality takes epistemological precedence in understanding the cosmos.[89] Laws of nature are the divinely willed, created, and sustained patterns of formation that enable humanity's covenant relations with God and others.

---

86. Maximus "follows the widespread philosophical and Christian tradition which sees man . . . as forming a microcosm . . . which reflects the created world," Thunberg, *Microcosm and Mediator*, 231.

87. *CD*, III/2, 21–27.

88. *CD*, III/2, 34ff. Similar to Maximus's concept of the *logoi*.

89. O'Donovan, *Resurrection*, 23.

11. Christ and Human Nature

In his treatment of anthropology, Barth reformulates the patristic understanding of human nature as consisting of the sum of a substantive set of static invariants that perdure through time, through the relationship of God to the human Jesus.[90] This relationship reveals God's: 1) election, becoming and remaining one with Jesus; 2) self-revelation, action, and glorification, in and through Jesus; 3) love addressed to Jesus, and through him to all who believe, and the whole creation; and 4) freedom and sovereignty which dwell in Jesus as their Bearer and Substitute.[91] What sin cancels is revealed perfectly in Jesus because "the nature of the man Jesus alone is the key to the problem of human nature."[92] In two significant statements concerning rationality, a central concept in natural law, Barth "places the contemplative and reflective reason of the creature in the service of the Creator's knowledge of the creature" and describes confessing Christ as "the basic act of man's God-given reason."[93] Thus reason that is apposite to human nature is directed not to itself, its origin, or its *telos* as such, but to its covenant partnership with God. We only truly know ourselves, and what is right and good about our being and acts, when we know God's knowledge of us. This knowledge is properly demonstrated in Jesus' covenant relationship with God. Jesus properly knew himself because he knew God's knowledge of him, even from childhood (Luke 2:49). Natural reason is theological in its orientation even though it commences with the knowing self, because reasoning about oneself finally leads to God and his determination of our existence when it is properly exercised. Conversely, human reason and inclinations that direct the self back to the self are incapable of indicating proper moral acts, goods, or ends. Appetitive natural inclinations are a form of the phenomenological approach dismissed.[94] "There can be no doubt that everywhere in [Paul's] Christ-Adam parallel . . . Christ is the One who actualised the human nature corrupted by Adam."[95]

---

90. Barth, *CD*, III/2, 40f.

91. Ibid., 41. The capitalization is Barth's.

92. Ibid., 43. "To find the . . . essential nature of man we have to look not to Adam . . . but to Christ." "The nature of Christ objectively conditions human nature," Barth, *Adam and Christ*, 24, 42–43.

93. Barth, *CD*, III/2, 44, III/4, 73.

94. Predispositions that lead to sin tend towards non-being, Wolf Krötke, "The humanity of the human person in Karl Barth's anthropology," in Webster, *Cambridge Companion to Karl Barth*, 165.

95. Barth, *CD*, III/2, 46.

Nonetheless, there are differences between Jesus' human nature and ours, so that a *direct* deduction from Christology to anthropology is impossible.[96] Again, these are not static qualities, but personal relations. Jesus' humanity is not characterized by our self-contradiction, self-deception, and sin. His humanity is the basis of our acceptance by God. As the Son of Man and Son of God, his relation as a human being to God is unique, providing the basis of our relation to God. Notwithstanding these differences, by living in this obedient covenant relationship with God, Jesus' humanity is: 1) the prototype of which ours is the copy; 2) sinless whilst ours is distorted; and 3) revelatory of humanity's original, basic, and good form, unlike our opaque nature. These three descriptions of true humanity's character, origin, and *telos* carry certain ethical implications.

First, Christ's prototypical humanity leads non-controversially to moral exemplarism.[97] Jesus' moral humanity is the dynamic event of his covenant relationship with God. When the archetype is dynamically actualist, the noun "copy" (our humanity being a copy of his archetypical humanity) implies the verb "copy!" (our active partaking in his covenant relationship with God), so that the conceptual center of moral exemplarism is our participation in and reproduction of Christ's Spirit-enabled covenant relationship to God, which our moral practices subsequently embody.

Second, Jesus' sinlessness was not a heroic human achievement but the maintenance of his true humanity through the Word and Spirit. Consequently, our humanity necessarily requires similar moral enabling. While Jesus' humanity, created by the Spirit (Luke 1:35), only existed in union with his divine person as the *Logos*, it is this same Word and Spirit that created and upheld Adam's sinlessness. Because Adam's sinlessness was not a static and innate quality, but a Spirit-maintained obedient relationship to God, moral existence is heteronomous and non-heroic, making it impure in Kantian terms.[98] Natural human inclinations are therefore dispositions created

---

96. Ibid., 47–54. The following argument is grounded in this text. Also, "anthropology cannot be Christology, nor Christology anthropology," 71.

97. Exemplarism is rightly criticized by Weinandy, *In the Likeness*, 13f, if Jesus' humanity is severed from his divinity, concurring with Barth, and Reimer's critique of Yoder.

98. Neder, *Participation*, 33, argues that in Barth genuine human existence is responding to God with actions "not within the range of its own inherent possibilities." This either mistakes human actions with sinful actions, or understands *pre-lapsum* humanity without the Spirit's enabling. Issler, "Jesus' Example. Prototype of the Dependent, Spirit-Filled Life," in Issler and Sanders, *Jesus in Trinitarian Perspective*, 189–225, rightly argues that Christ as model is due to his Spirit enabled humanity as last Adam, brother and example. Pneumatic Christology reflects the Biblical aversion to heroic ethics, as it locates the source of Jesus' moral achievement heteronomously.

and upheld by grace within the divine-human covenant relation. Natural inclinations are those created orientations and dispositions that maintain humanity's covenant relationship with God and facilitate human flourishing in God as the author and sustainer of life (Gen 1:28). Any inclination which lies outside this relationship, or which militates against it, is a serpentine intrusion into the proper character of humanity. Dispositions, inclinations, thoughts, acts, or decisions that have the effect of rending the covenant relationship are themselves rendered unnatural.

Third, because Jesus' good human nature is transparent, the opacity of our sinfulness no longer constitutes an impediment to understanding humanity's proper character. Aristotle's focus upon observable human phenomena cannot be taken as primary or definitive of human nature, because it is irrational to develop an anthropology and ethic from a flawed source whilst a perfect source is patent. Jesus plainly reveals good humanity, as well as bad humanity, by way of contrast.[99] In Levinasian terms, Jesus is the good transparent face that elicits our shame at our contrasting sin, and elects us to good action.[100]

Despite these three associations, a symmetrical and direct relationship between anthropology and Christology is rejected because the an/enhypostasia doctrine implies the priority of Christ's pre-existent divine nature over his human nature. Yet neither can the "phenomena of man" yield a proper view of humanity.[101] Nonetheless, Christ's two natures are in perfect union, revealed in the Johannine *I am* sayings and in his obedience to his threefold office as the person who is for God.[102] This relational understanding of human nature means that human phenomena need evaluation through the

---

In contrast, Chalier describes Kant's moral autonomy as "not alien to the subject, it is not imposed on the subject by an external source," *What Ought I to Do?*, 64. However, Spirit enabling is not Spirit imposition. Spirit Christology is explicit in the Synoptics and implicit in John according to Brown, *Miracles*, 320, while the opposite is argued regarding John by Burge, *Anointed Community*. Dunn, *Jesus and the Spirit*, 11-88, wrongly limits Jesus' pneumatic experience to his divine Sonship and unique charismatic/prophetic ministry.

99. Barth, *CD*, III/2, 52. By rejecting their election, people have "forfeited their true being," Neder, *Participation*, 20.

100. 2 Corinthians 3-4. The face confronts "the egoistic sedimentations of interestedness in being, prior to everything and the other, which . . . keeps us in a state of forgetfulness," Chalier, *What Ought?*, 103.

101. Barth, *CD*, III/2, §44.2, 71-132. H. A. G. Blocher, "Karl Barth's Anthropology," in Chung, *Karl Barth*, 101-102, says that Barth's grounding of anthropology on Christology is his "most original feature" even though denying a direct identification between them.

102. Barth, *CD*, III/2, 55-71.

relation between Jesus and God.[103] This relation reveals a six-fold determination of humanity as: derived from God; the object of God's deliverance; being for God's glory; under God's lordship; corresponding to God's actions for it; and being in service to God. This excludes naturalistic, ethical/idealistic, existential, and transcendent understandings of human nature, because they deal only with human phenomena and not human reality as related to God. These will be discussed later.

Consequently, because the source of Barth's anthropology is Christ, who is both the "Real Man" and God, godlessness is ontologically impossible.[104] The "godless man" is illusory because a human being only exists as a being with God: denying God is denying oneself.[105] The subject "human" has as an essential predicate "related to God." As a moon cannot be defined without reference to its planet, so God defines humanity. This means that Kantian moral autonomy is impossible. And because humanity and ethics are understood in an actualist fashion, and every human action is either for or against existing with God, good human action is necessarily theological.[106] God-directed actions constitute the fulfilling of human ontology, and anti-God actions constitute their emptying, so that the natural law thesis that Christian ethics is an imperative to be human becomes christologically grounded: "Be human the way Jesus is human in his relation to God." As that which is proper to a dog is to be dog-like, that which is proper to a human is to be Christ-like, in respect to his God-determined humanity. Any move towards Christ humanizes; any move away de-humanizes or "de-ontologizes." Christ is therefore the human ontological reality upon which moral exemplarism is grounded in its God-derived nature. As real ethics is philosophically parasitic upon realist ontology, Christian real ethics is parasitic upon realist human ontology—that is, the God-related humanity of Christ in whom humanity participates.

Because human ontology *is* Jesus Christ in his God-derived humanity, christological ethics becomes both theological and universal.[107] But Christ

---

103. Ibid., 73–95. "The human . . . exists . . . in relations," Krötke, "Barth's Anthropology," in Webster, *Cambridge Companion to Karl Barth*, 168. Barth retrieves his four-fold negation of phenomena by calling them "symptoms" (pathologies?) of human nature, *CD*, III/2, 198–202.

104. The "Real Man" is discussed in *CD*, III/2, §44.3, 132–202.

105. Ibid., 72–77. "Man *in abstracto*" is lost in sin as an ontological necessity, III/2, 146.

106. The divine-human relation is "ontologically decisive" for anthropology, *CD*, III/2, 135f. Milbank agrees by arguing that theology is the true sociology, i.e., humanity, *Theology and Social Theory*, 380.

107. "What is *Christian* is . . . identical with what is *universally human*," Barth,

as "Real Man" is also the one in whom *ta panta* exist, so that metaphysical ethical realism is also determined christologically.[108] This means that a christological understanding of human nature includes cosmological concerns. Both traditional anthropological (e.g., Calvin) and cosmological (e.g., Cicero) natural law are inadequate here.[109] Properly, they are defensible as forms of Christian natural law only when grounded upon Christ who is, ontologically, the real human, and metaphysically, the origin, basis, and coherent center of *ta panta*. Because godlessness is humanly impossible, it is also cosmologically impossible, because the cosmos is understood through christological anthropology. Consequently, Christ reconfigures cosmological reasoning away from Stoicism's cold legality towards warm personal covenantal relations. This is clear in the cosmological Christology of Colossians 1:15–20, a text that concludes with personal reconciliation, that is, covenant relations with God.

Because Barth's anthropology is Chalcedonian, it overcomes the attenuation of the divine nature in both radical ethics and anthropological natural law. As actualist, it shatters the classical view of static humanity and thaws out Stoicism's cold natural law. As relational and covenantal, the non-theological autonomous determination of natural inclinations and human moral agency is overcome. Because Christ is the "Real Man" whose humanity is consubstantial with ours, what is natural to his humanity is also real and natural to our humanity, so that a rapprochement of christo-ethical radicalism and natural law is possible.

III. Humanity as Summoned

Because our election is in and through the election of Christ the Word who speaks and summons the world into existence, being human is being

---

Christ and Adam, 43, italics original.

108. It may be here that Barth mistakes the incarnate Christ for the pre-existent Son, as it is theologically the latter who is the creator of all things. However, with Barth's strong doctrine of christological election, cited above, it is likely that he is at least consistent.

109. Natural law is "that apprehension of the conscience," Calvin, *ICR*, II.ii.22, 282, and "is right reason in agreement with nature," Cicero, *DE REPUBLICUS*, iii.xxii.33. Regarding reason (Cicero's emphasis), P. Pettit argues for a substantive moral theory of respectful co-rationalism: "Humans . . . are creatures of the word and can relate to one another in the co-reasoning that speech makes possible," Petit, "Substantive Moral Theory," in Paul et al., *Objectivism*, 25. Barth would likely rework this as rational covenantal conversation between God and humanity, i.e., the hypostatic union.

summoned by God.[110] A salient quote illustrates Barth's *logos* Christology at this point:

> He is to the created world and therefore ad extra what the Son of God as the eternal Logos is within the triune being of God. If the eternal Logos is the Word in which God speaks within Himself, thinks Himself and is conscious of Himself, then in its identity with the man Jesus it is the Word in which God thinks the cosmos, speaks with the cosmos and imparts to the cosmos the consciousness of its God.[111]

Because God thinks, speaks with, and is conscious of himself as the *Logos*, that same Word thinks, speaks with, and imparts to the cosmos its proper consciousness of God, such that "real" human nature is simply equivalent to "summoned."[112] This means that real human competencies are determined by their capacity to respond to that summons, and that those abilities that are contrary to the summons cannot be considered as real capacities of human creation, but mere phenomena. As the real Word, Jesus speaks the divine summons, and as the real human, he obeyed the divine summons.[113] Jesus remained really human as God's covenant partner through obedience to the divine summons. To be real is to be summoned by God, and we are "summoned because chosen."[114] This concept of summons unites both creation and redemption, because the gospel summons to recreation is a summons back to original creation, and both occur through the Word. The creational summons (Genesis 1) is echoed in the gospel summons (John 1:1, Mark 1:17, John 11:43, 2 Cor 5:17). As such, human beings are not the presupposition of their own existence, but are derived from and sustained by the gracious Word that brings them forth. This is determined christologically for two reasons.

First, Christ's humanity was summoned, or announced (Luke 1:26–38); and second, in his humanity he was the only one who properly responded to the divine summons in covenantal faithfulness (Luke 2:49; Heb 3:6; 1 Pet 2:22). Outside of Christ the summons is improperly heeded, and thus

---

110. Barth, *CD*, III/2, 147, italics added. Regarding election, *CD*, III/2, 142–7, and being summoned, 147–57. Taken together, they constitute human being as history, that is, Jesus Christ, 157–62.

111. Ibid., 147.

112. Barth, *CD*, III/2, 150, 152. This summons is the presupposition of human creation, the *ex nihilo* doctrine, 152–7.

113. This is contra Aristotle's corporate human self-enclosure in the *polis*, *Politics* I.I.1253a 1, Thomas's rationalism, *ST*, Q.94.2, 3, and Kant's autonomous ethics.

114. Barth, *CD*, III/2, 150.

The Christological Redetermination of Natural Law 245

a "phantom man" obscures the "real man."[115] Consequently, because Jesus constitutes in his own being the "real man," ethical naturalism can no longer be understood as a non-theistic concept, but becomes a christological one. Christ is the natural reality of humanity because he is its elected presupposition, and because he maintained this real humanity through obedience to the divine summons.[116]

Moreover, humanity as summoned by and to God is presupposed in Jesus' enhypostatic humanity, because his humanity was summoned into being (Luke 1:26–38) in union with the Word (John 1:14). Because his humanity was thus summoned and joined to his divinity, natural law grounded in human nature, and ethical naturalism as grounded in human facts, are freed from their self-enclosed character by the relation of Jesus' humanity to his divinity. Christ's incarnate life, as a dynamic event that was summoned into being, constitutes the true nature of humanity.[117] When considered from the viewpoint of the human subject, history is response, because Jesus Christ himself exists only as externally determined by the divine Word's decision to become incarnate.[118] Consequently, because human nature is constituted by such responsive actuality, the realization of innate human essence through acts of self-originating or self-determining actualization is displaced. Thus the being of humanity is "not merely the formal character of logos but the material character of being reached, determined and motivated by the divine Logos."[119] Humanity is not addressed by the *Logos* because it can hear, but can hear because it is addressed by the *Logos*. The capacity to hear is not the presupposition of the summons; the summons

---

115. Ibid., 75.

116. For Christ as presupposition, CD, III/2, 151. Christopher W. Gowans, "Virtue and Nature," in Paul et al., *Objectivism*, 28, defines naturalism as moral values being tied to natural facts, which themselves are determined by science. Barth would contest Christ as a knowable "fact" apart from faith. Regarding what constitutes nature, Hauerwas, *With the Grain*, argues that Gifford's understanding of natural theology was itself not "natural" but a specific species of Enlightenment rationality demanding of Christian theology, "Prove it!" Aquinas and Barth provide alternative approaches: see chapter 1.

117. Barth, CD, III/2, 158.

118. Ibid., 159–62. If Christ's human response is understood as wholly passive, acting only as determined by the divine nature, we skirt the edge of monothelitism. A pneumatic Christology safeguards Christ's humanity as *active* response. Human responsibility as *response*-ability means active subjectivity contains a degree of heteronomous determination, Anderson, *On Being Human*, 35–43, 56ff.

119. Barth, CD, III/2, 163–164. "Man is, as he hears this Word," 165. Chalcedon means Jesus is both the Word spoken, and the Word heard and obeyed as recapitulated Adam; Wingren, *Man and Incarnation*, 89.

is the presupposition of the capacity to hear: creation is for the covenant. Human capacities are gifts that enable us to respond to the divine summons.

Because each person is a "being in summons" by the divine *Logos*, human rationality is the capacity to respond to this divine Word. The Word spoke into nothing, and human hearing and reasoning became. Natural law's formal criterion of humanity—rationality—is seen to be materially inadequate here. The human *logos* comes into existence and functions properly only through its obedient hearing of the summons of the divine *Logos*.[120] Such hearing extends the act of creation, as an act that perdures through time, as a continual divine summons to become and be, and includes Christ's summons to follow him in life-fulfilling obedience (Mark 8:34–35). Natural law's formal human criterion of rationality is what corresponds in humanity to the *Logos*'s warm personal summons to live in free gratitude in faithful covenantal relations.

When this response is glad and grateful, it is "in the strictest sense, a natural human action" because human gratitude is the counterpoint to Christ who is, ontologically, grace.[121] This constitutes gratitude to God as a natural inclination that brings about human flourishing in correspondence to its natural ends. In Finnis, religion is one of the basic human goods indicated by the natural inclinations.[122] For Barth, however, gratitude is a response to an external Word, not an innate propensity in line with an innate good. What is natural for human existence is what corresponds and answers to the summons of the *Logos*, whether in creation (Genesis 1) or recreation (John 1), so that failure to thus respond drives it towards nothingness—non-flourishing. When human beings act according to traditional natural inclinations, they are responding to the divine summons embedded in creation to fully flourish (Gen 1:28–30). Yet because the covenant is the internal basis of such flourishing, only those inclinations and acts that do not mitigate the covenant are properly natural.

There is no doubt that Barth appears to downplay the phenomena of humanity such as time, culture, place, language, traditions and so on as mere modalities of being, not its essence.[123] In this sense he moves somewhat close to the ethical "view from nowhere" by replacing the universal humanity, will, and rationality of the Enlightenment with the universal humanity of Christ. As Kant sought the ground of ethics in a universal autonomous

---

120. John 1:1–4.

121. Barth, *CD*, III/2, 166: human εὐχαριστία corresponds to divine χάρις.

122. Finnis, *Fundamentals*, 50–51.

123. Bart, *CD*, III/2, 159, 249. This emphasis alienated Barth from Gogarten, Busch, *Karl Barth*, 193–194.

will, does Barth base humanity in a universal heteronomous Christology? Playing on Barth's understanding of ethics as action, his anthropology at this point begs the question, "But what about *me*, in *my* life, *my* history? What am *I* to do?"[124] What he is attempting, however, is an understanding of human nature and its relations that are proper to Chalcedonian Christology, not its phenomenological description.

Most significant is Barth's assertion that gratitude reveals humanity's first "own act," —humanity as true subject. Such gratitude fulfills the being of humanity as God's creature, for, being divinely grounded, gratitude has both its origin and goal in God. Gratitude can therefore meet the criteria for both protological and teleological natural law as a genuine human act directed by and corresponding to the goodness of God's grace. Failure to give thanks, to think thankfully (Rom 1:21), is irrational, associated with moral dissolution and the corruption and disintegration of human nature (Rom 1:18–32). As Romans 1:18–32 is a significant natural law text, thanksgiving acquires the character of a natural inclination—albeit one that is irrationally suppressed, yet renewed christologically (Rom 12:1–2).

Because gratitude is a true human act, humanity at this point constructs its own moral self. But as a response, gratitude possesses no autonomous status. Parasitic upon gratitude as humanity's first "own act" is Barth's understanding of human responsibility as a definite act, not a state or potentiality.[125] Such responsibility possesses four characteristics: 1) the knowledge of God;[126] 2) obedience to God so that "I am" becomes "I will";[127] 3) invocation to God; and 4) personal freedom consisting in this knowledge, obedience, and invocation. Freedom consists in fulfilling one's gifted responsibility to know, obey, and invoke God. Such freedom is the proper "creaturely mode" of humanity, the "decisive definition of what we mean when we describe man as subject," in contrast with the modalities of time, culture, place, language, and traditions, noted above.[128] But what is a subject?

---

124. However, in *CD*, III/4, §52–§56, concrete realities are considered such as marriage, children and neighbors, the protection of life, flora and fauna, sickness, legal punishment, war, and vocation. All such temporal matters "are enclosed by time," 569, which is shared by Christ, 577.

125. Barth, *CD*, III/2, 174–186.

126. Ibid., 193. Barth's "self knowledge is impossible apart from knowledge of God," Neder, *Participation*, 37.

127. Ibid., 180.

128. Ibid., 194.

A subject is "something which freely posits itself in its own being."[129] Human freedom consists in response to its election and summons by the Word of God. Humanity is, as it "performs such acts of responsibility."[130] Like his doctrine of God, this is an actualist and historical concept of the human subject over a substantialist view. Thus whilst freedom is the formal criterion of humanity, the material content is not empty, but consists in those acts proper to its election and divine summons. Freedom is the human correlate to the divine election and summons to be God's covenant partner. In this response humans act as real subjects, positing their being truly. Alternate choices constitute a renunciation of freedom and therefore a movement away from being a real subject. The "Real Man" is Christ because he freely responded in gratitude. As grace constitutes God as a Subject, gratitude constitutes humans as subjects. As the divine Subject, Christ exists in grace; as the human subject he exists in the free gratitude corresponding to this grace. By this free and responsible gratitude he placed himself in an obedient relation to his election, creation, and summons, and thus posited himself as a true human being and subject. Consequently, the four phenomenological symptoms of humanity briefly outlined above—namely, natural science, ethics/idealism, existentialism, and the quest for transcendence—are displaced. Each of these is now considered in relation to natural law.

First, regarding natural science, natural inclinations are often associated with endocrinologically determined drives such as self-survival and fulfillment of appetites. Christ's response to violence in his Passion disables this understanding. Likewise, the paraenesis of 2 Peter 2:12–22 equates unrighteous pleasure (v. 13) with irrational animal nature that is inclined towards death (v. 12). As natural inclinations indicate proper human nature, Peter's assessment—that pleasure which trends to godlessness is an animal and not human inclination—serves to limit the idea's usefulness. This implies that righteousness (v. 7), godliness (v. 9), and following the straight path (v. 15), are naturally and properly human. However, such qualities are not usually understood as natural inclinations but their opposites—heroic moral virtues that develop through practice, as in Aristotle. Thus a clear distinction must be drawn between innate and natural in the context of ethics: innate is that which is automatic and reflexive, and may or may not be determined by sin, whereas natural is that which corresponds to our election, creation, and summons by and to God. Christ's act of blessing his enemies

---

129. Ibid. Yet being a subject does not negate being an object—of God's love. Barth denies both self-realized human agency and divine sole agency, Webster, *Barth's Moral Theology*, 151–78.

130. Barth, *CD*, III/2, 175.

from the cross was a natural inclination because it was an act proper to him as a human subject. It was an act of "real humanity" and thus a natural act due to it being an act of knowing and obeying his election and summons by God. The natural good was to trust God and maintain human covenant relations, not retaliate with violence.

Second, because Christ's enhypostatic humanity is neither self-originating nor self-substantiating, the self-determination that is characteristic of ethics/idealism is negated. As Christ's humanity exists only in its divine determination, election, and summons, the ethical question, "What am I to do?" becomes Gethsemane's plea, "Not my will, but yours be done."[131] This trustful relation makes Christ's "real humanity" a correlate to this divine summons, and as our "real humanity" likewise exists by divine summons, natural law's concept of basic human goods as self-originating is arrested. Basic human goods are those goods to which we are divinely summoned. Because Christ is the fulfillment of the Law that is itself the second edition of creation's natural law, Christ enacts natural law in all his moral actions and determinations. Creation, Sinai, and the gospel all reveal the divine external summons to be human. Basic human goods thus become divine determinations, for human nature is identical with that "Real Man" who is elected and summoned to grateful obedience to God. What is misunderstood as an apparent heteronomous divine will is correctly understood as a gifted human inclination. In Barth, human determination takes on the characteristic of having its "beginning and its basis in another, higher determination"—God.[132] The idealism of ethics where my be*coming* is posited out of my own *being*, is replaced by my *being* determined by the divine summons to be*come* God's covenant partner, and thus experience human flourishing. Creation, election, and summons naturally incline humanity to the final good of covenantal fidelity to God. The proper self-determining actions that correspond to this *telos* are gratitude and free responsibility towards God.

Third, Barth understands existentialism as an attempted resolution of the conflict between naturalism and ethics/idealism. Existentialism argues that existence (nature) precedes essence (ethics/idealism), with the latter emerging from a courageous unconstrained decision. But when existence and essence are refracted through the doctrine of creation, human gratitude for its own existence, that is, for its own creation, becomes the essence of its being. Existence becomes essence, because existence is a divine gift that includes our essence to which we respond in gratitude. The essence of our

---

131. Matthew 26:39.
132. Webster, *Barth's Moral Theology*, 109.

humanity is given in our existence as creatures capable of responding to God's summons in free obedience and gratitude for that existence. As such, nature and ethics are not irreconcilable but co-inhere. And when this is understood christologically, human existence (mere facticity, nature, the *is*) and essence (self-created human identity, ethics/idealism, the *will*), the two poles around which existentialism orbits, is rendered redundant to the extent that in his free obedience, Christ posits his essence as a true human subject through gratitude.

Finally, transcendence as such is rejected because it permits a non-christological human determination of the material content of a formal metaphysical concept.[133] Chalcedonian Christology properly fills out divine transcendence through the imminence of Christ's actuality, because the hypostatic union discloses the fullness of the divine moral nature in a material form. Here the concept of transcendence is no longer formally definite yet materially empty, but both formally and materially determined by the actuality of Christ's historicity: "I and the Father are One."[134] Because Christ's humanity and divinity are inseparably united in the one hypostasis, the moral determinations of the divine/transcendent are expressed in the moral actions of the humanity of Jesus. Chalcedon's fourfold apophaticism means that not only Christ's immanent human nature, but also that nature's actions, are "unconfusedly, immutably, indivisibly, inseparably" united with his transcendent divine nature. That is, Christ's human *actions* are in union with his divine nature because of the *actualist* and historical view of divine and human natures rather than a substantive one.[135] Chalcedonian Christology historically anchors transcendent moral attributes in Jesus.

In summary, this attempt to develop the unrealized potential of Barth's christological anthropology means that; a) the received non-christological natural law tradition is disabled because its understanding of humanity is reduced to a description of human phenomena rather than real or essential humanity as theologically determined; and b) Anabaptist moral reasoning is saved from historicist criticism and provincialism by placing Christology within the greater concerns of universal human nature. By understanding humanity through the union of Christ's human nature with his divine nature, and his whole person in his relationship with God, a christologically actualist and theological determination of natural law is enabled. That which

---

133. Barth, *CD*, III/2, 132. In 128–132 he specifically criticizes Brunner's *Der Mensch im Widerspruch*.

134. John 10:30, also 1:14, 18.

135. Jesus' *work* is "the *being* of this man." He is not estranged from himself in his work, Barth, *CD*, III/2, 63–64, emphasis added.

is natural to humanity is its ineradicable relation to God, and its summons to grateful free obedience, exemplified in Christ.

b. *The Basic Form of Humanity*

Barth extends his central theological concept of the covenant, plus God's summons, to include relations between individual persons. Again, this is christologically grounded. Even though Jesus' humanity is uniquely for others' salvation, it nonetheless constitutes humanity's basic form: the "humanity . . . of each and every man, consists in the determination of man's being as a being with others."[136] This "being with others" is symmetrical and reciprocal and means that human relations constitute each person's basic form. In attacking Nietzsche's "I am," Barth enriches Buber's "I-Thou" through an actualist and covenantal "I am in encounter."[137] The content of this encounter, which constitutes humanity's basic form, is fourfold. In ascending order it is: 1) looking the other in the eye; 2) reciprocal speech and hearing; 3) mutual assistance; and 4) gladness, the inner soul of the three prior outward actions. Hearing the Thou is receiving "the call of the other" in their need and rendering help, similar to being elected as a moral agent by seeing the needy face of the transcendent other in Levinas.[138] Whereas sin blinds the eye to the Thou's needs, moral agency is elected and awakened when the Thou's needy face is seen.[139] Thus the source of the moral imperative "Thou shalt" in Barth is the form of Christ's humanity as the person for others, in contrast to the Law of God in the Old Testament, the self in Kant, and the other's face in Levinas.

---

136. Ibid., 243. "If it is not fellow-human . . . it is not human," 285. This also constitutes Barth's doctrine of the *imago Dei*, 323–324, III/1, 191–192 and man-woman relations, III/4, 116–240ff. This extends into the human realm our character as God's partners in the theological realm, III/1, 222, 226. Both realms are ethically important, III/4, 48–49.

137. Barth, *CD*, III/2, 231–47. This encounter is "the very root of my being," 247. As Safenwil's "red" pastor Barth likely had a social view of humanity early; Henri A. G. Blocher, "Karl Barth's Anthropology," in Chung, *Karl Barth*, 112–113. He questions whether Barth's "I-Thou" is Buberian, 113–119.

138. Barth, *CD*, III/2, 261–262. "Access to the face is straightway ethical," and "face and discourse are tied. The face speaks," Levinas, *Ethics and Infinity*, 85, 87.

139. Chalier on Levinas, *What Ought?*, 78–80. Barth's language also reflects such election: the "call" for help comes from the Thou, but the I consigns itself to "perdition" if it refuses help. The Thou elects, and the I is elected, to assistance, *CD*, III/2, 264, 271–272. Similarly, "since the Logos in incarnated, God has a face"; Zimmermann, *Theological Hermeneutics*, 286.

Significantly, "to be human . . . confessing both the need of assistance and the willingness to render it, is supremely *natural* and not unnatural" and "an ineluctable law of nature." Gladly helping others is the "*conditio sine qua non* of humanity."[140] Here is a remarkably strong definition of a universal "law of nature" grounded in human nature itself. Gladly giving and receiving help is a natural law of humanity. Such gladness mirrors in the human realm what gratitude is in the theological realm. The divine summons emerging from another is a call to fulfill humanity's essential social character. Both other persons (Gen 2:20–21) and the Lord (Ps 54:4) are our natural helpers. Barth proudly sees humanity as a family of lions rather than a lone tiger.

Gladness is basic because without it assistance degrades into legalism, and is thus no longer proper to true humanity: the cry for assistance is heard as a rancorous imposition, and giving it a grudging burden. Without gladness, the Thou is debased into an external fact that diminishes one's humanity, just as sin transforms God into an alien threat to one's freedom. Non-covenantal existence makes others aliens and potential threats to the self, whereas a covenantal understanding of humanity implies that God and others form the I and are therefore essential to the flourishing of the I. Without gladly seeing, hearing and assisting the external Thou as an inward constitutive element of itself, the I launches an assault upon its own humanity.

With echoes of Calvin, Barth's I-Thou mutuality is "the law of the Creator . . . given him as his own law, the law which he himself sets up, the law of his own freedom."[141] Gladly obeying this law of freedom is a grateful response to God's command. The Thou participates in the constitution of the I because the I only exists as an "I-Thou." To be an I is to acknowledge the Thou as an ineradicable constituent of the self and as a law of its own existence. Neither being owned by or owning the Thou, neither slave nor tyrant, the I and Thou are companions, associates, comrades, fellows, and helpmates.[142]

This "supremely natural" mutual assistance expresses the creation story, where helping and being helped accords with created humanity (Gen 2:20). The goodness of creation includes human interdependence (Gen 1:28, 31), which expresses in the symmetrical human realm what is true

---

140. Barth, *CD*, III/2, 264, italics added, 266–267. Barth' ethics of action ("to act accordingly") is based upon "to be human" showing his realism in the Ristian sense. Refusing the other's eye turns the "I" into a self-enclosed ego: one is no longer a real "I" nor has an eye, 264. As *CD* III/2 was first published in 1948, is this a reflection upon Nazism's Nietzschian and Wagnerian legacy?

141. Ibid., 268. Calvin's "law of our creation" becomes the I-Thou relation.

142. Ibid., 271.

in the asymmetrical theological realm, where humanity is in constant need of divine sustaining (Pss 33:20, 104:30). Both the Lord and others are our natural helpers. Because both sets of relations are proper to human nature, non-theological existence and non-social existence are unnatural and tend to nothingness. This I-Thou covenant partnership is humanity's true form, not unlike Aristotle's political existence, although Barth's *telos* is mutual assistance, whereas Aristotle's is social peace.[143]

Such an understanding of humanity's basic form concurs with Anabaptist tripolar theology that posits God, the self and the neighbor as the three essential elements in Christian confession.[144] This is contra modern historical consciousness in liberal democracy that prioritizes the self devoid of both God and the neighbor, and in forms of social democracy that prioritize the self and the neighbor devoid of God, or in Spiritualism and classical Christian confessionalism that posits God and the self devoid of the neighbor.[145] As ethics and law are naturalistic in the sense that they are derived from concepts of human nature, the better the concept of human nature, the better the ethic.[146] Such realism expresses the metaphysical claim of the singularity, self-consistency, and indivisibility of truth.[147] The argument that human nature is christologically determined, and that its basic form (gladly seeing, hearing and speaking, and assisting) is derived from Jesus' humanity in his covenantal relations with both God and others, constitutes a clear form of christological moral reasoning such as that found in Rist's understanding of naturalism. If humanity's basic form is an I-Thou "I am in encounter," an ethic of being-for-others follows trivially.

Given this form of humanity, it is clear that an ethics of action, "What am I do to?" must be answered so that the "I" stands as one subject within this covenantal I-Thou relation. Hence natural law as an ethic of real human nature (Rist) and the "law of our creation" (Calvin) must be understood socially. By calling the I-Thou relation an "ineluctable law of nature," Barth's rejection of natural law appears inconsistent. Moral realism appears to rear its head because in an actualist theology "the law of the Creator"[148] as an *ad extra* divine act becomes identical with God's *ad intra* being. Does his

---

143. Aristotle, *Politics*, I.I.1253a 1.

144. Augsburger, *Dissident Discipleship*, 7–22.

145. Liberal democracy is monistic in that it is "enslaved to one universally acclaimed good, that of individual self-determination," O'Donovan, "Subsidiarity," 19, cited by Reimer, *Mennonites and Classical*, 528.

146. Rist, *Real Ethics*, 61–62.

147. Lowe, *Survey*, 1–4.

148. Barth, *CD*, III/2, 268.

actualism here merge with a form of substantive realism, or is it simply an example of his dialectical method? Or by "law" is he simply placing the form of his ethics (law) ahead of its matter (gospel)? Whatever may be the case, at this point he appears to hold a form of natural moral law grounded in both creation and Christ. This natural "law of the Creator" bears significantly upon radicalism's ecclesiology as discussed in Part Two.

1. The Basic Form and Christo-Ethical Radicalism

Barth's social doctrine of humanity is an extension of his covenantal approach to theology. Sinai's two tables and Jesus' two commandments (Matt 22:37–40) both articulate these aspects of the covenant, which correspond to the metaphysical/theological and the anthropological aspects of natural law. But because the covenant is the internal basis of our creation, and natural law attempts to articulate our proper moral createdness, such covenantal relations take on a distinctly natural character. This covenantal nature of humanity—gratefully loving God and gladly loving neighbors, which finds its fullest expression in Jesus—finds an ecclesial expression in radicalism's willing congregationalism. What follows is an attempt to establish four elements of christo-ethical radicalism upon the basis of a christologically-determined natural law.

First, radicalism places ethics as a first principle of Christian confession rather than as an addendum to theological affirmations. As natural law ethics derives from human nature, and the form of human nature is Jesus in his covenant relations to both God and others, then our relation to God cannot be quarantined from our relations to others, even though they can be conceptually distinguished. To confess God means to acknowledge others, so that the radical inclusion of ethical articles in theological confessions is justified not only on christological covenantal grounds, but also on the basis of natural law.

Second, the radical critique of the Lutheran *sola fide* and its wholly forensic view of justification is upheld, for Jesus (*fide's* object) cannot be separated from his basic form of humanity as the person for others. Because the moral character of humanity is non-illusory, a wholly forensic view of the gift of Christ readily tends to a mild form of Docetism because his moral humanity is obscured behind legal categories. By prioritizing legal concepts, the relationship between Christ and the believer easily reduces to a contractual one. It also changes faith, because faith is now directed not to the whole Christ, but to his representative legal role. Christ, the object of faith, becomes less human than the believer, the subject of faith. A wholly forensic view tends to reduce the essential form of Jesus' humanity as a friend and advocate, a Thou, into an impersonal It. The I-Thou covenant becomes an I-It contract. If Jesus is a friend and advocate, an exclusively forensic view makes his advocacy wholly legal in nature, while possibly eliminating his friendship.

Because of Barth's act/being theme, the *act* of justification expresses Christ's *being* for others, which is humanity's basic form. Christ's justifying act was his supreme act of being for others, so that the object of justifying faith is Christ in his being-for-others basic humanity. And as the basic human form of the object of faith cannot be alien to the humanity of the subject of faith, justification cannot be reduced to a mere forensic category. If Jesus' basic form of humanity as the person for others is either surplus or unnecessary to the basic form of humanity for those who believe in and are justified through him, then his humanity is trivialized. Because justification and righteousness are covenantal and thus relational concepts, the righteousness of Christ consists in these covenant relations. As such, the I-Thou basic form of our humanity as being in a right relation with both God and others cannot exist *de jure* without being articulated *de facto* in the obedience of faith (Rom 1:5).

Third, because covenantal human I-Thou relations have their presupposition in Jesus, violence is excluded as improper to our nature because Jesus refused violence. To neglect—and neglect is the passive aggressive form of violence—the needy Thou's call is to "plunge myself into perdition, namely inhumanity," because this call constitutes his election of me to the realization of my humanity. As natural law is the law of our created humanity that orders it to its correct end, violence is an attack upon one's own humanity and election by the call of the needy other, leading to perdition. And as perdition is not our natural *telos*, violence is contrary to natural law.

Augustinian natural law, however, justifies violence when it is necessary to maintain social order, befitting its neo-Platonic character. Charles cites Augustine's distinction between personal attitudes of the heart (grounded in the Sermon on the Mount) and external action (argued from a pragmatic calculus) to justify "benevolent harshness" to conquer evil and facilitate social goods according to natural law.[149] His non-christological moral reasoning is also evident when he asserts that retribution is an aspect of the *imago Dei*, for he fails to note that the Pauline *imago Dei* is Christ whose non-retributive responses to provocation are cited as morally exemplary

---

149. Charles, *Retrieving the Natural Law*, 306. Yoder is rejected precisely because "in his conflation of the personal and the political," he "fails to distinguish between . . . Rom. 12 and . . . Rom. 13," 140, n. 113. Yet Romans 13:1–7 lies within the *inclusios* of enemy love and mercy, 12:12, 13:8–14; Yoder, *Politics*, 197–214.

acts. Where christological retribution is described in the New Testament, it is always eschatological and never morally exemplary: suffering is to result in patient endurance, not retribution.[150]

Admittedly, Charles does not defend violence but retribution. But his approval of Augustine's argument, which locks Jesus' words up in the heart, begs the question, "Why not lock up Locke, Aristotle, Thomas, Calvin, Cicero etc up in the heart, too?"

However, if the true form of humanity is grounded in Jesus' humanity as the person for others, then acts proper to human nature are precisely those that maintain the I-Thou relation. If tyranny is self-determined perdition and inhumanity, then the Anabaptist rejection of violence can be defended on a natural law basis as contrary to both the moral subject's proper end (which is not perdition) and its proper nature (which is not inhumanity). The *telos* of natural law is not Augustine's platonized social order, maintained by violence, but the realization of the christological form of glad humanity in I-Thou relations.

Fourth, the covenantal nature and form of humanity is more richly embodied in radicalism's covenantal and congregational polity than the ecclesial polity of either magisterial territorialism or Spiritualism. By legally coercing ecclesial relations, both Catholic and Reformation territorialism degraded the humanity of their citizens by stripping them of glad willingness. The I-Thou becomes an I-It. By averting ecclesial relations, Spiritualism also degraded the humanity of its adherents by stripping them of the same glad willingness. The I-Thou becomes a type of spiritual Nietzschian "I am."[151] Territorialism breaks the I-Thou relation by turning the social Thou into an external coerced It, whilst Spiritualism breaks it by turning the Thou into an external unnecessary It. By so doing, humanity's basic form degrades towards inhumanity and perdition.

Thus the affirmation that the basic form of covenantal humanity is glad, that people "meet gladly and in freedom," leads naturally to a willing church.[152] Such a form expresses in the ecclesial sphere the basic form of

---

150. E.g. Revelation 1:9, 6:11.

151. Jesus' "I am" is otherwise; "I am the good shepherd . . . [who] *lays down his life*," John 10:11, NIV.

152. Barth, *CD*, III/2, 271: "If humanity does not exist first and last in this freedom, it does not exist at all," 273. Barth does not draw out any ecclesiology at this point, but later in *CD*, IV/1, §62; IV/2, §67; IV/3.2; §72 and *Lecture Fragments*, §75. The apparent thinness of ecclesiology in *CD* is widely discussed. Neder, *Participation*, 81, n.1 sees Barth's ecclesiology as a function of his doctrines of election and Christology, and union with Christ. Biggar, *Hastening*, 123–45, suggests that ecclesiology is the "matrix" for Barth's treatment of ethics and character, although prioritizing the Word

humanity according to "the law of the Creator."[153] This church is the place where true humanization and the fulfillment of human goods occur, such that non-ecclesial existence is unnatural and trends towards dehumanization. Barth himself does not draw such conclusions due to his universal view of grace and humanity, yet his late affirmation of the baptism of those who believe trends that way.

II. Conclusion

Barth's basic form of humanity as an I-Thou social relation agrees somewhat formally with Aristotle's natural law, as well as with the radical emphasis upon human relations as confessionally significant. Yet his Chalcedonian Christology can enrich natural law's concerns about human sociality and the nature, form, and purposes of social goods by providing an historical example of such humanity that is universal, perfect, and theologically real. It also enriches radicalism because Christ's non-violent covenantal humanity not only resists reduction to ecclesiastical rules due to its universality, but

---

and our response to it. J. J. Buckley, "Christian community, baptism, and the Lord's Supper," *Cambridge Companion to Karl Barth*, 195–211, sees Barth dealing with the church under the Word of God (*CD* I), as the sacrament/sign of God's self-attestation in Jesus (*CD* II), as God's witness to the world through baptism and its moral life (*CD* III), through the work of the Spirit (*CD* IV), and as the place of invocation (*Lecture Fragments*). O'Neil, *Forming Moral Community*, v, argues that Barth "developed his theology as a deliberate attempt to shape the ethical life of the church." T. George, "Running Like a Herald to Deliver the Message: Barth on the Church and Sacraments," in Chung, *Karl Barth*, argues that Barth was first and foremost a "churchly theologian," 192. I contend that Barth's ecclesiology is implicit throughout the *CD* (see Hauerwas, *With the Grain*, 194), while explicitly central to his whole life. His concern with the church's proclamation began early: it constitutes §1 of the 1924 Göttingen Dogmatics, cost him his job at Bonn, and is central to the Barmen Declaration and his fight with the German Christians. *Church Dogmatics* itself is ecclesially archaeological and catholic, drawing richly on patristic, medieval, and reformation antecedents. His preference for "community" against "church" may betray anti-Catholic nervousness, while his doctrine of God's triumph over all sin tends to hide the witnessing church, as the "provisional representative of the whole world of humanity justified in Him," behind the world, *CD*, IV/1, 643. The church's self-understanding must be of a "new reality of world-occurrence concealed in Jesus Christ," yet manifestly *visible*, *CD*, IV/3.2, 721–26. *Church Dogmatics*'s trinitarian structure suggests that the unfinished third-article volume would have been ecclesial. The "voluntary . . . membership" of radicalism's ecclesiology, Yoder, *Royal Priesthood*, 279, shares with Barth a formal but not material social doctrine of willing I-Thou humanity. Barth early criticized Pietism's voluntary church as expressing the Enlightenment's absolutism of the individual, *Protestant Theology*, 113–24, but later affirmed it in the form of baptism by request, *Christian Life*, 47.

153. Barth, *CD*, III/2, 268.

also possesses a theologically real basis in the hypostatic union. Chalcedon's double consubstantiality means that Christ's divinity foregrounds rather than diminishes his humanity, because it makes that humanity universally normative. Christ's covenantal social form of humanity corresponds in the human realm to its covenantal spiritual form in the theological realm. Consequently, human moral action accords with its nature when it corresponds to Christ's glad seeing, hearing, and helping of others. The Anabaptist practice of non-violence is given a basis in human nature though Christ.

6. Conclusion

Does Barth exhibit a "classic christocentric weakness"?[154] Perhaps, but given his wider argument with bourgeois liberal Protestantism, the German Christians, and two world wars, such a focus exhibits his concern to determine ethics wholly theologically. His rejection of casuistry is likewise motivated by an aversion to supplanting God. Like Yoder, he seeks to redress an attenuation of the tradition.

I have argued that the criticism that Barth neglects human agency reflects a Kantian understanding that human moral autonomy is the essence of such agency. Barth is like the pre-modern Calvin, for whom possessing a teachable spirit is essential to the perfecting and humanizing process of sanctification, and of proper reasoning.[155] Here the undifferentiated self is not the center of moral agency, because the self only exists and is properly understood covenantally with both God and others.[156] For Barth, the undifferentiated self is illusory sinful nothingness. True human agency is maintained, but placed within God's agency in Christ. The double agency of our theologically determined but free responsibility corresponds to the double agency of Christ's hypostatic union as the active God and active human. The Word in flesh is the presupposition, enabling, and example of what constitutes true moral agency, so that natural human actions are those actions that we do in our circle that correspond to his actions in his circle. By locating ethics as one aspect of the doctrine of God and his self-election in Christ, Barth denies independent status to human moral action and approximates the early Anabaptist confessions that included ethics. The Word's eternal self-election to be incarnate means that his humanity is the presupposition of ours, so that protological natural law becomes christological.

154. MacDonald, *Metaphysics*, xvii, although acknowledging his debt to Barth.
155. Calvin, *ICR*, I.vii. 3, 77; 5, 81; III.iv, 546.
156. "Nearly all wisdom . . . consists of . . . knowledge of God and of ourselves," Calvin, *ICR*, I.i, 1, 35.

The Christological Redetermination of Natural Law 259

Consequently, because Christ's human nature is both Adamic and enhypostatic, human nature is derived from and related to the divine person and nature. This relegates human phenomena to secondary status, making rational and aesthetic inclinations, and especially appetitive drives, unreliable indicators in themselves of proper human goods. Consequently while "animal impulses should be given their rights," they are constrained within "their essential limitations and until there is a clear command to the contrary,"[157] because such created inclinations serve creation's fundamental covenantal character. Barth's insistence that Christ's obedience to his Father and his practice of being for others are natural, and reveal the basic spiritual and social goods essential for human flourishing, is right. This "I-am-in-encounter" basic form of humanity places the person inalienably within willing and glad social relations, so that the concept of the person as a self-enclosed atomistic entity in the tradition of Democritus, which informed Cartesian criticism and Newtonian mechanism, is displaced.[158]

Consequently, Barth's Chalcedonian actualism suggests that the concerns of natural law, both in its divine and human expressions, can be answered christologically in such a way that the Antiochene christological moral reasoning of the Anabaptist tradition finds substantial support.[159] His Christology challenges ethical idealism, romanticism and phenomenalism. Regarding idealism (Alexandria), Barth's Christology subverts abstract speculative metaphysical categories by reading them though christological actualism: here is the real God as real humanity. Regarding Romanticism (Berlin), Jesus' Spirit-enabled obedience to his Father displaces religious feelings of absolute dependence, and self-evident or intuitive apprehensions of what constitutes what is natural: here is true "religious" ethics.[160] Regarding phenomenalism (Antioch), it changes traditional concepts of observable natural inclinations and human reasoning by asserting that the nature and ends of humanity are revealed in Jesus' God-derived, God-directed, and other-directed enhypostatic humanity: here is proper human nature. All of this finds its presupposition in the eternal election of the eternal Word to

---

157. Barth, *CD*, III/4, 347. This is under the head "Respect for Life," § 55.1.

158. Polkinghorne, "The Demise of Democritus," in Polkinghorne, *Trinity and Entangled World*, 1–14.

159. Yoder's use, or neglect, of Barth's Chalcedonianism is worthy of further investigation.

160. Biggar argues that in Barth the Spirit calls humanity to "creaturely order and eschatological destiny . . . that fulfils the teleological structure of creaturely being," so that his ethics "does . . . espouse what could be called a version of natural law," *Hastening*, 164. Creation (Gen 1:1–2:25), incarnation (Luke 1:35), regeneration (John 3:5–6) and recreation (Rom 8:1–39) are all acts of the Spirit.

never not be incarnate as the one person Jesus Christ. Consequently, proper human action is revealed in the human Jesus (Antioch) and theological idealism is reframed through the divine *Logos* (Alexandria), united in the one Jesus Christ (Chalcedon).

Accordingly, the particularity of Jesus leads to sectarian ethics only when the presence of the divine nature and eternal *Logos* is denied its localization in him, and when his humanity is severed from ours. Chalcedon means that christo-ethical radicalism possesses universal scope, which is a primary concern of natural law. True humanity is christologically determined because Jesus' humanity is the eternally elected archetype of universal created humanity, consubstantial with our human nature, and the true example of covenant faithfulness with God and others. Because it is enhypostatic with the divine nature, it resists reduction to historicism and its attendant voluntarism. Barth's classically rich and historically grounded Chalcedonianism enables the possibility of the rapprochement of natural law and christo-ethical radicalism attempted here.

Conclusion

THIS PROJECT HAS SOUGHT to change the relationship between natural law and christo-ethical radicalism from a fraught conversation into a fruitful co-rationalism through Chalcedonian Christology. As such, it is a tentative answer to a broader set of questions about what constitutes moral goodness. Whether such goodness is understood to reside in metaphysics, which is so deeply entangled in contemporary ontotheological suspicion, or in history, which is so deeply entrenched in contemporary consciousness, Chalcedon provides a coherent theoretical Christology where a "single explanatory posit can do many explanatory jobs."[1] This is because the metaphysical *Logos* and the historical *sarx* coalesce in Jesus.

More narrowly, this thesis could be understood from two different general tendencies of these traditions. First, it can be understood as an attempt to bring together radicalism's christological ethical openness and classical orthodoxy's somewhat christological ethical reticence. This varying christological emphasis reflects each tradition's ecclesiology. Radicalism seeks primarily to articulate a moral vision for the church and not the world, while classical orthodoxy seeks to express a vision for the world plus the church. There are historical reasons for this: orthodoxy filled the vacuum of civility in European culture caused by Rome's political collapse, whereas radicalism filled the vacuum of monasticism in reformation Christianity caused by Rome's ecclesial collapse. Radicalism's open Christology is often closed to the world, whereas orthodoxy's closed Christology is open to the world.

Second, this project could be described as an attempt to unite the traditionally unembarrassed natural law emphasis of classical orthodoxy and its suspicion in christo-ethical radicalism.

Yet do these approaches in different ways both misunderstand the doctrines of creation and providence? Classicism often confuses creation,

1. Adams, *Christ and Horrors*, 2.

and thus natural law, with convention, due to reading divine providence as the maintenance of social order through the benevolent kindness of a heavenly Father. Its doctrine of creation tends to be christologically thin, perhaps due to an emphasis upon Christ's divinity that eclipses his created humanity as a morally normative example. Such theological ethics is often associated with dominant social classes: Augustine would likely not have written an eternal law defense of slavery if he himself were a slave.

On the other hand, radicalism's view of creation and natural law is often read through the prism of sin. Here it confuses the good creation of John 1:3 with the fallen world of John 1:10 rather than seeing true humanity in John 1:14. Creation and social convention are determined through the *cosmos* that opposes the *Logos*, rather than through the *sarx* that embodies the *Logos*. This is exacerbated by radicalism's experiential ecclesiology, and orthodoxy's use of natural law to justify violence and social conventions that depart from Christ. Such practices easily marginalize radicalism by politely placing it as a quaint ecclesial exhibit of a naïve pre-modern age, or by antagonistically rejecting it as a bleeding heart with an over-sensitive social conscience. The presence of oppositional personalities, as Martens describes Yoder, may feed into such marginality.

It can be argued therefore that magisterialism's natural law emphasis represents a nation's *volk*, while radicalism represents a nation's exiles. This is a socially constructivist view of theological ethics. If it historically reduces theology to a central focus of class conflict, it is a modern analysis. If it emotionally reduces theology to a decentered clash of wills, it is a postmodern analysis. Yet such an analysis is itself historicist, and could be expressed as either a radical or orthodox reading of theological ethics. So given this current unstable moral epistemology, it is open to a writer to propose his own approach to any problem with which he is confronted. In this I have chosen an ancient confession of the church—the Chalcedonian Definition—to give voice to the conviction that the disparity between natural law and radical ethics is at best a misunderstanding and at worst an unnecessary hostility. This is because Chalcedon is not only orthodox and catholic, but is so christologically, and that Christ's two hypostatically united moral natures are normative for ethics.

For this reason it is curious that both traditions tend to exhibit christological reticence in the face of negative appraisals of Christianity, although in different forms. Orthodoxy expresses its christological embarrassment through its tendency to reframe Christian ethics in the dominant speech of contemporary pluralistic voluntarism. It is linguistically reticent about Christ. It robustly speaks the prevailing moral language in the public sphere, and thus retains its social presence. Yet it needs to acknowledge that its commitment to orthodox Christology necessarily implies that Christ is ethically normative, and as such is universal, and that its reduction to voluntarist ethics will finally prove unhelpful because language shapes perception, and voluntarist language cannot but serve to relativize, and thus de-divinize, Christ. As such it is linguistic Arianism. Magisterialism's embarrassment readily places an unwarranted interdiction on christological public rhetoric.

Those radical groups that have adopted orthodoxy's strategy by using contemporary social justice and human rights language share this tendency.

On the other hand, radicalism's tendency to christological embarrassment is often expressed in social reticence and withdrawal from public discourse. Like an ecclesiastical mole, it hibernates in church burrows to avoid the long secular moral winter. Or in another image, it tends to lift the drawbridge on its ecclesial castle so that it can maintain confident Christian speech amongst its own populace. The challenge it faces is to recognize that Christ's moral humanity, as universally normative, cannot be limited to disciples, and must be lived in the public square. Radicalism's embarrassment readily places an unwarranted interdiction on Christian public engagement.

Yet what is attempted here is not so much a solution to a social problem confronting ecclesial traditions, but a theological solution to an ethical problem.

Natural law places both divine and human natures central in moral reasoning: the nature of both God and humanity are real, and this realism norms ethics, because ethics is philosophically a function of such natures. Chalcedon unites both these natures in the one person of Jesus, so that natural law breaks out of its speculative, rationalistic, or phenomenalistic fetters into the arms of Jesus, and radicalism's moral Christology bursts out of its ecclesial chains into the arms of universal humanity. Chalcedon means that both the law of human creation and divine reason and law coalesce in Christ's single person, because both his natures are consubstantial and historically revealed.

This project could be extended by further exploring a number of features noted along the way. These include Irenaeus's recapitulation second-Adam theology and the two hands of God in creation, Levinas's affirmation of the needy face of the particular other as the subject who elects us to moral agency, transposed into the face of Christ (2 Cor 3:12–18), an ethical doctrine of the Trinity by a greater integration of a *logos* Christology, a Reformed or Lutheran moral exemplarism which allays their soteriological fears, and a greater integration of pneumatology into natural law.

Chalcedon's double *homoousios* and *logos* Christology is offered here as the theological means of a rapprochement of natural law and radical ethics. Jesus' human nature, created and assumed by the divine Word, reveals humanity's natural inclination to both God and others in faithful covenant relations. Jesus' divine nature, uncreated yet graciously assuming the form of a human servant, reveals the moral being and acts of God. In terms of natural law, what is morally good and proper to both human and divine natures is located in the person and acts of Jesus. In terms of christo-ethical radicalism, the life of Jesus is universally normative because he is the divine Son and Word whose humanity is consubstantial with ours. Jesus' being and acts constitute the good and right of both God and humanity. "The Word became flesh and dwelt amongst us, full of grace and truth" (John 1:14).

Bibliography

Adams, Marilyn McCord. *Christ and Horrors: The Coherence of Christology.* Current Issues in Theology, No. 4. Cambridge: Cambridge University Press, 2006.
Adams, Robert Merrihew. *Finite and Infinite Goods: A Framework for Ethics.* New York, NY: Oxford University Press, 2002.
Aldridge, Larissa. "Should a Christian Believe in the Laws of Nature?" Presented at the Second Annual Australasian Christian Conference for the Academy and the Church, Queensland Theological College, Brisbane, QLD: 2010.
Anatolios, Khaled. *Athanasius: The Coherence of his Thought.* New York, NY: Routledge, 1998.
Anderson, Ray S. *On Being Human. Essays in Theological Anthropology.* Grand Rapids, MI: Eerdmans, 1982.
Aquinas, Thomas. *Corpus Thomisticum.* Textum Leoninum Romae 1892 editum. http://www.corpusthomisticum.org/sth2090.html.
———. *The Summa Theologica of St. Thomas Aquinas.* 2nd and rev. ed., 1920. Translated by the Fathers of the English Dominican Province. Online edition, © 2006 by Kevin Knight. http//www.newadvent.org.
Aristotle. *Politics.* Translated by Benjamin Jowett. Mineola, NY: Dover, 2000.
———. *Politics.* Translated by H. Rackham. Cambridge, NY: Harvard University Press, 1932.
———. *Rhetoric.* Translated by W. Rhys Roberts. Mineola, NY: Dover, 2004.
———. *The "Art" of Rhetoric.* Translated by J. H. Freese. Cambridge, NY: Harvard University Press, 1926, 1967.
———. *The Nicomachean Ethics.* Translated by David Ross. Revised by J. L. Ackrill and J. O. Urmson. Oxford: Oxford University Press, 1991.
———. *The Nicomachean Ethics.* Translated by H. Rackham. Cambridge, NY: Harvard University Press, 1932, 1998.
———. *The Politics of Aristotle.* Translated by Ernest Barker. Oxford: Clarendon, 1948.
Athanasius. "On The Incarnation of the Word." Edited by Archibald Robertson. In NPNF 2. vol. 4:36–67. Peabody, MA: Hendrickson, 2004.
Audi, Robert, ed. *The Cambridge Dictionary of Philosophy.* Cambridge: Cambridge University Press, 1996.
Augsburger, David. *Dissident Discipleship: A Spirituality of Self-Surrender, Love of God, and Love of Neighbor.* Grand Rapids, MI: Brazos, 2006.
Augustine. "The City of God." Translated by Marcus Dods. In NPNF 1, vol. 2:1–511. Grand Rapids, MI: Eerdmans, 1979.

———. "The Morals of the Catholic Church." Translated by Richard Stothert. In NPNF 1, vol. 4:41–63. Grand Rapids, MI: Eerdmans, 1979.

———. "On the Holy Trinity." Translated by Arthur West Haddan, revised by W. G. T. Shedd. In NPNF 1, vol. 3:1–228. Grand Rapids, MI: Eerdmans, 1978.

———. "Reply to Faustus the Manichaean [Contra Faustum Manichaeum]." Translated by Richard Stothert. In NPNF 1, vol. 4:155–345. Grand Rapids, MI: Eerdmans, 1887, 1979.

Ayres, Lewis. *Nicaea and Its Legacy. An Approach to Fourth-Century Trinitarian Theology*. Oxford: Oxford University Press, 2004.

Azkoul, Michael. *St. Gregory of Nyssa and the Tradition of the Fathers*. Texts and Studies in Religion. Lewiston, NY: Edwin Mellen, 1995.

Bahrim, Dragos. "The Anthropic Cosmology of St Maximus the Confessor." *Journal for Interdisciplinary Research on Religion and Science* 3 (2008) 13.

Barrett, C. K. *The Gospel According to John. An Introduction with Commentary and Notes on the Greek Text*. London: SPCK, 1975.

Barth, Karl. *Christ and Adam. Man and Humanity in Romans 5*. Translated by Tom Small. Edinburgh: Oliver and Boyd, 1956.

———. *The Christian Life, Church Dogmatics IV/4, Lecture Fragments*. Translated by Geoffrey W. Bromiley. Grand Rapids, MI: Eerdmans, 1981.

———. *Church Dogmatics. I/1 – IV/3.2*. Translated and edited by Geoffrey W. Bromiley et al. Edinburgh: T & T Clark, various dates.

———. *Ethics*. Translated by Geoffrey W. Bromiley, edited by Dietrich Braun. New York, NY: Seabury, 1981.

———. *The Humanity of God*. London: Fontana, 1967.

———. *Protestant Theology in the Nineteenth Century*. Valley Forge, PA: Judson, 1973.

———. *Witness to the Word*. Translated by Geoffrey W. Bromiley; Grand Rapids, MI: Eerdmans, 1986.

———. *The Word of God and the Word of Man*. Translated by Douglas Houton. New York, NY: Harper and Brothers, 1957.

Bathrellos, Demetrios. *The Byzantine Christ. Person, Nature and Will in the Christology of Saint Maximus the Confessor*. Oxford: Oxford University Press, 2004.

Bayer, Oswald. *Freedom in Response: Lutheran Ethics; Sources and Controversies*. Oxford Studies in Theological Ethics. Translated by Jeffrey F. Cayzer, edited by Oliver O'Donovan. Oxford: Oxford University Press, 2007.

Beasley-Murray, George R. *John*. WBC. 2nd ed. Nashville, TN: Thomas Nelson, 1999.

Biesecker-Mast, Gerald. *Separation and the Sword in Anabaptist Persuasion. Radical Confessional Rhetoric from Schleitheim to Dortrecht*. CHSS, vol. 6: Telford, PA: Cascadia, 2006.

Biesecker-Mast, Susan, and Gerald Biesecker-Mast, eds. *Anabaptists & Postmodernity*. CHSS, vol. 1: Telford, PA: Pandora, 2000.

Bennet, John C. *The Radical Imperative: From Theology to Social Ethics*. Philadelphia, PA: Westminster, 1975.

Berkouwer, G. C. *General Revelation*. Studies in Dogmatics. Grand Rapids, MI: Eerdmans, 1955, 1973.

Berkowitz, Peter. *Nietzsche: The Ethics of an Immoralist*. Cambridge, MA: Harvard University Press, 1995.

Bernstein, Richard J. *Beyond Objectivism and Relativism. Science, Hermeneutics and Praxis*. Philadelphia, PA: University of Philadelphia Press, 1983.

Betz, Hans Dieter. *The Sermon on the Mount*. Hermeneia. Minneapolis, MN: Fortress, 1995.
Biggar, Nigel. *The Hastening That Waits: Karl Barth's Ethics*. Oxford, Clarendon, 1993.
Biggar, Nigel and Rufus Black. *The Revival of Natural Law: Philosophical, Theological and Ethical Responses to the Finnis-Grisez School*. Aldershot: Ashgate, 2000.
Black, Rufus. *Christian Moral Realism. Natural Law, Narrative, Virtue and the Gospel*. Oxford: Oxford University Press, 2001.
Blough, Neal. *Christ in Our Midst. Incarnation, Church and Discipleship in the Theology of Pilgram Marpeck*. Kitchener, Ontario: Pandora, 2007.
Bockmuehl, Markus. *Jewish Law in Gentile Churches: Halakah and the Beginning of Christian Public Ethics*. Grand Rapids, MI: Baker, 2000.
Boersma, Hans. "Irenaeus, Derrida and Hospitality: On the Eschatological Overcoming of Violence." *Modern Theology* 19 no. 2 (2003) 163–80. *Religion and Philosophy Collection*, EBSCO*host*.
Boethius, Ancius. *The Consolations of Philosophy*. Translated by Victor Watts. London: Penguin Classics, 1999.
Boff, Leonardo. *Trinity and Society*. Kent, UK: Burns & Oates, 1988.
Bonhoeffer, Dietrich. *Act and Being. Transcendental Philosophy and Ontology in Systematic Theology*. Translated by Hans-Richard Reuter and H. Martin Rumscheidt, edited by Wayne Whitson Floyd, Jr. Dietrich Bonhoeffer Works, vol. 2. Minneapolis, MN: Fortress, 2009.
———. *Christology*. Translated by John Bowden. London, Collins, 1960.
———. *The Cost of Discipleship*, London: SCM, 1976.
———. *Ethics*. Translated by Neville Horton Smith, edited by Eberhard Bethge. New York, NY: Macmillan, 1965.
———. *Sanctorum Communio. A Theological Study of the Sociology of the Church*. Translated by Reinhard Kraus and Nancy Lukens, edited by Clifford J. Green. Dietrich Bonhoeffer Works, vol. 1. Minneapolis, MN: Fortress, 1996.
Boring, M. Eugene. "The Gospel of Matthew. Introduction, Commentary, and Reflections." In *The New Interpreter's Bible*, vol. 8. Nashville, TN: Abingdon, 1995.
Bornkamm, Günther, et al. *Tradition and Interpretation in Matthew*. Translated by Percy Scott. London: SCM, 1971.
Boyd, Craig A. *A Shared Morality: A Narrative Defense of Natural Law Ethics*. Grand Rapids, MI: Brazos, 2007.
Braaten Carl E. and Robert W. Jenson, eds. *Union with Christ. The New Finnish Interpretation of Luther*. Grand Rapids, MI, Cambridge, UK: Eerdmans, 1998.
Brown, Colin. *Miracles and the Critical Mind*. Grand Rapids, MI: Eerdmans, 1984.
Brunner, Emil. *The Divine Imperative*. Translated by Olive Wyon. London: Lutterworth, 1937.
———. *Man in Revolt*. Translated by Olive Wyon. London: Lutterworth, 1947.
Bultmann, Rudolf. *Theology of the New Testament*. Translated by Kendrick Grobel. Vol. 2. London: SCM, 1976.
Burge, Gary M. *The Anointed Community. The Holy Spirit in the Johannine Tradition*. Grand Rapids, MI: Eerdmans, 1987.
Burridge, Richard A. *Imitating Jesus. An Inclusive Approach to New Testament Ethics*. Grand Rapids, MI: Eerdmans, 2007.
Busch, Eberhard. *Karl Barth. His Life from Letters and Autobiographical Texts*. Translated by John Bowden. Grand Rapids, MI: Eerdmans, 1994.

Calvin, John. *Calvin's New Testament Commentaries*. Edited by David W. Torrance and Thomas F. Thomas. 12 vols. Grand Rapids, MI: Eerdmans, 1972, 1980.

———. *Institutes of the Christian Religion*. Translated by Ford Lewis Battles, edited by John T. McNeill. LCC, vol. 20, 2 vols. Philadelphia, PA: Westminster, MCMLX, 7th printing 1975.

———. *INSTITUTIO CHRISTIANAE RELIGIONIS, (BEROLINI, AUD GUSTUVUM EICHLER, MDCCCXXXIV)*. http//www.ccel.org/calvin/institutio1/age 187.html.

Carter, Craig. A. *The Politics of the Cross: The Theology and Social Ethics of John Howard Yoder*. Grand Rapids, MI: Brazos, 2001.

Chalier, Catherine. *What Ought I to Do? Morality in Kant and Levinas*. Translated by Jane Marie Todd. Ithaca and London: Cornell University Press, 2002.

Charles, J. Daryl. *Retrieving the Natural Law. A Return to Moral First Things*. Grand Rapids, MI: Eerdmans, 2008.

Chung, Sung Wook, ed. *Karl Barth and Evangelical Theology. Convergences and Divergences*. Grand Rapids, MI: Baker, 2006.

Cicero. *DE LEGIBUS*. Translated by Clinton Walker Keyes. Cambridge, MS: Harvard University Press, 1928, 1977.

———. *DE REPUBLICUS*. Translated by Clinton Walter Keyes. Cambridge, MS: Harvard University Press, 1928, 1977.

———. *The Republic and The Laws*. Translated by Niall Rudd. Oxford: Oxford University Press, 1998.

Collinson, Sylvia Wilkey. *Making Disciples. The Significance of Jesus' Educational Methods for Toady's Church*. Milton Keynes, UK: Paternoster, 2004.

Cooper, Adam. *The Body in St Maximus the Confessor. Holy Flesh, Wholly Deified*. Oxford: Oxford University Press, 2005.

Cooper, Adam G. "Maximus the Confessor on the Structural Dynamics of Revelation." *Vigiliae Christianae* 55 no. 2 (2001) 161–86. ATLA Religion Database with ATLASerials, EBSCOhost.

Crisp, Oliver D. *Divinity and Humanity: The Incarnation Reconsidered, Current Issues in Theology*. Cambridge: Cambridge University Press, 2007.

Cromartie, Michael, ed. *A Preserving Grace. Protestants, Catholics, and Natural Law*. Grand Rapids, MI: Eerdmans, 1997.

Cunningham, Lawrence S., ed. *Intractable Disputes About the Natural Law. Alisdair MacIntyre and Critics*. Notre Dame, IN: University of Notre Dame Press, 2009.

Curran, Charles E., ed. *Natural Law and Theology*, Mahwah, NJ: Paulist, 1991.

Curran, Charles E. and Richard McCormick, eds. *Readings in Moral Theology No. 7. Natural Law and Theology*. Mahwah, NJ: Paulist, 1991.

Dannals, Robert S. *Aspects of* Imitatio Christi *in the Moral Christology of Dietrich Bonhoeffer*. PhD diss., The Graduate Theological Foundation, Mishawaka, IN: 2005.

Davids, Peter. *The Epistle of James. A Commentary on the Greek Text*. TNIGTC. Exeter: Paternoster, 1982.

Davies W. D. and Dale C. Allison. *Matthew. A Shorter Commentary*. Edited by Dale C. Allison. London: T & T Clark International, 2004.

Davis, Kenneth R. *Anabaptism and Asceticism. A Study of Intellectual Origins*. SAMH, vol. 16. Pennsylvania, PA: Herald, 1974.

Davis, Stephen T., et al., eds. *The Incarnation: An Interdisciplinary Symposium on the Incarnation of the Son of God*. Oxford: Oxford University Press, 2002.

Dear, John. *The God of Peace. Toward a Theology of Nonviolence.* Maryknoll NY: Orbis, 1994.
Denny Weaver, J. *Anabaptist Theology in the Face of Postmodernity. A Proposal for the Third Millennium.* CHMS, vol. 2. Telford, PA: Pandora, 2000.
Dodd, C. H. *The Interpretation of the Fourth Gospel.* Cambridge: Cambridge University Press, 1972.
Dunn, James D. G. *Jesus and the Spirit. A Study of the Religious and Charismatic Experience of Jesus and the First Christians in the New Testament.* London: SCM, 1975.
———. *Romans 1–8.* WBC. Edited by David A. Hubbard et al. Dallas, TX: Word, 1988.
Ebeling, Gerhard. *Luther: An Introduction to His Thought.* Translated by R. A. Wilson. Philadelphia, PA: Fortress, 1970.
Ellis, George F. R. *A Universe of Ethics, Morality and Hope. Proceedings from the Second Annual Goshen Conference on Religion and Science.* Kitchener, Ontario: Pandora, 2003.
Engberg-Pedersen, Troels. *Paul and the Stoics.* Louisville, KY: Westminster John Knox, 2000.
Fee, Gordon. *The First Epistle to the Corinthians.* NICNT, edited by F. F. Bruce. Grand Rapids, MI: Eerdmans, 1988.
Finger, Thomas N. *Christian Theology: an Eschatological Approach.* Scottdale, PA: Herald, 1989.
———. *A Contemporary Anabaptist Theology: Biblical, Historical, Constructive.* Downers Grove, IL: InterVarsity, 2004.
Finnis, John. *Fundamentals of Ethics.* Oxford: Clarendon, 1983.
———. *Moral Absolutes: Tradition, Revision and Truth.* Washington DC: Catholic University of America Press, 1991.
———. *Natural Law and Natural Rights,* Oxford: Clarendon, 1980.
Ford, David F. "The What, How and Who of Humanity Before God: Theological Anthropology and the Bible in the Twenty-First Century." *Modern Theology* 27 no. 1 (2011) 41–54.
Ford, David F., and Graham Stanton, eds. *Reading Texts, Seeking Wisdom.* London: SCM, 2003.
Fowl, Stephen E. and L. Gregory Jones. *Readings in Communion: Scripture and Ethics in the Christian Life.* Grand Rapids, MI: Eerdmans, 1991.
Friedmann, Robert. *The Theology of Anabaptism.* SAMH, No. 15. Scottdale, PA: Herald, 1973.
Gardner, Richard B. *Matthew.* Believers Church Bible Commentary. Scottdale, PA: Herald, 1991.
Gorman Michael J. *Cruciformity: Paul's Narrative Spirituality of the Cross.* Grand Rapids, MI: Eerdmans, 2001.
Goyette, John, et al., eds. *St. Thomas Aquinas and the Natural Law Tradition. Contemporary Perspectives.* Washington, D.C: The Catholic University of America Press, 2004.
Grabill, Stephen J. *Rediscovering the Natural Law in Reformed Theological Thought.* Grand Rapids, MI: Eerdmans, 2006.
Grasso, Kenneth L. and Robert P. Hunt, eds. *A Moral Enterprise. Politics, Reason, and the Human Good. Essay in Honor of Francis Canavan.* Wilmington, DE: ISI, 2002.

Gregersen, Niels H. and Ulf Görman, eds. *Design and Disorder. Perspectives from Science and Theology.* Issues in Science and Theology. London: T & T Clark, 2002.

Grimsrud, Ted. "Anabaptism for the Twenty-First Century." *Mennonite Quarterly Review,* 80 no. 3 (2006) 373.

Grunlan, Stephen A. and Marvin K. Mayers. *Cultural Anthropology. A Christian Perspective.* 2nd ed. Grand Rapids. MI: Zondervan, 1988.

Gunton, Colin E. *Act and Being: Towards a Theology of the Divine Attributes.* London, SCM Press, 2002.

———. *The Barth Lectures.* Edited by P. H. Brazier. London: T & T Clark, 2007.

———. *The One, The Three and the Many: God, Creation and the Culture of Modernity.* Cambridge: Cambridge University Press, 1993.

———. *The Theology of Reconciliation.* London: T & T Clark, 2003.

Gurtner, Daniel M. and John Nolland, eds. *Built Upon the Rock. Studies in the Gospel of Matthew.* Michigan: http://books.google.com.au/books, 2008.

Haber, Joram Graf. *Doing and Being; Selected Readings in Moral Philosophy.* New York, NY: Macmillan, 1993.

Hall, Pamela M. *Narrative and the Natural Law. An Interpretation of Thomist Ethics.* Notre Dame and London: University of Notre Dame Press, 1994.

Harrington, Daniel J. *The Gospel of Matthew.* SACRA PAGINA. Minnesota: http://books.google.com.au/books, 1991.

Hauerwas, Stanley. *After Christendom? How the Church is to Behave if Freedom, Justice and a Christian Nation are Bad Ideas.* Sydney: Anzea, 1991.

———. *Character and the Christian Life: A Study in Theological Ethics.* San Antonio, TX: Trinity University Press, 1985.

———. *Christian Existence Today. Essay on Church, World and Living in Between.* Durham, NC: Labyrinth, 1988.

———. *A Community of Character: Towards a Constructive Christian Social Ethic.* Notre Dame, IN: University of Notre Dame Press, 1981.

———. *The Peaceable Kingdom. A Primer in Christian Ethics.* Notre Dame, IN: University of Notre Dame Press, 1983, 1986.

———. *Truthfulness and Tragedy. Further Investigations into Christian Ethics.* Notre Dame, IN: University of Notre Dame Press, 1977, 1985.

———. *With the Grain of the Universe. The Church's Witness and Natural Theology.* Grand Rapids, MI: Brazos, 2001.

Hauerwas, Stanley, et al., eds. *Theology Without Foundations: Religious Practice and the Future of Theological Truth.* Nashville, TN: Abingdon, 1994.

Hauerwas, Stanley, et al., eds. *The Wisdom of the Cross: Essays in Honor of John Howard Yoder.* Grand Rapids, MI: Eerdmans, 1999.

Hauerwas, Stanley, and L. Gregory Jones, eds. *Why Narrative? Readings in Narrative Theology.* Grand Rapids, MI: Eerdmans, 1989.

Hawthorne, Gerald D. *Philippians,* WBC. Edited by David A. Hubbard et al. Dallas, TX: Word,1983.

Hays, Richard B. *The Moral Vision of the New Testament. Community, Cross, New Creation. A Contemporary Introduction to New Testament Ethics.* New York, NY: HarperCollins, 1996.

Henriksen, Jan-Olav. *Desire, Gift, and Recognition. Christology and Postmodern Philosophy.* Grand Rapids, MI: Eerdmans, 2009.

Hershberger, Guy F., ed. *The Recovery of the Anabaptist Vision: A Sixtieth Anniversary Tribute to Harold S. Bender.* Eugene OR: Wipf and Stock, 2001.
Hiebert, Paul G. *Cultural Anthropology.* 2nd ed. Grand Rapids, MI: Baker, 1990.
Hittinger, Russell. *A Critique of the New Natural Law Theory.* Notre Dame, IN: University of Notre Dame Press, 1987.
Holsinger-Freisen, Thomas. *Irenaeus and Genesis. A Study of Competition in Early Christian Hermeneutics.* Journal of Theological Interpretation, Supplement I; Winona Lake, IN: Eisenbrauns, 2009.
Ingraffia, Brian D. *Postmodern Theory and Biblical Theology. Vanquishing God's Shadow.* Cambridge: Cambridge University Press, 1995.
Hubmaier, Balthaser. *Balthasar Hubmaier: Theologian of Anabaptism.* Translated by H.W. Pipkin and John H. Yoder. CRR, vol. 5. Scottdale, PA: Herald, 1989.
Irenaeus. "Against Heresies." In *ANF* vol. 1:315–567. Edited by Alexander Roberts and James Donaldson. Peabody, MS: Hendrickson, 2004.
Issler, Klaus and Fred Sanders. *Jesus in Trinitarian Perspective. An Introductory Christology.* Nashville, TN: B & H, 2007.
Jersak Brad and Michael Hardin, eds. *Stricken by God? Nonviolent Identification and the Victory of God.* Grand Rapids, MI: Eerdmans, 2007.
Jewett, Paul K. and Marguerite Shuster, eds. *Who We Are: Our Dignity as Human. A Neo-Evangelical Approach.* Grand Rapids, MI: Eerdmans, 1996.
Justin. "The Second Apology." In *ANF*, vol. 1:188–193. Edited by Alexander Roberts and James Donaldson. Peabody, MA: Hendrickson, 2004.
Käsemann, Ernst. *Commentary on Romans.* Translated by Geoffrey W. Bromiley. London: SCM, 1980.
Katongole, Emmanuel. *Beyond Universal Reason: The Relation Between Religion and Ethics in the Work of Stanley Hauerwas.* Notre Dame, IN: University of Notre Dame Press, 2000.
Keeling, Michael. *The Mandate of Heaven: The Divine Command and the Natural Order.* Edinburgh: T & T Clark, 1995.
Kelly, Anthony. *Aristotle on the Perfect Life.* Oxford: Clarendon, 1992.
Kelly, J. N. D. *Early Christian Doctrines.* 5th revised ed. London: A & C Black, 1977.
———. *The Epistles of Peter and Jude.* Black's New Testament Commentaries. Edited by H. Chadwick. London: A & C Black, 1969.
Kittel, Gerhard, ed. *Theological Dictionary of the New Testament.* Vol. 3. Translated and edited by Geoffrey W. Bromiley, edited by G. Kittel. Grand Rapids, MI: Eerdmans, 1965.
Klassen, William. *Covenant and Community: The Life, Writings and Hermeneutics of Pilgram Marpeck.* Grand Rapids, MI: Eerdmans, 1968.
Klassen, Walter, ed. *Anabaptism in Outline: Selected Primary Sources.* Scottdale, PA: Herald, 1981.
Koop, Karl, ed. *Confessions of Faith in the Anabaptist Tradition 1527–1660.* Translated by Cornelius J. Dyck et al. CRR, vol. 11. Kitchener, Ontario: Pandora, 2006.
Krahn, Corneius. *Dutch Anabaptism: Origin, Spread, Life and Thought, 1450–1600.* Scottdale, PA: Herald, 1981.
Kraus, Norman. *Evangelicalism and Anabaptism.* Scottdale, PA: Herald, 1979.
La Montagne, D. Paul. *Barth and Rationality. Critical Realism in Theology.* Eugene, OR: Cascade, 2012.
Lee, Philip J. *Against the Protestant Gnostics.* Oxford, NY: Oxford University Press, 1987.

LeMasters, Philip. *Discipleship for All Believers: Christian Ethics and the Kingdom of God*. Scottdale, PA: Herald, 1992.

Levinas, Emmanuel. *Ethics and Infinity. Conversations with Philippe Nemo*. Translated by Richard. A. Cohen. Pittsburgh, PA: Duquesne University Press, 1982.

Lightfoot, J. B., trans. and ed. *The Didache or Teaching of the Apostles*. http://www.earlychristianwritings.com/text/didache-lightfoot.html.

Lorenzen, Thorwald. *Resurrection and Discipleship. Interpretive Models, Biblical Reflections, Theological Consequences*. Maryknoll, NY: Orbis, 1995.

———. *Resurrection, Discipleship, Justice. Affirming the Resurrection of Jesus Today*. Malcon, GA: Smyth & Helwys, 2003.

Lossky, Vladimir. *The Mystical Theology of the Eastern Church*. Crestwood, NY: St Vladimir's Seminary, 1976.

Louth, Andrew. *Maximus the Confessor*. London and New York: Routledge, 1996.

Lowe, E. J. *A Survey of Metaphysics*. Oxford: Oxford University Press, 2002.

Luther, Martin. *Luther: Early Theological Works*. Translated and edited by J. Atkinson. LCC, vol. 16. London: SCM, 1962.

———. *Three Treatises*. Edited by Helmut. T. Lehmann. From the American Edition. Philadelphia, PA: Fortress, 1970.

McClendon Jnr., James Wm. *Systematic Theology. Ethics*. Nashville, TN: Abingdon, 1986.

———. *Systematic Theology II. Doctrine*. Nashville, TN: Abingdon, 1994.

McCormack, Bruce L. *Orthodox and Modern. Studies in the Theology of Karl Barth*. Grand Rapids, MI: Baker, 2008.

McCready, Douglas. *He Came Down from Heaven. The Preexistence of Christ and the Christian Faith*. Downers Grove: IL: InterVarsity, 2005.

MacDonald, Neil B. *Metaphysics and the God of Israel. Systematic Theology of the Old and New Testaments*. Grand Rapids, MI: Baker, 2006.

McDowell, John C. "One Person, Many Persons? Adding Up the Personality Disorder in Karl Barth's CD, I.1 §§8–9." Presented at Morling College, NSW: 2009.

McGrath, Alister E. *Iustitia Dei. A History of the Christian Doctrine of Justification*. 2nd ed. Cambridge: Cambridge University Press, 1998.

———. *Luther's Theology of the Cross*. Oxford: Blackwell, 1990.

———. *The Open Secret. A New Vision for Natural Theology*. Oxford: Blackwell, 2008.

———. *A Scientific Theology*. 3 vols. Edinburgh: T & T Clark, 2006.

MacIntyre, Alasdair. *After Virtue: A Study in Moral Theory*. 2nd ed. Notre Dame, IN: University of Notre Dame Press, 1984.

———. *Three Rival Versions of Moral Enquiry: Encyclopaedia, Genealogy and Tradition*. Notre Dame, IN: University of Notre Dame Press, 1990.

———. *Whose Justice, Which Rationality?* Notre Dame, IN: University of Notre Dame Press, 1988.

McIntyre, John. *The Shape of Christology*. London: SCM Press, 1966.

MacKenzie, Iain M. *God's Order and Natural Law: The Works of the Laudian Divines*. England: Ashgate, 2002.

McKenzie Ross H., and Benjamin Myers. "Dialectical Critical Realism in Science and Theology: Quantum Physics and Karl Barth." *Science and Christian Belief* 20 no. 1, (2008) 49–66.

Macquarrie, John, *The Principles of Christian Theology*. London: SCM, 1966.

Maritain, Jacques. *An Introduction to Philosophy,* London: Continuum, 2005.

Marbeck, Pilgram. *The Writings of Pilgram Marpeck*. Translated by William Klassen and Walter Klaassen. Scottdale, PA: Herald, 1978.
Marshall, Chris D. *Beyond Retribution: A New Testament Vision for Justice, Crime and Punishment*. Grand Rapids, MI: Eerdmans, 2001.
Martens, Paul. *The Heterodox Yoder*. Eugene, OR: Cascade, 2012.
Maximus the Confessor. *On the Cosmic Mystery of Jesus Christ. Selected Writings from St Maximus the Confessor*. Translated by Paul M. Blowers and Robert Louis Wilken. Crestwood, NY: St Vladimir's Seminary Press, 2003.
Melanchthon, P. *Melanchthon on Christian Doctrine: Loci Communes 1555*. Translated and edited by Clyde L. Manschrek. Grand Rapids, MI: Baker, 1965, 1982.
Milbank, John. *Theology and Social Theory. Beyond Secular Reason*. Signposts in Theology, Oxford: Blackwell, 1990.
Molnar, Paul D. *Divine Freedom and the Doctrine of the Immanent Trinity: In Dialogue with Karl Barth and Contemporary Theology*. London: T & T Clark, 2002.
Moltmann, Jürgen. *God in Creation. An Ecological Doctrine of Creation*. trans. M. Kohl; London: SCM Press, 1985.
———. *The Trinity and the Kingdom of God: The Doctrine of God*. London: SCM, 1981.
———. *The Way of Jesus Christ. Christology in Messianic Dimension*. Minneapolis, MN: Fortress, 1993.
Montgomery, John Warwick, ed. *Jurisprudence: A Book of Readings*. Strasbourg, France: International Scholarly, 1974.
Mott, Stephen Charles. *Biblical Ethics and Social Change*. New York/Oxford: Oxford University Press, 1982.
Mouw, Richard J. *The God Who Commands: A Study in Divine Command Ethics*. Notre Dame, IN: University of Notre Dame Press, 1990.
Murphy, Mark C. *God and Moral Law. On the Theistic Explanation of Morality*. Oxford: Oxford University Press, 2001.
Murphy, Mark C., ed. *Alasdair MacIntyre*. Contemporary Philosophy in Focus. Cambridge: Cambridge University Press, 2003.
Murphy, Nancey. *Theology in the Age of Scientific Reasoning*. Ithaca, NY: Cornell University Press, 1990.
Murphy, Nancey, et al., eds. *Virtues and Practices in the Christian Tradition: Christian Ethics after MacIntyre*. Notre Dame, IN: University of Notre Dame Press, 2003.
Murphy, Nancey, and George F. R. Ellis. *On the Moral Nature of the Universe. Theology, Cosmology and Ethics*. Minneapolis, MN: Fortress, 1996.
Murray, John Courtney. *We Hold These Truths: Catholic Reflections on the American Proposition*. Sheed and Ward, New York, 1960.
Murray, Stuart. *Biblical Interpretation in the Anabaptist Tradition*. Ontario; Pandora, 2000.
Nation, Mark. *John Howard Yoder: Mennonite Patience, Evangelical Witness, Catholic Convictions*. Grand Rapids, MI: Eerdmans, 2006.
Neder, Adam. *Participation in Christ. An Entry into Karl Barth's Church Dogmatics*. Columbia Series in Reformed Dogmatics. Louisville, KY: Westminster, 2009.
Nicgorski, Walter, ed. *Cicero's Practical Philosophy*. Notre Dame, IN: University of Notre Dame Press, 2012.
O'Day, Gail R. *The Gospel of John*. NIB, vol. 9. Nashville, TN: Abingdon, 1995.
O'Donovan, Oliver. *Resurrection and Moral Order: An Outline for Evangelical Ethics*. London: IVP, 1986.

O'Donovan, Joan Lockwood. "Subsidiarty and Political Authority in Theological Perspective." *Studies in Christian Ethics* 6 no. 1, 1993, 16–33.
Ollenburger, Ben. C., and Gayle Gerber Koontz, eds. *A Mind Patient and Untamed. Assessing John Howard Yoder's Contributions to Theology, Ethics and Peace-making.* Telford, PA: Cascadia, 2004.
O'Neil, Michael D. *Forming Moral Community. Christian and Ecclesiastical Existence in the Theology of Karl Barth.* PhD diss., Murdoch University, Perth, WA: 2008.
Origin. "Commentary on John." Edited by A. Menzies. In *ANF*, vol. 9. Peabody, MS: Hendrickson, 2004.
Outka, Gene and John P. Reeder, eds. *Prospects for a Common Morality.* Princeton, NJ: Princeton University Press, 1993.
Pannenberg, Wolfhart. *Anthropology in Christian Perspective.* Translated by Matthew J. O'Connell. Edinburgh: T & T Clark, 1999.
———. *Basic Questions in Theology.* Vol. 3. Translated by R. A. Wilson. London: SCM, 1973.
———. *Ethics.* Translated by Keith Crim. Philadelphia, PA: Westminster, 1981.
———. *Jesus—God and Man.* Translated by Lewis L. Wilkins and Duane A. Priebe. London: SCM, 1976.
———. *Metaphysics and the Idea of God.* Grand Rapids, MI: Eerdmans, 1971.
———. *Towards a Theology of Nature. Essays on Science and Truth.* Edited by Ted Peters. Louisville, KY: Westminster/John Knox, 1993.
Paul, Ellen Frankel, et al., eds. *Objectivism, Subjectivism and Relativism in Ethics.* Cambridge: Cambridge University Press, 2008.
Paul II, John. *Veritatis Splendor: On Certain Fundamental Questions of the Church's Moral Teaching.* Sydney: St Paul's, 1994.
Pelikan, Jaroslav. *Christianity and Classical Culture: the Metamorphosis of Natural Theology in the Christian Encounter with Hellenism.* New Haven, CT: Yale University Press, 1993.
Peters, Ted. *God—The World's Future. Systematic Theology for a Post-modern Era.* Minneapolis, MN: Fortress, 1992.
Perl, Eric David. *Methexis: Creation, Incarnation, Deification in Saint Maximus the Confessor.* PhD diss., Yale University, New Haven, CT: 1991.
Philips, Dirk. "Concerning the New Birth and New Creation: Brief Admonition and Teaching from the Holy Bible." In *Early Anabaptist Spirituality. Selected Writings.* The Classics of Western Spirituality. Translated and edited by Daniel Liechty. New York, NY: Paulist, 1994.
Pickard, Stephen, and Gordon Preece, eds; *Starting With the Spirit.* Hindmarsh, Australia: ATF, 2001.
Placher, William. *Unapologetic Theology: A Christian Voice in a Pluralist Conversation.* Louisville, KY: Westminster/John Knox, 1989.
Polkinghorne, John, ed. *The Trinity and an Entangled World. Relationality in Physical Science and Theology.* Grand Rapids, MI: Eerdmans, 2010.
Porter, Jean. *Natural Law and Divine Law: Reclaiming the Tradition for Christian Ethics.* Grand Rapids, MI: Eerdmans, 1999.
———. *Nature as Reason: A Thomist Theory of the Natural Law.* Grand Rapids, MI: Eerdmans, 2005.
Preece, Gordon R. *The Viability of the Vocation Tradition in Trinitarian, Credal and Reformed Perspectives. The Threefold Call.* Lewiston, NY: Edwin Mellen, 1998.

Rae, Murray, et al., eds. *Science and Theology. Questions at the Interface*. Edinburgh: T & T Clark, 1994.
Ramsey, Ian T., ed. *Christian Ethics and Contemporary Philosophy*. London: SCM, 1973.
Rasmussen, L. *Moral Fragments and Moral Community: A Proposal for Church in Society*. Minneapolis, MN: Fortress, 1993.
Reimer, A. James. *Mennonite and Classical Theology: Dogmatic Foundations for Christian Ethics*. Kitchener, Ontario: Herald, 2001.
Richardson, R. A. *Reading Karl Barth. New Directions for North American Theology*. Grand Rapids, MI: Baker Academic, 2004.
Ridderbos, Herman. *Paul: An Outliner of His Theology*. Translated by J. R. de Witt. Grand Rapids, MI: Eerdmans, 1975.
Rist, John M. *Real Ethics: Rethinking the Foundations of Morality*. Cambridge: Cambridge University Press, 2002.
Sattler, Michael. *The Legacy of Michael Sattler*. Translated and edited by John Howard Yoder. CRR, vol. 1. Scottsdale, PA: Herald, 1973.
Schneewind, Jerome B., *The Invention of Autonomy: A History of Modern Moral Philosophy*. Cambridge, Cambridge University Press, 1998.
Schockenhoff, Eberhard. *Natural Law and Human Dignity: Universal Ethics in an Historical World*. Translated by Brian McNeil. Washington, DC: Catholic University of America Press, 2003.
Schreiner, Susan E. *The Theatre of His Glory. Nature and the Natural Order in the Thought of John Calvin*. Grand Rapids, MI: Baker Academic, 1991.
Schürmann, Heinz, et al., eds. *Principles of Christian Morality*. Translated by Graham Harrison. San Francisco, CA: Ignatius, 1975.
Schweitzer, Albert. *The Quest for the Historical Jesus. A Critical Study of its Progress From Reimarus to Wrede*. Translated by W. Montgomery. 3rd ed. London: A & C Black, 1956.
Shults, F. LeRon, and Jan-Olav Henriksen, eds. *Saving Desire: The Seduction of Christian Theology*. Grand Rapids, MI: Eerdmans, 2001, http://www.amazon.com/dp/0802866263/ref=rdr_ext_tmb.
Simon, Yves R. *The Tradition of Natural Law. A Philosopher's Reflection*. Edited by Vukan Kuic. Bronx, NY: Fordham University Press, 1965, 2006.
Simons, Menno. *The Complete Writings of Menno Simons, c. 1496-1561*. Translated by Leonard Verduin. Edited by John C. Wenger. Scottdale, PA: Herald, 1956, 1974.
Slane, Craig J. *Bonhoeffer as Martyr. Social Responsibility and Modern Christian Commitment*. Grand Rapids, MI: Brazos, 2004.
Smith, James K. A. *Desiring the Kingdom. Worship, Worldview, and Cultural Formation*. Grand Rapids, MI: Baker, 2009.
Smith, James K. A., and James H. Olthuis, eds. *Radical Orthodoxy and the Reformed Tradition. Creation, Covenant, and Participation*. Grand Rapids, MI: Baker, 2005.
Snyder, C. Arnold. *Following in the Footsteps of Christ: the Anabaptist Tradition*. Traditions of Christian Spirituality Series. Edited by Philip Sheldrake. London: Darton, Longman and Todd, 2004.
Spohn, William C. *Go and Do Likewise: Jesus and Ethics*. New York, NY: Continuum, 1999.
Stauffer, Ethelbert, and Robert Friedmann. "The Anabaptist Theology of Martyrdom." *Mennonite Quarterly Review* 19 no. 3 (1945) 179-214. ATLA Religion Database with ATLASerials, EBSCOhost.

Steenberg, Matthew C. *Of God and Man. Theology as Anthropology from Irenaeus to Athanasius*. London: T & T Clark, 2009.

Storkey, Elaine. *Created or Constructed? The Great Gender Debate*. Sydney, NSW: UNSW Press, 2001.

Swartley, William M., ed. *The Love of Enemy and Nonretaliation in the New Testament*. Louisville, KY: Westminster/John Knox, 1992.

Taylor, Charles. *Sources of the Self. The Making of Modern Identity*. Cambridge: Cambridge University Press, 1989.

Thiel, John E. *Nonfoundationalism*. Minneapolis, MN: Fortress, 1994.

Thielicke, Helmut. *Living With Death*. Translated by Geoffrey W. Bromiley. Grand Rapids, MI: Eerdmans, 1983.

———. *The Ethics of Sex*. Translated by John W. Doberstein. Cambridge: James Clarke, 1964.

———. *Theological Ethics, vol. 1, Foundations*. Edited by William H. Lazareth. Grand Rapids, MI: Eerdmans, 1984.

Thompson, Michael B. *Clothed With Christ. The Example and Teaching of Jesus in Romans 12.1–5.13*. In JSNT, Supp. Ser. 59. Sheffield: Sheffield Academic, 1991.

Thunberg, Lars. *Man and the Cosmos. The Vision of St Maximus the Confessor*. Crestwood, NY: St Vladimir's Seminary, 1985.

———. *Microcosm and Mediator. The Theological Anthropology of Maximus the Confessor*. 2nd ed. Illinois: Open Court, 1995.

Tillich, Paul. *Systematic Theology, vol. 1: Reason and Revelation, Being and God*. Chicago, IL: Chicago University Press, 1966.

Torrance, A. *Person in Communion: Essays on Trinitarian Description and Human Participation,* Edinburgh: T & T Clark, 1996.

Torrance, Alan, ed. *The Doctrine of God and Theological Ethics*. Edinburgh: T & T Clark, 2006.

Torrance, Thomas F. *The Christian Frame of Mind: Reason, Order and Openness in Theology and Science,* Edinburgh: Handsel Press, 1985.

———. *Divine and Contingent Order*. Edinburgh: T & T Clark, 1998.

———. *Divine Meaning: Studies in Patristic Hermeneutics*. Edinburgh: T & T Clark, 1995.

———. *God and Rationality*. Oxford: Oxford University Press, 1971.

———. *The Ground and Grammar of Theology*. Edinburgh: T & T Clark, 2001.

———. *The Incarnation: Ecumenical Studies in the Nicene-Constantinopolitan Creed AD 381*. Edinburgh: Handsel Press, 1981.

———. *Incarnation. The Person and Life of Christ*. Edited by Robert T. Walker. Bucks, UK and Colorado Springs, USA: Paternoster and InterVarsity, 2008.

———. *Juridical Law and Physical Law*. Edinburgh: Scottish Academic, 1982.

———. *Reality and Evangelical Theology: The Realism of Revelation*. Downer's Grove, IL: InterVarsity, 1999.

———. *Space, Time and Incarnation*. Oxford: Oxford University Press, 1969.

———. *Theological Science*. Oxford: Oxford University Press, 1969.

———. *The Trinitarian Faith, The Evangelical Theology of the Ancient Catholic Church*. Edinburgh: T & T Clark, 1993.

Torrance, Thomas F., ed. *Belief in Science and in Christian Life: The Relevance of Michael Polanyi's Thought for Christian Faith and Life*. Edinburgh: Handsel, 1980.

Trainor, Brian T. *Christ, Society and the State*. Adelaide: ATF, 2010.

Treier, Daniel J. *Virtue and the Voice of God: Towards Theology as Wisdom.* Grand Rapids, MI: Eerdmans, 2006.
Vardy, Peter. *What is Truth?* Sydney: UNSW Press, 1999.
Volf, Miroslav. "'The Trinity is our Social Program': The Doctrine of the Trinity and the Shape of Social Engagement." *Modern Theology* (1998), vol. 14, 403–423. *Academic Search Premier*, EBSCO*host*.
Von Balthasar, Hans Urs. *Cosmic Liturgy. The Universe According to Maximus the Confessor.* San Francisco, CA: Ignatius, 2003.
Vysheslavtsev, B. P. *The Eternal in Russian Philosophy.* Translated by Penelope V. Burt. Grand Rapids, MI: Eerdmans, 2002.
Wainwright, William J. *Religion and Morality.* Ashgate Philosophy of Religion. England: Ashgate, 2005.
Ware, Timothy. *The Orthodox Church.* Middlesex: Penguin, 1985.
Webster, John. *Barth's Ethics of Reconciliation.* Cambridge: Cambridge University Press, 1995.
———. *Barth's Moral Theology: Human Action in Barth's Thought.* London: T & T Clark, 2004.
Webster, John, ed. *The Cambridge Companion to Karl Barth.* Cambridge: Cambridge University Press, 2000.
Weinandy, Thomas G. *Athanasius: A Theological Introduction.* England: Ashgate, 1988.
———. *In the Likeness of Sinful Flesh: An Essay on the Humanity of Christ.* London: T & T Clark, 1993.
Weissman, David. *Truth's Debt to Value.* New Haven, London: Yale University Press, 1993.
Wiebe, Ben. *Messianic Ethics: Jesus' Proclamation of the Kingdom of God and the Church in Response.* Scottdale, PA: Herald, 1992.
Williams, George Huntston. *The Radical Reformation.* Philadelphia, PA: Westminster, 1962.
Williams, George Huntston and Angel M. Mergal, eds. *Spiritual and Anabaptist Writers: Documents Illustrative of the Radical Reformation.* LCC, Ichthus edition. Philadelphia, PA: Westminster, 1957.
Wingren, Gustav. *Man and the Incarnation. A Study in the Biblical Theology of Irenaeus.* Translated by Ross Mackenzie. Edinburgh and London: Oliver and Boyd, 1959.
Wolterstorff, Nicholas. *Reason Within the Bounds of Reason.* 2nd ed. Grand Rapids, MI: Eerdmans, 1984.
Wright, David F., ed. *Essays in Evangelical Social Ethics.* Wilton, CT: Morehouse-Barlow, 1979.
Wright, N. T. *The Letter to the Romans.* NIB, vol. 10. Nashville, TN: Abingdon, 2002.
Yoder, John Howard. *Christian Attitudes to War, Peace, and Revolution.* Edited by Theodore J. Koontz and Andy Alexis-Baker. Grand Rapids, MI: Brazos, 2009.
———. *Preface to Theology: Christology and Trinitarian Method.* Grand Rapids, MI: Brazos, 2002.
———. *The Politics of Jesus.* Grand Rapids, MI: Eerdmans, 1972, 1980.
———. *The Politics of Jesus.* 2nd ed. Grand Rapids, MI: Eerdmans, 1994.
———. *The Priestly Kingdom: Social Ethics as Gospel.* Notre Dame, IN: University of Notre Dame Press, 1984.
———. *The Royal Priesthood: Essays Ecclesiastical and Ecumenical.* Edited by Michael G. Cartwright. Grand Rapids, MI: Eerdmans, 1994.

Zimmermann, Jens. *Recovering Theological Hermeneutics. An Incarnational-Trinitarian Theory of Interpretation*. Grand Rapids, MI: Baker, 2004.

Zizioulas, John D. *Being as Communion. Studies in Personhood and the Church*. Crestwood, NY: St Vladimir's Seminary, 1993.